James Macaulay

True Tales

Of Travel and Adventure, Valour and Virtue

James Macaulay

True Tales

Of Travel and Adventure, Valour and Virtue

ISBN/EAN: 9783337074579

Printed in Europe, USA, Canada, Australia, Japan

Cover: Foto ©ninafisch / pixelio.de

More available books at **www.hansebooks.com**

TRUE TALES

OF

Travel and Adventure, Valour and Virtue.

BY

JAMES MACAULAY, M.A., M.D.,

AUTHOR OF "ALL TRUE," "GREY HAWK,' ETC., AND
EDITOR OF "THE LEISURE HOUR."

WITH THIRTEEN ILLUSTRATIONS.

London:

HODDER AND STOUGHTON,
27, PATERNOSTER ROW.

MDCCCLXXXIV.

(All rights reserved.)

Printed by Hazell, Watson, & Viney, Limited, London and Aylesbury.

CONTENTS.

	PAGE
WILLIAM ADAMS, THE PIONEER ENGLISHMAN IN JAPAN	1
A STRANGE ELECTION AND A STRANGER AUCTION	13
CALIFORNIA'S FIRST START	18
AT THE COURT OF THE GREAT MOGUL	24
THE GREAT MOSQUE OF DELHI AND THE TAJ MEHAL AT AGRA	44
THE LAST OF THE GREAT MOGULS	50
THE STORY OF CLEOPATRA'S NEEDLE	54
A PERSIAN GRAND VIZIER	61
CAPTAIN WILLIAM PEEL'S RIDE THROUGH NUBIA	66
SARAWAK AND THE SOUDAN	75
THE VOYAGE OF THE "FOX"	82
PERILS IN THE ICE	96
A PARLIAMENTARY DEBATE IN TAHITI	103
ORIGIN OF THE GIPSIES	110
GARIBALDI, THE ITALIAN PATRIOT AND HERO	123
UNBEATEN TRACKS IN JAPAN	143
FRENCH ACCOUNTS OF ENGLISH NAVAL VICTORIES	155

Contents.

	PAGE
THE BATTLE OF THE NILE	167
THE BATTLE OF TRAFALGAR	175
LUTHER BEFORE THE EMPEROR	184
JUGGERNAUT IN 1806	189
LIFE-BOAT SERVICES	192
THE TALKING WOOD CHIP	211
EUSTACHE, THE NEGRO SLAVE	215
THE MONTYON PRIZE OF VIRTUE	221
REMARKABLE ESCAPE FROM THE MASSACRE AT CAWNPORE	228
THE SIEGE OF JERUSALEM BY TITUS	238
CAPTURE OF A SPANISH SLAVE SHIP	253
SAVED FROM A FLOATING SEPULCHRE	256
THE ORIGINAL ROBINSON CRUSOE	261
CAPTAIN DAMPIER AND THE BUCCANEERS	268
ARMINIUS VAMBÉRY'S TRAVELS IN ASIA	280
THE FATE OF A GERMAN WATCHMAKER IN BOKHARA	289
THE GALLANT DEFENCE OF RORKE'S DRIFT	292
HEROES OF THE VICTORIA CROSS	300
KAVANAGH'S DARING JOURNEY	310
THE LAST OF THE MAMELUKES	317
MAN OVERBOARD!	322
EARLY EXPLORING EXPEDITIONS IN AUSTRALIA	329
ACROSS AUSTRALIA FROM SEA TO SEA	337
THE DISCOVERY OF GOLD IN AUSTRALIA	345
HOW CHRISTIANITY WAS INTRODUCED INTO MANGAIA	349
TWO ATTEMPTS TO ASCEND CHIMBORAZO	360

Contents.

	PAGE
TWICE TO THE TOP OF CHIMBORAZO	369
THE WIDOW AND HER MONEY-BAGS	374
COMMODORE BYRON IN PATAGONIA	381
THE TRAVELS OF MARCO POLO	386
HOW BLAKE MADE VAN TROMP TAKE THE BROOM FROM HIS TOP-MAST	391
DAVID DOUGLAS, THE BOTANICAL COLLECTOR	397

LIST OF ILLUSTRATIONS.

	PAGE
THE DUTCH SETTLEMENT AT DESHIMA, JAPAN	12
THE TAJ MEHAL AT AGRA	46
THE PALACE AT DELHI	50
ARRIVAL OF THE GOOD SHIP "HARMONY"	97
GARIBALDI'S HOUSE AT CAPRERA	124
A JAPANESE WATER PICNIC	143
WRECK OF THE "INDIAN CHIEF," AND SERVICES OF THE RAMSGATE LIFEBOAT	198
REMARKABLE ESCAPE FROM THE MASSACRE AT CAWNPORE	234
"NO SOONER HAD I TAKEN THE GLASS IN MY HAND THAN I LOOKED TO SEE THE REFLECTION"	291
GALLANT DEFENCE OF RORKE'S DRIFT. THE MORNING AFTER THE CONFLICT	296
BLOWING UP OF THE CASHMERE GATE	305
DEPARTURE OF BURKE'S EXPEDITION FROM MELBOURNE	339
MANGAIA. HEATHEN CEREMONIES ON THE RETURN OF THE PLEIADES	356

WILLIAM ADAMS,
THE PIONEER ENGLISHMAN IN JAPAN.

IN the year of our Lord 1598, the Dutch East India Company sent out a fleet of five Hollanders "to traffic in the Indies." Great rumours were spread throughout Europe of the riches obtained by the Spanish and Portuguese in these far-distant parts of the world. Defying the bulls and interdicts of the Pope, and the threatenings of the nations protected by him, the Dutch, like the English, were resolved to seek their share in the good things made known by the navigators and discoverers of those times. So this Dutch fleet was equipped and sent forth, sailing from the Texel on the 24th of June, under the command of Master Jacque Mahay, as admiral, in the good ship *Erasmus*.

The chief pilot of the fleet was an Englishman, William Adams, born in "Gillingham, two miles from Rochester, and one mile from Chatham, where the Queen's ships do lie." This "Kentish man" was a true and loyal subject of Queen Elizabeth, but he was ready, like many Englishmen of that time, to serve wherever he had good opportunity, provided it was not among the Spaniards and other enemies of free and Protestant England. He gives account of himself and of his voyages in letters to his wife, which were fortunately preserved, and published by Purchas, the Collector of so many curious and valuable records of old travel and adventure.

Of his previous life, this is what Will Adams tells :—" I was from the age of twelve brought up in Limehouse, near London, being 'prentice twelve years to one master, Nicholas Diggins, and have served in the place of master and pilot in Her

Majesty's ships, and about eleven or twelve years served the Worshipful Company of Barbary Merchants, until the Indian traffic from Holland began, in which Indian traffic I was desirous to make a little experience of the small knowledge which God hath given me." He was thus a well-trained and experienced mariner, this pilot of the Dutch expedition under Admiral Jacque Mahay.

The fleet sailed on the 24th of June, as we are told; but as there is some confusion about exact dates in old style and new style reckoning, let it be about the middle of the year 1598. Voyages in those days were seldom swift, and provisions not of the most wholesome kind, so we are not surprised to learn that sickness broke out—scurvy, most likely—and they were glad to touch on the coast of Guinea for rest and refreshment. Before they sailed again, the Admiral and many of his men died. It was not till April of next year, 1599, that they reached the Straits of Magellan, having decided to reach the Indies by way of the South Seas. In so long a voyage the ships could not expect to keep in company, and Moka, on the coast of Chili, was appointed as the place of rendezvous. The *Erasmus* arrived here in due course, but after waiting till the month of November for her consorts, only one turned up, the pilot of which was a friend and countryman of Will Adams, "one Timothy Shotten, who had been with Master Cavendish in his voyage round the world."

Two of the ships were never heard of, and are supposed to have foundered at sea. A third fell into the hands of Spaniards, or pirates, for they were much the same in those days.

On the American coast the two remaining ships had hard times of it from the same enemies. The captain of the *Erasmus*, when on shore to purchase supplies for the half-starving crew, was attacked and slain, with several of his men, among whom, says Adams, was "my poor brother Thomas, and they left scarce so many men whole as could weigh our anchor." The sister ship fared no better. The captain and twenty-seven men were killed in another affair on that coast.

The brave and resolute survivors in the two ships chose new captains, and then "held a council as to what they should do to make their voyage most profitable. At last it was resolved to go for Japan; for by the report of Derrick Gerritson, who had been there with the Portugals, woollen cloth was in great estimation in that island; and we gathered, by reason that the Malaccas and the most part of the East Indies were hot countries, woollen cloths would not be much accepted. Therefore it was we all agreed to go to Japan."

A very wise and shrewd resolution, arrived at unanimously. There were no "cotton goods" in those days to export from our factories; the woollen manufacture and good broadcloth formed the staple of English trade in the rough old times when the Lord Chancellor literally sat upon a woolsack! Adams had made woollen stuff the substance of his share of the cargo, and probably had advised others to do the same.

On the 29th of November, 1599, the two ships, piloted by William Adams and Timothy Shotten, started on the long voyage across unknown waters. They bore up bravely before the south-east trade-wind, but so little did they know about winds and weather in these parts of the ocean, that this curious entry appears in the narrative, "The wind continued good for divers months"!

But after they got beyond the reach of the trade-winds, and after various perils and adventures in strange island channels, sailing northward from the equator, they gradually came to regions of stormy winds and angry seas. On the 24th of February the *Erasmus* parts finally from her consort, and Timothy Shotten is heard of no more. He is supposed to have gone down at sea—a less horrible fate than that of eight of his fellow-seamen, who had been killed and eaten by the natives of some cannibal island of the South Sea.

The *Erasmus* still held on towards Japan, and on the 24th of March Adams records : " We saw an island called

Una Colonna, at which time many of our men were sick and divers dead. Great was the misery we were in, having no more than nine or ten men able to go or creep upon their knees ; our captain and all the rest looking every hour to die. But on the 11th of April, 1600, we saw the high land of Japan near unto Bungo, at which time there were no more than five men of us able to go. The 12th of April we came hard to Bungo, where many country barques came aboard us, the people whereof we willingly let come, having no force to resist them ; and at this place we came to an anchor."

It was a sorry plight for them to be in on their first arrival at the long-sought land of hope and promise—Cipango, or Zipangu of old Marco Polo, the Venetian traveller, who had three hundred years before brought to Europe tales about its fabulous wealth and high civilization. These rumours had spread through Europe, and had kept alive the desire for better knowledge of the mysterious island. Since the first voyage of Columbus, the reaching of Cathay and Cipango, and all the rich regions of the Indies, had become a passion with voyagers and explorers, and merchant men were keenly watching the results of their enterprizes and explorations.

These Dutchmen were not, however, the first to see the golden islands, as they soon found to their cost. There were enemies in the country more to be dreaded than even the perils of the sea and the dangers of sickness, from which William Adams and his few and weakened comrades had been delivered.

"After we had been there" (in Bungo), wrote the English pilot, "from five to six days, a Portugal Jesuit, with other Portugals" (so they always then called the Portuguese), "and some Japanese, that were Christians, came from a place called Nagasaki, which was ill for us, the Portugals being our mortal enemies ; who reported that we were pirates, and were not in the way of merchandizing."

The Tycoon, or executive Emperor of Japan, was at that time at Osaka, and when the arrival of the ship at Bungo was reported to him, the crew thereof being not Portuguese nor Spanish, he ordered that the pilot and one of the seamen should be brought before him, the captain being too ill to move. The Jesuit and the Portugals had no doubt given a very dreadful account of these strangers, as being not only pirates, worthy of instant death, which was the penalty of that crime, but doubly deserving crucifixion, as being heretics, and foes of the true faith (of the Portugals).

It was a serious crisis, and Will Adams probably had small prospect of safety when he said good-bye to his sick captain and shipmates; nevertheless, adds he, " I commended myself into His hands that had preserved me from so many perils on the sea."

Brought before the Tycoon, and questioned through an interpreter, " I showed him," says Adams, " the name of our country, and that our land had long sought out the way by sea to the East Indies." Having explained that this was for purposes of commerce, the Tycoon asked whether our country had wars ? " I answered him, ' yea,' with the Portuguese and Spaniards, being at peace with all other nations."

Now the Tycoon, who had not long since succeeded to the dignity, had no love for Portuguese or Spaniards. His predecessor, Taiko-sama, had actually commenced a stern persecution of the Jesuit missionaries, as suspected of political intrigues as well as disturbers of the people, and several priests had been put to death in the year before he died. The Jesuits hoped that the new Tycoon would be less hostile, and, in fact, at the commencement of his rule there seemed to be full toleration. The missionaries made good use of their time. It is estimated that their export of silver alone at this epoch was about two millions of taels every year, besides gold and other valuables. At least, this is asserted by Kæmpfer, the early historian of Japan, who represents these Romish emissaries as keen traders under the guise of devout missionaries. Making due allowance for Kæmpfer being a Dutchman, there is no doubt that the Spanish and Portuguese Jesuits in those times knew how to make the best of both worlds, and the warrant of the Tycoon for the death of the three priests, still extant among the Imperial records, says that they were condemned to death for "having come from the Philippines to Japan under the pretended title of ambassadors, and for having persisted in my land, and preached the Christian religion against my decree."

All this was well known to the Tycoon, before whom William Adams now stood. He no doubt heard without displeasure that the new-comers were no friends of the Portugals or Spaniards, and were of a different religion from that which had proved troublesome to the empire. He gave orders that the two men should be kept in prison, and a little later he ordered that the ship be brought up to Osaka. For thirty-nine days Adams and his shipmate remained in custody, full of anxiety about the fate of themselves and their friends. The Jesuits used every means to influence the Tycoon, and when the *Erasmus* at length arrived they redoubled their cruel efforts, again affirming that these strangers were pirates and robbers, as well as foes to their people, and saying that "if justice was executed upon us it would terrify the rest of our nation from coming there any more." "To this intent," says Adams, " they daily sued to His Majesty to cut us off."

Perhaps their zeal overshot its mark; at all events, the heathen ruler proved more humane than the so-called Christian missionaries, for "the Emperor answered them, that because their two countries were at war, it was no reason why, to please Portugals, he should slay Dutch and Englishmen!" With keen satire the political appeal was thus disposed of, and though the Emperor made no reference to the religious differences, the charitable state of mind in the Jesuits can be easily guessed; while honest Bill Adams piously expresses his thankful feeling in the words, "Praised be God for ever and ever!"

When the ship arrived, the pilot and the seamen were received by their comrades with wonder and "much shedding of tears," for they had been told that Adams and his companion had long since been put to death. They were all treated with kindness and hospitality, and they soon recovered health and spirits; but they and their good ship were never again to return to Europe. The *Erasmus* was ordered to the city of Yeddo, the capital of the empire, and William Adams, whose bearing and character seem to have favourably impressed the Tycoon, was retained in the Imperial service. What became of the rest of the crew is not stated, but they probably served as seamen, or were otherwise employed in the land of their enforced residence. We know that they were ordered to be granted daily rations of rice, and twelve kobangs of gold a year, as an Imperial allowance. The captain, we also know, received permission to go as far as the Straits of Malacca in a native vessel, and he was killed in an action with the Portuguese, having joined the Dutch fleet there during the fight. None of the other seamen were allowed to leave Japan. Possibly the hint of the Jesuits had been taken, although not in their fatal intent, that the sending away of these men might bring others of their nation!

Several years passed, Adams growing in favour and influence at the Court of Yeddo, acquiring, no doubt, much knowledge of the people, and their ways and language, but never losing remembrance of his country and home in old England.

His time was turned to good account for his new masters. He had some skill in ship-building, and having built a vessel of 80 tons the Tycoon was greatly pleased. He afterwards built a larger vessel of 120 tons, and made a cruise as far as Miako Bay in her with a Japanese crew. But he astonished the natives by more than skill in manual craft. "Being in such grace and favour," he says, " by reason I taught him (the Emperor) some points of geometry and the mathematics, with other things, that what I said could not be contradicted. At the which, my former enemies, the Jesuits and Portugals, did greatly wonder, and entreated me to befriend them to the Emperor in their business; and so by my means both Spaniards and Portugals have received friendship from the Emperor, I recompensing their evil unto me with good."

What were the " other things " besides " the mathematics " which he showed to the Emperor we are left to conjecture, but the narrative carries a very useful lesson to the young as to the importance of a knowledge of practical geometry in all its branches, as well as skill in the use of various tools and instruments, and as much acquaintance as can be gained with arts and sciences, as well as with mere grammar and literature, whether in living or dead languages. How few of the boys educated in our public schools could have risen to the position and obtained the honour of Will Adams, the apprentice lad of Limehouse! With fair natural ability, he had always a thirst for knowledge, and desire to add to his " experience " in whatever circumstances he found himself.

The year 1609 brought two events which caused a mighty commotion in Japan, and in which Adams took no unimportant part. A Spanish galleon, the *San Francisco*, returning from Manilla to Acapulco in Mexico, and having on board the Governor of the Philippines, was wrecked on the coast of Japan. Of the crew, one hundred and sixty souls perished. The remainder, including the Governor, were very kindly treated. The larger vessel, of 120 tons, built by Adams, was placed at their disposal by the Emperor, and fitted out with every means for proceeding on their voyage, which they did in the same year, returning, it appears, to Manilla. How the very name of " Spanish galleon," and such places as Manilla and the Philippines, and Acapulco in Mexico, conjure up visions of dollars and gold-pieces, and the rich freights of the Argosies of those days! No wonder that pirates abounded, and that in time of war the privateers scoured all the seas of the world in quest of prizes!

This was what brought two Dutch privateers to the seas of Japan, in the same year that the Spanish galleon was wrecked there. The Dutchmen came to look after a Portuguese ship which ran yearly from Macao to the land of the Tycoon.

They missed their prize, but they found themselves very well treated ; and professing willingness to engage in lawful and peaceable trade, the port of Firando was ceded to them for this purpose, through the good offices and intercession of William Adams. They returned to Europe to make arrangements for the opening of regular trade, and Adams took advantage of the opportunity for sending letters home. These are the letters which have found an abiding and interesting place of record in the pages of Purchas.

The Dutch East India Company must have watched anxiously and waited wearily for the ships sent out by them so long ago as 1598, and must have wondered why no tidings ever came of them. Adams, and the other survivors of the crew of the *Erasmus*, must also have often wondered what people at home were saying of them, whether they were still anxiously looked for, or given up as hopelessly lost. There was at least a hope of opening communication with the lands and people to which their thoughts and affections so often had been travelling. The disappointment at not being allowed to depart with the Dutch ships must have been great, but if these got to Holland in safety there was hope of his being heard of by his family and friends, and of receiving tidings through those who would come to Japan. Meanwhile he is in good quarters so far as outward affairs go. Through the kindness and generosity of the Emperor he has a living "like unto a lordship in England, with eighty or ninety husbandmen, who are as my servants and slaves,"—living the life, in fact, of a country squire or nobleman. He has a high opinion of the people and nation where his lot is now cast. " The people are good of nature, courteous above measure, and valiant in war." And as to the government, " I think no land better governed in the world by civil policy." So he urges his countrymen to come to trade, and have dealings with such a people, ending that letter with a touching utterance of patient submission and pious prayer about what was still nearest to his heart, the thought of his dear wife and children. "Patiently," he writes,

"I wait the good will and pleasure of God Almighty, desiring all those to whom this letter may come, to use means to acquaint my good friends with it, and so my wife and children may hear of me; by which means there may be hope that I may see them before my death—which the Lord grant to His glory and my great comfort. Amen."

This was written and sent in 1611. How the next year passed with him we do not hear, but in 1613 the startling news came to Yeddo that an English ship had arrived, and was at anchor in the port of Firando. The Governor of that place sent for Adams, in the meantime treating the newly-arrived Englishmen with marked attention. Adams found the ship to be the *Clove* of London, belonging to the East India Company, and commanded by Captain John Saris, who was furnished with a letter from King James I., and suitable presents for the Emperor, whose friendship and good offices he was charged to seek, in order to arrange a treaty of commerce. The good ship *Clove* had left the Thames so far back as April 18th, 1611, and had spent more than two years in the voyage, trading at various ports, as the custom then was, and not reaching Firando till the 11th of June, 1613. Captain Saris little knew how efficient and influential a fellow-countryman he was to find in Japan. After consultation, and despatch of various messages, it was arranged that the captain and ten of his Englishmen should attend the Emperor at Yeddo, to which place they set out early in August, bearing the royal letter and the presents. The interview and audience came off splendidly. The Tycoon was delighted with the frank and dignified bearing of Captain Saris, and with the advice of Adams a treaty was concluded between the Emperor of Japan and the King of Great Britain, by which the most important privileges were granted—far beyond what had ever before been conceded to a foreign power, and, in fact, beyond what are now possessed. The tone of the whole treaty may be gathered from the first article, which was as follows :—" We give free license to the subjects of the King of Great Britain—viz., Sir Thomas Smith,

Governor, and the Company of the East India Merchants and adventurers, for ever safely to come into any of our ports of our Empire of Japan, with their ships and merchandize, without any hindrance to them or their goods; and to abide, buy, sell, and barter, according to their own manner with all nations; to tarry here as long as they think good, and to depart at their pleasure." Other articles of the treaty gave freedom from customs, tolls, and duties; liberty of transit by sea or land; right to build and to possess property; orders for instant payment for all goods delivered; dispensing with permits and passports, and a variety of other rights and privileges, the extent and liberality of which the more surprise us, from knowing the subsequent history of Japanese relations with foreign nations. But the Tycoon of that period, Tyeyas, was an enlightened and liberal ruler, and he had for his chief adviser in the matter William Adams. Captain Saris took his departure, highly gratified by his reception, and bearing a letter from the Tycoon to King James, offering a hearty welcome to his subjects, complimenting the English people for their worthiness and their skill in navigation, and promising that "in their honourable enterprise of discoveries and merchandizing, they shall find the said Tycoon further them according to their desires."

The chief station or headquarters of the English trade was to be at the port of Firando, where the Dutch also had their factory. William Adams seems to have entered the employment of the East India Company, and to have resided at Firando as interpreter in the English factory, which was under the charge of a Mr. Richard Cookes, as consul and manager. He probably remained there till his death, which is supposed to have been in or about the year 1619. He had long resigned himself to perpetual exile, and we have no doubt that the consolation of true piety, which marked his whole character, sustained and cheered him. His name will always be remembered with respect and honour.

It does not belong to this article to follow further the course of events in Japan. After the death of Adams, and after sustaining loss in their Japanese trade, the East India Company retired from the station, and the factory at Firando was voluntarily abandoned. It was given up just in time. Not long after a new policy succeeded in the Government of Japan. The persecution of the Christians, of which they had had before some experience, broke out with great fierceness. The intrigues and misconduct of the Romish priests and missionaries no doubt provoked the attack, and caused an illiberal and intolerant treatment of all foreigners. The Portuguese and Spaniards were forcibly expelled, and the Dutch were permitted to remain only under the most humiliating conditions, their traders being confined to the island of Deshima, near Nagasaki. They were not allowed to set foot on any other part of the soil of the Empire, and when carrying a tribute to the Emperor, they were conveyed in closed carriages, without being permitted to hold communication with the people. "Not a Christian shall remain in Japan," had been the declaration of an Imperial edict, and the Dutchmen imprisoned at Decima hardly owned themselves as Christians. The Japanese had borne long enough the interference of meddlesome foreigners, and in 1637 an Imperial interdict was published, of which one clause thus runs :—"No Japanese ship or boat whatever, nor any natives of Japan, shall presume to go out of the country; and whosoever acts contrary to this shall be put to death, and the ship and goods shall be forfeited; and all Japanese who return from abroad shall be put to death."

Thus commenced the policy of exclusion and seclusion which marks the history of Japan for the next two centuries. In 1673 the English made an attempt to reoccupy their former factory; but there was no William Adams now at Court to be their advocate with the Emperor. The Dutchmen at Decima did not choose to remember that they owed their introduction to Japan to the English pilot, and they had the craft to inform the Government that the English King,

THE DUTCH SETTLEMENT OF DESIMA, OR DESHIMA, JAPAN.

Charles II., was married to the daughter of the King of Portugal. The old religious animosity was thus awakened, and the Japanese authorities courteously, but firmly, refused permission for the English to trade. The Dutch retained a monopoly of commerce, such as it was, at Deshima, until intercourse with the outer world was again opened by the United States of America, little more than thirty years ago. The events that have since occurred are recorded in many well-known books, among which we may name Mr. Mossman's "Land of the Rising Sun"; Miss Bird's "Japan" (Murray); and a bright little book by Sherard Osborne, R.N., "A Cruise in Japanese Waters" (Blackwood and Sons).

A STRANGE ELECTION AND A STRANGER AUCTION.

IN May 1862, William Talcott, an employé in the Pony Express Company, went to look for his ponies in the nearest range of mountains, which was the Toyabe range, in Nevada, United States. He took with him an Apache Indian boy, who had been purchased not long before in Arizona for a jack-knife and a pair of blankets. When in search for the ponies they struck a seam of greenish quartz, which Talcott thought something like what he had seen in a rich mining region. They carried bits of the rock to the house of a Mr. O'Neill, and there they were seen by Mr. Vanderbosch, an intelligent Dutchman, who immediately pronounced a favourable opinion as to the "indications of silver" contained in them. The traces of silver were slight, but there were metals usually found in connection with silver, especially antimony and galena, or lead ore. Specimens were sent to Virginia city, to be tested by assay, with such results as to attract immediate attention.

Among those who heard of the discovery was one David Buel, an enterprising miner and frontier's-man, who had spent much of his time among the Indians of California. He started, along with two friends, for the Reese River, as a small stream in the locality had been called by a miner of the name of Reese. This party of three prospected at several localities, especially near a spot where the city of Austin was soon to rise. Talcott's friends were also busily prospecting, and had made a settlement, which they called Pony Lodge, in remembrance of the incident of Talcott and the Indian boy seeking the strayed ponies.

It is curious that the celebrated western explorer and pathfinder, Colonel Fremont, had passed near these places, but his route lay a little further to the south, and so he missed being the discoverer of the new silver mines in that part of Nevada.

Vanderbosch, Buel, O'Neill, Veatch, and many other miners were now hard at work "prospecting" and "locating" in various localities, and some of the claims turned out to be rich in silver ore. But we are not concerned with mining operations in this narrative. We pass over the time that intervened between the first discoveries, and the foundation of Austin, as the chief place in the district.

Now it is a peculiarity of the American people that they carry with them into every new territory their municipal and political institutions. A "city" of only a few houses, and inhabitants consisting only of rough miners, must have a Mayor and Common Council, with meetings, and election excitements. No American can live without making speeches, or hearing them, without holding office, or voting somebody else into office. Austin was not exempt from this notable feature of American life.

The city charter was passed with due solemnity in April 1864. Public rejoicings followed, as a matter of course. There was great excitement at that period touching the political issues of the day. At Austin, Republicans and Democrats were pretty equally divided, the latter being known chiefly by the name of Copperheads. The election of Mayor would test the numerical strength of the two hostile parties. Every man felt that not only local, but national interests, were concerned in the result.

There were two candidates, pretty fairly matched, for the contest. On the Democratic side was David Buel, already mentioned,—" Uncle Davy," as his fellow-citizens familiarly called him,—a man of imposing presence, six feet four in height, and large in proportion, and with a frank, off-hand manner that endeared him to his fellow-miners. Mr. J. Ross-Browne, an American traveller, who knew Buel well, says that he was acting as "Government Indian Agent on the Klamath Reservation" when he first met with him. "I found him a remarkable man in more respects than one. He was a man of grand presence, of indomitable spirit, of superior intelligence, and of great energy of character. He was an honest Indian agent, the rarest work of God that I know of." A more popular candidate could not have been chosen for his side. It was expected that his personal claims would have carried a large portion of the Republican votes, and doubtless would have done so at any other time. But party feeling then ran high, and the Copperheads were regarded as little more than traitors to the National and Union cause.

The other candidate was Charles Holbrook, a young man of good character and great business capacity. He had recently erected a handsome store, built of cut granite, and was one of the chief merchants of the rising town. His integrity was undoubted, his professions great, and his political faith Ultra-Union. So his chances were not to be despised in an election which seemed likely to turn on public, more than personal, qualifications. Each side was confident of success.

As usual on such occasions, betting was largely made on the result. One of these bets was of a somewhat eccentric kind. Dr. Herrick made an agreement with Mr. R. C. Gridley to the following effect :—If Buel wins, Herrick is to carry a sack of flour from Clifton to Upper Austin, the distance being about a mile and a half, and uphill all the way. If Holbrook is elected, Gridley is to carry a sack of flour from Upper Austin to Clifton, having the advantage of the down-hill grade.

The battle was exciting, and was zealously and honourably fought out on both sides. The betting did no harm, but rather helped to keep the people in good humour, especially when not for money, but for such a wager as the carrying of the sack of flour!

Holbrook, the Republican candidate, was elected by a clear majority. The sentiment of the people was sound, when it came to the great question of maintaining the Union at all hazards.

Gridley, true to his engagement, was on hand at the appointed time and place, with his sack of flour. The whole population turned out to witness the novel performance. Laughter and good humour prevailed on all sides. Winners and losers fraternized, and enjoyed the fun with equal gusto, . A grand procession was formed, headed by an energetic band of music. The newly-elected officials, including His Honour the Mayor, mounted on horseback, followed the musicians. Next to them walked the hero of the scene, the redoubtable Gridley, with the sack of flour on his back. On each side marched a standard-bearer, carrying high the flag of the Union. Never was seen such a lively crowd in Austin. "Go it, Gridley;" "Stick to it, Gridley;" "Never say die, Gridley;" were the encouraging words which greeted him as he plodded on under his load.

On arriving at Clifton, it was suggested by some enterprising genius, whose speculative spirit kept pace with his patriotism, that the sack of flour should be sold for the benefit of the Sanitary Commission. This was a charitable work of which the good offices were devoted to the sick and wounded of both sides, in the war and after. The proposition met with unbounded applause. An empty barrel was quickly found, and an auctioneer mounted on its end. The bidding was lively, but only in small amounts, so that no large number of dollars was offered for the flour. The auctioneer said

a Stranger Auction. 17

that the reserve price had not been reached, and announced that another auction should be held at Austin. The sack of flour was taken up again, Gridley insisting on being the voluntary porter. The procession was re-formed, and marched off this time to the tune of "Dixie."

The most uncompromising Copperhead was now won over, and all united in common sympathy for the suffering soldiers, and in real regret for the strife in their common country. It was a clever stroke of policy for the Republicans.

The procession halted in front of the store owned by His Honour the Mayor. By this time the crowd was enormous, and the enthusiasm great. The miners from outlying claims had gathered to the town, the business men had come from their stores, women and children from their cottages and cabins.

The sack of flour was once more put up at auction, with a general hurrah. This time the bidders were in earnest. They bid up twenties, and fifties, and even hundreds, some bidding against themselves in their eagerness! Republicans and Democrats vied in the contest. The best feeling prevailed, and three thousand dollars was the result.

The purchaser, amidst vociferous applause, donated his purchase back to the Sanitary Fund. A third auction was held on the following day. The result on this occasion was nearly two thousand dollars.

The excitement fanned the patriotic fire in the breast of Gridley. He resolved to make an institution of the sack of flour at auction. He would immortalise it; he would gather a munificent sum as a donation for the sick soldiers, gathering also a reputation for himself.

So Gridley set out on a tour with his sack of flour. It was sold at Virginia City for eight thousand dollars, at Sacramento for ten thousand dollars, and at San Francisco for about fifteen thousand dollars. "I was witness," says Mr. Ross-Browne, in one of his books of travel, "to the procession in San Francisco. It was the notable event of the times. Never did Montgomery Street present a more imposing appearance. The beauty and fashion of the city were there, and so was Gridley, decked out in glorious array, the observed of all observers. Thus did he draw the superfluous cash from the pockets of the generous public, and thus did he good service to the cause of humanity and freedom. All honour to Gridley!"

The grand finale was a gift of one hundred thousand dollars to the Sanitary Commission! It was a noble speculation, the humble origin of which we have narrated, as connected with the Mayor's election at the little Nevada town of Austin.

On the strength of his fame, Gridley became interested, along with other experienced financiers, in the establishment of a bank in Austin, sufficient capital being raised in New York to commence it, under the name of the "First National Bank of Nevada."

CALIFORNIA'S FIRST START.

THE rapid increase of population and wealth in that part of Western America known as "The Great Pacific Slope" is one of the most notable events in the history of the world. At the time when Queen Victoria began her reign, the land of California was to Englishmen, and even to the people of the United States, a *terra incognita*. In fact, before the Mexican war, when General Jackson commanded the American army of invasion, these regions had attracted little notice. They were far too remote to tempt the most adventurous emigrants, and seemed divided from the rest of the continent by unpassable mountains and impossible distance. Here and there, in the southern part of the region, a few Mexican squatters had ranchos of unbounded extent, with cattle that were killed only for their hides. Over the whole region wild tribes of Indians roamed, numbering at that time perhaps hundreds of thousands. Gradually adventurous hunters trappers, and traders came to the country; but forty years ago, in 1844, the whole white and half-breed population of California did not exceed seven or eight thousand, with about an equal number of domesticated Indians. The whole vast territory was little better than a wilderness.

In 1845 the American Congress declared Texas to be annexed to the Republic, as Mexico owed a debt of some million of dollars, a debt which could neither be paid nor repudiated. The war which followed led to further annexation, and the American flag was planted in California. Under the protection of that flag, and in the confidence which it gave, people from the States, and emigrants of other nationalities, began to appear, streams of emigration waggons slowly travelling over the pathless prairies and across the rugged mountains, toward the lands of the west. In two or three years the population had doubled. Among the earlier emigrants was one Captain Sutter, who had a large farm on the Sacramento River, where he had planted himself, building a fort, which he called New Helvetia.

An event was soon to occur, apparently purely accidental, but which now, on looking back upon it, will be recognized as the providential means used by the Ruler of the world for great and beneficial purposes. It had the effect of changing the whole face of the country, of attracting the attention and stirring the feelings of men, not only in America, but in distant lands, and of drawing multitudes to people a region hitherto almost uninhabited, and providing homes, amidst riches and plenty, for vast numbers of the human race. In the course of a few years this event produced results which a century might not have effected in the ordinary march of civilization and rate of progress.

In the winter of 1847-8 this Captain Sutter was building a saw-mill on the south branch of the Sacramento River. Mr. James Marshall, the contractor to erect the mill, one day let water into the tail-race, in order to deepen the channel. With the water was borne some sand and mud, which was deposited. On looking down, Marshall saw little bright grains among the sand. Picking some of it up, examining it, and noticing its weight, he was certain that he had particles of gold in his hand. Eager with excitement, he ran to tell Sutter what he had found. The captain, on hearing his words, and observing his excited manner, thought at first he had gone mad, and kept an eye on his loaded rifle. Marshall soon satisfied him that he was all right, and gave him the gold to examine for himself. Both were now alike excited, and they hastened to the place, vowing to each other the utmost secrecy. But they did not know that they had been observed. A Mormon soldier, who happened to be within sight, was attracted by their movements, and closely watched them from a concealed spot. He was one of a band who had been in the Mexican war, and with his companions was on his way back to the States. The soldiers soon ascertained for themselves what was the cause of excitement in Sutter and Marshall. The secret was out, and rumour began its usual course, with more than usual speed and enlargement. The news spread far and wide that gold was to be had for the picking up in the sands of the " Rio de los Americanos," as that branch of the Sacramento was called in the country. Birds of prey do not more rapidly and mysteriously see or scent from afar the place of feeding than men become aware of the existence of gold.

Before many days had passed, many hundreds of people could be seen from Sutter's saw-mill, and swarms more day by day arriving in the neighbourhood, armed with spades, shovels, knives, sticks, and wooden bowls, all searching in the stream and the soil for the hidden treasure. As the news spread, the rush increased—Spaniards, Mexicans, Americans. Then the tidings reached remote places; towns were deserted, ships left crewless. An American clergy-

California's First Start.

man—Dr. Todd, of Pittsfield—who visited California some years after, and heard on the spot the legends of those days, thus describes the events :—" Oregon on the north, the Sandwich Islands on the west, Peru and Chili on the south, poured in their eager diggers. Then China felt the thrill, and her people flocked over ; Australia sent her convicts and rascals ; and adventurers from all parts of the earth, having nothing to lose, flew to California. The Mexican war had just been closed, and thousands of young men from the soldiery went to the land of gold. The Eastern States caught the fever, and emigrant waggons uncountable hastened over the deserts, leaving the bones of men and of animals to bleach along their path.

"On—on, to the land of gold ! Ho, for California ! Ships went tossing round Cape Horn full of young men. England, Germany, France, Italy, sent multitudes. At once the east (of the United States) was aroused, and sent fifty thousand men a year for five successive years, and invested ninety-two millions of dollars before any return was made. In a time incredibly short there was at least a quarter of a million of the wildest, bravest, most daring, and most intelligent young men digging for gold. There was no female society, there were no homes to soften or restrain, no laws, no police, and no magistrates. From the lakes of the north to the Gulf of Mexico, from the lumber-mills of Maine to the settler on the Indian territories, the whole land was moved."

This is no exaggerated statement of the excitement caused by the reported gold discoveries. We well remember the influence of the news even in London Numbers of young men left their situations, and shop-keepers gave up trade, in the hope of getting rich in a more rapid and certain way. It was no uncommon sight to see shutters closed, and a notice posted or chalked up, "Gone to the diggings," or " Off to California " !

Nothing was thought of by these adventurers beyond the

hope of getting gold for the searching. Whether the search would be successful, or whether the game would pay, was seldom considered. It was a far-off land, where there were neither houses nor shops, clothing nor food. Fabulous sums are reported to have been paid for the most trifling articles. As a rare luxury, a so-called " saloon," composed of tarpaulin, could now and then hang out the sign "Potatoes this day," and crowds flocked to the costly entertainment. Apples are known to have sold for five dollars apiece in gold! " Easy come, easy go," it was with such expenditure!

Worse than costly living, was the fearful gambling among the diggers. Fortunes made in a day were lost in a night in these infamous gambling dens.

Now and then rumours came of new places where gold had been found. Once, for instance, it was reported that a rich field was in Oregon, in the black sand near the seashore. In two days eight vessels from San Francisco were advertised to sail for the Gold Bluffs. The excitement died at once when thousands had been disappointed.

Long afterwards there were still fresh reports and repeated failures. Who does not remember the Fraser River excitement? It was a thousand miles away, up in British Columbia. Hundreds started off at once, in the next month nine thousand five hundred went, and in three months from the first notice nearly twenty thousand had gone from California!

This article is not intended to be historical nor statistical, so we say nothing here about the amount of gold that has been obtained since the first year of its being discovered, nor of the growth of California in population or in resources. Neither are we going to moralize about the lust of gold, nor the habits and character of the digger. Let it suffice to say that here, as in Australia, and in all countries and periods of the world, the miner's and digger's career is, on the whole, not to be admired or envied. A few find wealth, but the fate of the vast majority is poverty and

California's First Start.

disease, disappointment and disaster. The object in recalling this strange time of excitement is not to deal with personal conditions, but to refer to the providential circumstances by which a new region of the world was occupied, and a mighty increase made in the population and wealth and influence of the great American Republic. That Republic now bears dominion from the Atlantic to the Pacific Ocean, and by the peopling of the Pacific Slope has added a vast territory, available for supporting millions of civilized and Christian men. For with all the faults and vices that prevail among men of every race and clime, it is pleasant to think that the influence of the United States is, on the whole, conducive to the peace and prosperity, the civilization and progress of the human race.

One curious and remarkable incident we must mention before closing this article. At first the digging or gathering of gold and of silver, which was discovered in the Nevada ranges not many years after, was at best a rude and mechanical work. For continuing the mining with success and profit, Art had to be used, both in providing machinery and by introducing chemical processes. In the latter case the use of an enormous quantity of mercury or quicksilver is required. It will add to our admiration of the providential arrangement to which we have referred when it is stated that the discovery of vast stores of quicksilver was also the result of what we call a lucky accident. Not long before the gold discovery, a Mexican officer met a tribe of Indians with their faces resplendent with vermilion colour. He knew that this paint comes from cinnabar, an ore of quicksilver. By a bribe, he induced the Indians to show him the place where they got the ore. What followed, and how from the ore the mercury is obtained, and how the rich mines have been utilised, need not here be described; but we cannot avoid remarking how seasonable this discovery also was, and how it worked along with the gold discovery in securing the settlement of the great State of California.

AT THE COURT OF THE GREAT MOGUL.

IN the year A.D. 1600, the first charter was granted to the East India Company by Queen Elizabeth. The trade of England with India continuing to increase, King James the First resolved to send an ambassador, or special envoy, to the Emperor of Hindustan, commonly called the Great Mogul. The object of the embassy was to obtain a treaty of peace and amity between the King of Great Britain and his Indian Majesty; to secure for English subjects freedom of trade in all ports of India; and in various ways to advance the commercial interests of England, by such protection and privileges as could be granted by the mighty Ruler of the East.

The Mogul of this period was Jehan Guire, the tenth in descent from Timour-Leng (the lame prince), better known as Tamerlane, the renowned conqueror. Timour married the only daughter of those nations or tribes of Great Tartary called Moguls. Hence the name borne by the conquerors and rulers of Hindustan, or Indostan, the country of the Hindus, or Indians. By successive conquests these rulers now bore sway over all the regions from China to the Caspian, and from the mountains to the sea. Candahar, Cashmere, Cabul, the Punjab, Agra, Delhi, Gwalior, Gujerat, Bengal, these are but a few of the principalities and powers mentioned as being under the dominion of Shah Selim Jehan Guire, the Great Mogul, at the beginning of the seventeenth century. The rulers in different regions were not all of the Mogul race; some were Persians, Arabs, or Turks, while other territories were left under their native Indian rajahs or kings, who were tributaries of the Mohammedan Suzerain, the Great Mogul.

Sir Thomas Roe was the ambassador sent by James

At the Court of the Great Mogul.

the First, having with him many curious and valuable articles from the western world as presents, and accompanied by a small retinue, including a chaplain and an artist. Sir Thomas kept a minute journal of his travels, and of his residence at the court of the Mogul, portions of which are published in various old collections of travels, both in English and foreign languages. The journal extends over three years—1614, 1615, 1616. Even at this distance of time, and under the strangely-altered conditions of English intercourse with India, there are many things recorded by Sir Thomas Roe full of interest.

On March 6th, 1614, the Lizard light was lost sight of, and the course begun for the Cape of Good Hope. On the 26th the African coast was descried; Cape Bodajor east by south on the 27th; April 14th the Line was crossed; May 2nd the tropic of Capricorn; and on June 21st they arrived at the Cape. Saldanha Bay and Penguin Island were the only places at which anchor was cast. At Saldanha the natives are described as "the most barbarous people in the world," "eating carrion," "having no clothes but skins wrapped upon their shoulders," and "their houses but a mat, rounded at the top like an oven, which they turn as the wind changes, having no door to keep it out." There are, at the same time, "cows in abundance, antelopes, baboons, pheasants, wild geese, ducks, and many other sorts." On the Isle of Penguin "is a sort of fowl of that name, that goes upright, his wings without feathers, hanging down like sleeves faced with white. They do not fly, but only walk in parcels, keeping regularly their own quarters. They are a sort of mixture of beast, bird, and fish, but most bird!" The Table Mountain is described as "11,853 feet high." "The bay is full of whales and seals."

They did not stop at the Cape, and on July 8th sighted Madagascar, and anchored on the 22nd at Molalid, one of the Comorese Islands. Of the Arab people inhabiting these islands, with their government, customs, products, and their trade with the Mozambique mainland, details are given. On

August the 2nd they weighed and stood for Socotora; recrossing the equinoctial line northward on the 10th; making Cape Guardafui, at the entrance to the Red Sea, on the 18th, and coming to anchor in Delicia Bay, Socotora, on the 24th August. Socotora, or Socotra, is the Dioscuria of the ancients, well known in their commerce and navigation. The people then, as now, being Mohammedans, were ruled by an Arab Sultan, son of a great sheikh in Arabia Felix. The king received the English embassy with much courtesy, coming to the shore on horseback with about three hundred men, armed some with muskets, some with bows, and all with good swords." "He had a very good turban, but was barefooted." " He was so absolute that no man could sell anything but himself, his people sitting about him very respectfully." Mr. Boughton, one of the embassy, went to see the king's house at the chief town—Tamara. He found it "such as would serve an ordinary gentleman in England. The lower rooms served for warehouses and wardrobe, some changes of robes hanging about the walls, and with them about twenty-five books of their law, religion, history, and saints' lives. No man was permitted to go upstairs to see his wives, which were three, nor the other women; but the ordinary sort might be seen in the town, with their ears full of silver rings." For dinner Mr. Boughton had fowl with rice, and for drink water and " cahu, black liquor, drank as hot as could be endured "—no doubt *café noir*, or coffee, with which evidently Sir Thomas Roe was not acquainted. A priest was at service in the mosque, which they visited. Some remains were seen of crosses and images, showing that Christians formerly had been in the island. Some of the older inhabitants of the island were seen—a poor, unclothed, savage people. Aloes and certain gums seemed the chief trade products of the island.

They weighed anchor on August 31st, and steered their course for Surat, where they landed on the 26th of September. Surat, near the mouth of the river Taptee, which flows

At the Court of the Great Mogul.

into the Gulf of Cambay, was in old times the chief port on the western side of India, being then, as Bombay now is the first place reached by all voyagers by the Red Sea route. It is still the favourite port for the embarcation of Mohammedan pilgrims to Mecca. On the arrival of the English ambassador, he was received by the principal officers of the town in an open tent. Much discussion took place as to the payment of duties, and searching the persons of the servants of the ambassador; but at last all were permitted to proceed to a house provided for them, where they remained till the 30th of October, " suffering much," says Sir Thomas Roe, " from the Governor, who by force searched many chests, and took out what he thought fit." What caused so long a tarrying as five weeks is not explained, but possibly the Governor had despatched swift messengers to announce the arrival of the unusual and important strangers on the coast.

They left Surat " on the 30th aforesaid," and travelled very leisurely northward towards Ajmere, or Adsmere as Sir Thomas calls it, where the Court of the Mogul then was. It was not till near the middle of the seventeenth century, under Shah Jehan, son of Jehan Guire, that new Delhi rose near the ruins of the ancient Delhi, and attained to the magnificence it reached in and after the reign of Shah Jehan, of his son Aurungzebe, and of later Moguls.

Of the journey to Ajmere we must give very brief notice, as our space will be better occupied with particulars about the Mogul and his court. On the third day after leaving Surat they entered the kingdom of " Pardassha, a pagan lord of the hills, subject to nobody,"—for there were some of the ancient people, as everywhere in mountain countries, who long retain freedom and independence. Six days from Surat, at Nunderbar, they tasted bread for the first time on the journey, as " the Banians who inhabit the country make no bread, but only cakes. The country is plentiful, especially of cattle, the banians killing none or selling any to be killed. One day I met ten thousand bullocks loaded with corn, in one drove, and most days after lesser parcels." At one place, having pitched the tents outside a town or village, "the king's officers attended me all night with thirty horse and twenty shot (armed men), for fear of the robbers on the mountains, because I refused to remove into the town." The towns were mostly collections of mud-built huts, with stone buildings occasionally, when there were persons of importance or wealth. On the fourteenth day they reached "Brampore," "which I guess to be 223 miles from Surat." At Batharpore, a village two miles short of Brampore, there was a prince, or rajah, to whose presence he was conducted. "The officer told me as I approached I must touch the ground with my head bare, which I refused, and went on to a place right under him, railed in, with an ascent of three steps, where I made him reverence, and he bowed his body; so I went within, where were all the great men of the town, with their hands before them like slaves. The place was covered overhead with a rich canopy, and under foot all with carpets. It was like a great stage, and the prince sat at the upper end of it. Having no place assigned, I stood right before him, he refusing to admit me to come up the steps, or to allow me a chair. Having received my presents, he offered to go into another room, where I should be allowed to sit; but, by the way he made himself drunk out of a case of bottles I gave him, and so the visit ended."

In some parts of the journey, ruins of great extent and apparent magnificence were seen, "fair towers, many pillars, and innumerable houses, but not one inhabitant." This was in the country of Rama, "a prince newly subdued by the Mogul, or rather brought to own subjection." This was in the time of Echar Shah, father of Jehan Guire. Rama was said to be lineally descended from Porus, the Indian king, overcome by Alexander the Great. The rest of the journey was in a north-westerly direction "to compass the hills," but after that due north again, the whole distance to Ajmer being estimated at

At the Court of the Great Mogul. 29

about 418 English miles. Ten months had passed since the Embassy left England, and at last they had come near the presence of the Great Mogul. We now use the words of Sir Thomas Roe.

January the 10th, I went to court at four in the afternoon to the Durbar, where the Mogul daily sits to entertain strangers, receive petitions and presents, give out orders, and to see and be seen. And here it will be proper to give some account of his court. None but eunuchs come within that king's private lodgings, and his women, who guard him with warlike weapons. These punish one another for any offence committed. The Mogul every morning shows himself to the common people at a window that looks into the plain before his gate. At noon he is there again to see elephants and wild beasts fight, the men of rank being under him within a rail. Hence he retires to sleep. After noon he comes to the Durbar aforementioned. After supper at eight of the clock he comes down to the Guzalcan, a fair court, in the midst whereof is a throne of free stone, on which he sits, or sometimes below in a chair, where none are admitted but of the first quality, and few of them without leave. Here he discourses of indifferent things very affably. No business of state is done anywhere but at one of these two last places, where it is publicly canvassed, and so registered; which register might be seen for two shillings, and the common people know as much as the council; so that every day the king's resolutions are the public news, and exposed to the censure of every scoundrel. This method is never altered unless sickness or drink obstruct it; and this must be known, for if he be unseen one day without a reason assigned, the people would mutiny; and for two days no excuse will serve, but the doors must be opened, and some admitted to see him to satisfy others. On Tuesday he sits in judgment at the Jarruco, and hears the meanest person's complaints, examines both parties, and often sees execution done by his elephants.

Before my audience, I had obtained leave to use the customs

of my country. At the Durbar I was conducted right before him; entering the outward rail, two noble slaves met to conduct me nearer. At the first rail I made a low reverence, at the next another, and when under the king a third. The place is a great court, to which all sorts of people resort. The king sits in a little gallery overhead; ambassadors, great men, and strangers of quality within the inmost rail under him, raised from the ground, covered with canopies of velvet and silk, and good carpets under foot. The next degree, like our gentry, are within the first rail, the commonalty without in a lower court, yet so that all may see the king. In fine, it is rising by degrees like a theatre. His reception was very favourable, but needs not particularizing.

The next day being the 12th of March, I went to visit the king, and delivered him a present, where I saw abundance of wealth, but being of all sorts put together without order, it did not look so regular. The same day the son of Rama, the new tributary before mentioned, did his homage, touching the ground three times with his head. The thirteenth at night I had audience at the Guzalcan, and pressed to have the peace and commerce with England settled after a solemn manner, and all the articles settled, which the Mogul ordered should be done. The fifteenth I went again in the evening to the Norose, and according to the Mogul's order chose my place of standing, which was on the right hand of him on the rising of the throne, the Prince and young Rama standing on the other side; so I had a full view of what was to be seen—presents, elephants, horses, and women. The twenty-third the Mogul condemned one of his own nation upon suspicion of felony; but being one of the handsomest men in India, and the evidence not very clear against him, he would not suffer him to be executed, but sent him to me in irons for a slave to dispose of at my will. This is looked upon as a great favour, for which I returned thanks: adding, that in England we had no slaves, nor thought it lawful to make the image of God equal to a beast, but that I would use him as a servant, and if he behaved himself well,

At the Court of the Great Mogul.

give him his liberty. This the Mogul was well pleased with. The twenty-sixth I went to the Guzalcan, and delivered the articles I had drawn up, which were referred to Asaph Chan, who a while after sent to me to remove from the standing I had taken before the king, because I stood alone, and that was not the custom. I refused at first, but he insisting I should rank myself among the nobility, I removed to the other side, to the place where only the Prince and young Rama were; which more disgusted Asaph Chan, who persuaded the Prince to complain of me, which he did; but the Mogul having heard their complaint, and my answer, that I removed by Asaph Chan's order, answered, I had done well, and they were in the wrong to offer to displace me in his sight. So I kept my place in quiet.

The substance of the articles delivered to the Great Mogul was: 1. That there be perpetual peace and amity between the King of Great Britain and His Indian Majesty. 2. That the subjects of England have free trade in all ports of India. 3. That the governors of all ports publish this agreement three times upon the arrival of any English ships. 4. That the merchants and their servants shall not be searched, or ill used. 5. That no presents sent to the Mogul shall be opened. 6. That the English goods shall not be stopped above twenty-four hours at the custom-house, only to be there sealed and sent to the merchant's house, there to be opened and rated within six days after. 7. That no governor shall take any goods by force, but upon payment at the owner's price; nor any taken upon pretence of the king's service. 8. That the merchants shall not be hindered selling their goods to whom they please, or sending them to other factories, and this without paying any other duty than what is paid at the port. 9. That whatsoever goods the English buy in any part of the Mogul's dominions, they may send down to the ports without paying any duty more than shall be agreed on at the port at shipping them, and this without any hindrance or molestation. 10. That no goods brought to any port shall be again opened, the

English showing a certificate of their numbers, qualities, and conditions, from the governor or officers of the place where they were bought. 11. That no confiscation shall be made of the goods or money of any English dying. 12. That no custom be demanded for provisions during the stay of English ships at any port. 13. That the merchants' servants, whether English or Indians, shall not be punished or beaten for doing their duty. 14. That the Mogul will punish any governor or officer for breach of any of these articles. 15. That the English ships shall suffer all others to pass and repass freely to the Mogul's ports, except their enemies; and that the English ashore shall behave themselves civilly as merchants. 16. That they shall yearly furnish the Mogul with all rarities from Europe, and all other such things as he shall desire at reasonable prices. 17. The English to pay the duty of $3\frac{1}{2}$ per cent. for goods reasonably rated, and 2 per cent. for pieces of eight, and no other duty elsewhere. 18. That the English shall be ready to assist the Mogul against all his enemies. Lastly, That the Portuguese may come into this peace within six months; or if they refuse, the English to be at liberty to exercise all hostilities against them. These were the articles presented, but they were delayed and opposed, and what was the conclusion we shall see hereafter.

The 31st of March the Mogul dined at Asaph Chan's house, all the way from the palace to it, which was an English mile, being laid under foot with silks and velvets sewed together, but rolled up as the King passed. They reported the feast and present cost six lecks (lacs) of rupees, which is £60,000 sterling.*

From this time Sir Thomas Roe continues his journal as before; but there being nothing in it remarkable for many days, all the business being soliciting for money due to merchants, and such other affairs, in which there is nothing worth

---

* Thevenot says a lac is 100,000 rupees, and a rupee worth a crown French and five sols, after which rate the six lacs must have been in those days at least £150 000 sterling. The rupee is now less than 2s.

At the Court of the Great Mogul. 33

observing, *that part is thought fit to be wholly left out here, as it was also done by Purchas in his account of this embassy.

The month of July passed most away in soliciting the prince to sign and seal the articles I had presented to the king, of which an abstract was given before. On the 13th at night I went to the Durbar to visit the king, who sent Asaph Chan to tell me he was informed I had an excellent painter at my house, which I told him was only a young man that drew upon paper, and that very indifferently; however, I promised to bring him to His Majesty, who at this time used so many expressions of kindness to me that all men were amazed at it, and proffered me anything I would ask for in his kingdom. I went from him to Asaph Chan's house, where I continued till the king came out again, when I was conducted back to him, carrying with me Mr. Hughes, the supposed painter, with whom the king had some discourse. After this I presented the king with a curious picture I had of a friend of mine, which pleased him highly, and he showed it to all the company. The king's chief painter being sent for, pretended he could make as good; which I denying, a wager of a horse was laid about it between me and Asaph Chan, in the Mogul's presence and to please him; but Asaph Chan afterwards fell off. This done, the Mogul fell to drinking of Alicant wine I had presented him, giving tastes of it to several about him, and then sent for a full bottle, and drinking a cup, sent it to me, saying, it began to sour so fast it would be spoiled before he could drink it, and I had none. This done, he turned to sleep; the candles were popped out, and I groped my way out in the dark.

Nothing remarkable happened till August the 6th: I was sent for to the Durbar, where I had much talk with the king, who asked me many questions to satisfy his curiosity, and bid me come to the Guzalcan at night, and I should see my picture so exactly copied, that I should not know the one from the other. I came at night, and he showed me six pictures, five of them painted by his own painter, all pasted upon a board, and so like, that by candle-light I could scarce know one from another. Neither did I at first sight know my own, at which the Mogul was much pleased; but looking closer upon them I showed it, and the difference between it and the others. The Mogul was overjoyed, and I surprised at their art, not thinking they could have performed so well; and the king, after many civilities, promised me his own picture.

The 17th I went to visit the king, who as soon as I came in, called to his women, and reached out his own picture set in gold, hanging at a gold wire chain, with one pendant of foul pearl, which he delivered to Asaph Chan, warning him not to demand any reverence of me, but what I was willing to make; it being the custom, whensoever he bestows anything, for the receiver to kneel down, and put his head to the ground, which has been required of the ambassadors of Persia. Asaph Chan came to me, and I offered to take it in my hand; but he made signs to take off my hat, and then he put it about my neck, leading me right before the king. I understood not his meaning, but feared he would require the custom of the country mentioned above, which they call Size-Da, and was resolved rather to return my present than submit to it. He made signs to me to give the king thanks, which I did after my own manner; whereupon some officers called to me to make the Size-Da, but the king in the Persian tongue said, No, no. So I returned to my place; but that you may judge of the king's liberality, this gift was not worth in all £30; yet was it five times as good as any he gives in that sort, and looked upon as a special favour. For all the great men that wear the king's image, which none may do but those to whom it is given, receive only a medal of gold, as big as a sixpence, with a little chain of four inches to fasten it on their heads, and this at their own charge; some set it with stones, or adorn it with pendants of pearls.

The 2nd of September was the king's birthday, and kept with great solemnity. On this day the king is weighed against some jewels, gold, silver, stuffs of gold, silver, and silk,

At the Court of the Great Mogul.

butter, rice, fruit, and many other things, of every sort a little, which is all given to the Bramas or Bramans. The king commanded Asaph Chan to send for me to this solemnity, who appointed me to come to the place where the king sits at Durbar, and I should be sent for in; but the messenger mistaking, I went not till Durbar time, and so missed the sight; but being there before the king came out, as soon as he spied me, he sent to know the reason why I came not in, since he had ordered it. I answered according to the mistake, yet he was very angry, and chid Asaph Chan publicly. He was so rich in jewels, that I own in my life I never saw such inestimable wealth together. The time was spent in bringing his greatest elephants before him; some of which being lord elephants, had their chains, bells, and furniture of gold and silver, with many gilt banners and flags carried about them, and eight or ten elephants waiting on each of them, clothed in gold, silk, and silver. In this manner about twelve companies passed by most richly adorned, the first having all the plates on his head and breast set with rubies and emeralds, being a beast of wonderful bulk and beauty. They all bowed down before the king, making their reverence very handsomely; this was the finest show of beasts I ever saw. The keepers of every chief elephant gave a present. Than having made me some favourable compliments, he rose up and went in. At night, about ten of the clock, he sent for me. I was then abed. The message was, that he heard I had a picture which I had not showed him, desiring me to come to him and bring it; and if I would not give it him, he would order copies of it to be taken for his women. I got up, and carried it with me. When I came in, I found him sitting cross-legged on a little throne, all covered with diamonds, pearls, and rubies. Before him a table of gold, and on it about fifty pieces of gold plate, all set with jewels, some very great and extremely rich, some of them of less value, but all of them almost covered with small stones. His nobility about him in their best equipage, whom he commanded to drink merrily, several sorts of wine standing by in great flagons. When I drew near, he asked for the picture. I showed him two; he seemed astonished at one of them, and asked whose it was. I told him a friend of mine that was dead. He asked if I would give it him. I answered I valued it above all things, but if His Majesty would pardon me, and accept of the other, which was an excellent piece, I would willingly bestow it on His Majesty. He thanked me, and said he desired none but that picture, and if I would give it him, he should prize it above the richest jewel in his house. I replied, I was not so fond of anything, but I would part with it to please His Majesty, with other expressions of respect. He bowed to me, and said it was enough, I had given it him; that he owned he had never seen so much art, so much beauty, and conjured me to tell him truly, whether ever such a woman lived. I assured him there did, but she was now dead. He said he should show it his women, and take five copies, and if I knew my own I should have it again. Other compliments passed, but he would restore it, his painters being excellent at copying in water-colours. The other picture being in oil, he did not like. Then he sent me word it was his birthday, and all men made merry, and asked whether I would drink with them. I answered, I would do whatsoever His Majesty commanded, and wished him many happy days, and that the ceremony might be renewed a hundred years. He asked me whether I would drink wine of the grape, or made, whether strong or small. I replied, what he commanded, but hoped it would not be too much, nor too strong. Then he called for a gold cup full of mixed wine, half of the grape and half artificial, and drank; causing it to be filled again, and then sent it by one of the nobles to me with this message, that I should drink it off twice, thrice, four or five times for his sake, and accept of the cup and appurtenances as a present. I drank a little, but it was stronger than any I ever tasted; insomuch that it made me sneeze, which made him laugh; and he called for raisins, almonds, and sliced lemons, which were brought me on a gold plate, bidding me

At the Court of the Great Mogul. 37

eat and drink what I would, and no more. I made reverence for my present after my own manner, though Asaph Chan would have had me kneel, and knock my head against the ground; but His Majesty accepted of what I did. The cup was of gold, set all about with small rubies and Turkey stones, the cover with large rubies, emeralds, and Turkey stones in curious works, and a dish suitable to set the cup on. The value I know not, because the stones are many of them small, and the greater, which are many, not all clean; but they are in number about two thousand, and the gold about twenty ounces.

Thus he made merry, and sent word he esteemed me more than ever he had done, and asked whether I was merry at eating the wild boar sent me a few days before, how I dressed it, what I drank, assuring me I should want for nothing in his country: the effects of all which his public favours I presently found in the behaviour of all his nobility. Then he threw about to those that stood below two chargers of new rupees, and among us two charges of hollow almonds of gold and silver mixed; but I would not scramble, as his great men did, for I saw his son take up none. Then he gave sashes of gold and girdles to all the musicians and waiters, and to many others. So drinking, and commanding others to do the same, His Majesty and all his lords became the finest men I ever saw, of a thousand several humours. But his son, Asaph Chan, two old men, the late King of Candahar, and myself forebore. When he could hold up his head no longer, he laid down to sleep, and we all departed.

Seven months were now spent in soliciting the signing and sealing of the articles of peace and commerce set down above, and nothing obtained but promises from week to week, and from day to day; and therefore on the 3rd September, the English fleet being hourly expected at Surat, I went to the prince, and delivered him a memorial containing the articles I desired him to give an order to be observed for the unloading of the ships. The articles were,

First, That the presents coming for the king and prince

should not be opened at the port, but sent up to court sealed by the custom-house officers.

Secondly, That curiosities sent for other presents, and for the merchants to sell, should also be sent up to court sealed, for the prince to take the first choice.

Thirdly, That the gross merchandize be landed, reasonably rated for the custom, and not detained in the custom-house; but that the merchants paying the custom have full liberty to sell or dispose of it; and that the ships be supplied with provisions without paying custom.

On the 4th, Asaph Chan sent me back my first articles, after so long attendance and so many false promises, some of them altered, others struck out, and an answer, that there was no articling at all, but it was enough to have an order from the prince, who was Lord of Surat, to trade there: but for Bengala or Syndu, it should never be granted. Notwithstanding all this vexation, I durst not change my method of proceeding, or wholly quit the prince and Asaph Chan: therefore I drew up other articles, leaving out what was displeasing in the former, and desiring Asaph Chan to put them in form, and procure the seal, or else to give me leave to apply myself to the king, to receive his denial, and depart the country. The substance of the new articles was as follows. That all the subjects of the Mogul should receive the English in friendly manner; to suffer them to land their goods peaceably; to furnish them with provisions for their money, without paying any customs for them; to have liberty, after paying custom for their goods, to sell them to any person, and none to oblige them to sell any under rate; to have liberty to pass with such goods to any parts, without anything being exacted further of them more than at the port; to have the presents for the Mogul and prince sealed without opening, and sent to the ambassador; to have the goods of any that die secured from confiscation, and delivered to the other English factors; and in short, that no injury in any sort be offered to any of them.

The 8th of this month, Asaph Chan sent me word in plain

terms he would procure nothing for me sealed; but I might be satisfied with an order signed by the prince: which made me resolve to apply myself directly to the prince, and apply no more to Asaph Chan. Accordingly I was with the prince the 10th, and the 11th he sent me an order, but so altered from what I had given in, that I sent it back. But at night I received a new order from the secretary, containing all my articles; though some words were somewhat ambiguous, which the secretary interpreted favourably, and at my request, writ to the Governor of Surat, explaining them to him as he had done to me. He gave me many assurances of the prince's favour; and being a man not subject to bribery, I gave the more credit to him. So I accepted of the order, which, when translated, I found very effectual. The 16th I visited the prince, resolving to seem wholly to depend on him, till I had heard what entertainment our ships met with. I found him sad for fear of Prince Pervis coming to court, be being but eight cosses from it; but the power of Normahal, the favourite queen, diverted it, and he was ordered away directly to Bengala. The Mogul was retired, but whither no man could certainly tell.

Several days passed in soliciting the king and great ones, and paying court to them, without anything remarkable; till on the 9th of October I received letters from Surat with an account that four English ships were arrived there.

The ships brought much merchandise, but difficulties were made in disposing of them, for want of the treaty having been formally signed and sealed. It was evident that Asaph Chan and the other courtiers hindered the Mogul from carrying out his original purpose of settling matters favourably. In fact, Sir Thomas Roe had to leave, after long delay, without accomplishing what the embassy had been sent to do. But this is not the main object of our narrative, which is chiefly to report some of the strange records given of the proceedings at the court of the Mogul. In the following year the ambassador was more fortunate in witnessing the ceremonies at the celebration of the royal birthday, especially the public weighing, which is thus described :—

The 1st of September being the king's birthday, with the solemnity of weighing him, I was conducted into a fine garden, where besides others there was a great square pond with trees set about it, and in the midst of it a pavilion or tent, under which were the scales the king was to be weighed in. The scales were of beaten gold, set with small stones, rubies, and turquoises; they hung by chains of gold, and for more surety there were silk ropes. The beams were covered with plates of gold. The great lords of the nation sat about the throne on rich carpets, expecting the king's coming out. At length he appeared covered with diamonds, rubies, and pearls. He had several strings of them about his neck, arms, wrists, and turban, and two or three rings on every finger. His sword, buckler, and throne were also covered with precious stones. Among the rest I saw rubies as big as walnuts, and pearls of a prodigious magnitude. He got into one of the scales, sitting on his legs like a tailor. Into the other scales to weigh against him, were put several parcels, which they changed six times. The country people told me they were full of silver, and that the king that day weighed 9,000 rupees. Then they put into the same scale gold and precious stones; but being packed up I saw them not. After that he was weighed against cloth of gold, silks, calicoes, spices, and all other sorts of precious commodities, if we may believe the natives, for all those things were packed up. Lastly, he was weighed against honey, butter, and corn; and I was informed all that was to be distributed among the Banians; but I think that distribution was not made, and all those things were carefully carried back. They told me all the money was kept for the poor, the king using to cause some to be brought at night, and to distribute that money among them very charitably. Whilst the king was in one of the scales, he looked upon me and smiled, but said never a word, perhaps because he did not see my interpreter, who could not get in with me. After being weighed,

At the Court of the Great Mogul. 41

he ascended the throne. Before him there were basins full of almonds, nuts, and all sorts of fruit artificially made in silver. He threw about a great part of them, the greatest noblemen about him scrambled for them. I thought it not decent to do so; and the king observing it, took up one of those basins which was almost full, and poured it out into my cloak. His courtiers had the impudence to thrust in their hands so greedily, that had I not prevented them, they had not left me one. Before I came in, they had told me those fruits were of massive gold; but I found by experience they were only silver, and so light, that a thousand of them do not weigh the value of £20. I saved the value of ten or twelve crowns, and those would have filled a large dish. I keep them to show the vanity of those people. I do not believe the king that day threw away much above the value of £100. After this solemnity, the king spent all the night a-drinking with his nobles: I was invited, but desired to be excused, because there was no avoiding drinking, and their liquors are so hot they will burn a man's inside.

The Journal kept by Sir Thomas Roe ends rather abruptly, the concluding portion having been lost. The last entry is as follows:—

"January the 30th the Dutch came to court with a present of several rarities brought out of China. They were not permitted to come near the third ascent. The prince asked me who they were. I told him they were Dutch, and lived at Surat. He asked whether they were our friends. I answered, they were a nation that depended on the King of England, and were not well received in all parts; that I knew not what brought them thither. Since they are your friends, said he, call them. I was forced to send for them to deliver their presents. They were placed near our merchants, without holding any discourse with them."

Sir Thomas Roe seems soon after this to have left the court of the Mogul, not without sending reports to the East India Company. The first letter, dated at Adsmere or Ajmere, January 25th, 1615, was as follows:—

"At my first audience, the Mogul prevented me in speech, bidding me welcome as to the brother of the king my master; and after many compliments I delivered His Majesty's letter, with a copy of it in Persian; then I showed my commission, and delivered your presents, that is, the coach, the virginals, the knives, a scarf embroidered, and a rich sword of my own. He sitting in his state could not well see the coach, but sent many to view it, and caused the musician to play on the virginals, which gave him content. At night, having stayed the coachman and musician, he came down into a court, got into the coach, and into every corner of it, causing it to be drawn about. Then he sent to me, though it was ten o'clock at night, for a servant to put on his scarf and sword after the English fashion, which he was so proud of, that he walked up and down, drawing and flourishing it, and has never since been without it. But after the English were come away, he asked the Jesuit whether the King of England were a great king, that sent presents of so small value, and that he looked for some jewels; yet rarities please as well; and if you were yearly furnished from Frankfort, where there are all sorts of knacks and new devices, a hundred pounds would go further than five hundred laid out in England, and be more acceptable here. This country is spoiled by the many presents that have been given, and it will be chargeable to follow the example. There is nothing more welcome here, nor did I ever see men so fond of drink, as the king and prince are of red wine, whereof the governor of Surat sent up some bottles, and the king has ever since solicited for more: I think four or five casks of that wine will be more welcome than the richest jewel in Cheapside; large pictures on cloth, the frames in pieces, but they must be good, and for variety some story with many faces. For the queen, fine needle-work toys, bone laces, cut-work, and some handsome wrought waistcoats, sweet-bags, and cabinets will be most convenient. I would wish you to spare sending scarlet, it is dear to you, and no better esteemed here than stammel. I must add, that any fair

China bedsteads, or cabinets, or trunks of Japan, are here rich presents.

This place is either made, or of itself unfit for an ambassador; for though they understand the character, yet they have much ado to understand the privileges due to it, and the rather because they have been too humbly sought to before."

The latest letter to the Company ends in similar strains of disappointment.

"I will settle your trade here secure with the king, and reduce it to order, if I may be heard; when I have so done, I must plead against myself, that an ambassador lives not in fit honour here. I could sooner die than be subject to the slavery the Persian is content with. A meaner agent would, among these proud Moors, better effect your business. My quality often for ceremonies, either begets you enemies, or suffers unworthily. The king has often demanded an ambassador from Spain, but could never obtain one, for two reasons; first, because they would not give presents unworthy their king's greatness; next, they knew his reception should not answer his quality. I have moderated according to my discretion, but with a swoln heart. Half my charge shall corrupt all this court to be your slaves.

The best way to do your business in this court is to find some Mogul that you may entertain for a thousand rupees a year, as your solicitor at court. He must be authorised by the king, and then he will serve you better than ten ambassadors. Under him you must allow five hundred rupees for another at your port to follow the governor, and customers, and to advertise his chief at court. These two will effect all, for your other smaller residencies are not subject to much inconveniency."

Such is the account of the first intercourse of the English with the Great Mogul. The son of Jehan Guire moved his court to Delhi, where a new and magnificent capital was built near the site of the more ancient city.

THE GREAT MOSQUE OF DELHI, AND THE TAJ MEHAL AT AGRA.

THE first European whose visit to new Delhi is recorded was a Frenchman, M. Bernier, who was there in the time of Aurungzebe, grandson of Jehan Guire. The history of his voyage to the East Indies is full of curious matter, and his account of the new capital, and also of the city of Agra, has much interest, as being the earliest description of places so familiar in subsequent annals of India. We quote on this ground the Frenchman's description of the two celebrated buildings so often described by later travellers — the great Mosque of Delhi, and the Taj Mehal at Agra—the latter being the tomb of Shah Jehan's favourite wife Normahal.

The great Mosque is seen afar off in the midst of the town, standing upon a rock, flatted to build upon, and to make round about a large place for four long and fair streets to end upon, and answering to the four sides of the Mosque—viz., one to the principal gate, or frontispiece, another behind that, and the two others to the two gates that are in the middle of the two remaining sides. To come to the gates, there are twenty-five or thirty steps of fair and large stones going round about, except the back part, which is covered with other great quarry-stones to cover the unevenness of the cut rock. The three entries are stately, there is nothing but marble, and their large gates are covered with copper-plates exceedingly well wrought. Above the principal gate, which is much statelier than the two others, there are many small turrets of white marble as well without as within; that in the middle is much bigger and higher than the two others. All the rest of the Mosque, I mean from these three domes unto the great gate, is without covering, because of the heat of the country; and the whole pavement is of large squares of marble. I grant willingly, that this structure is not according to the rules and orders of

The Great Mosque of Delhi. 45

architecture, which we esteem is indispensably to be followed; yet I observe nothing in it that offends the eye; but rather find all to be well contrived, and well proportioned: and I do even believe, that if in Paris we had a church of this way of architecture, it would not be disliked, if there were nothing else in it but that it is of an extraordinary and surprising aspect, and because that, excepting the three great domes and all the turrets, which are of white marble, it appears all red, as if all were nothing else but great tables of red marble, though it be nothing else but a stone very easy to cut, and which even flaketh off in time.

This Mosque it is to which the king repaireth every Friday (which is the Sunday of the Mahometans) to pay his devotion. Before he goes out of the fortress, the streets he is to pass are constantly watered because of the heat and dust. Two or three hundred musqueteers are to stand and make a lane about the gate of the fortress, and as many more on the sides of a great street that ends at the Mosque. Their musquets are small, but well wrought, and they have a kind of scarlet-case with a little streamer upon them. Besides there must be five or six cavaliers well mounted ready at the gate, and ride at a good distance before the king, for fear of raising dust; and their office is to keep off the people. Things being thus prepared, the king is seen to come out of the fortress seated upon an elephant richly harnessed, under a canopy with pillars painted and gilded; or else on a throne shining of gold and azure, upon two beamś, covered with scarlet or purfled gold, carried by eight chosen and well accoutred men. The king is followed by a body of Omrahs, some of which are on horseback, some in a palekey. Among these Omrahs there are many Mansebdars, and mace-bearers, such as I have before spoken of. And though this be not that splendid and magnificent procession, or rather masquerade of the Grand Seignor (I have no properer name for it), nor the warlike order of our kings, it being altogether of another fashion, yet for all that there is something great and royal in it.

So much for the Mosque of Delhi; now for the Taj Mehal.

You may represent to yourself, that at the going out of the city of Agra eastward, you enter into a long and broad paved street, which riseth gently, and hath on one side a high and long wall, making the side of a square garden that is much

THE TAJ MEHAL AT AGRA.

bigger than our Place Royal, and on the other side a row of new houses arched, such as those of the principal streets of Delhi above spoken of. Having gone the length of half the wall, you shall find on the right hand of the side of the houses a great gate well made, by which one enters into a caravan-serah, and over against it, on the wall's side, a stately gate of

The Taj Mehal at Agra.

a great square pavilion, by which you enter into the garden between two conservatories built up with free-stone. This pavilion is longer than it is large, built of a stone-like red marble, but not so hard. The frontispiece seems to me very magnificent, after their way, and as high as that of St. Louis in the street of St. Anthony. It is true you do not there see columns, architraves, and cornishes, cut out after the proportion of those five orders of architecture so religiously observed in our palace : it is a different and particular kind of structure, but such an one as wants no agreeableness even in the unusualness of its contrivance, and which, in my opinion, would very well deserve a place in our books of architecture. It is almost nothing but arches upon arches, and galleries over galleries, disposed and ordered a hundred different ways; and yet all appears stately, well enough contrived and managed. There is nothing that offends the eye ; on the contrary, all is pleasing, and a man cannot be weary in beholding it. The last time I saw it, I was there with one of our French merchants, who also could not behold it enough. I durst not tell him my thoughts of it, apprehending it might have spoiled my gust, and framed it according to that of Indostan. But he being lately come from France, I was very glad to hear him say, " He had never seen anything so august and bold in Europe."

After you are somewhat entered into the pavilion to pass into the garden, you find yourself under a high vault made like a cap, which hath galleries round about and below, on the right and left side, two divans or causeys, made up of earth of eight or ten foot high. Opposite to the gate there is a great arch quite open, by which you enter into an alley, which cuts almost the whole garden into two equal parts. This alley is by way of terrass so large, as that six coaches can pass on it abreast, paved with great squares of hard stone, raised some eight feet above the garden-plots, and divided in the middle by a channel walled up with free-stone, having jets of water at certain distances. After you have gone twenty-five or thirty paces upon this alley, turning your eye to behold the entry, you see the other face of the pavilion, which, though it be not comparable to that which looks to the street, yet wants not its stateliness, being high and of a structure approaching the other. And on both sides of the pavilion, along the wall of the garden, you see a long and profound gallery by way of terras, supported by many low columns near one another. And in this gallery it is, that during the season of the rains, the poor are permitted to enter, who come there thrice a week, receiving alms from a foundation made there by Shah-Jehan for ever.

Advancing further in this alley, you discover at a distance before you a great dome, where is the sepulchre, and below on the right and left hand you see divers alleys of a garden set with trees, and several parterres covered with flowers. At the end of this alley, besides the dome before you, you discover on the right and left two great pavilions, built of the same stone, and consequently, looking all red as the first. These are great and spacious square edifices, made by way of terrass opening by three arches, and having at the bottom the wall of the garden, so that you march under them as if they were high and large galleries.

I shall not stay to describe unto you the ornaments within these pavilions, because in respect to their walls, ground-plot, and pavement, they are not so much unlike the dome, which I am going to delineate to you, after I shall have observed, that between the end of the alley (which we have spoken of) and the dome, there is a pretty large space of a floor, which I call a water-parterre, because that the diversely cut and figured stones you march upon, are there instead of the box-wood of our parterres. And it is from the midst of this parterre, that you may conveniently see a part of this edifice, where the sepulchre is, which remains now to be considered.

It is a great and vast dome of white marble, which is near the height of that of our Val de Grace in Paris, surrounded with many turrets of the same matter, with stairs in them. Four great arches support the whole fabric, three of which are visible, the fourth is closed in by the wall of a hall, accom-

The Taj Mehal at Agra. 49

panied with a gallery, where certain Mullahs (entertained for that end) do continually read the Alcoran, with a profound respect to the honour of Taje-Mehalle. The mould of the arches is enriched with tables of white marble, wherein are seen engraven large Arabian characters of black marble, which is very agreeable to behold. The interior or concave part of this dome, and the whole wall from top to bottom is covered with white marble; and there is no place which is not wrought with art, and hath not its peculiar beauty. You see store of agat, and such sort of stones as are employed to enrich the chapel of the great duke of Florence; much jasper, and many other kinds of rare and precious stones, set a hundred several ways, mixed and enchased in the marble that covers the body of the wall. The squares of white and black marble, that make the floor, are likewise set out with all imaginable beauty and stateliness.

Under this dome is a little chamber inclosing the sepulchre, which I have not seen within, it not being opened but once a year, and that with great ceremony, not suffering any Christian to enter, for fear (as they say) of profaning the sanctity of the place: but really by what I could learn, because it hath nothing rich or magnificent in it.

There remains nothing else, than to take notice of an alley in the fashion of a terrass (we follow the old spelling), twenty or twenty-five paces large, and as many or more high, which is betwixt the dome and the extremity of the garden, whence you see below you, at the foot of it, the river Jumna running along a great campaign of gardens, a part of the town of Agra, the fortress, and all those fair houses of the Omrahs that are built along the water. There remains no more, I say, than to cause you to observe this terrass, which taketh up almost the whole length of one side of the garden, and then to desire you to judge, whether I had reason to say, that the Mausoleum, or tomb of Taje-Mehalle, is something worthy to be admired. For my part I do not yet well know whether I am not somewhat infected still with Indianism; but I must needs say, that

I believe it ought to be reckoned amongst the wonders of the world, rather than those unshapen masses of the Egyptian pyramids, which I was weary to see after I had seen them twice, and in which I find nothing without, but pieces of great stones ranged in the form of steps one upon another, and within nothing but very little art and invention.

THE LAST OF THE GREAT MOGULS.

HAVING given an account of the first contact of the English with the mighty ruler known as the Great Mogul, it will be interesting as a contrast to mention the fate of the last of the Moguls, who died a prisoner and an exile in British Burmah in 1863.

But it may be useful first to devote a brief paragraph to the story of the dynasty of the Mogul Emperors of Delhi.

Baber, the founder of the dynasty, was descended from both Ghengiz Khan and Tamerlane, the mighty conquerors and terrible scourges of earlier times. The conquest of Delhi by Tamerlane was in the year 1398. During five days he gave up the city to massacre, and every male above fifteen years of age was slaughtered by his savage troops. It was after this the city became a heap of ruins, till a new Delhi was built by the descendants of Baber, as we have already stated. In the time of Baber and of his son Humdyun (1526—1556) the Mogul dynasty was not firmly established, the Afghan power having for a time successfully contested the sovereignty. But the third of the Mogul rulers, Akbar, subdued every opponent, and became the ruler not only of almost all Hindostan, but also of Cashmere and Kandahar. Akbar's reign (1556—1605) nearly coincided with that of our Queen Elizabeth. He was succeeded by his son Jehan Guire, to whose court Sir Thomas Roe came

THE PALACE AT DELHI.

The Last of the Great Moguls.

as Ambassador from James I. The next ruler was Shah Jehan, third son of Akbar. He was the builder of New Delhi. To him succeeded his brother Aurungzebe, under whom the Mogul Empire seemed to increase in glory, but really passed its zenith. Jehan-Guire, Shah Jehan, and Aurungzebe were, all three of them, monsters of vice and cruelty, and the dynasty became contemptible as well as infamous, though still possessing mighty power. By frequent conflicts with Hindu princes, to whom Akbar had wisely left some form of independence, and still more by attempting to reduce the Mohammedan kingdoms of the Deccan, the rulers of Delhi began to lose their supremacy. Shah Alum, the successor of Aurungzebe, had to make concession to the Mahrattas, who now first appeared as a formidable power in India. Their power grew till they became the real rulers of Delhi. From 1718 to 1803 this influence remained, the history of India meanwhile being enlivened by the invasion of Nadir Shah in 1748, and the irruption of an Afghan force under Ahmed Shah, better known as Durani, who in 1757, in the battle of Paniput, for a time checked the Mahratta power.

The wars and revolutions of these generations reduced India to a sad state of anarchy, and its conquest by some foreign power seemed the only safety for the oppressed and impoverished people. The story of the gradual rise and progress of English rule under Clive, Warren Hastings, and Wellesley, we cannot recount here, but only tell that in 1803 Lord Lake took Delhi, and rescued Shah Alum II., the fourteenth Mogul Emperor, from the Mahrattas, whose power for further mischief was broken by the decisive battle of Assaye, one of Wellington's early victories. From this time the Great Mogul at Delhi became a vassal or tributary of the English, receiving a pension of £150,000 yearly, the Emperor still retaining a nominal sovereignty, under which there was an attempt to restore the native rule, in the person of Mohammed Shah, the seventeenth and last in the imperial dynasty founded by Baber. The overthrow of this attempt was the turning-point of the terrible crisis in English history known as the Indian Mutiny.

The capture of Delhi broke the neck of the rebellion, and from that moment the restoration of British rule was assured

The gist of the story of the mutiny can be told in a few sentences, although volumes would not exhaust all the narrative of that epoch of danger and disaster, of heroism and triumph. After the great Sikh war ended, the Sepoy army, which had for generations been led from victory to victory, with extra batta and unlimited loot, in the peaceful years which followed led a comparatively idle life. They were pampered and spoiled, and discipline was sadly relaxed. Becoming insolent and high-minded, they became the ready tools of designing men. Some of the native princes were alarmed by the annexations in Lord Dalhousie's time. Mohammedan ambition helped to fan the smouldering discontent. Under these circumstances the regulation was issued, in 1856, that all Bengal Sepoys were to be enlisted for general service. In 1857 the new Enfield rifles were introduced into the Indian army, and immediately the report was spread that the cartridges were greased with the fat of pigs and of cows, that Mohammedans and Hindus might alike be defiled. This was the spark that set the inflammable materials ablaze. The horrors of the massacres and other events that followed need not be recalled. Most of the mutinous regiments made for Delhi, and there proclaimed a native empire. When an English army, reinforced by the troops raised by John Lawrence in the Punjab, commenced the siege of Delhi, there was not a man in India who did not say, "It must be taken in a month, or our empire is gone." It was not taken for several months, for the place was full of troops, and the military stores were unbounded. With true British endurance the siege was kept up, and with true British valour the storming of the stronghold was at length effected. The rebels might have resisted long, but they soon took to flight. The victors were too few and were too exhausted at once to pursue the fugitives, but some were slain or captured, and among the prisoners was the aged king. His life was spared because the officer to whom he surrendered had pledged his word to that effect. Some of his sons, greater miscreants, if possible, than the father, met with swift and merited doom. The old man and two young princes were taken as prisoners to Rangoon, after a trial in which the guilt of the king as the instigator of many atrocities was clearly proved.

The capture of Delhi, and the pursuit and dispersion of the rebel forces there, did not prevent the subsequent campaigns in Oude and Rohilcund, but even the recovery of Lucknow was a less important event than that of the ancient city of the Great Mogul.

We are indebted to the *Leisure Hour* for the only notice that we have seen of the ex-king in his last days. In that magazine, in the number for July 1862, appeared a photograph of the king and two of his sons, and of the prison at Rangoon where they were confined, sent by the officer whose duty it was to inspect the prisoners. In his communication he says : "These prisoners are no other than 'the last of the Great Moguls' and his family. They reside in the small house adjoining the main guard, as shown in the drawing. It is surrounded by a paling about fifteen feet high. In the court-yard were several attendants, and upon going up the ladder and entering one of the small rooms into which the house is divided, I saw the ex-king sitting down on a bed, robed in true Oriental undress, smoking a hubble-bubble. He looked vacantly at me, said nothing, but put out his hands and bent his head slightly to one side, and assumed an aspect as if to express, 'See here the pitiable condition I am come to!' He looked very old, and as if he was fast sinking. His two sons, Gewun Buksh and Shah Abbas, were in the verandah. I send a photograph of the whole party. Previous to the mutiny or rebellion our government allowed the king £150,000 a year, the total expense incurred now is under £500!"

The old king died, as we have said, in 1863. These sons were treated kindly, and instructed by English teachers. What was their subsequent career need not here be recorded. We have seen the end of the last of the Great Moguls!

THE STORY OF CLEOPATRA'S NEEDLE.

AMONG the remarkable objects to be seen in London few have more romantic interest than the Egyptian obelisk on the Thames embankment, popularly known as Cleopatra's Needle. It is wonderful for its size, being by far the largest quarried stone in England ; and it is more wonderful for its character and history, having been prepared by workmen two centuries before the Israelites were delivered by Moses from their bondage in Egypt. It was set up before the great temple of the sun, at Heliopolis, by Thothmes III. The hieroglyphics, or sacred inscriptions in the columns on its four sides, were carved by order of that monarch, and the columns of hieroglyphics on the sides of the central record were added by order of Rameses II., the Pharaoh of "the oppression," so that on this obelisk on the Thames embankment may be read records carved by the two mightiest of the kings of ancient Egypt.

Before describing the historical record, it is worth saying a few words about the obelisk, viewed merely as a gigantic monument, and as a specimen of architecture and of masonry.

First, in regard to its size. It is sixty-eight feet five-and-a-half inches long, and from the base—which measures about eight feet—it tapers upwards to the width of five feet, when it ends in a pointed pyramid seven feet in height. This is the usual form of an obelisk, the tapering point being sometimes called a pyramidion, or pyramid-like structure, the sides of which are

The Story of Cleopatra's Needle.

generally inclined at an angle of sixty degrees. The top was originally covered with gold, as is mentioned in the inscription. The substance of this obelisk is that form of granite known as Syenite, being taken from the quarries of Syene in Upper Egypt. Taking the density of Syenite, and the size of the tapering monument, the estimate of the whole mass is about one hundred and eighty-six tons. This is about ten times the weight of the largest block of stone at Stonehenge, which was the heaviest monolith, or single piece of wrought stone, in England before the arrival of this Egyptian monument.

In the great Pyramids may be seen some enormous masses, but the largest do not approach the size and weight of this obelisk. There are also huge blocks of masonry in the ruined walls of the Temple at Jerusalem, but these, also, are comparatively small and light. One has been measured twenty-six feet long, six feet high, and seven feet wide, a block of solid limestone, estimated to weigh about ninety tons. This is still less than half the weight of Cleopatra's Needle.

Although larger by far than any other stone in England, this obelisk is surpassed in size and weight by many stones in the country from which it came. The column of red granite, known as Pompey's Pillar, is in length about one hundred feet, and its girth round the base twenty-eight feet, the weight of the monolithic shaft being estimated at about three hundred tons. Even more gigantic than Pompey's Pillar is a block of carved granite found on the plain of Memphis, which, next to Thebes, was the most important city in Upper Egypt in ancient times. This block is a gigantic statue, lying face downwards, and partly covered with sand and rubbish. The head is about ten feet long, and the body in proportion, all carved from one mass of granite, the total weight of which is estimated at about four hundred tons.

There is yet one more monument which was more colossal than this prostrate statue, but it is not now of its full weight or dimensions. The great obelisk in the Piazza of St. John Lateran, at Rome, was originally one hundred and ten feet long, and therefore the longest monolith ever known to have been quarried. It was also the heaviest, weighing, as it does, about four hundred and fifty tons, or more than twice the weight of the London obelisk.

By what mechanical contrivances these gigantic blocks were quarried, and with what tools the hard syenite was worked, we do not very clearly know. Enough has been discovered, however, to get a general idea of the modes of procedure. In the quarries at Syene may yet be seen an unfinished obelisk, still connected with the parent rock, with traces of the workmen's tools so plainly seen on the surface, that one might suppose the men to have been hastily called away, and that they intended soon to return to their work. This unfinished obelisk shows the mode in which the huge monoliths were separated from the native rock. In a sharply cut groove, marking the boundary of the stone, are holes, evidently designed for wooden wedges. After these had been firmly driven into the holes, the groove was filled with water. The wedges, gradually absorbing the water, swelled, and cracked the granite from end to end.

The block once detached from the rock, was pushed forwards on rollers made of the stems of palm trees, from the quarries to the edge of the Nile, where it was surrounded by a large timber raft. It lay by the river side till the next rising of the waters, when the raft floated with its precious burden, and was conveyed down the stream to the city where it was to appear as a monument. Here it was again pushed upon rollers, up an inclined plane, to the front of the temple or other site. The pedestal had previously been placed, and a firm causeway of sand, covered with planks, formed an incline up which the mass was rolled. By levers, and ropes, made from the palm-fibre, the obelisk was hoisted into an upright position. This is as much as is known about the architectural and mechanical arrangements connected with the ancient Egyptian monuments. In one bas-relief at El-Bershel is a representation of the transit of a monument, a colossal

The Story of Cleopatra's Needle. 57

figure upon a sledge, with four rows of men dragging it by ropes, urged by the whips of task-masters.

The Syenite granite being extremely hard, is capable of taking a high polish. The carvings are always in hollow relief, as the inscriptions, if projected in high relief, would have been more liable to be chipped off. They are always arranged with great taste in vertical columns, and they were carved after the obelisk was placed in its permanent position. The tools for this work must have been admirable, and we know that, from earliest times, there has been great skill in the manufacture and the tempering of metals.

Thothmes III. erected four great obelisks at Heliopolis, and probably others in different parts of Egypt. Of the two pair known as Pharaoh's Needles and Cleopatra's Needles, the former were removed from Heliopolis to Alexandria by Constantine the Great. Thence one was taken to Constantinople, where it now stands at the Almeidan. Being only fifty feet high, it is thought that the lower part was broken, and that the part remaining is only the upper half of the original obelisk. The other was taken to Rome, and is that which stands in front of the Church of St. John Lateran.

The well-known obelisk in the Place de la Concorde, at Paris, is one of two which Rameses II. erected before the Temple of Luxor. It is seventy-six feet high, or seven-and-a-half feet higher than the obelisk in London.

That which stands in front of St. Peter's at Rome, in the great Piazza, was erected by Menephtah, the son and successor of Rameses II. It is about ninety feet high, and in size is reckoned the third obelisk in the world. The second in size is still standing at Karnak, about one hundred feet high, a companion obelisk having fallen to the ground. The largest of all, as already stated, is that of the St. John Lateran, at Rome.

It would take a long time to tell how the various obelisks now in Europe and in other lands (for the Turks and the Americans also have these monuments) came into the hands of their present possessors. The story of Cleopatra's Needle, so far as ownership is concerned, may be briefly told. After the defeat of the French in Egypt, first by Nelson, who destroyed their fleet in Aboukir Bay, and then by Sir Ralph Abercrombie and his troops, it occurred to many of the officers, naval and military, that this column might be taken to England, and set up as a trophy of their Egyptian victories. After considerable expenditure, both of labour and money, the idea was abandoned, the commanders not heartily taking to the scheme. They contented themselves with getting part of the pedestal disinterred and erected, with a space chiselled out of the surface, into which a brass plate was inserted, on which was engraved a short account of the British triumphs.

When George IV. came to the throne, Mehemet Ali, then ruler of Egypt, formerly made a gift of the obelisk to the king, as his ally and friend. King George had more unromantic sentiments, and more congenial ways of spending money. The offer was renewed to King William IV., with the handsome addition of offering to ship the monument free of charge. The compliment was declined with thanks. In 1840 the government announced its desire to bring the gift of Mehemet Ali to England, but the opponents of the Ministry of the day urged " that the obelisk was too much defaced to be worth removal," and the proposal was not carried out. In 1851 the question was again broached in the House, and the appearance of the obelisk would have been a memorable incident in the Great Exhibition in Hyde Park, but the estimated outlay of £7,000 was deemed too large an outlay of public money. In 1853 the Crystal Palace Company expressed their readiness to be at the expense of bringing the obelisk to be an ornament of their Egyptian Court, but the design fell through, on the ground of its being against precedent to allow what was national property to be used for the benefit of a private company. This seemed rather a dog-in-the-manger policy, but we suppose it is necessary that the custodians of public property must avoid making bad precedents. In 1867 the new Khedive sold the ground on which the obelisk lay to a Greek merchant, who insisted on its removal from his property. The Khedive appealed to the English authorities to take possession of it, otherwise the title to the monument must lapse. The appeal had no effect, and it was evident that if the monument ever came to England it would not be at the cost of the Government or the nation. If no private munificence interposed, the obelisk would be broken up for building material, as the owner of the ground now threatened.

Meanwhile, there was one public-spirited Englishman, an old soldier who admired Abercromby and his army of Egypt, and who never had forgotten the original purpose of the removal. General Alexander had often pleaded with the Government, and the learned societies, and with the public through the press, and now he went to Egypt to visit the spot. He found the prostrate obelisk almost buried in the sand, but through the assistance of Mr. Wyman Dixon, C.E., he had it uncovered and examined.

On returning to England, General Alexander stated the case to his friend, Professor, now Sir Erasmus Wilson, the eminent surgeon. The question of transport was discussed by them, along with Mr. John Dixon, C.E. The result was that Professor Wilson signed a bond to pay £10,000 to Mr. Dixon on the obelisk being erected in London. The Board of Works offered the site on the Thames Embankment, and Mr. Dixon set about his part of the contract.

Early in July 1877 he arrived at Alexandria, and on examination found the monument in better condition than had been usually stated in the discussions on its removal. He adopted the plan of encasing the obelisk in an iron water-tight cylinder about 100 feet long, which, with its precious burden, was set afloat by digging to it a short canal. The *Olga* steam-tug was engaged for towing the cylinder, and the voyage from the harbour of Alexandria was begun. For twenty days the passage was propitious, but a storm arose in the Bay of Biscay, and as the cylinder threatened to sink, and to involve the *Olga* in the catastrophe, there was nothing for it but to sever the connection. The captain returned to England under the impression that the cylinder with its heavy freight had gone to the bottom, and great was the vexation and disappointment. It turned out, however, that the cylinder had floated safely, and after drifting on the surface for about sixty hours was sighted by the steamer, and towed to Vigo on the Spanish coast. After a few weeks' delay, and glad payment of salvage, the obelisk arrived in the Thames, to be set up in its present position. Many will remember the excitement of those few days, and the whole nation rejoiced in the successful termination of an affair in which few had previously shown any interest.

The hieroglyphic inscriptions on the obelisk we consider of less importance than might have been anticipated,—always excepting the one fact which they reveal as to Thothmes III. being the builder. His cartouche, with the name, occurs four times, once on each side, at the top of the central column of hieoglyphics. We know that this Thothmes reigned more than 3,000 years ago. He and his armies overran Palestine two centuries before Moses was born. His was a long reign, about fifty-four years, and he was the greatest perhaps of all Egyptian kings, although Sesostris, or Rameses II. has even more fame as a foreign conqueror. Possibly Jacob and Joseph, certainly Moses and Aaron, and the Greek philosophers, Pythagoras and Plato, and the ancient travellers and historians, have gazed on this very monument. But the inscriptions themselves do not greatly increase our feeling of reverence or admiration. Thothmes boasts of his ancestry, as being the son of Horus, and the descendant of the Sun. The obelisk is dedicated to the rising sun. There were different divine names for the sun at rising, at midday, and at going down. The inscription bears many pictures of objects, the symbolic meanings of which are known to students of hieroglyphics, chiefly representing attributes or abstract ideas,—such as the arm for power, the beetle for life, the lion's head for victory, and so on. The literal translation of the inscription on one of the sides is as follows :—" Horus, powerful Bull, beloved of Ra (the Sun), King of Upper and Lower Egypt. His father set up for him a great name, with increase of royalty, in the precincts of Heliopolis, giving him the throne of Seb (Saturn of the Latins), the dignity of Kheper (the sacred beetle, emblem of majesty), son of the Sun, Thothmes, the Holy, the Just, beloved of the benner (sacred bird), of An (or On) ever-living."*

Since the obelisk came to London the wonderful discovery has been made of the actual bodies of Thothmes III., of Rameses II., and other mighty monarchs of Old Egypt, in a rocky sepulchre at Deiv-el-Bahari. The royal mummies are now ranged in order at the Boolak Museum, near Cairo.

A PERSIAN GRAND VIZIER.

IN Oriental histories, ancient and modern, the career of the great minister of state known as the Grand Vizier is seldom without strange romance. The story of Mirza Tekee, Persian Plenipotentiary at the Conference of Erzeroum, is an example of the wonderful vicissitudes seen in the life of these high dignitaries. The purpose of this conference was to arrange the disputed boundaries between the Turkish and Persian dominions. The survey of the countries, and the proceedings of the conference lasted for some years, but we are not here concerned with the geographical and political matters under discussion. The Grand Vizier of Persia, Mirza Tekee, was one of the ablest and most interesting of the personages who assembled at Erzeroum, and an account of his early career and of his tragic end has been given by the Hon. Robert Curzon, in his book of travels in Armenia.

Mr. Curzon, then the private secretary to Sir Stratford

* The detailed account of the inscriptions, with much valuable matter, will be found in a little book published by the Religious Tract Society, " Cleopatra's Needle," with exposition of the hieroglyphics and illustrations, by the Rev. James King, M.A.

Canning, afterward Lord Stratford de Redcliffe, was appointed joint Commissioner for England, along with Colonel Williams, the distinguished hero of Kars, during the Russian war. There were also Russian and Turkish Commissioners. Their joint labours settled the frontier and arranged affairs, but the settlement was of short duration, and the regions have since been exposed to various troubles and wars. However, our present subject is Mr. Curzon's account of his Persian colleague, the Persian Grand Vizier.

Mirza Tekee was the son of the cook of Bahmas Meerza, brother of Mohammed Shah, and governor of the province of Tabriz. The cook's little boy was brought up with the children of his master and educated with them. Being a clever boy, as soon as he was old enough he was put into the office of accounts, under the commander-in-chief, the famous Emir Nizam, who was employed in organizing and drilling the Persian army in the European style.

Tekee became Vizier ul Nizam, or the governor's adjutant-general as we would say, and having the confidence of the old Emir, he did as he pleased, and amassed great wealth. It was partly because of his being rich that the Shah of Persia chose him to be his representative at the Erzeroum congress, for he had no intention of paying him any salary, but sent him with flattering speeches and promises, none of which he intended to fulfil. The cunning old prime minister at Teheran, Hadji Meerza Agassi, who was sedulously employed in feathering his own nest, was jealous of Mirza Tekee, and very glad to get him safe out of the way.

The Turks and Persians, as everybody knows, hate each other religiously, which seems always the worst sort of hatred. The Soonis and the Shiahs, the two great divisions of the Mohammedan world and creed, are, as it were, the Papists and Protestants of that religion. If these two countries, Turkey and Persia, are at peace for a time, the smouldering flame is sure to break out again at the first convenient opportunity, and it will do so till the end of time.

The Turks, who disliked Mirza Tekee with more than common aversion, from his dignified bearing and stately manners, gave out various accusations against him and against members of his household. A fanatical mob of many thousand indignant Soonis surrounded all that quarter of the town of Erzeroum where Tekee, the illustrious Shiah, then was, attacked the Plenipotentiary's house, and kept it in a state of siege for some hours. Volleys of rifle-shots were fired at the windows, while from within Mirza Tekee only permitted his servants to fire blank cartridges. Izmet Pacha, the Governor of Erzeroum, a drunken old Turk, sat on horseback as well as he could, but would not interfere in the disturbance, though he had all his troops, amounting to several thousands, under arms. For his misconduct on this occasion he was turned out of his governorship. Colonel Williams, at great personal hazard, did all he could to quell the tumult and to protect Tekee. The Turks swore they must have blood, and demanded that one of the Persians, at least, must be delivered up to them as a victim, upon which they promised to withdraw. Colonel Williams could be no party to such a compromise, but the servants of Tekee laid hold of a poor man in the house and thrust him out to the mob. It was a man who had called that morning to say he was going to Tabriz, and would be happy to take charge of any message or letter. The servants knew nothing of him, and they saved their own lives by the sacrifice of this poor fellow, who was killed by the mob. Another Persian, a merchant, was killed the same day in another part of the town, where he had no knowledge of the disturbance at Tekee's house. The mob continued to assault the place, and breaking down the doors effected an entrance, pillaging and destroying all that they could get hold of. Mirza Tekee was saved only by barricading himself in a room at the back of the house, where he and his servants defended themselves for many hours, till the mob dispersed with their booty. The Sultan afterwards sent Mirza £8000 in repayment of the loss sustained by this outrage.

When the treaty was signed between Turkey and Persia Mirza Tekee returned to Tabriz. On the death of the Emir Nizam he succeeded to the office of commander-in-chief.

During the last illness of Mohammed Shah, his brother, Bahman Meerza, had been intriguing in hopes of succeeding to the throne. But his intrigues being discovered and baffled, he escaped to Tiflis, under Russian rule, where he knew he would be welcomed. It is the policy of Russia, in the East, to receive and pension rival claimants and rebels, in expectation of their being possibly turned to useful account in the future.

Mirza Tekee now found his occasion. He marched to Teheran at the head of his army, and seated the young Prince Noor Eddin, upon the throne. Noor Eddin was grateful; he gave to Tekee his sister in marriage. He also got possession of the vast territorial estate of Hadji Meerza Agassi, the prime minister of Mohammed Shah. The Hadji had been Mohammed's tutor, and rose to be one of the most famous of the Viziers of that monarch, whose chief amusement, in his latter years, was to shoot sparrows with a pistol! When the Hadji became rich his master squeezed him, as our Henry VIII. did Cardinal Wolsey, but as he still retained a considerable treasure in gold, silver, and jewels, he thought it prudent to retire to Kerbela, where he died in the odour of sanctity in 1851. Thus the way was clear for Tekee to be Grand Vizier.

He was now seated on the pinnacle of prosperity. The extent of the possessions which the Shah handed over to him from the plunder of his predecessor, the Hadji, was so great as to be almost incredible, and was such as would have yielded the revenue to a king.

Mirza Tekee had, nevertheless, or rather the more on account of his prosperity, enemies at court. His chief enemy was the Shah's mother, a lady who in Turkey and Persia, and in other Oriental lands, usually enjoys an extraordinary degree of power, wealth, and dignity. If she likes to do good she can do much good, if she likes to do evil she can do much evil, whether to the state or to individuals.

The Persian Grand Vizier.

Between those who were partizans and the friends of Bahman Meerza, the late Shah's brother, and those who hated the strong government of Mirza Tekee, a powerful party of malcontents was growing, who got hold of the weak mind of the young Noor Eddin. Although he owed everything to the Vizier at his coming to the throne, he now allowed him to be destroyed by his enemies. Permission was given to him to go to Koom, where he had an estate. This was the form in which his banishment from court was announced.

So secretly had the conspiracy worked that Tekee's suspicions do not seem to have been aroused. His young wife followed him, with all her train, looking forward to the pleasure of living with her husband for a while in the quiet retirement of a beautiful place in the country. But when she arrived within sight of the town of Koom, a messenger came out to meet her, and the news that he brought was that Mirza Tekee had been killed by the order of her brother, the Shah. The assassins sent for this cruel deed found the minister in his bath on their arrival, and there they opened his veins and held him till he bled to death. No charge was made against him, and no crime ever proved. It was an instance of foul murder by the Shah, who thus destroyed one of his ablest and most honest subjects, at the instigation of some of the most infamous and worst.

This tragic event happened in 1851, about the time when the representatives of all nations were assembled in London, at the opening of the Great Exhibition, the festival of the world's peace and industry. In our happy land we know little of what is passing in the dark places of the earth, which are full of the habitations of cruelty. Such was the career and such the fate of a Grand Vizier.

CAPTAIN WILLIAM PEEL'S RIDE THROUGH NUBIA.

LET the reader join me in paying a tribute of respect to the memory of the sailor son of the great statesman—Sir Robert Peel—William Peel, as noble an Englishman as ever served in the British navy, whose career of honour and usefulness was too early closed. There are many who still remember the sad sorrow when the news came that the commander of the naval brigade in the time of the Indian Mutiny had fallen a victim to small-pox. Of his gallant services at that crisis, as well as in the Crimean war and on other occasions, this is not the place to give a record. Suffice it to say that in his profession he always well sustained the reputation of the name that he bore, and of the illustrious house to which he belonged.

It is not so generally known that he published a book descriptive of a journey made by him in one of the intervals of public service, "A Ride through the Nubian Desert." It was as long ago as 1851 that he went there, but recent events in that region of the world give a fresh interest to the record of that journey. He saw and described many of the places of which the names are now more familiar to us, and some of the matters referred to have an enduring importance.

The character of the man, and the spirit in which he went forth on this journey, appear in his opening chapter. Speaking of his companions in the voyage to Egypt he says, "Some have gone to India, some to Afghanistan, others to China and to Borneo,—all to uphold the character of England, to administer justice, to extend commerce, or to defend and expand our empire. I embarked with the object of travelling in the Soudan, hoping, by the blessing of the Almighty, to help to break the fetters of the negro, to release him from the selfish Mussulman, from the sordid European; to tell him there is a God that made us all, a Christ that came down and died for

Ride through Nubia.   67

all." And again, on the last parting at Cairo, he says, " They left me at Cairo, thinking I was bound for pleasure, all except one, to whose kind and honoured friendship I had confided my views. I watched them all depart; to me it was another trial. I felt tired of Egypt, and turned with horror from the natives, for whom I had no sympathy; in despair from the rapid flowing Nile, whose current must be stemmed for many hundred miles. I was in most wretched health, and the question rose why I should go. Europe seemed so inviting, her civilization so intelligent, her Christianity so genial. But four days sufficed to restore my health, and in the quiet rides to Shoubra, unsurpassed by those of any city, along the banks of the mysterious Nile, all my high hopes returned."

He had sailed from England for Alexandria on the 20th August, 1850, in the good steamer *Pottinger;* and after stopping six hours at Gibraltar and forty at Malta, reached the Egpytian port on the 4th September. That day they all embarked in the canal boat on the Mahmondieh canal, and towed to Afteh on the Nile. There they changed to a steamer, and arrived at Cairo the following evening. Such was the mode of transit at that time.

Cairo having been explored, and a Firman and Couwass or Commissionaire being procured, with the help of Mr. Murray, the Consul-General, he sailed, at sunset of September the 11th, from Boolak, the port of Cairo, in a dahabieh, or Nile boat, for Korosko. He had previously had an interview with the Viceroy, Abbas Pacha, a true friend of England and the English, to whom he was already personally known, and who showed much interest in his projected journey.

In eleven days from Cairo they arrived at Assouan, the ancient Syene, the frontier post between Egypt and Nubia, where the river commences its unbroken flow through the valley of the Nile. While viewing with admiration the natural and historical scenes, the sympathy of our traveller is called forth by the condition of the labouring people. " The villages of the fellahs are a collection of huts made of unburnt bricks or date leaves stuccoed with mud, about eight feet high, pulverised by the sun, a heap of dirt and dust standing on the accumulated rubbish of centuries. A grove of date trees surrounds them, which readily marks their site, and their appearance at a distance is often improved by a number of pigeon houses built like turrets. And this is the abode of a human being, the fellah of Egypt, who goes to his work day after day, from early dawn till dark, working naked in the sun, often without even a covering to his head or loins, standing all day in the water, raising it by a bucket, digging a trench with his hands, or cutting the mud with his feet; and his labour is not for himself, but for a grinding master. With all this he preserves the beauty of the human form, his countenance is serene, and he answers the passing traveller with a pious and graceful salutation. To say that he is happy because he knows no better, is it not making his condition worse? The women are frightfully ugly, and their dress most dismal—a large sheet or wrapper of dull blue drawn over the head and body, and held across the face. See them squatting on the banks when they go to fill their water-jars, uttering a mourning cry, they look like evil spirits waiting to be carried across the river of death."

Such are the poor fellaheen of Egypt, but such is the lot of poverty and labour all the world over, only here there is little to raise the spirit above its depressing surroundings. Happily there are efforts now being made to improve their condition, and Christian missions are bringing to many of these sons and daughters of toil new comforts and hopes, which the religion of the false prophet failed to effect for them.

But we must pass on to Nubia or the Soudan. Captain Peel's only companion was Churi, a Maronite of the Lebanon, from whom he had taken lessons in Arabic and Italian in London, and whom he persuaded to accompany him on his journey. Churi had been at an early age sent from his own country to be educated at the college of the Propaganda at Rome; a good linguist, and a man of probity and intelligence,

Ride through Nubia.   69

With him Captain Peel travelled, not in Egypt only, but in the Sinaitic Desert and in the Holy Land, and his companionship is spoken of with commendation and gratitude.

Korosko was reached on September 27th, at noon of the sixteenth day after leaving Cairo, and on the following day the journey through the desert began, in the direction of Berber. The party consisted of the Captain and Churi, the couwass, and an Egyptian cook, an Arab guide, and four Arab attendants or camel drivers. There were thirteen dromedaries to carry the travellers, with their baggage and water.

It was a weary, dreary journey through this parched and barren wilderness. Here are some of the entries in the Journal :—" We marched in silence, our camels advancing in line abreast over the broad pavement of closely-packed sand. There was not a blade of grass, not even a withered straw, the remnant of some partial winter vegetation, and the heat was intense, a hot south wind blowing from the rocks with the breath of a furnace, and the sand glaring with light. We halted at seven o'clock that night, but only to feed the camels; there was no time to make a fire, we, therefore, drank water and ate onions for our dinner. The march was then resumed. I never was more fatigued; my tongue was parched, and the throat painfully swollen from the hot wind. We came to a halt at twenty minutes past one o'clock, when I stretched my poor body on the sand to sleep, and my mind wandered by the side of rippling streams in the earthly paradise of England. At 5.15 a.m., having drunk only water for our breakfast, we were again on the march, and went on till 8.20 under the sickening heat of a morning sun without food. Our halting place was on the side of a hill, under a deep ledge, which afforded shade till noon. The Arabs told us we were to sleep, and showed us the example, but the mind was too active, and I felt the necessity of supporting the body with food.

" I eagerly asked what we had brought, and then first learned that we had come to cross this desert without a stick of firewood, with no meat, no eggs, no vegetables, for even the onions were gone! I turned with the fierceness of an African tornado. What was the use of a couwass? What was the use of a cook? What was the use even of my faithful Churi? The cook and the couwass retired, but Churi's temper is imperturbable, and he loves me too well to care for my hasty words. He said he had tried his best; he said he thought I knew there were none of these things. The fierce passion soon fell at his soft answer, and I asked kindly to know what there really was besides our tea and coffee. There was only a bag of rice and some stale bread, which we had bought at Emé, and had baked in the sun. We then made a fire with camels' dung, and boiled the coffee and rice. This was our only food in crossing the desert, and it came twice a day; it was boiled rice and coffee in the morning, boiled tea and rice in the evening. Churi's diet was still more simple, for he confined himself almost entirely to soaked bread and water. The thermometer here at noon, under the shade of the deep rock, and held apart from the side, was 108° of Fahrenheit."

So they went on day by day, and at sunset on the 1st October arrived at the wells of Mourad, three reservoirs of brackish water in the middle of this desert. These wells are in a little amphitheatre, formed by the high surrounding hills. Some trees grew in the water-courses formed in the rainy season from these heights. Next day the journey was resumed across plains of sand, interrupted occasionally by rocky ridges, arriving at length at Aboo Hamed, on the edge of the desert, but on the banks of the Nile.

The river at Aboo Hamed is of great breadth, and in the centre is a chain of islands highly cultivated. There are no boats, and the people swim across the stream on inflated skins, gathering their clothes in a high turban round the head; or they form rafts of grass and the green straw of the doora, which they bring for the fodder of the camels, and on them they place their other produce.

A short distance below the Nile turns sharp to the westward, running over beds of rock, causing rapids which prevent navigation. It is to avoid this great detour that this line of communication lies straight through the Nubian desert.

From Aboo Hamed to Berber the course runs in a straight line, at times close to the river; and when there is a bend, the path stretches across some high plain, but all sense of weariness is removed by the sight of the delicious Nile, which runs through the midst, tracing a line of the deepest green. The islands, as well as the lands on either bank, are richly cultivated and highly productive, at least after reaching Kenaniet, where the camels had green food for the first time since leaving Korosko.

Above Kenaniet the country is no longer threatened by the sands of the desert, and the inundation fertilizing a wide plain. It is like a second Egypt.

Berber, or Barbar, was reached on October 11th, after travelling with the same long journeys, but not at the same rapid pace as through the desert. This is the capital and also the limit of Nubia. The people are still called Barbaras, whence, probably, the Greek word " barbarians." All above is the country of the Soudan. The native name of Berber is also El Moukharef. The governor of Berber at that time was an Albanian, who received the travellers hospitably. The Arabs were dismissed, and as they had served willingly and faithfully, a good backshish was added, that they might have an entertainment before the return journey. Enough was given to buy a sheep and other materials for a feast. The day wore on, and the poor camel drivers continued near the tent. "We asked them if they had roasted the sheep. They expressed astonishment, and said there was nothing for them to eat. The guide was sent for, and though clearly convicted before them all of having kept the money, it was impossible to raise a blush on his hardened face. He seemed only surprised at our taking up his roguery so warmly! The piastres were then given to the others, amidst great clamour and abuse of the guide; but five minutes after, knowing each would have done the same, they and the conductor were in perfect harmony."

On the 12th October, with a favourable northern wind, they set sail in a boat for Khartoum, passing Shendy on the morning of the 16th, and reaching Khartoum soon after sunrise on the 23rd October, exactly six weeks after leaving Cairo. Their home was made at the Roman Catholic Mission, the vicar-general, the chief of which, was absent, but two brethren of the mission showed every hospitality and attention. The reception was also cordial on the part of Latif Pacha, governor-general of the upper provinces, of which this is the capital. "Khartoum, on the conquest of the country, only a few years back, did not even exist. It is now a very rising city, with an excellent bazaar, several gardens and date-tree plantations, and a large fleet of dahabiehs. From its position, it would soon, under good government, become a place of first-rate importance." This was said in 1851, and Captain Peel adds, "I am one of those who believe that an English government and a handful of Englishmen could make Egypt and the Nile the means of civilizing Africa and conferring blessings on the world. Under English rule cities would rise up at Assouam and at Khartoum, whose influence would be felt over the whole interior. I know, alas! the spirit of the age is against such thoughts; and there are even men who would wish to abandon our empire; but I speak the voice of thousands of Englishmen who, like myself, have served their country abroad, and who do not love her least, who will never consent to relinquish an empire that has been won by the sword, and who think the best way to preserve it is by judicious extension."

Latif Pacha tried hard to dissuade the travellers from proceeding beyond Berber, saying much about the perils and risk of the journey to Labeyed or Obeid, the capital of Kordofan. But when he found them resolved to go there, he gave every advice and assistance. The Cairo couwass being invalided, the governor sent his own couwass, and gave a letter to Abd-

Ride through Nubia. 73

el-Kader, the ruler of the province of Kordofan. The Sheik Ali Abd El Wacked, head of Ababdeh Arabs, the most powerful of the tribes in all Egypt, had the courtesy to come to see them set out on their journey, and gave letters to some of his people in the country.

In ten days they arrived at Obeid, meeting on the way several gangs of slaves on their route to Khartoum. The Arab escort was well armed, every one in the country carrying spears, and some having also firearms.

A house was given to the travellers, near that of the governor, and here they remained some days. They then announced their wish to go on to Darfoor, but the governor objected to this, without having obtained the leave of the Sultan. But he gave way, after some dissuasion, and agreed that they should proceed to the frontier, and there wait the permission of the ruler of Darfoor. But a severe attack of fever and ague put an end to this plan. Captain Peel and Churi were both prostrated, and it was not till the end of November that they were able to move out of the house.

The reports in his journal about Obeid are chiefly valuable as showing the extent of the slave trade. The only other trade of importance is in gum-arabic, which is collected at certain seasons of the year. But at all times slaves are bought and sold. Here is one extract from the captain's note-book: "Monday morning, November 10th, 1851. Scene opposite my windows, which look into Government court-yard. Five male slaves just arrived, their necks in a wooden triangle at the end of a long heavy pole, which was attached to a camel during the march; also one female slave bound by the feet. I believe the number of slaves brought every year to Khartoum and Obeid, and thence sent to Egypt, is very great. Some are also sent from Darfoor to Siout. These slaves were caught by the Arabs in some mountains to the southward. In the afternoon they were stripped, examined, made to walk —in fact, critically examined like beasts—in the government court-yard. And how did they behave? Like beasts? I watched them closely, unseen, and cannot conceive how men could have behaved with such propriety, or shown more touching dignity. There was no fear, nor was there any momentary pride to show muscular strength; they held themselves mechanically, letting others bind their limbs, and marched no further than the very line. When inspection was finished, they wrapped their scant clothing with decency round their waists, and took no notice of the flowing robes or gorgeous turbans of their masters. As men, physically, they were their superiors, in heart and feeling it is mockery to make comparison, in courage unquestionably not inferior; but they have no self-reliance or moral strength, and in the onward march of the world, from the position of their country and its climate, have been left behind."

Kordofar was a rich and populous negro land when conquered by the Egyptians, now sixty years ago. The excesses of the troops, and the exactions of the rulers have ruined it. The people have been regarded both by Egyptians and by Arab traders as only fair game for being hunted and kidnapped for slavery. The government retained its power at that period only by terror. The sale of firearms or of gunpowder was forbidden, and the people were kept down by the Egyptian garrison. So things remained till near our own time. On the return journey Captain Peel found that "all the boats of Khartoum had gone on the annual slave-hunting expedition up the White Nile!"

We conclude with quoting Captain Peel's general estimate of the Arab tribes in Africa. "All that I have seen," he says, "of the Arabs has made me form a very bad opinion of them. There is little elevating in their character, and they are essentially avaricious. Hospitality is their redeeming feature; it is a law universally acknowledged, and accorded without stint or afterthought to any traveller. They have respect for the Mohammedan religion, even when themselves ignorant or neglectful of its precepts. Hence, negroes on their pilgrimage to Mecca, with their wives and children, travel afoot from remotest regions of Africa without fear, and without any money, whilst their pagan countrymen are being hunted and sold into slavery around them. Hadji, or pilgrim, is a title that gives them sure protection."

The road these people take is to Suakim, a port on the Red Sea, about ten days' journey from the Nile, where they embark and go almost direct across to Mecca. It is a stream of human beings constantly flowing and continually increasing, for while the Mohammedan religion seems fading in the East, it is making astonishing progress through the negro nations. We little know with what fiery zeal the missionaries of this religion are propagating their faith; already it extends in an unbroken line from the Red Sea to the Atlantic; and wherever it comes, it falls as a blight upon the country, turning the warm heart of the negro into selfishness and suspicion, and forming the most dangerous barrier to the enterprise of the traveller. In returning, between Khartoum and Berber, Captain Peel saw, in a hollow where some water still remained from the rains, above two thousand camels, all together, organized into troops, and attended only by a few Arabs. Other scenes and incidents were met with, but we have quoted enough to interest the reader in this ride through the Nubian desert and journey to the Soudan.

SARAWAK AND THE SOUDAN.
THE STORY OF RAJAH BROOKE.

THE position of Egypt and of the Soudan may be very different when this book is read from what it was when written. But, apart from passing events, there is a permanent interest, of no common kind, in the following letter written by Rajah Brooke in reference to the work of General Gordon in the Soudan. It gives an authentic summary of the great work done in Borneo by the uncle of the writer, the first Rajah Brooke. It shows what can be done by a wise and brave Englishman in foreign lands, even when alone and unsupported by the power and resources of his own country. We may criticize details in the lives of such men, but must admire the result of their enterprise and spirit in bringing civilization to regions long given over to barbarism.

In 1838, when my uncle, Sir James Brooke, first anchored his yacht off the coast of Borneo, he found a condition of things existing on the coast not unlike that which has necessitated the abandonment of the Soudan. The country was under the government of the Sultan of Brunei, a potentate whose authority over Sarawak was characterized by the same abuses which have driven the Soudanese to revolt. His government was a system of Bashi-Bazoukery plus slave-raiding, with this difference, that in Sarawak, unlike the Soudan, the slave-raids were undertaken by the orders and under the direction of the Sultans or Rajahs of Brunei. Their agents scoured the country in all directions, kidnapping children, and young girls to supply their harems. The tribes, provoked at last beyond endurance, rose in revolt, and at the time when my uncle arrived at Sarawak the insurgents were confronting the forces of the Sultan very much as those of the Mahdi are now confronting the troops of the Khedive. Sir James Brooke interposed between the combatants. He won the confidence of the leaders of the revolt, and undertook to act as mediator between them and their Sovereign. The Sultan of Brunei conceived a great liking for my uncle, and without much difficulty it was arranged that the Sultan should abandon his claims over the revolted region. Sarawak became independent, the Bashi-Bazoukery from Brunei ceased to trouble the tribes, and the homes of the villagers were no longer laid desolate in order to supply victims for the Sultan's pleasure. The bag-and-baggage policy was unsparingly applied, and Sarawak, stripped of all the agents of the executive authority of the Sultan of Brunei, was left as independent as the Soudan will be when General Gordon has completed the amputation of "the dog's tail."

But, instead of leaving Sarawak in a state of native anarchy, that province was saved for civilization by the transfer of all the prerogatives of the Brunei Sultans to my uncle. A free grant of sixty miles of coast-line was made to Sir James Brooke to govern as seemed to him good. The task of establishing a civilized government in that wild and savage region was no child's play. It was in miniature identical with that which would lie before General Gordon if, after the completion of the evacuation, he were established, as has been suggested, as Lord Protector of Khartoum and the Valley of the Niles. To begin with, he was face to face with a population long cruelly oppressed and but yesterday emancipated. He was an Englishman and a Christian in the midst of a mixed population of Moslems and heathens. The Malays on the coast correspond to the Arabs of the Soudan, while the Dyaks inland resemble the negro population. These Dyaks should properly be divided into two classes—the peaceful and the savage; the latter, best known as the head-hunting Dyaks, carried on a species of warfare, which may be described as the Bornean counterpart of the razzias of the slave-hunters against whom Gordon waged unsparing war. Of the slave-trade in the African sense there was little in Sarawak, but the Dyaks of the hills, in their hunts for heads, contrived to inflict as much misery upon their neighbours as even Zebehr has brought about in the heart of Africa. It is very extraordinary what a passion the Dyaks had for heads. When remonstrated with, they replied that it was the custom of their ancestors, which it was their duty to hand down unimpaired to posterity. It was really the women who were at the bottom of it; no Dyak woman would ever marry a man who could not display as a trophy at least one human head. As long as the taking of human life was an indispensable condition preliminary to marriage, head-hunting prevailed, and all attempts to suppress it by killing the men were utterly unavailing; it was only when you carried the war into the homes of the women, and burnt their finery and all their household goods, that head-hunting went out of fashion. Few Englishmen have any idea of the extent to which this head-hunting was carried on. Immense flotillas of head-hunters' canoes would sally forth from the rivers and cruise along the coast, proceeding sometimes as far as 400 miles from home. On such an expedition, sometimes 7,000 men would be engaged; each canoe carried about sixty warriors. They landed wherever they saw a village on the coast, slew man, woman, and child, and carried off their heads in triumph. It is difficult to exaggerate the misery produced over vast regions by these head-hunting expeditions, but they were an established custom in the country, they had existed from time immemorial. Sir J. Brooke, however, worked patiently on, and he had a marvellous faculty of winning the confidence of the natives. His material resources were very limited; aid from Government, except an occasional man-of-war on the coast, he had none. He had his yacht and a private fortune, which, when all was realized, did not amount to more than £30,000; yet from that small beginning he succeeded in building up a kingdom considerably larger than Scotland, in which at this moment the authority of the law is as supreme as in Hyde Park.

The way in which this work was accomplished was very simple. Sir J. Brooke had little difficulty in securing the support and devotion of the Malays on the coast, who were sufficiently enlightened to see the benefit of a settled government, and to welcome the rule of a just and upright Governor, foreigner though he was. From this nucleus he worked along the coast, and gradually drew inland. The Dyak tribes who were weak, and were constantly plundered by the head-hunters of the interior, naturally rallied round the new Rajah, and assisted him in attacking their enemies. This was very simple, but very practical. The Rajah's secret was the protection of the oppressed, and the conversion of the victims of the head-hunters into instruments for the suppression of head-hunting. By small degrees, pressing forward step by step, the domain of order and peace was pushed inland until over the

Sarawak and the Soudan. 79

whole of the free-grant territory head-hunting was extinct. The work was not done with rosewater, but by dint of sheer hard fighting ; but the whole of the blood shed in suppressing the custom was nothing compared with the carnage of a single head-hunting expedition. Operations against head-hunters are comparatively rare now. It is more than two years now since I had to lead an expedition against some young fellows who, more for sport than anything else, had revived the custom of their ancestors, and had to be burned out in consequence. I know few more striking scenes in the world than the departure of an expedition against the head-hunters. The advance is made in the first instance by water, for the rivers are the only highways of Sarawak. A summons is sent round to the tribes who are exempted from taxation on condition of rendering military service. They assemble in thousands, each man bringing his own provisions of rice and salt, sufficient for three weeks' campaign; they bring their own arms and their own canoes. At the appointed time the whole force, varying, according to circumstances, from 6,000 to 15,000 men, embark on board some 300 to 500 canoes. The signal for starting is generally given by the firing of a gun ; in a moment the whole flotilla is in motion ; every paddle strikes the water when the flash is seen, and a great wave stirred by the thousand paddles lashes the shore as the expedition departs on its errand of vengeance. The cost of such an expedition is next to nil; the men render their services without pay, and they find their own rations. The Dyaks supply the rank and file of fighting men under their own chiefs; the Malays supply the central or body-guard. The great advantage which we possess is the control of the rivers, which afford us access to all parts of the country. From these we operate as a base.

If any one who saw Sir J. Brooke drop anchor forty-six years ago off the coast of Sarawak had been told that in the year 1884 the representative of that Englishman would be reigning with undisputed authority over the whole of the Principality of Sarawak, maintaining peace and enforcing the law, levying taxation, equipping forces, and exercising all the functions of sovereignty, he would have naturally regarded the prophecy as ridiculously absurd; but what would have been his amazement if he had been informed that not only would all those things be accomplished, but that the foreign Government established with the unassisted resources of that solitary Englishman would have suppressed the most cherished institutions of the natives, converted the head-hunting Dyaks, for the most part, into peaceable citizens, suppressed piracy, established schools, and created a commercial value at £1,000,000 annually, and is about to completely eradicate slavery. Such, however, is a simple statement of an accomplished fact.

This, I am told, is absolutely unique; Sarawak stands alone, but I do not see why, with the experience of Sarawak before us, we should despair of accomplishing similar results in the Soudan. General Gordon, or whatever other Englishman might be appointed ruler of Khartoum,—though it may be difficult to find another so suitable as Gordon,—would have advantages far greater than those which sufficed for the founding of the Principality of Sarawak. He would occupy a commanding position at the junction of the two Niles, from which with the steamers already in his possession he could dominate the country on both banks of both streams for a thousand miles. He would have in the storehouses and arsenals of the late Government a vast stock of necessary material for arming and equipping such native forces as might be necessary to assert his authority and to suppress slave-raids. He would have no English troops, and he would be much better without them; he must rely upon native strength; he might, of course, have a few friends as a personal staff, but his administrators, like his soldiers, would be drawn from the Soudan. (The staff in Sarawak consists of about thirty Europeans.)

I do not think there would be any insuperable difficulty in dealing with the slave-raids on the same principle that we have dealt with the head-hunters. Of course, if you clear out

Sarawak and the Soudan. 81

not only the Egyptian soldiers and Bashi-Bazouks, but also the English officer who superintends the evacuation, you hand the Soudan over to the unchecked domination of the slave-traders and slave-hunters; in short, you do in the Soudan what would have been done in Sarawak if when the authority of the Sultan of Brunei was withdrawn no other authority had been set up in its place. In Sarawak that would have meant handing over the whole territory to the atrocity of the head-hunters. Are you prepared to sanction as great an infamy in the Soudan ? It is even worse in the Soudan, for there you have had a semi-civilized Government, and you have a great waterway open to the commerce of the world, which will then be used almost exclusively for the slave trade. Sultan will fight against sultan, tribe will prey upon tribe, the whole of the Nile valley will be one scene of bloodshed and desolation. Surely, if this can be avoided it ought not to be allowed to take place. Why not let General Gordon stay in Khartoum, with instructions to do what he can with such resources as he finds to his hand ? England would have no responsibility for him any more than she has for me; the trade of the Nile is rich enough, surely, to pay the moderate expenses of the simple but efficient Government which is all that is required. There is no need to aim at a great scheme at first. Khartoum, and as much of the Soudan as can be covered by the range of a field-piece on the deck of a steamer, would form the nucleus of a kingdom which might grow hereafter until it included almost all the provinces of the now abandoned empire. That, however, is for the future : the question of the hour is whether Khartoum and the Nile are to be handed over to the slave trade or saved for civilization. The experience of Sarawak seems to me to justify a hope that the latter alternative may yet be found practicable.*

* This paper, by Rajah Brooke, appeared in the *Pall Mall Gazette* of March 1st, 1884.

THE VOYAGE OF THE "FOX,"
AND DISCOVERY OF THE FATE OF SIR JOHN FRANKLIN.

THE search for Sir John Franklin and his lost men and ships occupies a large space in the history of modern Arctic exploration. It was in 1845 that Her Majesty's ships, *Erebus* and *Terror*, under captains Sir John Franklin and Crozier, were sent to endeavour to find a way from the North Polar Sea, through Behring's Straits, into the Pacific Ocean. This was the famous "North-West Passage," which had been the dream of the early Elizabethan age, and in search of which in recent times many gallant seamen had volunteered to sail. John and James Ross, Parry, Richardson, and many others went forth, from 1818 to 1840, and laboured and suffered much, in unavailing efforts to carry out to completion this desire of their countrymen, and of men of science all over the world.

European geographers knew that Behring's Straits were navigable; that the Mackenzie River discharged itself into a salt-water sea; and that Baffin's Bay separated Greenland from the North American Continent. The object was to connect these three known points, and to discover an open way round North America to the Indies.

When the expedition set forth, in 1845, there was a very sanguine though unfounded confidence in an easy success. So much had been discovered in previous voyages; the ships were so well equipped and well manned, that no one seems to have expressed any doubt that the Admiralty order was quite sufficient to insure its achievement. Previous difficulties, hardships, and failures were ignored; no cautions were given as to establishing depôts as they advanced, in case of retreat being necessary, or to afford information to those who might have to seek them; no overland expeditions were organized to co-operate from the North American mainland; and no means of rescue provided, in case the ships were lost, and in case the crews had to retire upon the Hudson's Bay territories. They sailed amidst boundless enthusiasm, and everyone expected to hear of them again from a very different region of the world.

When the winter of 1847 closed, and no tidings of Franklin and his comrades had ever come, people began to feel uneasy. Two winters had already passed, and the ships were only provisioned up to the spring of 1848. Then the search for Franklin was commenced. No better proof exists of the vigour and perseverance with which it was prosecuted, year after year, for eleven long years, from 1848 to 1859, than the comparison of Arctic charts and maps at the beginning and close of the period. More was done in the way of geographical discovery in those regions in these few years than in two centuries previously. Every channel and inlet seemed to be penetrated; every island and shore searched, in that vast Arctic archipelago, before their energies were turned in the right direction. The ships were used chiefly as affording the basis of operations, the officers and men passing the most of their time in expeditions on foot over the frozen lands, in seeking first to save the lives of the one hunded and forty missing comrades, and, when this seemed hopeless, to solve the mystery of their fate. America joined with England in the noble efforts. No less than forty thousand miles, it is estimated, were journeyed over by upwards of one hundred sledging expeditions, often at terrible risks and always with extreme hardships.

The history of these various exploring voyages and expeditions will ever hold a high place in the annals of the British navy. The records of hair-breadth escapes from wreck and famine; of firm, manly reliance in God and their own energy; of proofs of a courage which no danger could daunt, and an endurance which no suffering could subdue, thrill the landsman as he reads them, and must ever stimulate future generations of seamen to emulate such deeds of "high emprize." If any proofs are wanted that the seamen of our time have in no way fallen off in the enterprise, hardihood, and courage of their forefathers, they will be found in the narratives of modern Arctic exploration, and especially in the expeditions in search of Sir John Franklin.

But while the interest of these narratives will always remain, it must be confessed that there is, also, in some degree, a sameness in their perusal. The battling with waves and icebergs; the long, dreary Arctic winters; the details of geographical discovery in regions so inhospitable and unfruitful, all this would pall on the taste were it not the hope ever springing up of a successful issue to the search for the lost explorers. The later volumes of this library of Arctic travel leave a painful and wearisome impression on the mind, and people began to feel, as it were, a relief, when a narrative was advertised with the title of "The Last of the Arctic Voyagers," almost wishing it to be the last as well as the latest of these fruitless expeditions. The Admiralty and the Government of the day recognized the state of public opinion, and refused to sanction further search at the nation's approval and cost.

Then came the voyage of the good ship *Fox*. At the darkest hour of public despair as to the search the light of a new hope arose. The devoted wife of Franklin was not discouraged by the adverse decision of the naval authorities. She, with the aid of a few sympathizing friends, resolved to have another expedition, and in Captain, now Sir Leopold, M'Clintock, she found a leader worthy of the adventure. To this voyage we owe the discovery of the only authentic document which rewards the long search for the lost expedition. Other tidings have since been gleaned, and other relics recovered, but the romance of the successful search belongs to the "Narrative of the discovery of the fate of Sir John Franklin and his companions," as told by M'Clintock. Here is the substance of the story.

It was in the summer of 1857 that the little steam yacht *Fox*, screw fitted, and only of 177 tons burden, set out on her perilous mission. She left Aberdeen on the 1st of July, and by the 8th of August, under sail and steam, she was striving to find a way through the great belt of broken ice which streams down from Baffin's Bay into the Atlantic Ocean. Satisfied, after a close examination of many miles of its margin, that no passage across the Bay towards Lancaster Sound could be forced, the *Fox's* prow was turned northward, and an attempt made to go round Melville Bay. But before the "middle ice" could be rounded, the short summer had passed, and wintry weather set in. On the 7th of September, after gallant efforts to cut, bore, or warp through the pack, the *Fox* was frozen in, and there was no alternative but to drift with the ice where it listed. She remained thus enchained with frozen fetters till April 17th, 1858, never moving from her involuntary moorings. In these eight dreary months she drifted helplessly far south of the Arctic Circle, which she had so gaily entered. During the 242 days she had been impacted in the ice, she had travelled no less than 1,385 miles, the longest drift on record.

We can imagine the wild grandeur of this scene of solitude, when the little ship, a mere speck on the vast frozen sea, was thus drifting helplessly southward. There were only twenty-five souls on board, all told, twenty-two of the crew, with the captain, and Lieutenant Hobson second in command, and Captain Allen Young, an experienced Arctic navigator, sailing master. We can enter into the feelings of the gallant captain, as he writes in his Journal—

" Everything around us is painfully still, excepting when an occasional iceberg spilts off from the parent glacier ; then we hear a rumbling crash like distant thunder, and the wave occasioned by the launch reaches us in six or seven minutes, and makes the ship roll lazily for a similar period. I cannot imagine that within the whole compass of nature's varied aspects there is presented to the human eye a scene so well adapted for promoting deep and serious reflection, for lifting the thoughts from trivial things of every-day life to others of the highest import.

The glacier serves to remind one at once of time and of eternity—of time, since we see portions of it break off to drift and melt away; and of eternity, since its downward march is so extremely slow, and its augmentations behind so regular, that no change in its appearance is perceptible from age to age. If even the untaught savages of luxuriant tropical regions regard the earth merely as a temporary abode, surely all who gaze upon this ice-overwhelmed region, this wide expanse of 'terrestrial wreck,' must be similarly assured that here 'we have no abiding place.'"

It needs, indeed, a noble enthusiasm, a steadiness of purpose, to carry men bravely through such scenes, the awfulness of which was enhanced by darkness, monotony, and the constant dangers of a winter's drift in that polar pack. All their visions of success in 1857 were gone—all hope of returning home in 1858, with the important news which their eager hopes assured them they should obtain, deferred until 1859. Yet M'Clintock neither bewails his misfortune nor doubts his ultimate success—all his fears, when he expresses any, are for " poor Lady Franklin; how disappointed she will be!" At last, after long months of imprisonment, the day of release came for the little *Fox*, but was a day indeed of frightful danger. On Saturday, the 24th of April, Captain M'Clintock writes :—

" It is now ten o'clock in the evening; the long ocean swell already lifts its crest five feet above the hollow of the sea, causing its thick covering of icy fragments to dash against each other and against us with unpleasant violence. It is, however, very beautiful to look upon the dear old familiar ocean swell! It has long been a stranger to us, and is welcome in our solitude. If the *Fox* was as solid as her neighbours, I am quite sure she would enter into this ice-tournament with all their apparent heartiness, instead of audibly making known her sufferings to us. Every considerable surface of ice has been broken into many smaller ones. With feelings of exultation I watched the process from aloft. A floe-piece near us, of one hundred yards in diameter, was speedily cracked so as to resemble a sort of labyrinth, or, still more, a field-spider's web. In the course of half an hour the family resemblance was totally lost; they had so battered each other, and struggled out of their original regularity. The rolling sea can no longer be checked. ' The pack has taken upon itself the functions of an ocean,' as Dr. Kane graphically expresses it."

By midnight the *Fox* was striving for sweet life through this rolling sea of ice. Sunday, the 25th of April, came in; the swell was ten feet high, the shocks from the ice so severe that the crew could hardly keep their feet on deck, and the vessel had to be steered very nicely so as to keep her sharp stem towards the charging masses. Still, aided by the screw and steam, the stout yacht fought her way outwards to the open sea; an iceberg was passed, it was nearly seventy feet high, and " crashing through the pack," while from the small water space left in its wake the seas were throwing spray quite over its summit—a pretty good proof of the fearful commotion through which the *Fox* was seeking a way. The swell still increased, and rolled along more swiftly—an ugly sea, thickly strewn with heavy ice.

At sea! writes Captain M'Clintock on the next day, " It has pleased God to accord to us a deliverance in which His merciful protection contrasts, how strongly! with our own utter helplessness." It appeared as if the mercies vouchsafed during the long, long winter and mysterious ice-drift " had been concentrated and repeated in a single act; and, after yesterday's experience," he adds, " I can understand how men's hair has turned grey in a few hours." The *Fox*, however, passes out of the ice in Davis's Strait only to refit in Greenland, and again enter it a month afterwards. Men so stanch deserved to succeed. The middle-ice was cleared; the Esquimaux stories from Pond's Bay about white men and ships disposed of by personal examination; Lancaster Sound reached; Beechey Island, the great Arctic store depôt, visited; and on August 16th they sailed up Barrow's Strait. That night the *Fox* " was battling against a strong wind with *sea*," and so unusually clear of ice was this channel that on the 17th the gallant captain writes :—

"17th.—Last night battling against wind and *sea*, in rain and fog. To-day much loose ice is seen southward of Griffith's Island. The weather improved this afternoon, and we shot gallantly past Limestone Island, and are now steering down Peel Strait, all of us in a wild state of excitement—a mingling of anxious hopes and fears!

18th.—For twenty-five miles last evening we ran unobstructedly down Peel Strait, but then came in sight of unbroken ice, extending across it from shore to shore! It was much decayed, and of one year's growth only; yet as the strait continues to contract for sixty miles further, and it appeared to me to afford so little hope of becoming navigable in the short remainder of the season, *I immediately turned about for Bellot Strait*, as affording a better prospect of a passage into the western sea discovered by Sir James Ross from Four River Point in 1849. Our disappointment at the interruption of our progress was as sudden as it was severe. We did not linger in hope of a change, but steered out again into the broad waters of Barrow's Strait."

This rapidity of decision, when combined with correct judgment and great nerve, is the most essential qualification in the Arctic navigator, who has no time to cast about, lest the right moment slip away. Success rewarded the captain's attempt to reach Bellot Strait, and with but little hindrance he had within seventy hours repassed Barrow's Strait, visited Leopold harbour, secured the depôt established there by Ross in 1848, and sailed down Regent's Inlet into the entrance of the remarkable strait which cleaves North Somerset and Boothia. Here, happily for the *Fox* and her gallant company, as we believe, they found the sea to the westward of Boothia still choked with ice, and Captain M'Clintock was obliged to be satisfied with wintering in the very excellent position which had been vouchsafed to him, for while his retreat to Baffin's Bay was open annually in his rear, the coasts of King William's

The Voyage of the "Fox."

Land were only 150 miles distant from Bellot Strait in his front.

The winter of 1858-59 was an unusually severe one in 72 deg. north, and its severity was augmented by the position of their winter quarters. The lofty granitic cliffs of Bellot Strait, with the hills, 1,500 feet high, of Murchison Promontory, on the one side, and those of North Somerset on the other, formed a funnel through which the storm and the snow-drift seemed to be ever revelling in wildest mood, while the deep waters of the strait rolled ever to and fro with fierce rapidity, chasing and grinding the heavy ice borne into it from that hopeless western sea. " Even when we have a calm night," says M'Clintock, " we can hear the crushing sounds of the drift ice in Bellot Strait, and it emits dark chilling clouds of hateful, pestilent, abominable mist."

The sun of 1859 had hardly thrown his light over North Somerset when we find Captain M'Clintock and his comrade, Allen Young, braving a temperature of 48 deg. minus of Fahrenheit, or 80 deg. below the freezing point of water, in sledging parties to the westward and southward. The great object of Captain M'Clintock's visit to these frozen wilds seemed at once to be within his grasp, for from Esquimaux he recovered many relics of the Franklin Expedition, all of which they assured him came from a party of " starving white men " who had reached an island in the mouth of the great river (Montreal Island), after their ship had been crushed by the ice in the sea to the west of King William's Land. This one ship, for they knew not of a second, must have been either the *Erebus* or *Terror*, and their intelligence confirmed Captain M'Clintock in directing his principal division of sledges to the search of King William's Land, while the uncertainty as to the fate of the second vessel compelled him to detach his able comrade, Young, to search the shores of Prince of Wales Land, in case she might have been there wrecked or beset.

Early in April every man, dog, and sledge that could possibly be spared from the *Fox* started upon their final and momentous duty. Allen Young faithfully accomplished all the work assigned him in spite of many difficulties and much suffering. He found no trace of Franklin's Expedition, but he discovered 380 miles of coast-line, established the insularity of Prince of Wales Land, and connected Sir James Ross's furthest in 1848 with the shores of Bellot Strait.

On the other hand, Captain M'Clintock, Lieutenant Hobson, and Carl Petersen explored the entire coast of King William's Land, as well as the west coast of Boothia and the estuary of the Great Fish River, and, above all, they discovered at Point Victory a document—the only document as yet found—in which the death of Franklin and the achievements and loss of his expedition are at last revealed to us. From that record, the relics found, the information now brought home, as well as Esquimaux reports, which Carl Petersen's cross-examinations rectify to a very considerable extent, we are able to put together the following facts, and they briefly account for the *Erebus* and *Terror* up to the period of their abandonment by the crews, and of the subsequent fate of those gallant men. The tale is briefly as follows:—

The *Erebus* and *Terror*, under Franklin and Crozier, in the same year (1845) that they left England, proceeded up Barrow's Straits; entering Wellington Channel (of which we then only knew the southern headlands), they sailed up that remarkable straight to the 77th degree of north latitude, some miles further than was attained by Her Majesty's ships *Assistance* and *Pioneer*, under Captains Belcher and Osborn, in 1852. From the northern outlet of Wellington Channel Franklin was obliged to retrace his steps southward, and this, in all probability, owing to his finding the path to the westward hopelessly blocked with ice. He discovered, however, a new channel between Bathurst and Cornwallis Island, and must have re-entered Barrow's Straits very near the point at which the expedition of 1850, under Captains Austin and Ommanney, wintered—namely, Griffith's Island.

Having accomplished this almost unparalleled extent of

The Voyage of the "Fox."

Arctic navigation in the open season of 1845, Franklin proceeded to Beechey Island, and there, as we have long known, passed his first winter, with the loss of only three men out of the entire complement of 129 souls in the expedition. In that exploration of 1845 Franklin discovered fully 500 miles of new coast-line, and explored two channels, of a combined length of 250 miles; subsequently, searching parties have gone over and rediscovered nearly every inch of this ground, and it is strange, that, throughout its whole extent, the Franklin Expedition should have erected no cairn, placed no record; and, still more so, that they should have again sailed from Beechey Island for a second effort in accomplishment of their task—the discovery of the North-West Passage—without placing in some of the many cairns erected around their winter quarters a statement of their past success and of their future intentions.

We can account for such a fatal omission but in one way, that they were so confident of reaching Behring's Straits or the American continent that it was never deemed possible others would follow on their footsteps to aid or assist them, and that, if the anxiety of the leader led him even to contemplate the possibility of failure in carrying his followers to the Pacific, he supposed, when his expedition had outstayed its time from England, that the same steps for his relief would be repeated as had been carried out when John Ross was missing in the *Victory*—that parties would be merely sent overland down the Great Fish and other rivers to rescue him.

At any rate, in 1846, without placing any record at Beechey Island, the Franklin Expedition sailed to reach the American continent, at or near the Great Fish River, whence to Behring's Straits the ground had been already explored. The concurrent testimony of all the Arctic navigators who have subsequently visited the seas round Cape Walker and Prince of Wales Land, go to maintain that it was down between that land and North Somerset that Franklin found his way to the south. Great success again attended this second cruise of the intrepid navigator, and it was not until he had accomplished 250 miles down a new strait, which now bears the name of Franklin, that his expedition was overtaken by winter and beset in the ice. They were only twelve miles from and in sight of Cape Felix, a headland of what was then supposed to be a promontory of the continent of America, and known as King William's Land. The second winter, that of 1846-47, was passed in this tantalizing position; but considering how large had been their success in each of the previous summers that they had passed in the Arctic zone there was everything to cheer the officers and men and assure them of perfect success in 1847, the more so that Cape Herschel, the point at which the connection of the Pacific and Atlantic oceans would be established, was *barely ninety miles distant.*

We are, therefore, not astonished to find the officer in charge of a sledge party which left the *Erebus* in May 1847, describing their condition in the expedition to be "All well, Sir John Franklin in command." The trail of the sledge party, as shown by certain cairns, indicated that it went to the south-west, very probably to connect the coast-line with Cape Herschel, and to cheer up the ship's companies with the glorious intelligence that they had really discovered the long-sought passage. So far all was indeed well, but the summer of 1847 must have been one of those "close seasons," of which our Arctic sailors have had such trying experience. The ships appear to have drifted a very short distance to the south-west, and to have been constantly beset. Sickness seems to have broken out, Sir John Franklin died as early as the 12th of June, and we are appalled to find, when the spring of 1848 dawns upon the expedition, that, since leaving Beechey Island, no less than twenty-one souls had perished, nine of whom were officers.

We need not say that scurvy and starvation must have been rife during that winter of 1847-48, for we find in Captain M'Clintock's narrative ample testimony to show that even in his small crew, in spite of a far more nutritious and liberal dietary than ever Franklin's crews could have had, scurvy was making steady and fatal inroads during even a second winter in the ice. This fearful loss of life, and the fact that the expedition was only provisioned to the spring of 1848, obliged Captains Crozier and Fitzjames to direct a retreat and abandonment of the ships, and as they had no choice, they led one hundred and five poor starving sailors and officers away from the *Erebus* and *Terror* on the 22nd of April, and did not reach the land, though only fifteen miles distant, until April 25th—a sad proof of how weak or encumbered with sick they must have been.

On that 25th of April they write that they start on the morrow, the 26th, for the Fish River! The next time they were seen or heard of alive was by some Esquimaux, who were sealing on King William's Land; the "*starving white men*" were then only about forty in number, all, with exception of a chief, "a tall, stout man," were dragging at a sledge; they were hungry and thin; they purchased seal's flesh; they fell down and died as they marched along! What became of this forlorn hope of forty individuals we will presently relate, but how they had suffered up to the point at which these Esquimaux met them, the wreck-strewn beaches of King William's Land but too sadly tell. An abandoned boat, with two skeletons in it, only half-way from the *Erebus* and *Terror* to Cape Herschel, indicated some attempt to return towards the ships, or such weakness that they could no longer drag what was so essential to them in the ascent of such a stream as the Great Fish River. Another skeleton was discovered some miles beyond Cape Herschell, and Heaven only knows whether the bleaching bones of the unaccounted for sixty individuals lie under the snows of King William's Land, or in the depths of its ice-encumbered sea. Clothing, sledge gear, and personal equipment of all descriptions were found on that west coast of King William's Land by Captain M'Clintock and Lieutenant Hobson, but no provisions; this fact alone only too painfully brings home to us the melancholy end of the unfortunate crews of the *Erebus* and *Terror*.

Of the "forlorn hope" seen in the spring by the Esquimaux

we have a clue in the visit of Mr. Anderson to Montreal Island, at the mouth of the Great Fish River in 1855, and the traces he found all went to corroborate the report gleaned from the natives, by Dr. Rae, in 1854—that in the summer of the same year, and subsequent to the period that the natives had seen them alive, the corpses of thirty white men, and some graves containing others, were discovered in one spot, near the great river, and five more dead bodies on an adjacent island. Some of these dead white men were in a tent; others under a boat turned over for shelter, and the officer was again recognized by his having a telescope and double-barrelled gun near him. Nothing can be more circumstantial than this evidence, and it all goes to prove that, although some portion of the starving crews reached the continent of America, at the entrance of the Great Fish River, that they there perished of starvation, and on Captain M'Clintock's visit to Montreal Island, every vestige or relic of them had been swept away by the natives, although in 1855 traces of Europeans having been there were pretty numerous.

Apart from an official record contained in a cylinder, and already damaged by iron rust, not a single journal, log, or manuscript was discovered calculated to give any additional information as to the proceedings of the lost expedition. Indeed, it was not until the retreating party reached King William's Land that the idea seems to have struck the officers commanding, that any record of their past acts or future intentions ought to be left in cache; and, instead of a carefully prepared document being brought from the ships and left at Cape Victory, they merely opened the usual official notice, which Commander Gore had placed there in 1847, and in the bitter temperature of an Arctic April day, Captains Crozier and Fitzjames added a few brief, though graphic, sentences, in which all we shall probably ever know of that sad tale is revealed to us.

Yet we will not blame them; suffering, disease, and starvation had doubtless caused all their thoughts and feelings to be concentrated in the one great idea of saving their lives in that forthcoming summer. It was far more than they could all hope to do, and the strong would assuredly have preferred to drag a sick shipmate rather than a load of logs or journals ; nay, more, had they even carried such dead weight to the shore, would they not, we ask, have placed them under the cairn at Cape Victory, around which, we are told, there was a pile of abandoned clothing and equipment, indicative of weakness, and a desire to lighten themselves of every encumbrance ? That a few prayer-books and religious works, capable of being carried in the pocket, were discovered in the abandoned boat, is true ; but that only shows how utter must have been the exhaustion of our starving sailors, when they parted with the last solace of men, who knew their days were numbered.

All goes to prove that in the ships was left all further record of the voyage of the *Erebus* and *Terror*. One vessel indubitably sank when the ice broke up; the other was evidently carried round Capes Crozier, or Herschell, into the haunts of the Esquimaux, and one party of these savages distinctly pointed out that she had been lying upon that coast within a somewhat recent date. In 1859 this wreck had likewise disappeared, for every part of the coast was narrowly examined for her; the ice had either swept her off the beach, and she had then probably sunk in deep water, or the natives had applied fire to detach the wood and metal, in which she was a mine of wealth to them.

Such is the tale of Captain M'Clintock, and grateful ought every one to be that at last such conclusive intelligence was gained of an expedition, the search for which has called forth so much zeal and self-sacrifice. The official acknowledgment from the Admiralty, of the services of Lady Franklin's expedition, very justly says that Captain M'Clintock has rendered important service " *in bringing home the only authentic intelligence of the death of Sir John Franklin, and of the fate of the crews of the* Erebus *and* Terror," and his Sovereign gracefully evinced her high appreciation of the gallant officer's services, by an Order in Council granting him sea-time for every day he commanded the *Fox* yacht, as if his pendant had been flying on board one of Her Majesty's ships!—a handsome compliment, right worthily bestowed. The return voyage of the *Fox* to England was a prosperous one, and the little craft was sold to be used as an Arctic sealing vessel.

The writer of the notice in the *Times* of Captain M'Clintock's book, himself evidently well acquainted with Arctic affairs, and to whom we are indebted for valuable information, states that neither the captain, nor Allen Young, the sailing master, would accept any recompense for their services from private hands, and that of the £10,000 which the expedition cost, about £7,000 came from Lady Franklin's own purse. The gold medal of the Royal Geographical Society was presented to her as an honourable recognition of her husband's services in discovering the North-West Passage, and the monuments in Westminster Abbey and Waterloo Place recall the memory of Franklin, Crozier, Fitzjames, and their gallant comrades, who fell in the execution of a duty which had been assigned to them by their countrymen. The services of M'Clintock, with the good ship *Fox*, will always hold an honourable place in the records of Arctic voyages and travels.

PERILS IN THE ICE.

IN the year 1770 the Society of the Moravian Brethren first established mission stations on the coast of Labrador. Every year since that date a ship has been sent from the Thames, sometimes for the conveyance of passengers, but always for carrying the stores necessary for the life and comfort of the dwellers in those remote settlements. The records of these voyages are preserved in the Periodical Accounts published by the Society. Many remarkable events appear in

ARRIVAL OF THE GOOD SHIP "HARMONY."
[*Page* 97.

these records, the ships having been often exposed to great perils, and having met with memorable adventures, in times both of war and peace. Through the protection of Divine Providence, in all the years that have passed, the voyage has been made in safety, although the ships have encountered the dangers common to those seas and coasts. One of the most perilous voyages was that of the year 1817, in the *Jemima*, the predecessor of successive ships which, under the name of the *Harmony*, have continued the voyages from 1818 to the present time.

The *Jemima* reached Stromness from London on the 14th of June, and thence had a favourable voyage across the Atlantic. Up to the end of June all went well, but a few days later the record, as given by Brother Kmoch, a veteran missionary who was on board, bears a more stirring character :—

Between the 4th and 5th of July we heard and saw many ice-birds. This bird is about the size of a starling, black, with white and yellow spots, and is met with about 200 English miles from the Labrador coast. When the sailors hear it, they know that they are not far from the ice. It flies about a ship chiefly in the night, and is known by its singular voice, which resembles a loud laugh.

7th.—The morning was cold and rainy. In all directions drift-ice was to be seen. In the afternoon it cleared up a little, and we entered an opening in the ice, looking like a bay. The continual rustling and roaring of the ice reminded us of the noise made by the carriages in the streets of London, when one is standing in the golden gallery of St. Paul's Cathedral. The mountains and large flakes of ice take all manner of singular forms, some resembling castles, others churches, waggons, and even creatures of various descriptions. As we or they changed positions, the same objects acquired a quite different appearance ; and what had before appeared like a church, looked like a huge floating monster. Sitting on deck, and contemplating these wonderful works of God, I almost lost myself in endeavouring to solve the question,—" for what purpose these exhibitions are made, when so few can behold them, as they so soon vanish, by returning to their former fluid and undefined state?" But surely everything is done with design, though short-sighted man cannot comprehend it. Having in vain exerted ourselves to penetrate through the ice, we returned at night into the open sea.

14th.—Land was discovered ahead. It was the coast of Labrador, sixty or eighty miles south of Hopedale. We were close to the ice, and, as a small opening presented itself, the captain ventured to push in, hoping, if he could penetrate, to find open water between the ice and the coast. For some time we got nearer to the land, but were obliged at night to fasten the ship with two grapnels to a large field. This was elevated between five and six feet above the water's edge, and between fifty and sixty feet in thickness below it. It might be three hundred feet in diameter, flat at the top, and smooth as a meadow covered with snow. The wind has but little power over such huge masses, and they move very slowly with the current. There are small streams and pools of fresh water found in all those large pieces. Our situation now defended us against the smaller flakes, which rushed by and were turned off by the large field without reaching the ship. We were all pleased with our place of refuge, and lay here three whole days, with the brightest weather, and as safe as in the most commodious haven; but I cannot say that I felt easy, though I hid my anxiety from the party. I feared that a gale of wind might overtake us in this situation, and carry fields larger than that in which we lay, when the most dreadful consequences might ensue; and the sequel proved that I was not much mistaken.

On the 17th the wind came round from the south, and we conceived fresh hopes of the way being rendered open for us.

18th.—The weather was clear, and the wind in our favour; we therefore took up our grapnel, got clear of our floating haven, and again endeavoured to penetrate through some small openings. Both we and the ship's company were peculiarly

Perils in the Ice.

impressed with gratitude for the protection and rest we had enjoyed, and the warmth of a summer's sun felt very comfortable among these masses of ice. The clearness of the atmosphere to-day caused them to appear singularly picturesque. It seemed as if we were surrounded by immense white walls and towers. In the afternoon we had penetrated to the open water, between the ice and the land, but we durst not venture nearer, as the sea is here full of sunken rocks, and the captain knew of no harbour on this part of the coast. Having found another large piece of ice convenient for the purpose, we fastened the ship to it. In the evening a thick fog overspread us from the north-east, and we were again quite surrounded by ice, which, however, was soon after dispersed by a strong north-west wind.

In the night, between the 19th and 20th, we were driven back by a strong current to nearly the same situation we had left on the 17th, only somewhat nearer the coast. On the 20th, the morning was fine, and we vainly endeavoured to get clear, but towards evening the sky lowered, and it grew very dark. The air felt so oppressive that we all went to bed, and every one of us was troubled with uneasy dreams. At midnight we heard a great noise on deck. We hastened thither to know the cause, and found the ship driving fast towards a huge ice-mountain, on which we expected every moment to suffer shipwreck. The sailors exerted themselves to the utmost, but it was by God's merciful providence alone that we were saved. The night was exceedingly cold, with rain, and the poor people suffered much. We were now driven to and fro at the mercy of the ice, till one in the morning, when we succeeded in fastening the ship again to a large field. But all this was only the prelude to greater terrors. Deliverance from danger is so gratifying that it raises one's spirits above the common level. We made a hearty breakfast, and retired again into our cabins. At one o'clock the cook, in his usual boisterous way, aroused us by announcing dinner, and putting a large piece of pork and a huge pudding upon the table, of which we partook with a good appetite, but in silence, every one seemingly buried in thought, or only half-awake. Shortly after, the wind changed to north-east and north, increasing gradually, till it turned into a furious storm. Top-masts were lowered, and everything done to ease the ship. We now saw an immense ice-mountain at a distance, towards which we were driving, without the power of turning aside. Between six and seven we were again roused by a great outcry on deck. We ran up, and saw our ship, with the field to which we were fast, with great swiftness approaching towards the mountain; nor did there appear the smallest hope of escaping being crushed to atoms between it and the field. However, by veering out as much cable as we could, the ship got to such a distance that the mountain passed through between us and the field. We all cried fervently to the Lord for speedy help in this most perilous situation, for if we had but touched the mountain, we must have been instantly destroyed. One of our cables was broken, and we lost a grapnel; the ship also sustained some damage. But we were now left to the mercy of the storm and current, both of which were violent; and exposed likewise to thick masses of ice, which floated all around us.

The following night was stormy and dreadfully dark, the heavens covered with the blackest clouds driven by a furious wind, the roaring and the howling of the ice as it moved along, the fields shoving and dashing against each other, were truly terrible. A fender was made of a large beam, suspended by ropes to the ship's sides, to secure her in some measure from the ice, but the ropes were soon cut by its sharp edges, and we lost the fender. Repeated attempts were now made to make the ship again fast to some large field; and the second mate, a clever young man, full of spirit and willingness, swung himself several times off upon such fields as approached us, endeavouring to fix a grapnel to them, but in vain, and we even lost another grapnel on this occasion. The storm indeed dispersed the ice, and made openings in

Perils in the Ice.

several places; but our situation was thereby rendered only still more alarming, for when the ship got into open water, her motion became more rapid by the power of the wind, and consequently the blows she received from the ice more violent. Whenever, therefore, we perceived a field of ice through the gloom, towards which we were hurried, nothing appeared more probable than that the violence of the shock would determine our fate, and be attended with immediate destruction to the vessel. Such shocks were repeated every five or ten minutes, and sometimes oftener, and the longer she remained exposed to the wind, the more violently she ran against the sharp edges and spits of the ice, not having any power to avoid them. After every stroke we tried the pumps, to find whether we had sprung a leak; but the Lord kept His hand over us, and preserved us in a manner almost miraculous. In this awful situation, we offered up fervent prayers to Him, who alone is able to save, and besought Him that, if it were His Divine will that we should end our lives among the ice, He would, for the sake of His precious merits, soon take us home to Himself, nor let us die a miserable death from cold and hunger, floating about in this boisterous ocean.

It is impossible to describe all the horrors of this eventful night, in which we expected every approaching ice-field to be fraught with death. We were full ten hours in this dreadful situation, till about six in the morning, when we were driven into open water, not far from the coast. We could hardly believe that we had got clear of the ice; all seemed as a dream. We now ventured to carry some sail, with a view to bear up against the wind. The ship had become leaky, and we were obliged to keep the pump a-going, with only about ten minutes' rest at a time. Both the sailors and we were thereby so much exhausted that, whenever any one sat down, he immediately fell asleep.

During the afternoon the wind abated, and towards evening it fell calm. A thick mist ensued, which, however, soon dispersed, when we found ourselves near a high rock, towards which the current was fast carrying us. We were now in danger of suffering shipwreck among the rocks, but, by God's mercy, the good management of our captain succeeded in steering clear of them; and after sunset the heavens were free from clouds. A magnificent northern light illumined the horizon, and, as we were again among floating pieces of ice, its brightness enabled us to avoid them. I retired to rest, but, after midnight, was roused by the cracking noise made by the ice against the sides of the vessel. In an instant I was on deck, and found that we were forcing our way through a quantity of floating ice, out of which we soon got again into open water. The wind also turned in our favour, and carried us swiftly forward towards the Hopedale shore. Every one on board was again in full expectation of soon reaching the end of our voyage, and ready to forget all former troubles. But, alas! arriving at the same spot from which we had been driven yesterday, we found our way anew blocked up with a vast quantity of ice. The wind also drove us irresistibly towards it. We were now in a great dilemma. If we went between the islands, where the sea is full of sunken rocks, we were in danger of striking upon one of them, and being instantly lost; again, if we ventured into the ice, it was doubtful whether the ship would bear many more such shocks as she had received. At length the former measure was determined on, as, in case of any mishap, there might be some possibility of escaping to shore.

After encountering a succession of further perils and disappointments for three additional weeks, the *Jemima* was brought safely into Hopedale harbour on the 9th of August.

To the foregoing narrative the following remarks are appended by the editor of the "Periodical Accounts":—"The captain and mate report that, though for these three years past they have met with an unusual quantity of ice on the coast of Labrador, yet, in no year since the beginning of the Mission, has it appeared so dreadfully on the increase.

The colour likewise of this year's ice was different from that usually seen, and the size of the ice-mountains and thickness of the fields immense, with sand-stones embedded in them. As a great part of the coast of Greenland, which for centuries has been choked up with ice, apparently immovable, has, by some revolution, been cleared, this may perhaps account for the great quantity alluded to."

A PARLIAMENTARY DEBATE IN TAHITI.

AFTER the people of Tahiti and the other Windward Islands of the South Sea had received the religious teaching of the Christian missionaries, they sought instruction as to the principles and practice of civil government. The chiefs declared their readiness to give up their personal and despotic rule, and to adopt a suitable constitution and just laws. There was much consultation and deliberation, and at length, at the request of the chiefs, the missionaries prepared a draft of a constitution and of a code of laws, to be submitted for the approval of the chiefs. The advice given was to summon a conference of the chiefs and leading men, and to discuss the proposals offered for their consideration.

Accordingly, an assembly was convened, consisting of the adult male members of the royal family of Tahiti, the same of the principal chiefs, these being hereditary legislators; to whom were added, as representatives of the people, two members from each Mataaina or district, appointed by the people themselves. The place of meeting was at Papaoa, as being convenient of access for the members from other islands, as well as those in Tahiti. Mr. Nott, the senior missionary, was requested to act as president or speaker. The other missionaries were present, but took no part in the proceedings, and there were also present Mr. Tyerman and Mr. Bennett, a deputation from the London Missionary

Society, then on a tour round the world, for the purpose of visiting the various stations of that Society. Except the president, all the members were natives, and it was the first native parliament of the Windward Islands, held for the purpose of legislation and government. In old times no council had met except for unholy or warlike conference.

The draft of the code had been previously prepared by Mr. Nott, at the request of the chiefs and people, the general principles and specific enactments having been frequently and fully canvassed in several conferences, and recognized by all present as the basis of the literal form in which the same should be embodied and promulgated. This code, thus adopted, consisted of about forty articles, which appeared to comprehend all the necessary provisions for maintaining social order, promoting public welfare, and securing the rights and privileges of all ranks among the community, with regard to life, liberty, and property. For instance, in regard to theft, upon conviction there was to be reparation fourfold, and for repetition of the offence, hard labour, to the extent of five years as the maximum punishment. For drunkenness, the first offence was dealt with by public admonition, and hard labour after subsequent convictions. The enactments against tattooing and other former customs were repealed, leaving persons to act as they pleased in matters not injuring their neighbours.

For executing the laws many magistrates or judges were appointed, there being two, at least, for each district, besides seven supreme judges for Tahiti, and two for Eimeo. Juries were to consist of six persons, peers of the accused. Many of the articles were agreed to after considerable discussion, the most protracted of the debates being that on the question of capital punishment for murder. The question lay between punishment by death or perpetual banishment to some uninhabited island, the latter alternative being adopted unanimously. It is this debate that we are going to report, as showing the intelligence and earnestness, the good sense and good feeling, displayed forty years ago by these untutored natives of the South Sea Islands.

Before giving the summary of the debate, as recorded by Messrs. Tyerman and Bennett, who were present during the two days over which it extended, let us recall a somewhat analogous state of affairs which might have been witnessed in a European assembly, equally without previous experience in parliamentary procedure.

In the course of the great continental war of the early part of this century, Sicily fell into the hands of the English, and without any previous political education or preparation for liberty was placed under a constitution modelled after that of Great Britain. " No words," says a traveller, " can describe the scenes which daily occurred upon the introduction of the representative system into Sicily. The House of Parliament, neither moderated by discretion nor conducted with dignity, bore the resemblance of a receptacle for lunatics, instead of a council for legislators, and the disgraceful scenes so often seen at the hustings in England were here transferred to the floor of the Senate. The president's voice was unheeded and unheard; the whole House at times rose; partisans of different antagonists mingled in the fray, when the ground was literally covered with combatants, kicking, biting, and scratching. Such a state of things could not last; indeed, this constitutional synod was dissolved the very first year of its creation, and martial law established."

Similar scenes would probably be witnessed in an Irish parliament, under Home Rule! What caused the congress in Tahiti to present so totally different an aspect, and display so different a spirit? It was because many of the chiefs and people were truly Christian men, whose character was ennobled, and whose conduct was regulated by the truths and the spirit of the Gospel. In the whole proceedings of that assembly there was a propriety and earnestness that might put to shame even our own parliament in some of its debates.

On the question being proposed, whether exile for life to a desolate island should be the penalty on conviction for murder, Hitoti, the principal chief of Pape, stood up, and, bowing to the president and the assembly, said : "No doubt this is a good law; but a thought has been growing in my heart for several days, and when you have heard my little speech you will understand what it is. The laws of England, from which country we have received so much good of every kind, must they not be good ? And do not the laws of England punish murderers by death ? Now, my thought is that as England does so it would be well for us to do so. That is my thought."

Perfect silence followed this short but earnestly spoken address. And it may be observed here that, throughout the whole eight days' meetings of this assembly, in no instance were two speakers on their legs at once ; there was not an angry word uttered by one against another, nor did any assume the possession of more wisdom or authority than the rest. In fact, none controverted the opinion of a previous speaker, or even commented on it, without some respectful commendation of what seemed praiseworthy in it, while, for reasons which he modestly but manfully assigned, he deemed another sentiment better.

After looking round to see whether anybody were already up before him, Utami, the principal chief of Buanaauia, rose and thus addressed the president : "The chief of Pape has said well that we have received a great many good things from the kind Christian people of England. Indeed, what have we not received from Beretane ? Did they not send us the true gospel ?—But does not Hitoti's speech go too far ? If we take the laws of England for our guide, then must we not punish with death those who break into a house ?—those who write a wrong name ?—those who steal a sheep ? And will any man in Tahiti say that death should grow for these ?—No, no ; this goes too far ; so I think we should stop. The law, as it is written, I think is good ; perhaps I am wrong ; but that is my thought."

After a moment or two of stillness, Upuparu, a noble, intelligent, and stately chief, stood forth. It was a pleasure to look upon his animated countenance and frank demeanour, without the smallest affectation either of superiority or condescension. He paid several graceful compliments to the former speakers, while, according to his thought, in some things each was right, and each was wrong. "My brother, Hitoti, who proposed that we should punish murder with death because England does so, was wrong, as has been shown by Utami. For they are not the laws of England which are to guide us, though they are good;—the Bible is our perfect guide. Now, *Mitti Trutu* (the Missionary Crook) was preaching to us on (naming the day) from the Scripture, 'He that sheddeth man's blood, by man shall his blood be shed'; and he told us that this was the reason of the law of England. My thought, therefore, is not with Utami, but with Hitoti (though not because the law of England, but because the Bible, orders it), that we ought to punish with death every one found guilty of murder."

There was a lively exchange of looks all through the assembly, as if each had been deeply struck with the sentiments of the speaker, especially when he placed the ground of the punishment of death, not upon English precedent, but Scripture authority. Another chief followed, and " rising, seemed a pillar of state," one whose aspect, and presence, and costume of dress (richly native) made the spectators forget even him who had just sat down. His name was Tati; and on him all eyes were immediately and intensely fixed, while, with not less simplicity and deference to others than those who had preceded him, he spoke thus : " Perhaps some of you may be surprised that I, who am the first chief here, and next to the royal family, should have held my peace so long. I wished to hear what my brethren would say, that I might gather what thoughts had grown in their breasts on this great question. I am glad that I waited, because some thoughts are now growing in my own breast which I did not bring with me. The chiefs, who have spoken before me, have spoken well. But is not the speech of Upuparu like that of his brother Hitoti—in this way? If we cannot follow the laws of England in all things, as Hitoti's thoughts would perhaps lead us, because they go too far,—must we not stop short of Upuparu, because his thought goes too far likewise? The Bible, he says, is our perfect guide. It is. But what does that Scripture mean, 'He that sheddeth man's blood, by man shall his blood be shed'? Does not this go so far that we cannot follow it to the end, any more than we can follow the laws of England all the way? I am Tati; I am a judge; a man is convicted before me; he has shed blood; I order him to be put to death; I shed *his* blood; then who shall shed *mine?* Here, because I cannot go *so* far, I must stop. This cannot be the meaning of those words. But, perhaps, since many of the laws of the Old Testament were thrown down by the Lord Jesus Christ, and only some kept standing upright,—perhaps, I say, this is one of those which were thrown down. However, as I am ignorant, someone else will show me that, in the New Testament, our Saviour, or His apostles, have said the same thing concerning him that sheddeth man's blood as is said in the Old Testament. Show me this in the New Testament, and then it must be our guide."

Much cordial approbation was evident at the conclusion of Tati's speech, and its evangelical appeal seemed to remove some difficulty and doubt respecting the true Scriptural authority applicable to the case.

Next rose Pati, a chief and a judge of Eimeo, formerly a high priest of Oro, and the first who, at the hazard of his life, had abjured idolatry. " My breast," he exclaimed, "is full of thought and surprise and delight. When I look round at this *fare bure ra* (house of prayer) in which we are assembled, and consider who we are that take sweet counsel together here, it is to me all *mea huru e* (a thing of amazement), and *mea faa oaoa te aau* (a thing that makes glad my heart). Tati has settled the question; for is it not the gospel that is our guide?

and who can find directions for putting to death ? I know many passages which forbid, but I know not one which commands, to kill. But then another thought is growing in my breast, and, if you will hearken to my little speech, you shall know what it is. Laws to punish those that commit crime are good for us. But tell me, why do Christians punish ? Is it because we are angry, and have pleasure in causing pain ? Is it because we love revenge, as we did when we were heathens ? None of these: Christians do not love revenge ; Christians must not be angry ; they cannot have pleasure in causing pain. Christians do not, therefore, punish for these. Is it not that, by the suffering which is inflicted, we may prevent the criminal from repeating his crime, and frighten others from doing as he has done to deserve the like ? Well then, does not everybody know that it would be a greater punishment to be banished for ever from Tahiti, to a desolate island, than just, in a moment, to be put to death ? And could the banished man commit murder again there ? And would not others be more frightened by such a sentence than by one to take away his life ? So my thought is that Tati is right, and the law had best remain as it has been written."

One of the *taata rii*, or little men, a commoner, or representative of a district, now presented himself, and was listened to with as much attention as had been given to the lordly personages who preceded him. He said : " As no one else stands up, I will make my little speech, because several thoughts have been growing in my breast, and I wish you to hear them. Perhaps everything good and necessary has been said already by the chiefs ; yet, as we are not met to adopt this law or that law because one great man or another recommends it, but as we, the *taata rii* just the same as the chiefs, are to throw all our thoughts together, that out of the whole heap the meeting may make those to stand upright which are best, whencesoever they come—this is my thought. All that Tati said was good ; but he did not mention that one reason for punishing (as a Missionary told us when he was reading the law to us in private) is to make the offender good again if possible. Now, if we kill a murderer, how can we make him better? But if he be sent to a desolate island, where he is all solitary, and compelled to think for himself, it may please God to make the bad things in his heart to die, and good things to grow there. But, if we kill him, where will his soul go?"

Others spoke to the same purport, and, in the result, it was unanimously determined that banishment, not death, should be inflicted on murderers. It followed, of course, that the extreme exercise of magisterial power, to take away life, was excluded from every other case.

ORIGIN OF THE GIPSIES.

WITH SPECIAL ACCOUNT OF A SCOTTISH COLONY OF THEM.

AT the beginning of the reign of Queen Victoria it was estimated that the gipsies in Great Britain numbered about 18,000. In all Europe, it is supposed there were not fewer than 700,000 at that period. There were few or none then in the New World, but they have since found their way to the United States of America. Everywhere they have always retained peculiar and well-marked characteristics, easily recognized, and distinguishing them from the people of the countries where they wander and reside.

Where did these people come from? Many opinions have been held, and many theories propounded, and not a few books written, in reply to this question. After all that has been said on the subject, those who maintain their Indian origin have much the strongest proofs on their side. There are no authentic records or historical documents to appeal to, but taking the evidence arising out of the appearance of the people, their habits and customs, their superstitions, and, above all, their language, there is little doubt of their having originally emigrated from the far East.

Origin of the Gipsies. 111

The notion that they are descendants of Israel is wholly untenable. There are only a few words in their language resembling Hebrew, and they have not a ceremony peculiar to the Hebrew race in every land. They have also few words resembling "Coptic," and in Egypt they are deemed as strangers to the present time, although their name seems to indicate a connection with that country. Everywhere, in Europe, Asia, or Africa, they use a language peculiar to themselves; more or less modified by that of the people among whom they dwell. In fact, they remain, as they always have been, a distinct race in this western world.

Although history does not reveal their origin, it states very clearly when they first made their appearance in Europe. About 1410 they were first seen in southern and central Germany; in 1418 they were found in Switzerland; in Italy they are mentioned in 1422; and in France in 1427. In the reign of Henry VIII., from Statutes passed against them, they must have been for some time in England, although the time of their coming is unrecorded. It is remarkable that in the earliest notices of them, when they were in Europe, they are spoken of as black, especially the women, and they evidently were of darker hue then than now, an additional evidence of their Indian origin, before their complexion was affected by the climate and life of the countries to which they had migrated.

All these facts point to the conclusion, which has been a current belief for many generations, that these people were Asiatic Indians, driven from Hindostan in consequence of the terrible persecution of Timur Beg, or Tamerlane, the Tartar invader, who, in 1408 and 1409, ravaged the Indian peninsula, and put to the sword hundreds of thousands of the inhabitants. It is rational to suppose that numbers of those who escaped from these hordes of ruthless invaders should seek to save their lives by flying from their native land, to become wandering strangers in other countries. The Brahmins and other higher castes would sooner die than go into exile, and many of the Indian chiefs and people were able to make terms with

Origin of the Gipsies.

their Mohammedan conquerors. But the outcast Sudres were a poor and degraded people, looked on as the basest of the human race; and with ferocious troops seeking their destruction, they had every motive to leave, and none to stay in Hindostan. They fled to save their own lives and the lives of those dear to them.

By what track the ancestors of the gipsies found their way to Europe we cannot determine. But it may be presumed that they passed over the southern Persian deserts, and along the Persian Gulf to the mouth of the Euphrates, thence to Bussorah, and into Arabia, and thence into Egypt. Their appearance in Europe corresponds with the time at which the invasion of Timur Beg would have driven them from India.

It is needless to adduce the many proofs which philology and ethnology has accumulated in proof of the Indian origin and associations of the race. Long lists of words have been published, showing the identity and resemblance of gipsy words with those of Hindostanee. Writers in different countries of Europe have done this, and it is remarkable how many of the words are the same, notwithstanding the diversity of the tongue of the countries where the comparison has been made. Two or three incidental notices will be more to the point than elaborate lists of words.

Bishop Heber, in his Journal, says: "On the other side of the river" (in north-west India) "was a large encampment of wretched tents of mats, with a number of little hackeries, panniers, ponies, goats, etc., so like gipsies that on asking what they were, I was not surprised to hear Abdallah say they were gipsies; that they were numerous in the north-west provinces, living exactly like the gipsies in England; that he had seen the same people both in Persia and Russia; and that in Persia they spoke Hindostanee the same as here." Abdallah said that by desire of Sir Gore Ouseley he had talked with some of them when he was in Persia, and found they could understand and answer him.

In a letter to Sir Joseph Banks, President of the Royal

Origin of the Gipsies.

Society, read to the Society of Antiquaries in London, in 1785, Mr. Marsden speaks with certainty of "the identity of the Gipsy or Cingari or Hindostanee language," adding "that through the mountains of Nubia and on the plains of Roumania these tribes have conversed for centuries in a dialect similar to that spoken to this day by the gipsies in England."

Lord Teignmouth once said to a young gipsy woman in Hindostanee, " Tue burra tetschur," " Thou art a great thief." She immediately replied, " No, I am not a thief; I live by fortune-telling." An Indian missionary was in the house of the Rev. James Crabb, of Southampton, when a gipsy woman was present. After talking with her he expressed his conviction that her people must once have known well the Hindostanee tongue.

These are sufficient instances to show the truth of the alleged origin of the language. To argue that they are not of Indian origin because they do not speak Hindostanee with correctness, would be as absurd as to deny that they are natives of England because they speak very incorrect English.

I have mentioned the name of Mr. Crabb, of Southampton, long well known as "The Gipsies' Friend," because he was the first who made systematic efforts to civilize and improve them, and whose labours induced many benevolent persons to take interest in their social and religious welfare. Much in this way has been done since, and is still being done, notably by Mr. George Smith, of Coalville, and others who have written on the condition of the gipsies, and laboured on their behalf. But the services of Mr. Crabb, the pioneer in this good work, deserve lasting remembrance. From a little book published by him in 1832, entitled "The Gipsies' Advocate," we extract a chapter containing letters from a correspondent, a clergyman in Scotland, giving an account of a tribe then located in a parish of that country. The letters are as follows :—

Kirk Yetholm, a small village in the county of Roxburghshire, upon the borders of the two kingdoms of England and Scotland, has been long known, and somewhat celebrated, as the favourite residence or head-quarters of the largest colony in Scotland of that singular and interesting race of people the gipsies, whose origin is involved in so much obscurity and doubt. It is not, perhaps, correct to say that the "muggers" or "tinkers" of Kirk Yetholm are the pure, unmingled gipsy race, whose forefathers, upwards of four centuries ago, emigrated to Europe from the East. As in England, so also in Scotland, from their intermixture with the natives of the country, and with other wanderers like themselves, they are now less distinguishable as a peculiar race. Still, however, their language, their erratic and pilfering propensities, and, in general, their dark or dusky complexion, black piercing eyes, and Hindoo features, sufficiently betray the original of this despised and long-neglected race. At what period they first settled in Kirk Yetholm I have not been able to ascertain. The family of Fa, or Fall (a name renowned in gipsy story), seems to have been the first, which probably was about the beginning of the last century. Whether or not they have any intercourse with the gipsies in other parts of the country I am unable to say; I have at least no evidence that they have. That they have a peculiar language is a subject on which I have no doubt; though they themselves deny the fact, and seem astonished at the question. I do not mean to say that it is a regularly formed and complete language, but they are able to converse in words unknown to others.

I find that the slang or language used by the Kirk Yetholm gipsies is very much the same with the language spoken by the English and Turkish gipsies, a fact which identifies the colony residing in Kirk Yetholm with the same people in other parts of the world. The number of gipsies in the parish of Yetholm is about one hundred. It would appear, however, that the gipsy population of this place is fluctuating. In 1798, from the statistical report of the minister of the parish at that period, there were only fifty-nine. In 1818, there were one hundred and nine. In 1831, upwards of one hundred; and, in a few years more, this number may be considerably diminished

The Gipsies of Kirk Yetholm. 115

or increased. Their occupations are various. Two of the families are "horners" or "spoonmakers," who manufacture horn into spoons; one a travelling tinker; another a travelling cooper; the rest are "muggers," or "potters," as they prefer being called, who carry earthenware about the country for sale. Some of them also make baskets or besoms for sale. The spoons fabricated by the horners are very generally used by the poor, and farmers purchase a considerable number of them before autumn for the use of the reapers. With the exception of the individuals of this profession, whose occupation is better attended to at home, all the others are absent from home, with their families, from eight to nine months in the year.

It is needless, I suppose, to describe a gipsy tent, which is the same in England as in Scotland. They usually prefer for pitching their tents the least frequented parts of the country, and where they may have some convenient shelter. It is the business of the women to carry about and to dispose of the articles which they have for sale. The men, in the meantime, remain with their horses and carts, or occupy themselves in fishing or poaching, in both of which they show much dexterity. Occasionally two or more families travel together. They seldom remain longer than a few days in one place, and I believe they very rarely or never travel on the Sabbath. They leave their head-quarters very early in spring, probably the beginning of March, and return usually after the winter has fairly commenced, about the end of November. They seem to enjoy the best of health; and the older women of the tribe are supposed to possess much skill in the management of wounds and diseases. The only species of country work in which they engage with others is that of reaping, and for this purpose many of them return about the beginning of autumn, to hire themselves to those farmers who will engage them. At home they usually conduct themselves in a quiet and peaceable manner, and their quarrels are chiefly among themselves. These are very violent whilst they last, and the occasion or ground of quarrel is seldom known but to themselves. On these occasions especially they are addicted to profane and dreadful imprecations. Their character for truth and honesty does not stand high. But they have enemies enough to proclaim their faults, and these faults, it must be confessed, are neither few nor small.

The greater number of writers, in Scotland at least, when speaking of or alluding to this unfortunate race, seem scarcely able to discover expressions sufficiently strong to manifest their abhorrence of them. This is in some respects unjust. It is granted that they are idle, disorderly, vicious, and unrestrained; without almost any knowledge of religion. But it might also be recollected that this will always be the character, more or less, of those who live as they do—a very wandering life; and it becomes, therefore, the duty of society to inquire what they can do to reclaim them from their erratic mode of life—the grand source of almost all their vicious habits.

The gipsies are not destitute of good qualities. They have a species of honour, so that if trusted, they will not deceive or betray you. They are grateful for any attention that is shown them; so that I believe there are few instances of those who have treated them with kindness receiving any injury at their hands. Many pleasing instances could be mentioned, and several instances have come under my own observation, of their grateful sense of favours conferred, and at any length of time will remember an act of kindness shown to themselves or relations. They are very sensible of the dislike which is generally entertained against them, and would frequently conceal the fact that they belong to a separate race: whereas, formerly, it would appear they were rather proud of being regarded as a peculiar tribe, and this feeling is not altogether extinct among them.

I do not think that the gipsies of Kirk Yetholm are much addicted to drunkenness. There are particular seasons and occasions indeed when they drink to excess, and at such times may be guilty of dreadful extravagances; but I am not aware

The Gipsies of Kirk Yetholm. 117

that there is one habitual drunkard here. A deep and dark spirit of revenge seems to be the worst trait in their characters; and at their merry-makings or carousals, which are now, however, of rare occurrence, when their blood is heated with whiskey, this revengeful spirit is most apt to exhibit itself. Most or all of the gipsy parents have been married, I believe; the greater number, however, in an irregular manner. The majority of the children have been baptised. They almost invariably intermarry in their own tribes, and are generally dissatisfied when this is not the case. The interior of their houses is usually dirty, and the furniture of a very mean description; there are, however, some very pleasing exceptions to this observation. You rarely find them, except when very poor, destitute of a blazing fire, which they seem to regard, and with reason, too, as one of the greatest comforts of life. Most of the tribe can read; many, however, very indifferently; but all of them seem very sensible of the benefits of education. The parents generally express themselves as extremely desirous that their children should be instructed, and they speak of education as the only legacy which a poor man has to leave his children.

In Scotland, it will be remembered, that a person who cannot read, and even write also, is rarely to be met with. Still, however, there are many of the gipsy children not sent regularly to school, even during those few months they remain at home; and those of them that attend, during many months are travelling in the country, and are extremely apt to forget all they have been taught, and in the following winter must probably commence the same course of instruction anew. Generally they are remarked as clever children; and considering the many disadvantages under which they receive instruction, the progress they make is surprising. The parents are in general very much attached to their children. This, indeed, is one of those features of their character which distinguish their tribe wherever it is found. Nevertheless, so anxious are they that their children should be instructed, that they have again and again expressed their utmost willingness to part with them for this purpose, and to leave them at home during the summer months, that they might attend school, but lament their inability to maintain them. Most of the children have attended the Sabbath school during their continuance at home. Latterly a considerable number have attended church, most of them only occasionally; some of them, however, with exemplary regularity. The ideas entertained generally on religious subjects are extremely limited and erroneous. Indeed, how can they be expected to be otherwise than deplorably ignorant of religion, when it is considered that their education is so very defective, and that during eight or nine months out of the twelve they are houseless wanderers, with none to care for them, and none to instruct them? If we discover so much ignorance amongst our own residents, and our own church-going population, there is no wonder the gipsy is totally ignorant, as in many instances he is, of the very first principles of Christianity. Still they seem to profess a general respect for religion. I am not aware that they entertain on this subject any sentiments peculiar to themselves. Like all persons whose knowledge of every substance is extremely contracted, and who entertain a confused belief of the truth of religion, without knowing what it really is, they are very superstitious. Nor am I sure that their superstition differs much from that of the ignorant in general. They believe in apparitions and witchcraft, and in the existence of invisible beings, capable of doing them an injury. They have also a belief in omens. They hold it to be very ominous of evil, before commencing a journey, to meet with certain animals early in the morning, or with persons possessing certain features or deformities, and on such occasions they will unload their carts or asses, and wait a more auspicious season for their journey. They all profess to belong to the established church of Scotland. Most of them have Bibles or New Testaments, or at least the tattered remains of some portions of the Scriptures in their possession. It will be understood, of course, that in these remarks I speak generally. As a proof that they are not universally destitute even of ponderous folio Bibles, I may mention rather an interesting fact, which occurred during the late vacancy of the parish of Yetholm, or that interval of time which elapsed between the death of the preceding clergyman of the parish and the appointment of his successor. The deceased minister's family had left the parish, and carried with them the usual pulpit Bible. It happened that on the Sabbath following the removal of the Bible, a young clergyman from a distance, an entire stranger in the parish, was appointed to officiate : it appears also that the absence of the Bible was not discovered by the elders or church officers until the moment almost when it was necessary that the minister should be in the pulpit; upon this, as there was no time to send to any distance, the elders immediately proceeded to the nearest cottages, to inquire if a Bible of something like orthodox dimensions could be procured. One cottage after another was entered, without being able to furnish what was wanted. The next was the cottage of a gipsy. Probably they lingered before the door, doubtful whether to enter or not. They did enter, however, and thence returned with a folio Bible of the largest dimensions, and with copious notes.

One circumstance in the character of the gipsies I think ought not to be omitted. I allude to their manners. While these in most instances are rude and uncultivated, displaying only a bold and fearless independence, there are individuals among them who, judging from their manners alone, might have been bred at court. This is scarcely too exaggerated a description. In addressing their superiors, no matter how elevated in rank, they display the utmost self-possession, and most perfect propriety of behaviour. They express themselves tolerably well, and without hesitation or awkwardness.

Perhaps there is among them too much display, but their movements are natural and even graceful. Like a late departed monarch, his present gipsy majesty is the most polished of all subjects. The whole of this (royal) family indeed, male and female, are rather remarkable for this freedom and polish of manner. His Majesty, moreover, who is now an old man, without any family, and who never removes from home, is also a regular hearer at church.

Kirk Yetholm, therefore, has some pretensions to the name, which it has sometimes received, of the metropolis of the gipsy kingdom in Scotland. It is alluded to as their favourite residence in the following lines by Leyden :—

> "On Yeta's banks the vagrant gipsies place
> Their turf-built cots, a sunburnt swarthy race ;
> Through Nubian realms their tawny line they bring,
> And their brown chieftain vaunts the name of king.
> With loitering steps from town to town they pass,
> Their lazy dames rocked on the panniered ass.
> From pilfered roost or nauseous carrion fed,
> By hedge-rows green they strew the leafy bed.
> While scarce the cloak of tawdy red conceals
> Their fine-turned limbs which every breeze reveals.
> Their bright black eyes through silken lashes shine,
> Around their neck their raven tresses twine.
> But chilling damps and dews of night impair
> Its soft sleek gloss and tan the bosom bare.
> Adroit the lines of palmistry to trace,
> Or read the damsel's wishes in her face.
> Her hoarded silver store they charm away,
> A pleasing debt for promised wealth to pay."

The practice alluded to in these lines is, I believe, almost totally laid aside. Kirk Yetholm I may mention is a small village, containing about four hundred inhabitants, and situated a short mile from the boundary which separates the two kingdoms of England and Scotland. The boundary here is either a trifling stream, or more generally a mere imaginary line.

> "A river here, there an ideal line,
> By fancy drawn divides the sister kingdoms ;
> On each side dwells a people similar,
> As twins are to each other, valiant both,
> Both for their valour famous through the world."

There is another and larger village in the parish, called Town Yetholm, perhaps one of the most beautifully-situated villages in Scotland. It is distant from the other less than half a mile. They are placed on opposite sides of a valley, through which flows a wild romantic stream, called the "Bowmont Water." The parish lies at the foot of the Cheviot range of mountains, is small though populous, at a considerable distance from any town, peacefully secluded, and embosomed amid pastoral hills, which are smooth and green to the summit. The secluded situation of the parish, and the immediate vicinity of Kirk Yetholm, more especially to England on one side, and to the wild and pathless range of the Cheviot on the other, may perhaps be given as reasons why the gipsies originally chose this as their favourite haunt. If at any time pursued by the hand of justice, it was easy, the work of only a few minutes, to cross from the one kingdom to the other; or if the magistrates on both sides of the border were on the alert, the nimble-footed gipsies were soon safe from their pursuit among the wild valleys of the neighbouring mountains. It is very generally said that the gipsies of late years, probably since the end of the last century, have lost character very much. I will not inquire at present what truth there may be in this, but if it be the case, several reasons may be assigned for it. Many lawless and desperate characters, not belonging to the tribe, have from time to time connected themselves with it, and initiated them into practices formerly unknown among them. Their greater poverty also of late years may be another cause of their increased immorality, and the severe and unfeeling treatment of them by society may be regarded as a third cause of their more depraved and lawless condition of late years.

The gipsies are at present known as a wild and semi-barbarous race, "whose hand is against every man's, and every man's hand against them," who are feared and dreaded by others, as setting all law, character, religion, and morality at defiance, and unfortunately there is but too much truth in the description. The original and fruitful source of all the vicious habits and unfortunate peculiarities of this tribe has already been stated to be their loose, irregular, and wandering mode of life, and the natural consequences of this mode of life have been aggravated, it would appear of late years, by the causes above mentioned.

There is nothing obviously in the native character, blood, or constitution of the gipsy, to render him more desperate and vicious than others. They are neither better nor worse, I conceive, than other members of society would be were they placed in similar circumstances. Their wandering, for instance, exposes them to many peculiar temptations, idleness and rapine lead them frequently into scenes of mischief and wickedness, and necessarily leave them ignorant, uneducated, and uncivilized. Withdraw them, therefore, from this mode of life, and at as early an age as possible, before they have acquired the bad habits of the tribe, and you save them from innumerable evils, and probably render them valuable members of society; and several cases fortunately can be referred to of gipsies, who, owing to some peculiar circumstances, have been separated from their tribe, acquiring domestic habits, residing contentedly at home, and in no way to be distinguished from the rest of the community: and an equal or greater number of cases might be adduced of individuals in no way connected with the tribe, and who in early life had been trained to domestic habits, associating themselves with it, and acquiring all their disorderly and vicious habits. Let society, therefore, do their duty to these houseless wanderers, regard them not as an outcast and infamous race, but stretching forth to them the hand of reconciliation, say by their altered conduct, let us be friends and brothers, and as the poor, and ignorant, and immoral, let a civilized, a religious, and a benevolent society grant to them the privileges of education, and the means of improvement. Until this be done, they must naturally expect to have their properties injured, and perhaps even their own persons insecure. And they have a fine class of subjects to work upon; a people who will be grateful for any attention that is shown them, and the more so as they have been little accustomed to kindness; and a people whose capabilities of improvement are very great.

It is obvious that the rest of the community would be no small gainers by a change which is here contemplated. They would render their own homes, their persons and property, more secure, while they would discharge a long-neglected duty to a most interesting and unfortunate portion of their brethren. It cannot and ought not to be said, that such an attempt will be unsuccessful until it has been fairly tried and failed. But by the blessing of God it will succeed. Let Christians, uniting together, implore the divine blessing of God on their undertaking, go forward in their great Redeemer's name, and let them manifest how highly they value the privileges they enjoy, by their earnest and persevering efforts to bring these almost heathen wanderers in a British land, to share the comforts of social life, and the inestimable blessings of the gospel of the Son of God.

Amidst all that has been done and said concerning the gipsies in more recent years, these old records, preserved by good Mr. Crabb, of Southampton, will be read with interest, and studied with advantage.

GARIBALDI, THE ITALIAN PATRIOT AND HERO.

THE name and deeds of Garibaldi will always have a romantic interest. Few men ever had a life of more perpetual peril and adventure, by sea and land. In his early years it was the mere natural love of excitement that moved him, but from the time that he was acquainted with public events, he became, above all, a true patriot and a lover of freedom. Born in the days of the first Emperor Napoleon, he lived to see the fall of Napoleon III. The Italy of his childhood, divided and oppressed by tyrants, domestic and foreign, he lived to see united and free. He was one of the chief actors in the second great revolutionary epoch of modern Europe. Of the new kingdom of Italy he was truly one of the founders, for without the enthusiasm which he inspired, the plans and counsels of statesmen would have had little influence. He was the popular idol and hero in the heroic age of young Italy. Had he died, as Cavour died, when his main work was accomplished, it might have been better for his future fame. Noble in nature, generous in feeling, prompt in action, he was also easily impressionable, and liable to be misled by evil advisers. But the mistakes of his closing years will be readily forgiven and forgotten in the record of the grand events of his earlier life, a few incidents of which I will narrate.

Guiseppe, or Joseph Garibaldi, was born at Nice in July 1807. His father was a seaman, as his father before him had been. Joseph took to the sea as to his native element, being always about the shore and the ships, and becoming a powerful and skilful swimmer, an accomplishment which enabled him to save life on various occasions. The little book-learning that he obtained was through the influence of a worthy priest, his mother's brother. The only subjects for which he showed taste or aptitude were languages and mathematics, the knowledge of the latter serving him in good turn when once, like Louis Philippe and other notable men in exile and poverty, he had to earn his living by teaching.

Of his mother, Rosa Ragiundo, he always spoke with tender and grateful remembrance. To her inspiration he said that he owed his patriotic feelings. She was a devout woman also, after her creed, and he records that "in his greatest dangers by land or sea, his imagination conjured up the picture of a pious woman prostrated at the feet of the Most High, interceding for her beloved son."

When still a boy, he made several trips in his father's trading vessel, a brig, to Rome, Odessa, and Constantinople. His

GARIBALDI'S HOUSE AT CAPRERA. [Page 124.

taste for naval pursuits being fixed, he entered the Sardinian navy, and remained several years in the service. He rose to be lieutenant, and might have become a naval captain in command of a ship quietly cruising about in the Mediterranean. But a more stirring career was destined for him. At Marseilles he met with one whose name is also imperishably associated with the story of new Italy, Joseph Mazzini. By his influence the course of his life was changed. Mazzini was by nature a dreamer and a schemer, and by conviction and circumstance he became the arch-conspirator for the liberation of his country from foreign sway. He easily gained the young and generous Garibaldi to be a sharer of his enthusiasm and an instrument of his plots. At first Mazzini planned a descent on the Italian coast by sea, but the discovery of the scheme led to his expulsion from Marseilles. A raid upon the Savoy frontier was then planned from Geneva, but this also proved a futile scheme, Garibaldi ascribing the failure to treachery on the part of the Polish General, Romorino. We next hear of him on board the Royal frigate, *Eurydice*, off Genoa, in hope of seizing the vessel by raising mutiny among the crew. At this moment, having heard of a plot to storm the barracks of the Carbineers, he went on shore to join in the attack, but the attempt miscarrying, he found himself irreparably compromised. Not daring to go back to his ship, he fled to Nice, and thence across the frontier, taking refuge as an exile at Marseilles. At this great seaport it was easy for him to obtain employment. He went one voyage to the Black Sea, another to Tunis, where he even entered the service of the Bey, but soon tiring of this, he sailed in the *Nageur*, a vessel of Nantes, for Rio Janeiro. This was in 1836, when only in his twentieth year.

South America was a region well suited for the restless and adventurous spirit of the young exile now landed on its shores. The Wars of Independence were over, and the conflicts between the parent states of Europe and their colonies ended, but had been succeeded by fiercer fights and more lasting enmities than those which had marked the struggles for freedom. Garibaldi was soon drawn into the strife. He took service with the Republic of Rio Grande do Sul, a vast territory belonging to Brazil, but then in rebellion against that empire. Probably it was the mere name of Republic that attracted him to take the side of rebellion, for he could know nothing of the rights of the contest. We suppose this from the fact of his giving the name of "Mazzini" to a small privateering boat, with a crew of twelve men, of which he took the command. By aid of this he soon took possession of a larger and better armed vessel, his first prize seized from the enemy.

In the months which followed, he had a succession of hair-brained adventures and hair-breadth escapes, sometimes victorious against incredible odds, winning battles, storming fortresses, and keeping the Brazilian government in perpetual panic by his raids both on sea and land.

It was at this period that he first formed a band of irregulars, drawn to him and kept to his standard by personal admiration and attachment. Most of these were countrymen of his own, Italian exiles or emigrants. There was little of military discipline or stern rule, but the courage and endurance, the clemency and disinterestedness of the chief inspired all the band with sympathetic fidelity and daring. This was the origin of Garibaldi's Italian legion, which reappeared with fresh life at various periods of his career.

The Imperial resources of Brazil at length proved too powerful for the struggle to be successfully maintained. On one occasion, being severely wounded, Garibaldi fell into the hands of a Spaniard, who treated him with brutal cruelty, and he escaped death only by the intervention of the Governor of the district.

·At a later time his little flotilla of armed boats was overtaken by a hurricane, and he landed on the coast of Santa Caterina, wrecked and forlorn, having seen the bravest and best of his men shot down or drowned, and the means of further resistance no more to be found.

It was at a season of depression and disaster, when his

fortune seemed at the lowest ebb, that he fell in with his Anita, who became his devoted wife, and his faithful companion, amidst all the troubles and vicissitudes of his career, till parted by her death in the sadly tragic manner to be presently described This was not the first kind womanly heart that had pitied and comforted the young Italian. He tells with gratitude how, when thrown into a dungeon by the cruel Spaniard, when wounded and a prisoner, his life was saved and his sorrows soothed by the gentle ministrations of a good angel of charity, by name Madame Alleman. Now, in Anita he had such a helper and comforter always at his side, a woman as brave and enduring as she was gentle and tender. After the birth of her firstborn, Menotti Garibaldi, in September 1840, she went through all the perils and hardships of the closing scenes of that war, with the infant and his father. The sight of her sufferings, and the hopelessness of altering the fortune of an ill-conducted contest, led him to take leave of his Republican friends of Rio Grande, and he went, for a short interval in his adventurous career, to live at Montevideo. Here he gained a living for himself and loved ones by teaching mathematics, and by the business of a general broker—employment little to his taste.

At this time war broke out between the Republic of Uruguay and Buenos Ayres. As he had received the hospitable protection of the former State, he felt in honour bound to adopt her cause when appealed to. His reputation for skill and daring being well known, he was offered the command of the fleet of the young Republic, an absurdly imposing offer, for they had only a few small fishing boats on the river Parana. Garibaldi made the best of the circumstances; if he had not a fleet he would find one. Setting out in the night, with muffled oars, he entered a creek where an armed sloop of the enemy was at anchor. He boarded and captured her, with the whole crew, without any loss, as they were surprised by the sudden attack. A second vessel fell into his hands after a sharp engagement. He was then urged by persons high in power in the Montevidean government to make an expedition against the still strong fleet of Buenos Ayres, in the Parana river. The affair seemed so desperate, that it has been not without reason asserted that the object of the planners was to get rid of Garibaldi by exposing him to certain danger, they being jealous of his rising fame and influence. He made the best of his desperate position, and escaped from this conflict, not only with his life, but also "with honour, the only thing that was not lost." There being no longer hope of success by sea, Garibaldi organized another Italian legion, numbering three or four hundred men. This band performed deeds of wonderful daring, and rose to such distinction that, as a mark of honour, they were allowed precedence over all the other troops of the Republic.

At the close of its exploits grants of land were made to the survivors, but they refused them, at least Garibaldi in their name refused, saying that "the triumph of the Republican cause was the sole stimulus of their exertions." This reply shows the disinterested spirit of the man, but we think the men of the legion deserved all the reward that they could get for their heroic bravery and willing endurance in long and difficult contests. Their hundreds had almost always to contend with as many thousands, as was literally the case in more than one battle where the opposing forces were under General Rosas.

On one occasion Rosas advanced near Montevideo, having three thousand troops. Garibaldi had three hundred, about two hundred having been despatched by him to the neighbourhood of Montevideo, for the protection of his wife, whose safety was threatened by this invasion. The fight was maintained long against fearful odds. The legion succeeded in piercing the centre of Rosas' force, and dividing them into two. Anita at this moment coming up with the two hundred men, attracted by the firing, fell suddenly on the left division of the army of Rosas, who little knew the small number of the assailants, and fled in confusion. Next day Garibaldi attacked the right suddenly at Las-Trés-Croces (The Three Crosses), and drove them back. The camp at Bayada was carried the same night by a sudden assault, and Garibaldi returned next day with his beloved wife to Montevideo.

Her heroism on this occasion endeared her more than ever to her husband, to whom she was soon again to present a son. The child was born slightly lame, in consequence of the terrible fatigues and exertions of those days and nights.

It was, doubtless, the remembrance of that time of anxiety in his young married life that added intensity to the grief and implacable indignation against the Austrians, who in after years brought premature death to his Anita, when in a similar condition.

All through her life she shared the perils and adventures of her noble husband. At times, when left alone, she displayed the same undaunted spirit. More than under the excitement of the journeys or the battlefield, this cool courage was remarkable when she remained in charge of the farmhouse near Montevideo. The worst danger she then incurred was not from the enemy's attacks, but from the invasion of an armed band of mutineers, whose pay from the Republic was in arrears, and who, on finding Garibaldi absent, threatened to kill the wife and her children. By her coolness and tact she turned them from their rage, and sent them away full of admiration for her, and of hope that their grievances would be redressed.

On one occasion both husband and wife had a narrow escape. Rosas was eager to obtain possession of a foe so troublesome, and hearing that Garibaldi was then at his home, he made a sudden inroad into Uruguay, in hope of surprising him. On reaching the house unobserved, the cry arose, "He is taken." "Not yet," he replied, as he ran out and threw himself into a skiff at the bottom of his garden, whence he hurriedly pushed off into the stream. His pursuers got a boat as quickly as possible, but he had a good start, and, eluding their chase, he shortly afterwards arrived at Montevideo, where his wife and children had fortunately preceded him a few days before.

The story of the conflicts of these South American wars would be a narrative of romantic interest, so far as personal adventures are concerned, but the wars themselves are not worthy of detailed record. As Milton said of our own conflicts in the days of the Saxon Heptarchy, they have no more interest for living men now than "the struggles of kites and crows"! The rude guerilla warfare of Garibaldi's early life in the western world has importance now chiefly because he there was trained for the exploits on the larger and loftier field of European conflict. In his own native land he was soon to display the same dauntless courage, the same fertility of resource, and the same magnetic influence on the minds of others which had made him the hero of Montevideo.

Two other incidents only we mention, as showing his cleverness and his audacity in irregular war. He was equally ready in resource by sea as by land, and it was there that some of his most adventurous deeds were witnessed. On one occasion, at night, he had the ingenuity to make two of the enemy's vessels assail each other, to their irreparable injury. Steering his light vessel boldly down between them, he suddenly, by means of a pair of long sweeps, arrested and backed his course, after delivering a broadside at each, leaving them in the surprise and darkness of the night furiously firing at each other, till the stratagem was understood.

His last encounter at sea was one of the most daring and decisive. With two small vessels he encountered three of superior force, which Rosas sent to attack when the others were in port. Garibaldi, beating to quarters, ordered his crews to reserve their fire till within musket shot. A well-directed broadside at so short a range had deadly effect, and staggered the assailants. Another broadside was then coolly ordered by Garibaldi to be aimed at the rigging, and masts and sails came down by the board. In the confusion he then grappled with the enemy's ships, and boarded them, he leading the onset, cutlass in hand. In less than twenty minutes he drew the three ships into port.

One of them afterwards escaped, but was recovered by a singular stroke of audacity. He followed her in a swift fishing boat to reconnoitre her, and see if she was much damaged during the fight, as he thought she had been. They pursued him when far from land, and his boat grounded when returning to shore. He managed to escape by swimming to land, dragging the boat. It was night by this time, and he ordered his men to take the boat for a considerable distance along the coast, whence he again pushed off and gained the sea-board of the enemy. The crew of the ship were asleep, and utterly unprepared for the new assault, when Garibaldi and his men quickly cleared the deck with their cutlasses. Most of the crew were below, and surrendered. At daylight Garibaldi returned with the vessel into harbour, mooring it alongside of its companions already captured. Such was a specimen of the mingled stratagem and audacity of the man. He was now to appear on a field worthier of his name.

News came from Europe which thrilled the hearts of Italian patriots, whether emigrants or exiles, in the New World. Changes had taken place which altered the whole condition and prospects of their native land. There was a new Pope, Pius IX., who at first professed himself to be patriotic and liberal. In France a Republic had been proclaimed, after the flight of the Orleans king, Louis Philippe. There was a wave of revolution rolling over the whole of the continent, and constitutions, or promises of them, were being wrested from the reluctant despots of old dynasties. " After me the deluge," Metternich used to say, but it had come in his time. Austria was convulsed with insurrectionary movements. With its enormous army and impregnable fortresses, it could still keep firm hold of its Italian provinces, but these could no longer remain tamely submissive. When Naples was preparing to resist the brutal tyranny of its Bourbon king, and Sicily had risen in open and successful revolt, northern

Italy was ripe for insurrection against the Austrian yoke. The Milanese drove the garrison under Marshal Radetzky from their city, after five days' continuous fighting, and throughout all Lombardy the people were preparing to strike for freedom and independence. A party of Austrian cavalry and Hungarian artillery, on their way from Pavia to Milan, with six pieces of cannon, were attacked by the populace at Binasco. The Austrians fled, but the Hungarians cried "Vive l'Italia," and joined the insurgents.

It was time for the King of Sardinia to declare himself. Charles Albert must either lead the movement, or himself be removed by the national leaders. He proclaimed war against Austria, and then Venice and all the territories so long held in bondage by the House of Hapsburg were united in a common cause, and, so far as Austria was concerned, the independence of Italy was no longer a dream of patriots and poets.

Such was the state of affairs while Garibaldi was yet in far-off Uruguay. The struggle for independence had begun, but Italy had yet to see years of conflict, and to pass through many trials and disappointments before the final triumph.

All these movements were becoming known to the Italian exiles throughout the world. Garibaldi had early heard rumours of the Pope's liberal professions, and as far back as October 17th, 1847, he wrote a letter from Montevideo to the Nuncio Bedini, offering to his Holiness his services, with his comrades of the Italian legion of South America, in case of war with Austria being resolved upon. The letter was referred to the Pontifical Government at Rome. But Garibaldi, after waiting in vain for a reply from Nuncio or Pope, could no longer brook suspense or delay. With immense difficulty he gathered sufficient means to enable him to sail for Europe, along with his brave friend Anzani, having with them eighty-five men and two cannon, leaving the remainder of his legion to follow how and when it could.

He reached Nice in July 1848, and hastening to Genoa and Milan, learned the true position of affairs. His offer of services

Garibaldi, the Italian Patriot and Hero. 133

to Charles Albert was received coldly, owing to his supposed sympathies with the irreconcilable republicanism of Mazzini. The truth was, that after being defeated at Mortara and Custozza, Charles Albert had lost all hope of successful insurrection, and had accepted an armistice, which saved Piedmont from invasion.

There was still a provisional government at Milan, to which Garibaldi transferred his offer of service, and placed himself at the disposal of Mazzini.

A proclamation was issued, declaring the king a traitor to the cause of Italian independence, and announcing that "the royal war was at an end, and that of the people was now to begin." This Mazzinian proclamation was little better than idle bravado. With small and dispirited bands of guerilla troops success was hopeless. After maintaining for some time a gallant but unavailing struggle in the mountains, Garibaldi crossed the frontier into Switzerland, where already many of his men had found refuge.

A new turn of events called him back to Italy. Pius the Ninth had begun to throw off his cloak of pretended liberalism, and his popularity had departed. Pressed hard by his disaffected subjects, who assassinated his minister, Rossi, as the supposed cause of his withholding constitutional rights, and being himself threatened in his palace at the Quirinal, the Pope fled to Gaeta. A Roman Republic was proclaimed, with a Triumvirate at its head, Mazzini being the leading spirit. A brief gleam of glory rests on this episode of Roman history. The people used their triumph with the utmost moderation, and there was every prospect of peaceful and orderly rule. But a cloud rose in an unexpected quarter of the political horizon, and the sky of hopeful promise was speedily overcast.

The French Government, although itself Republican, maintained towards the sister Republic of Rome an ambiguous policy. Even Cavaignac had been induced to send succour to the Pope, and when Louis Napoleon succeeded to the Presidency he declared his hostility in the strongest manner, in the hope, probably, of gaining the support of the clerical party in France to his own selfish interests. It was a cruel and disgraceful business, French troops sent to join with the mercenaries of the King of Naples to suppress the Roman Republic and restore the Papal tyranny.

Now was the time for Garibaldi to reappear on the scene. His exploits at this crisis were full of daring, but could avail only to delay the catastrophe. He drove back the French from Porta Pancrazio, in the last days of April 1849. The Neapolitan army was routed in the campaign of Velletri, with a rapidity which astonished and amused all Europe. But this was like the farce preceding the tragic drama that was to be witnessed at Rome. The French army had been reinforced, and appeared before the eternal city with power and determination to take possession at all hazard and loss. The General, Oudinot, was instructed to proclaim that he came as the friend, not the foe, of the Roman people, and that his only object was to save the city from anarchy.

The Triumvirs hesitated until the French shells fell round St. Peter's, and even lodged in the library of the Vatican. Mazzini, with his love of learning and taste for art, fearing probably the reproach of allowing the treasures of the city to be destroyed, felt inclined to come to terms. But Garibaldi was determined to resist to the last, and the people were with him. The details of the gallant defence throughout a three months' siege, with occasional sorties, when heavy losses were inflicted on the besiegers, it is needless now to relate. On the 13th of July, 1849, the French entered the city as conquerors, having first threatened to lay St. Peter's and all the historic monuments of the place in ruins. " Let them perish," said Garibaldi, " rather than independence and freedom be lost." But Mazzini consented to sign terms of capitulation. While the French troops were entering the city in one direction, with triumphant martial music, Garibaldi, with his band of devoted volunteers, sorrowfully marched out at the other side, towards Terracina. A French officer, with a strong body of troops, presented himself before the Constituent Assembly, then presided over by the Prince of Canino, a Buonaparte, and summoning them to disperse, the Republic was at an end.

General Oudinot, on receiving the keys of Rome, sent one of his officers to lay them at the feet of the Holy Father, and at the same time sent a division of his troops in pursuit of Garibaldi. These were kept at bay for some time, and defeated at Turin, Orvieto, and other places; but the heroic chief, with his diminished band, had to cross the Apennines, retiring before overwhelming odds. New foes here awaited him. The Austrians were in large force ready for his destruction. He sought a brief respite in the small republic of San Marino, but no respect was paid to the rights of this puny state by his relentless pursuers. He reached the shore, in hope of finding some way of reaching Venice, which still was resisting the Austrian siege, but some Austrian ships in the offing hindered the attempt. By his request, those of his followers who still adhered to his fortunes, however desperate, dispersed for their own safety. Some of his nearest friends, including Ugo Bassi and Ciceruacchi, falling into the hands of the Austrians, were shot by them, without any form of trial, not even a military court martial, an act of wicked and wanton barbarism.

It was at this time that Garibaldi lost the loving and faithful partner of his life. While making her way along the banks of a small stream near Chioggio, in the territory of Ravenna, she was seized with the pangs of labour. Mother and child perished in that lone place, unaided in that sad hour; and after hastily interring them, the husband again set out, an utterly grief-stricken man.

Meeting here and there with a few friends, they had to assume disguises and adopt many stratagems to elude their bloodthirsty pursuers. For some weeks he wandered among the forests and ravines of the Apennines, sleeping by day and moving by night. At last, wearied and worn out, having crossed from the Adriatic to the Mediterranean, he was found, with a single attendant, by some carbineers of the Sardinian army. They took him to Nice, when the people, on hearing who was the prisoner, received him with acclamation. He was permitted to see his children, two sons and a daughter, and a few of his friends. The rumour of his being in the city disturbed the authorities, who became quickly anxious to get rid of him. They sent him to Genoa, where La Marmora was in command. The veteran general treated the fugitive with honourable respect, and letters, which were long afterwards published in the Italian journals, prove that already between these two brave men there had sprung up the warmest mutual esteem and sympathy. La Marmora supplied him with ample means for his going to Tunis, where he was willing to take refuge, obtaining also a pension for him from the Turin Government, who were no doubt glad thus to rid themselves of a troublesome guest.

There was no more at the time for Garibaldi to do in the cause of Italian independence. Charles Albert had resigned in favour of his son, Victor Emanuel, who had the will, but not yet the power, to gain his country's freedom. The disastrous defeat at Novara closed the prospect for that period. Venice had capitulated after heroic resistance, and the whole of northern Italy was again under the hated power of the Austrians.

In a letter to a friend, on the eve of his departure for Tunis, Garibaldi wrote: "I sail to morrow on board the *Tripoli*, for Tunis. I have seen what you and your generous colleagues have done for me. I charge you to express my gratitude to them. I have no reason to complain of any one. I believe we live in times in which resignation is necessary, for we are in times of bitterness. Remember me to all the brave defenders of the Italian cause."

Tunis afforded him no lasting resting-place. The relentless hostility of those who feared him followed him there.

Garibaldi, the Italian Patriot and Hero. 137

He was too near the theatre of his past efforts, and his name might keep alive the desire for insurrection. He must leave the shores of the Mediterranean, and become an exile again across the Atlantic. He went this time to the United States, where he expected among Republicans to find hospitality and sympathy.

It would be painful to give details of the life of the hero of Italian independence, when a refugee in the United States. Few took any notice of the illustrious exile. For some time he gained his living as a chandler or candle-maker on Staten Island, near New York. When his place of residence became known, vile agents, at the instigation of despotic governments, followed him with insults, hoping probably to incite him to violence. He had to move about armed to protect his life. One of his persecutors is said to have been a lawyer, whom the chances of political life afterwards lifted to notoriety at Washington, and who was even sent as ambassador to a European court. Garibaldi felt the annoyance so much as to leave his retreat, at the sacrifice of his little property, and he returned to his former haunts in South America. Finding no suitable employment there, he became sailor again, and once actually carried coals from Newcastle to Genoa. By intercession of friends he was allowed to remain on this side of the Atlantic, and went to Caprera, a small island near the Sardinian coast, when he settled down as a farmer, in a home where many English visitors saw him in his later peaceful years. There was yet, however, to be a stormy interval of war, and work in fields more in accordance with his impetuous spirit and his early fame.

On the 1st of January, 1859, at the usual reception of the ambassadors in the Tuilleries by Louis Napoleon, all Europe was thrown into excitement and alarm. It was the custom of this Imperial personage to utter words on this annual ceremony, not impromptu, but deeply planned by his advisers. It is asserted by those best qualified to judge that these utterances were for the most part made with financial rather than political purpose; at all events, it came to pass that the funds on every Stock Exchange in Europe rose or fell according to the report, flashed by the electric wires, of what Louis Napoleon said on New Year's day at the Tuilleries.

On this occasion there was more perceived than words to make money on the Stock Exchange. "I regret," he said to the Austrian ambassador, "that my relations with your government are not so amicable as I could have wished." The phrase, however ambiguous, convinced the diplomatists that war was intended. Vague declarations in the official *Moniteur* kept the event in doubt, but preparations for war were going on quietly and unceasingly. Sardinia was arming as well as France, and the Austrian government knew what this meant. The Sardinians were informed that continued preparation would be regarded as a menace, and, in fact, a declaration of war. The English foreign minister, Lord Malmesbury, induced the Austrian emperor to restrain hostilities for a week, and in the interval the French troops were already crossing the Alps, or steaming for Genoa.

A revolution in Tuscany preceded more important events. A popular demonstration in Florence, designed apparently to force the Grand Duke Leopold to declare himself openly on the side of Italy, led to the retirement of that prince to Elba. Victor Emanuel, of Piedmont, was then declared Dictator, and the army unfurled the Italian tricolour flag. Parma, Modena, and other principalities followed the example of Tuscany, and the Austrian rulers had to retire from all places not under the guns of the great fortresses of the army of occupation.

Louis Napoleon, who had issued a rhetorical proclamation before quitting Paris, addressed another on his arrival at Genoa to the army of Italy. It thus began: "Soldiers, I come to place myself at your head to conduct you to the combat. We are about to second the struggles of a people now vindicating its independence, and to rescue it from foreign oppression. This is a sacred cause, which has the sympathies of the civilized world. I need not stimulate your ardour. Every

Garibaldi, the Italian Patriot and Hero. 139

step will remind you of a victory." In the Via Sacra of ancient Rome inscriptions were chiselled in marble reminding the people of their exalted deeds. It is the same to-day. In passing Mondovi, Marengo, Lodi, Castiglione, Arcole, and Rivoli, you will, in the midst of these glorious recollections, be marching in anothing Via Sacra. The proclamation thus concluded : " The new army of Italy will be worthy of her elder sister !"

The interference of Lord Malmesbury, perhaps well meant, but certainly mischievous, prevented Austria from meeting the French before they arrived on Italian soil. They had thus time to take up good positions on the plains of Piedmont, instead of being assailed amidst the passes of the Alps. It is not our purpose to give any narrative of the Franco-Austrian war, nor of those campaigns of which the battles of Magenta and of Solferino formed the crowning events. The Austrian armies were overmatched by the French troops headed by their most experienced generals, and with the whole population of northern Italy in insurrection.

After Solferino, when there was enormous slaughter on both sides, the abrupt termination of hostilities caused surprise everywhere. When victories such as were jubilantly celebrated in Paris had been gained, it seemed strange that the conqueror should not follow up his advantages. But Louis Napoleon had gained all that he wanted. He had brought new glory to the French army, and had himself appeared as a successful general. He had posed as a friend of Italian liberty and independence, and had risked enough to justify his claim for the Italian maritime provinces to be annexed to France as the price of his assistance !

In addressing their own serfs and senates the French and Austrian Emperors represented the cessation of hostilities to have been the result of foreign intervention. But there was no truth in this statement. The real fact is, that the French ruler had gained all that he went to war for, and he might have broken his power in the attempt to attack the yet unthreatened Quadrilateral and other Austrian strongholds. Let us believe, in accordance with his early associations, that he was sincere in his wish to aid the Italians to throw off the Austrian yoke. But his conduct in regard to Rome and other Italian difficulties proved how, in the main, his objects were personal and selfish. At all events, this was the view taken by General Garibaldi, who had thrown himself heart and soul into the conflict, and who now saw with regret the war concluded, without results to justify so much bloodshed, or worthy of so great efforts. But we must briefly refer to the part taken by him in the war of Sardinian independence.

As soon as there seemed prospect of hostilities, Garibaldi had made offer of his services to the Sardinian government. General de la Marmora, as head of the army, declined to receive him, not so much on his own motion as on account of foreseeing difficulties in regard to the regular troops. Victor Emanuel and his minister Cavour promptly met the difficulty by giving Garibaldi independent command, uncontrolled by official rules or routine. Hence he took no part in the campaigns already described, but took his own line in attacking and harassing the Austrians. He had no sooner raised his standard than all the enthusiastic Italian patriots flocked to join him, reinforced by volunteers from Switzerland and other countries. Acting at first with Cialdini, the only Sardinian general whom he had fraternal sympathy with, he assailed the Austrians at Vercelli, and this was the earliest success of the war, " rather to the chagrin," we are told, " of the French protectors of the Italian cause." Other combats followed, and the Austrian generalissimo, Gyulai, dispatched Urban, one of his fiercest fighting generals, to encounter Garibaldi, who now established himself at Como. Louis Napoleon announced that he was going to send General Niel to co-operate with the irregular leader, but it was a false report, and no support was given by the French to Garibaldi's movements. At Como and at Bergamo the Austrians were repulsed, and Garibaldi led his volunteers, now called the Chasseurs of the Alps, in triumph to Brescia. Here he issued a proclamation, signed by him, "General Garibaldi, Commissioner of his Sardinian Majesty." The Austrian General, Urban, an old leader in the Hungarian war, proved a formidable foe, with troops well equipped and armed, and outnumbering the Italian free corps. Many of Garibaldi's men were killed or disabled in the conflicts at this time. It would be tedious to give details of the war, but one incident in an early encounter is worthy of being recorded. Garibaldi heard that Urban had shot one of his men who had been taken prisoner. Hearing of this atrocity, he ordered two of his Austrian prisoners of war to be shot, and then he called one of the oldest of the prisoners before him, and said, "I set you at liberty. Go to General Urban, and tell him that since he has caused one of my soldiers to be shot, I have shot two of his; and let him be assured that if I learn that a single prisoner is executed again, I swear to shoot every one who may fall into my hands, be he Marshal or Emperor of Austria." He was determined that his men, although irregular troops, should be treated as soldiers and as prisoners of war. And the Austrian General respected his determination.

With his Chasseurs of the Alps, Garibaldi did more to molest the Austrians than any general in the allied ranks, and although the French Emperor in his proclamations ignored him, his merits and services were honourably recognized by the sovereign whom he served, and his movements reported in the *Piedmontese Gazette*. Foreign journals everywhere rang with his exploits, which were finished only when peace was declared.

Of the events of the latter years of the life of Garibaldi, for reasons referred to at the beginning of this article, we do not here speak in detail. He lived to see the dream of his youthful enthusiasm more than realized, and Italy united, as well as independent and free, from the Alps to the Calabrian Gulf. When the French were compelled, by troubles of their own, to withdraw the army of occupation, so long shamelessly retained at Rome, Victor Emanuel entered the capital as King of Italy. The head of the ancient House of Savoy then ruled as a constitutional monarch over the whole peninsula. Garibaldi was a member of the Italian Parliament, but he never was an intelligent or hearty supporter of the new order of affairs. His sympathies were too much with his early Mazzinian and Republican friends, not understanding how, as in England, a constitutional monarchy is the safest and best of all republics. He never rightly appreciated the wisdom and prudence of Count Cavour and the other true statesmen who placed the fortunes of his country on a sure foundation. Possibly in some points the more impetuous and single-minded impulses of the heroic patriot might have saved Italy from some of its subsequent troubles. He would have driven the Pope away from Rome, and not have left him in the Vatican as the disturber of peace and the intriguer against the country's truest welfare. But into these political and religious questions we do not now enter. We leave Garibaldi, as we love to think of him in his peaceful retreat in the Island of Caprera, after having nobly helped to obtain for Italy its freedom and independence. His appearances in the Roman chamber were not always conducive to a higher estimate of his prudence or judgment, although he was always the honest, upright, generous patriot. It was in this aspect, as well as in admiration of his personal heroism, that his visit to England was marked by an outburst of popular enthusiasm such as has rarely been witnessed. Kings and emperors might have envied such a triumph. And in spite of weaknesses and faults of character, no man in modern times is remembered with more honour and respect that the Italian hero and patriot, Joseph Garibaldi.

A JAPANESE WATER PICNIC.

UNBEATEN TRACKS IN JAPAN.

IF old Will Adams, whose adventures in Japan were recorded in the first pages of this book, or if Kæmpfer, the early Dutch historian, or any of the Tycoons or Mikados of other days could behold their land now, they would indeed be struck with amazement. Foreigners are no longer excluded, but are everywhere seen, and the natives, from the Emperor to the humblest official, affect European or American manners, education, and even dress. On the waters are iron-clad war ships and bustling steamboats; on the land are railroads and telegraphs; while schools, colleges, newspapers, and all the appliances of modern civilization are rapidly transforming the nation. The Christian religion is not only tolerated, but has many true and zealous followers and teachers. The learning and science of the west are diligently cultivated, and young Japan has even the tendency to imitate the new-fangled notions of our time, and, like our own agnostics, look up to some of the lesser lights of modern research as greater men than Bacon or Newton. The change and the growth in mental culture may have been too rapid, but things will right themselves in the long run, and the Japanese will learn what is solid and sound, as well as what is showy and superficial in literature and in philosophy.

It is not pleasant to see ancient national customs and manners disappear, except those that are inherently evil and hurtful. Throughout the islands, and among the masses of the populations the old ways and usages and costumes will long remain, but many changes for the better have already been introduced from the foreigners. It is good, for instance, that the Daimios or feudal chiefs, with their bands of armed retainers, no longer oppress the peaceable people, but that all subjects of the Emperor are under new laws, administered by responsible magistrates. It is good to see policemen, and postmen, and other officials of social order in the great towns.

Not much change can be expected in the personal and domestic life of the people, and Japan will continue to present features of strange novelty to travellers from Europe. The physical aspect of the country cannot be changed any more than that of the natives with their almond-shaped eyes and olive-coloured complexions. It will be long also before railways and coaches displace the ordinary vehicles and modes of travel.

The *kuruma*, a light species of "Bath chair," is still the common carriage in streets and on highways, while boats pulled by men harnessed for swimming may still be seen on the lakes and bays. The grandeur and the beauty of the scenery all travellers speak of, and some have said that it was worth going to Japan, if only to see their celebrated mountain, Fuji-Yama, a mountain more picturesque and more gigantic than the peak of Teneriffe. Here is the testimony of one of the most enterprising of travellers, Mrs. Bishop, better known as Isabella Bird, author of the charming and instructive book, "Unbeaten Tracks in Japan." (J. Murray).

"It would be treachery to many delicious memories were I to omit to say that Fuji, either as a cone of dazzling snow, or rosy in the autumn sunrise, or as a lofty spiritual presence far off in a veil of mist, or purple against the sunset gold, is one of the great sights of Tôkiyô.* Even of Shiba, that dream of beauty, among whose groves the city hum is unheard, one might weary, but of Fuji never, and as time goes on, he becomes an infatuating personality, which raises one above the monotonous clatter and the sordid din of mere material progress. One vision of Fuji I shall never forget. After spending an afternoon alone among the crowds which throng the great temple of Kwannon at Asakusa, as I turned a corner at dusk to go down a hill, my *kuruma*-runner looked round and said, "Fuji!" and I saw a glory such as I had not seen before in Japan. The heavens behind and overhead were dark and covered with clouds, but in front there was a clear

* Tôkiyô is the modern capital, in which the ancient Yedo is merged.

sky of pure, pale green, into which the huge cone of Fuji rose as a mass of ruddy purple, sublime, colossal, while above the green, which was streaked with some lines of pure vermilion, the clouds were a sea of rippling rose-colour, and in the darkness below, at the foot of a solemn, tree-covered embankment, lay the castle moat, a river of molten gold, giving light in the gloom. Actual darkness came on, and still Fuji rose in purple into the fading sky, lingering in his glory, and never, while the earth and heavens last, will just the same sight be seen again."

Here is part of the account of a journey in the great plain of Yedo, made in a *kuruma*, or "one-man gig." There were two other *kurumas*, one for Ito, the guide and interpreter; the other for the baggage. The agreement was to go to Nikkô, ninety miles, in three days, without change of runners, for eleven shillings each.

"Blithely, at a merry trot, the *kuruma*-runners hurried us away from the kindly group in the Legation porch, across the inner moat and along the inner drive of the castle, past gateways and retaining walls of Cyclopean masonry, across the second moat, along miles of streets of sheds and shops, all grey, thronged with foot-passengers and *kurumas*, with packhorses loaded two or three feet above their backs, the arches of their saddles red and gilded lacquer, their frontlets of red leather, their "shoes" straw sandals, their heads tied tightly to the saddle-girth on either side, great white cloths figured with mythical beasts in blue hanging down loosely under their bodies; with coolies dragging heavy loads to the guttural cry of *Hai! huida!* with children whose heads were shaved in hideous patterns; and now and then, as if to point a moral lesson in the midst of the whirling diorama, a funeral passed through the throng, with a priest in rich robes, mumbling prayers, a covered barrel containing the corpse, and a train of mourners in blue dresses with white wings. Then we came to the fringe of Yedo, where the houses cease to be continuous, but all that day there was little interval between them. All had open fronts, so that the occupations of the inmates, the "domestic life," in fact, were perfectly visible. Many of these houses were roadside *chayas*, or tea-houses, and nearly all sold sweetmeats, dried fish, pickles, *mochi*, or uncooked cakes of rich dough, dried persimmons, rain hats, or straw shoes for man or beast. The road, though wide enough for two carriages (of which we saw none), was not good, and the ditches on both sides were frequently neither clean nor sweet. Must I write it? The houses were mean, poor, shabby, often very squalid, the smells were bad, and the people looked ugly, shabby, and poor, though all were working at something or other."

The country is a dead level, and mainly an artificial mud flat or swamp, in whose fertile ooze various aquatic birds were wading, and in which hundreds of men and women were wading too, above their knees in slush; for this plain of Yedo is mainly a great rice-field, and this is the busy season of rice-planting; for here, in the sense in which we understand it, they do not "cast their bread upon the waters." There are eight or nine leading varieties of rice grown in Japan, all of which, except an upland species, require mud, water, and much puddling and nasty work. Rice is the staple food and the wealth of Japan. Its revenues were estimated in rice. Rice is grown almost wherever irrigation is possible.

The rice fields are usually very small and of all shapes. A quarter of an acre is a good sized-field. The rice crop planted in June is not reaped till November, but in the meantime it needs to be "puddled" three times,—*i.e.*, for all the people to turn into the slush, and grub out all the weeds and tangled aquatic plants, which weave themselves from tuft to tuft, and puddle up the mud afresh round the roots. It grows in water till it is ripe, when the fields are dried off. An acre of the best land produces annually about fifty-four bushels of rice, and of the worst about thirty.

On the plain of Yedo, besides the nearly continuous villages along the causewayed road, there are islands, as they may be called, of villages surrounded by trees, and hundreds of pleasant oases on which wheat ready for the sickle, onions, millet, beans, and peas, were flourishing. There were lotus ponds too in which the glorious lily, *Nelumbo nucifera*, is being grown for the sacrilegious purpose of being eaten ! Its splendid classical leaves are already a foot above the water. A species of *Sagittaria* is also grown in water for food, but both it and the lotus are luxuries. There are neither hedges nor fences anywhere, but the peasant proprietors are well acquainted with their boundaries, and no land-gluttons have arisen yet to add "field to field." Except that in some cases horses and oxen are used for ploughing the rice-fields, the whole cultivation is by hand, and not a weed is to be seen. Rows of the *Paulownia Imperialis*, grown for the sake of the lightness of its wood, which is used for making clogs, do not improve the somewhat monotonous landscape.

After running cheerily for several miles, my men bowled me into a tea-house, where they ate and smoked while I sat in the garden, which consisted of baked mud, smooth stepping stones, a little pond with some gold fish, a deformed pine, and a stone lantern. Observe that foreigners are wrong in calling the Japanese houses of entertainment indiscriminately "tea-houses." A tea-house or *chaya* is a house at which you can obtain tea and other refreshments, rooms to eat them in, and attendance. That which, to some extent, answers to an hotel is a *yadoya*, which provides sleeping accommodation and food as required. The licenses are different. Tea-houses are of all grades, from three-storied erections, gay with flags and lanterns, in the great cities and at places of popular resort, down to the roadside tea-house, with three or four lounges of dark-coloured wood under its eaves, usually occupied by naked coolies in all attitudes of easiness and repose. The floor is raised about eighteen inches above the ground, and in these tea-houses is frequently a matted platform with a recess called the *doma*, literally " earth-space," in the middle, round which runs a ledge of polished wood called the *itama*, or "board space," on which travellers sit while they bathe their soiled feet with the water which is immediately brought to them; for neither with soiled feet nor in foreign shoes must one advance one step on the matted floor. On one side of the *doma* is the kitchen with its one or two charcoal fires, where the coolies lounge on the mats and take their food and smoke, and on the other the family pursue their avocations. In almost the smallest tea-house there are one or two rooms at the back, but all the life and interest are in the open front. In the small tea-houses there is only an *irori*, a square hole in the floor, full of sand or white ash, on which the live charcoal for cooking purposes is placed, and small racks for food and eating utensils; but in the large ones there is a row of charcoal stoves, and the walls are garnished up to the roof with shelves, and the lacquer tables and lacquer and china ware used by the guests. The large tea-houses contain the possibilities for a number of rooms which can be extemporised at once by sliding paper panels, called *fusuma*, along grooves in the floor and in the ceiling or cross-beams.

When we stopped at wayside tea-houses the runners bathed their feet, rinsed their mouths, and ate rice, pickles, salt fish, and "broth of abominable things," after which they smoked their tiny pipes, which give them three whiffs for each filling. As soon as I got out at any tea-house, one smiling girl brought me the *tabako-bon*, a square wood or lacquer tray, with a china or bamboo charcoal-holder and ash-pot upon it, and another presented me with a *zen*, a small lacquer table about six inches high, with a tiny teapot with a hollow handle at right angles with the spout, holding about an English tea-cupful, and two cups without handles or saucers, with a capacity of from ten to twenty thimblefuls each. The hot water is merely allowed to rest a minute on the tea-leaves, and the infusion is a clear straw-coloured liquid with a delicious aroma and flavour, grateful and refreshing at all times. If Japanese tea "stands," it acquires a coarse bitterness and an unwholesome astringency.

Milk and sugar are not used. A clean-looking wooden or lacquer pail with a lid is kept in all tea-houses, and though hot rice, except to order, is only ready three times daily, the pail always contains cold rice, and the coolies heat it by pouring hot tea over it. As you eat, a tea-house girl, with this pail beside her, squats on the floor in front of you, and fills your rice bowl till you say, "Hold, enough!" On this road it is expected that you leave three or four *sen* on the tea-tray for a rest of an hour or two and tea.

All day we travelled through rice swamps, along a much-frequented road, as far as Kasukabé, a good-sized but miserable-looking town, with its main street like one of the poorest streets in Tôkiyô, and halted for the night at a large *yadoya*, with downstairs and upstairs rooms, crowds of travellers, and many evil smells. On entering, the house-master or landlord, the *teishi*, folded his hands and prostrated himself, touching the floor with his forehead three times. It is a large, rambling old house, and fully thirty servants were bustling about in the *daidokoro*, or great open kitchen. I took a room upstairs [*i.e.*, up a steep step-ladder of dark, polished wood], with a balcony under the deep eaves. The front of the house upstairs was one long room with only sides and a front, but it was immediately divided into four by drawing sliding screens or panels, covered with opaque wall papers, into their proper grooves. A back was also improvised, but this was formed of frames with panes of translucent paper, like our tissue paper, with sundry holes and rents. This being done, I found myself the possessor of a room about sixteen feet square, without hook, shelf, rail, or anything on which to put anything—nothing, in short, but a matted floor.

My bed is merely a piece of canvas nailed to two wooden bars. When I lay down the canvas burst away from the lower row of nails with a series of cracks, and sank gradually till I found myself lying on a sharp-edged pole which connects the two pair of trestles, and the helpless victim of fleas and mosquitoes. I lay for three hours, not daring to stir lest I should bring the canvas altogether down, becoming more and more nervous every moment, and then Ito the guide and interpreter called outside the *shôji*, "It would be best, Miss Bird, that I should see you." What horror can this be? I thought, and was not reassured when he added, "Here's a messenger from the Legation, and two policemen want to speak to you." On arriving I had done the correct thing in giving the house-master my passport, which, according to law, he had copied into his book, and had sent a duplicate copy to the police-station, and this intrusion near midnight was as unaccountable as it was unwarrantable. Nevertheless the appearance of the two mannikins in European uniforms, with the familiar batons and bull's eye lanterns, and with manners which were respectful without being deferential, gave me immediate relief. I should have welcomed twenty of their species, for their presence assured me of the fact that I am known and registered, and that a Government which, for special reasons, is anxious to impress foreigners with its power and omniscience, is responsible for my safety.

Miss Bird travelled over many remote parts of the empire, especially in the northern island, where the aboriginal race of Ainos still form the chief portion of the population. She describes in glowing terms the scenery of these regions, as in the following letter written from Volcano Bay, Yezo, in September:

"It was a heavenly morning. The deep blue sky was perfectly unclouded, a blue sea with diamond flash and a 'many-twinkling smile' rippled gently on the golden sands of the lovely little bay, and opposite, forty miles away, the pink summit of the volcano of Komono-taki, forming the south-western point of Volcano Bay, rose into a softening veil of tender blue haze. There was a balmy breeziness in the air, and tawny tints upon the hill, patches of gold in the woods, and a scarlet spray here and there heralded the glories of the advancing autumn. As the day began, so it closed. I should like to have detained each hour as it passed. It was thorough enjoyment I visited a good many of the Mororan Ainos, saw

Unbeaten Tracks in Japan. 151

their well-grown bear in its cage, and tearing myself away with difficulty at noon, crossed a steep hill and a wood of scrub oak, and then followed a trail which runs on the amber sands close to the sea, crosses several small streams, and passes the lovely Aino village of Maripu, the ocean always on the left and wooded ranges on the right, and in front an apparent bar to farther progress in the volcano of Usu-taki, an imposing mountain, rising abruptly to a height of nearly 3,000 feet, I should think.

"In Yezo, as on the main island, one can learn very little about any prospective route. Usually when one makes an inquiry, a Japanese puts on a stupid look, giggles, tucks his thumbs into his girdle, hitches up his garments, and either professes perfect ignorance, or gives one some vague secondhand information, though it is quite possible that he may have been over every foot of the ground himself more than once. Whether suspicion of your motives in asking, or a fear of compromising himself by answering, is at the bottom of this, I don't know; but it is most exasperating to a traveller. In Hakodaté I failed to see Captain Blakiston, who has walked round the whole Yezo sea-board, and all I was able to learn regarding this route was that the coast was thinly peopled by Ainos, that there were Government horses which could be got, and that one could sleep where one got them; that rice and salt fish were the only food; that there were many 'bad rivers,' and that the road went over 'bad mountains'; that the only people who went that way were Government officials twice a year, that one could not get on more than four miles a day, that the roads over the passes were 'all big stones,' etc., etc. So this Usu-taki took me altogether by surprise, and for a time confounded all my carefully-constructed notions of locality. I had been told that the one volcano in the bay was Komono-taki, near Mori, and this I believed to be eighty miles off, and there, confronting me, within a distance of two miles, was this grand, splintered, vermilion-crested thing, with a far nobler aspect than that of '*the*' volcano, with a curtain range in front, deeply scored, and slashed with ravines and abysses whose purple gloom was unlighted even by the noonday sun. One of the peaks was emitting black smoke from a deep crater, another, steam and white smoke from various rents and fissures in its side, vermilion peaks, smoke, and steam, all rising into a sky of brillant blue, and the atmosphere was so clear that I saw everything that was going on there quite distinctly, especially when I attained an altitude exceeding that of the curtain range. It was not for two days that I got a correct idea of its geographical situation, but I was not long in finding out that it was not Komono-taki! There is much volcanic activity about it. I saw a glare from it last night thirty miles away. The Ainos said that it was 'a god,' but did not know its name, nor did the Japanese who were living under its shadow. At some distance from it in the interior rises a great dome-like mountain, Shiribetsan, and the whole view is grand.

" After passing through miles of scrub and sand we came quite suddenly upon the agricultural settlement of Mombets, where the Government has placed a colony of 600 Japanese, and the verses apply, 'The valleys are so thick with corn that they laugh and sing—the wilderness and the solitary place shall be glad for them, and the desert shall rejoice and blossom as the rose.' For two miles, careful manuring and assiduous hand labour have turned a sandy waste into a garden, a sea of crops without a weed, hundreds of acres of maize, wheat, millet, beans, tobacco, hemp, egg plants, peaches, apricots, pumpkins, and all the good things of Northern Japan, beautiful and luxuriant, with a good bridle road, fenced from the crops by a closely-cropped willow hedge, and numbers of small, neat Japanese houses, with gardens bright with portulacas, red balsams, and small yellow chrysanthemums, all glowing in the sunshine, a perfect oasis, showing the resources which Yezo possesses for the sustenance of the large population.

" I have not seen above three or four Japanese together since I left Hakodaté, and I was much impressed with their ugliness, the lack of force in their faces, and the feeble *physique* of both men and women, as compared with that of the aborigines. The Yezo Japanese don't look altogether like the Japanese of the main island. They are as the colonists of Canada or Australia as compared with the small farmers of England, rougher, freer, more careless in their dress and deportment, and they are certainly affected, as people always are, by the cheapness and abundance of horses, which they ride cross-legged, in imitation of the Ainos. Till I reached Mombets, all the Japanese I have seen have led a life of irregular and precarious industry, very different from that of the peasant proprietors of the main island; and in the dull time they loaf and hang about 'grog shops' not a little, and are by no means improved by the habit of lording it over an inferior race.

" A little beyond Mombets flows the river Osharu, one of the largest of the Yezo streams. It was much swollen by the previous day's rain; and as the ferry-boat was carried away, we had to swim it, and the swim seemed very long. Of course, we and the baggage got very wet. The coolness with which the Aino guide took to the water without giving us any notice that its broad, eddying flood was a swim, and not a ford, was very amusing.

" From the top of a steepish ascent beyond the Osharugawa, there is a view into what looks like a very lovely lake, with wooded promontories, and little bays, and rocky capes in miniature, and little heights, on which Aino houses, with tawny roofs, are clustered; and then the track dips suddenly, and deposits one, not by a lake at all, but on Usu Bay, an inlet of the Pacific, much broken up into coves, and with a very narrow entrance, only obvious from a few points. Just as the track touches the bay, there is a road-post, with a prayer-wheel in it, and by the shore an upright stone of very large size, inscribed with Sanskrit characters, near to a stone staircase and a gateway in a massive stone-faced embankment, which looked much out of keeping with the general wildness of the place. On a rocky promontory in a wooded cove, there is a large, rambling house, greatly out of repair, inhabited by a Japanese man and his son, who are placed there to look after Government interests, exiles among 500 Ainos. From among the number of rat-haunted, rambling rooms which had once been handsome, I chose one opening on a yard or garden with some distorted yews in it, but found that the great gateway and the *amado* had no bolts, and that anything might be appropriated by any one with dishonest intentions; but the house-master and his son, who have lived for ten years among the Ainos, and speak their language, say that nothing is ever taken, and that the Ainos are thoroughly honest and harmless. Without this assurance I should have been distrustful of the number of wide-mouthed youths who hung about, in the listlessness and vacuity of savagery, if not of the bearded men who sat or stood about the gateway with children in their arms.

" The next morning was as beautiful as the previous evening, rose and gold instead of gold and pink. Before the sun was well up I visited a number of the Aino lodges, saw the bear, and the chief, who, like all the rest, is a monogamist, and, after breakfast, at my request, some of the old men came to give me such information as they had. These venerable elders sat cross-legged in the verandah, the house-master's son, who kindly acted as interpreter, squatting, Japanese fashion, at the side, and about thirty Ainos, mostly women, with infants, sitting behind. I spent about two hours in going over the same ground as at Biratori, and also went over the words, and got some more, including some synonyms. The *click* of the *ts* before the *ch* at the beginning of a word is strongly marked among these Ainos. Some of their customs differ slightly from those of their brethren of the interior, specially as to the period of seclusion after a death, the non-allowance of polygamy to the chief, and the manner of killing the bear at the annual festival. Their ideas of metempsychosis are more definite, but this, I think, is to be accounted for by the influence and proximity of Buddhism. They spoke of the bear as their chief god, and next the sun and fire. They said that they no longer worship the wolf, and that though they called the volcano and many other things *kamoi*, or god, they do not worship them. I ascertained beyond doubt that worship with them means simply making libations of *sake*, and 'drinking to the god,' and that it is unaccompanied by petitions, or any vocal or mental act.

"These Ainos are as dark as the people of southern Spain, and very hairy. Their expression is earnest and pathetic, and when they smiled, as they did when I could not pronounce their words, their faces had a touching sweetness which was quite beautiful, and European, not Asiatic. Their own impression is that they are now increasing in numbers after diminishing for many years. I left Usu sleeping in the loveliness of an autumn noon with great regret. No place that I have seen has fascinated me so much.

FRENCH ACCOUNTS OF ENGLISH NAVAL VICTORIES.

ABOUKIR AND TRAFALGAR.

THE records of our great naval victories are familiar in all books of history in the hands of English readers. But there is a curious interest in seeing how the same events are described by the losers as well as the gainers of great battles. We select two of the greatest English victories in modern times, the battles of Aboukir or the Nile, and of Trafalgar, as viewed through French spectacles.

The account of the battle of Aboukir we take from the work of M. Denon, chief of the Savans who accompanied the French army to Egypt in 1798, and remained throughout the campaigns of General Bonaparte in that country. The dedication of the work is in the following terms : " To Bonaparte. To combine the lustre of your Name with the splendour of the Monuments of Egypt is to associate the glorious annals of our own time with the history of the heroic age, and to reanimate the dust of Sesostris and Menes, like you Conquerors, like you Benefactors. Europe, by learning that I accompanied you in one of your most memorable expeditions, will receive my work with eager interest. I have neglected nothing to render it worthy of the Hero to whom it is inscribed, by VIVANT DENON."

THE BATTLE OF ABOUKIR.

On the morning of the 1st of August we were masters of Egypt, Corfu, and Malta ; and the security of these possessions, annexed to France, seemed in great measure to depend on the thirteen ships of the line that we had with us. The powerful English fleets which were cruising in the Mediterranean could not be supplied with stores and provisions without much difficulty and enormous expense.

Bonaparte, who was sensible of all the advantages of such a position, was desirous to secure such advantages by bringing our fleet into the harbour of Alexandria, and offered two thousand sequins to any one who should accomplish this. It is said that several of the captains of merchantmen had sounded, and had found a passage for the fleet into the old harbour. The evil genius of France, however, counselled and persuaded the admiral to moor his ships in the Bay of Aboukir, and thus to change in one day the result of a long train of successes.

In the course of the afternoon chance led us to Abu-Mandur, a convent at the end of a pleasant walk from Rosetta along the river side. When we had reached the tower which commands the monastery, we descried a fleet of twenty sail. [There were really only fifteen, including a small brig.] To come up, to range themselves in a line, and to attack, were the operations of a few minutes. The first shot was fired at five

English Naval Victories. 157

o'clock, and shortly after our view of the movements of the two fleets was intercepted by the smoke.

When night came on we could distinguish somewhat better, without, however, being able to give an account of what passed. The danger to which we were exposed, of falling into the hands of the smallest troop of Bedouins which might come that way, did not withdraw our attention from an event by which we were so strongly interested. Rolls of fire incessantly bursting from the mouths of the cannon evinced clearly that the combat was dreadful, and supported with an equal obstinacy on both sides.

On our return to Rosetta we climbed on the roofs of the houses, where, at ten o'clock, we perceived a strong light, which indicated a fire. A few minutes after we heard a terrific explosion, followed by a profound silence. As we had seen a firing kept up, from the left to the right, on the object in flames, we drew a conclusion that it was one of the enemy's ships, which had been set fire to by our people, and we imputed the silence to the retreat of the English, who, as our ships were moored, were exclusively in possession of the range of the bay, and who, consequently, could persevere in or discontinue the combat at pleasure.

At 11 P.M. a slow fire was kept up, and at midnight the action again became general. It continued till two in the morning. At daybreak I was at the advanced posts, and ten minutes after the fleets were once more engaged. At nine o'clock another ship blew up. At ten, four ships, the only ones which were not disabled, and which I could distinguish to be French, crowded their sails and quitted the scene of the battle, in the possession of which they appeared to be, as they were neither attacked nor followed. Such was the phantom produced by the enthusiasm of hope.

I took my station again at the tower of Abu-Mandur, whence I counted twenty-five vessels, half of which were shattered wrecks, and the others incapable of manœuvring to afford them assistance. For three days we remained in this state of cruel uncertainty. We cherished illusion, and spurned at all evidence, until at length, the passage across the bar being cut off, and the communication with Alexandria intercepted, we found that our situation was altered, and that, separated from the mother country, we were become the inhabitants of a distant colony, where we should be obliged to depend on our own resources for subsistence until the peace.

We learned, in short, that the English fleet had surrounded our line, which was not moored sufficiently near to the island to be protected by the batteries; and that the enemy, formed in a double line, had attacked our ships one after the other, and had by this manœuvre, which prevented them from acting in concert, rendered the one half a witness to the destruction of the other half.

We learned that it was the *Orient* which blew up at ten o'clock at night, and the *Hercule* the following morning; and that the captains of the ships of the line, the *Guillaume Tell* and *Genereux*, and of the frigates *La Diane* and *La Justice*, perceiving that the rest of the fleet had fallen into the enemy's hands, had taken advantage of a moment of lassitude and inaction on the part of the English to effect their escape. We learned, lastly, that the 1st of August had broken the unity of our forces, and that the destruction of our fleet, by which the lustre of our glory was tarnished, had restored to the enemy the empire of the Mediterannean; an empire which had been wrested from them by the matchless exploits of our armies, and which could only have been secured to us by the existence of our ships of war.

Such is M. Denon's account of the Battle of Aboukir. We now give a French narrative of the Battle of Trafalgar.

A book published many years ago, "The Memoirs of a French Serjeant," gives the history and achievements of Robert Guillemard,—a sailor on board the French fleet at the battle of Trafalgar, and supposed to be the person who shot Lord Nelson. His claim to be the author of that memorable deed, seems to be confirmed by the promotion

and the honours to which he was raised in his country.*
He went to the Russian campaign with Napoleon in 1812,
and in that expedition, so disastrous to the French, he was
taken prisoner, and sent to Siberia, where he remained till
the peace of 1814 restored him to liberty, and his native
France. We quote the account of the battle of Trafalgar,
out of a great variety of adventures detailed in the Serjeant's
book.

BATTLE OF TRAFALGAR.

I was beginning to get tired of being at Cadiz, as were my
companions, and nothing indicated that a change would soon
occur. It was said that we were to sail for the Channel,
to protect the landing of the troops in England, which everybody talked of at the time; but an English squadron, known
to be commanded by Nelson, blockaded Cadiz, and prevented
us leaving the bay; and there was a report that Vice-Admiral
Villeneuve had received express orders to come to action.
On the 20th October, however, there was a vague rumour
in circulation that we were to leave our position next day
and attack the English. The frequent signals made by the
Bucentaure (the admiral's ship), the meeting of all the
captains of the fleet on board it, and the manœuvres and
preparations of the different vessels, indicated that these
reports were not without foundation. In fact, on the 21st
of October, at ten in the morning, the combined fleet left
Cadiz to offer battle to the English. It consisted of thirty
vessels, of which ten Spanish ships occupied the left flank.
Six frigates, French and Spanish, formed the wings of this
splendid fleet, and had orders to assist the vessels that required it during the action. Our line occupied more than
a league in extent, and towards twelve o'clock had come up

* In an account, however, of this battle, published in the *Gibraltar
Chronicle* of November 9th, 1805, it is stated that the Frenchman who gave
the fatal wound to Nelson was shot by Mr. Pollard, midshipman of
the *Victory*, and was seen to fall out of the mizen-top. He may have
been only wounded, and recovered to receive his pension.

within cannon-shot of the English squadron, which was nearly of equal strength. The two fleets manœuvred for more than an hour, for the purpose of choosing their positions and terminating the preparations for a battle that was henceforth inevitable. The *Redoubtable* was in the centre, and a little in front of the French line, which by the admiral's last orders had been formed in a semicircle. Immediately in front of him was an English three-decker, carrying a vice-admiral's flag, and consequently commanded by Nelson. This vessel occupied in the English fleet the same position which the *Redoubtable* did in ours. All at once it made signals, which were instantly answered, and advanced with full sail upon us, whilst the other vessels followed its example. The intention of its commander was evidently to cut our line by attacking the *Redoubtable*, which presented its flank, and discharged its first broadside. This was the signal for action. The English vessel returned the fire; and at the same moment, there began along the whole of the two lines a fire of artillery, which was not to cease, except by the extermination of one of the two squadrons. Already cries of suffering and death were heard on the decks of the *Redoubtable*. By the first discharge, one officer, and more than thirty sailors and soldiers, were killed or wounded. This was the first time I had been in action; and an emotion I had never felt till now made my heart beat violently. Fear might form an ingredient in the feeling, but it was mingled with other sentiments which I could not account for. I was grieved that I was kept in a post where I had nothing else to do but to fire my gun upon the enemy's deck. I should have desired a more active duty, to be allowed to go over the ship, and to work one of the cannon.

My desires were soon gratified. All our top-men had been killed, when two sailors and four soldiers (of whom I was one) were ordered to occupy their post in the tops. While we were going aloft, the balls and grape-shot showered around us, struck the masts and yards, knocked large splinters from

English Naval Victories.   161

them, and cut the rigging in pieces. One of my companions was wounded beside me, and fell from a height of thirty feet upon the deck, where he broke his neck. When I reached the top, my first movement was to take a view of the prospect presented by the hostile fleets. For more than a league extended a thick cloud of smoke, above which were discernible a forest of masts and rigging, and the flags, the pendants, and the fire of the three nations. Thousands of flashes more or less near continually penetrated this cloud, and a rolling noise pretty similar to the sound of continued thunder, but much stronger, arose from its bosom. The sea was calm, the wind light, and not very favourable for the execution of manœuvres. When the English top-men, who were only a few yards distant from us, saw us appear, they directed a sharp fire upon us, which we returned. A soldier of my company and a sailor were killed quite close to me; two others who were wounded, were able to go below by the shrouds. Our opponents were, it seems, still worse handled than we, for I soon saw the English tops deserted, and none sent to supply the place of those who must have been killed or wounded by our balls. I then looked to the English vessel and our own The smoke enveloped them, was dissipated for a moment, and returned thicker at each broadside. The two decks were covered with dead bodies, which they had not time to throw overboard. I perceived Captain Lucas motionless at his post, and several wounded officers still giving orders.

On the poop of the English vessel was an officer covered with orders, and with only one arm. From what I had heard of Nelson, I had no doubt that it was he. He was surrounded by several officers, to whom he seemed to be giving orders. At the moment I first perceived him, several of his sailors were wounded beside him, by the fire of the *Redoubtable*. As I had received no orders to go down, and saw myself forgotten in the tops, I thought it my duty to fire on the poop of the English vessel, which I saw quite exposed and close to me   I could even have taken aim at the men

I saw, but I fired at hazard among the groups I saw of sailors and officers. All at once I saw great confusion on board the *Victory;* the men crowded round the officer whom I had taken for Nelson. He had just fallen, and was taken below covered with a cloak. The agitation shown at this moment left me no doubt that I had judged rightly, and that it really was the English admiral.

An instant afterwards the *Victory* ceased from firing; the deck was abandoned by all those who occupied it; and I presumed that the consternation produced by the admiral's fall was the cause of this sudden change. I hurried below to inform the captain of what I had seen of the enemy's situation. He believed me the more readily, as the slackening of the fire indicated that an event of the highest importance occupied the attention of the English ship's crew, and prevented them from continuing the action. He gave immediate orders for boarding, and everything was prepared for it in a moment. It is even said that young Fontaine, a midshipman belonging to the *Redoubtable*, passed by the ports into the lower deck of the English vessel, found it abandoned, and returned to notify that the ship had surrendered. As Fontaine was killed a few moments afterwards, these particulars were obtained from a sailor, who said he had witnessed the transaction. However, as a part of our crew, commanded by two officers, were ready to spring upon the enemy's deck, the fire recommenced with a fury it never had had from the beginning of the action. Meanwhile, an English eighty-gun-ship placed herself alongside of the *Redoubtable* to put it between two fires; and a French ship of the same force placed itself abreast of the *Victory* to put it in the same situation. There was then seen a sight hitherto unexampled in naval warfare, and not since repeated—four vessels, all in the same direction, touching each other, dashing one against another, intermingling their yards, and fighting with a fury which no language can adequately express. The rigging was abandoned, and every sailor and soldier put to the guns. The officers themselves had nothing to provide for, nothing to order, in this horrible conflict, and came likewise to the guns. Amidst nearly four hundred pieces of large cannon all firing at one time in a confined space—amidst the noise of the balls, which made furious breaches in the sides of the *Redoubtable*—amongst the splinters which flew in every direction with the speed of projectiles, and the dashing of the vessels, which were driven by the waves against each other, not a soul thought of anything but destroying the enemy, and the cries of the wounded and the dying were no longer heard. The men fell, and if they were any impediment to the action of the gun they had just been working, one of their companions pushed them aside with his foot to the middle of the deck, and without uttering a word, placed himself with concentrated fury at the same post, where he soon experienced a similar fate.

In less than half an hour our vessel, without having hauled down her colours, had, in fact, surrendered. Her fire had gradually slackened, and then ceased altogether. The mutilated bodies of our companions encumbered the two decks, which were covered with shot, broken cannon, matches still smoking, and shattered timbers. One of our thirty-six pounders had burst towards the close of the contest. The thirteen men placed at it had been killed by the splinters, and were heaped together round its broken carriage. The ladders that led between the different decks were shattered and destroyed; the mizen-mast and main-mast had fallen, and encumbered the deck with blocks and pieces of rigging. Of the boats placed forward, or hung on the sides of our vessel, there remained nothing but some shattered planks. Not more than one hundred and fifty men survived out of a crew of about eight hundred, and almost all these were more or less severely wounded. Captain Lucas was one of the number. It was five o'clock when the action ceased. I went over the ship, where everything presented a prospect of desolation. Calm despair was painted on the countenances of those who had escaped from this terrible scene.

In the evening, English long-boats came to take away the remainder of our crew, to be divided among the vessels of the fleet; and I was taken on board the *Victory*. There I learned the death of Nelson; he had been wounded on the right shoulder by a ball, which penetrated obliquely, and broke the spine of the back. When taken to the cock-pit, he ordered his surgeon, Mr. Betty, to inform him of his situation without concealment or ceremony. He learned, without the least emotion or regret, that he had only an hour to live, called for his captain (Captain Hardy), and after inquiring about the situation of the two fleets, expressly forbid him to let the English fleet know of his death, and directed the vessels to be brought to anchor as soon as the action was over, on the very spot where it was fought. Captain Hardy promised to obey his orders implicitly, but he did not like to assume the responsibility. He made signals that the admiral was dead, when Lord Collingwood took the command, and did not judge proper to come to anchor, which, perhaps, might have been dangerous on account of the gale that came on that night. The death of Nelson was regarded by the English as a public calamity, the bitterness of which could not be allayed by the victory they had obtained. The sailors deplored him as a father; the officers as a commander, whose talents had caused the glory and prosperity of their country, and whose place would not for a long period be filled by an admiral of equal merit. He whose loss is regretted by an entire nation, he whose death is deplored by old sailors, usually little susceptible of sentiments of attachment, should necessarily inspire some interest, even in an enemy; hence, as a man, I could not help sharing in some degree the affliction that prevailed on board the *Victory;* while, as a Frenchman, I had reason to rejoice at an event that had delivered my country from one of her most dangerous enemies. At any rate, from the moment in which he received his wound, and the position of the wound itself, I could not doubt for a moment that I was the author; and I have ever since been

English Naval Victories. 165

fully convinced of it. But though the shot that had brought down this admiral had rendered a service to my country, I was far from considering it as an action of which I had a right to boast. Besides, in the general confusion, every one could claim the honour; I might not be believed; so that I was afraid of furnishing my companions with a subject of ridicule, and did not think proper to mention it to them, nor to the French officers I saw on board the *Victory*. It was in this manner, that more than once in the course of my life, carelessness and false shame have deprived me of advantages I might have justly claimed. A very strong gale arose in the evening, and blew through the night with extreme violence, and soon scattered the wrecks of our vessels which covered the sea.

We did not learn the particulars of the action till next day. Five French vessels were unable to come into action; the greater part of the Spanish ships would not fight; and the rest of the fleet sustained with the most distinguished courage the attacks of an enemy now become superior in number, for the whole of the English fleet were engaged. The Spanish three-decker, the *Santissima Trinidada*, commanded by Admiral Gravina, was sunk after an obstinate resistance against three English vessels; the admiral was taken up wounded, and died some time afterwards at Cadiz. When he saw all the masts of the *Trinidada* shot away, he exclaimed, —" I was lately in a ship, I am now in a fortress, and shall not abandon it till it sinks under me." This he did. The *Aigle*, a French 74, fought also against three English ships, lost almost all its crew, was taken, and was stranded during the night upon the Spanish coast, where both French and English were drowned together. The *Indomptable* foundered at sea, with fifteen hundred wounded men on board, not one of whom was saved. The *Intrepide*, commanded by the brave Infernet, was also sunk, after a terrible resistance to several vessels who came up successively to cannonade it. Infernet was picked up, along with one of his sons, and was taken on board an English vessel, where he astonished the officers by his language, equally remarkable for its freedom, bluntness, spirit, and originality. The *Achille,* in which was a detachment of the 67th regiment, was set on fire during the action. The English who were fighting it cleared off; and of eight hundred men, who formed the crew, not more than twenty found an opportunity of escaping. When all hopes of stopping the progress of the flames were gone, and death seemed inevitable, to avoid waiting for it, several officers blew out their brains; others threw themselves into the flames that were consuming the forepart of the ship, several sailors went to the storeroom, gorged themselves with brandy, and by the most complete drunkenness endeavoured to throw a veil over the disaster that was about to terminate their existence. Towards six o'clock in the evening the fire reached the gunroom, the vessel blew up, and everything disappeared. Upon any other occasion, the unfortunate crew could easily have been saved; but without troubling themselves about their fate, the two fleets in their vicinity thought of nothing but their mutual destruction. I need not enumerate all the vessels that perished. It is sufficient to state, that the combined fleet was totally annihilated, and that it fought with such obstinacy that of all those that were engaged in action, the English could only save, I believe, one single vessel : the rest all perished at sea, on the coast, or by fire.

The day after the action, they brought on board the *Victory* Vice-Admiral Villeneuve, who had displayed so much intrepidity, talent, and patriotism. The English received him with the marks of respect due to bravery and merit in misfortune. He was wounded in the right hand, and seemed quite terror-struck at his defeat, and careless of the respectful attentions that were shown him. The same day, he caused an inquiry to be made if there were any non-commissioned officers among the French prisoners on board ; not one was found. He then asked for a military man of any rank, who could write easily what he should dictate ; I offered myself. After a short examination, he told me that I should act as his secretary till further orders, and ordered me to come daily to the chamber that had been allotted to him.

Let us now see English accounts of these two naval victories.

THE BATTLE OF THE NILE.

THE enemy's fleet was first discovered by the *Zealous*, Captain Hood, who immediately communicated, by signal, the number of ships, sixteen, lying at anchor in the line of battle, in a bay upon the larboard bow, which we afterwards found to be Aboukir Bay. The Admiral hauled his wind that instant, a movement which was immediately observed and followed by the whole squadron, and at the same time he recalled the *Alexander* and *Swiftsure*. The wind was at this time N.N.W., and blew what seamen call a topgallant breeze. It was necessary to take in the royals when we hauled upon a wind.

The admiral made the signal to prepare for battle, and showed that it was his intention to attack the enemy's van and centre as they lay at anchor, according to the plan before developed. His idea in this disposition of his force, was, first, to secure the victory, and then to make the most of it, as circumstances might permit. A bower cable of each ship was immediately got out abaft, and bent forward. We continued carrying sail, and standing in for the enemy's fleet in a close line of battle. As none of the officers were acquainted with Aboukir Bay, each ship kept sounding as she stood in.

The enemy appeared to be moored in a strong compact line of battle, close in with the shore, their line describing an obtuse angle in its form, flanked by numerous gun-boats, four frigates, and a battery of guns and mortars on an island in the van. This situation of the enemy seemed to secure to them the most decided advantages, as they had nothing to attend to but their artillery, in their superior skill in the use of which the French so much pride themselves, and to which indeed their splendid series of land victories was in general chiefly to be imputed.

The position of the enemy presented the most formidable obstacles: but the admiral viewed these with the eye of a seaman determined on attack; and it instantly struck his eager and penetrating mind, that where there was room for an enemy's ship to swing, there was room for one of ours to anchor. No farther signal was necessary than those which had been made. The admiral's designs were as fully known to his whole squadron, as was his determination to conquer, or perish in the attempt.

The *Goliath* and *Zealous* had the honour to lead inside, and to receive the first shot from the van ships of the enemy, as well as from the batteries and gun-boats with which their van was strengthened. These two ships, with the *Orion*, *Audacious*, and *Theseus*, took their stations inside the enemy's line, and were immediately in close action. The *Vanguard* anchored the first on the outer side of the enemy, and was opposed within half pistol shot to *Le Spartiate*, the third in the enemy's line. In standing in, our leading ships were unavoidably obliged to receive into their bows the whole fire of the broadsides of the French line, until they could take their respective stations; and it is but justice to observe, that the enemy received us with great firmness and deliberation, no colours having been hoisted on either side, nor a gun fired, till our van ships were within half gun shot.

At this time the necessary number of our men were employed aloft in furling sails, and on deck, in hauling the braces, etc., preparatory to our casting anchor. As soon as this took place, a most animated fire was opened from the *Vanguard*, which ship covered the approach of those in the rear, that were following in a close line. The *Minotaur*, *Defence*, *Bellerophon*, *Majestic*, *Swiftsure*, and *Alexander*, came up in succession, and passing within hail of the *Vanguard*, took their respective stations by the stern, by which means the British line became inverted from van to rear.

The Battle of the Nile. 169

Captain] Thompson, of the *Leander*, of 50 guns, with a degree of judgment highly honourable to his professional character, advanced towards the enemy's line on the outside, and most judiciously dropped his anchor athwart hawse of *Le Franklin*, raking her with great success; the shot from the *Leander's* broadside, which passed that ship, all striking the *L'Orient*, the flag-ship of the French commander-in-chief.

The action commenced at sunset, which was at 31 minutes past 6 P.M., with an ardour and vigour which it is impossible to describe.

At about seven o'clock total darkness had come on; but the whole hemisphere was, at intervals, illuminated by the fire of the hostile fleets. Our ships, when darkness came on, had all hoisted their distinguishing lights, by a signal from the admiral.

The van ship of the enemy, *Le Guerrier*, was dismasted in less than twelve minutes; and in ten minutes after, the second ship, *Le Conquerant*, and the third, *Le Spartiate*, very nearly at the same moment, were also dismasted. *L'Aquilon* and *Le Souverain Peuple*, the fourth and fifth ships of the enemy's line, were taken possession of by the British at half-past eight in the evening.

Captain Berry, at that hour, sent Lieutenant Galway of the *Vanguard*, with a party of marines, to take possession of *Le Spartiate*, and that officer returned by the boat the French captain's sword, which Captain Berry immediately delivered to the admiral, who was then below, in consequence of a severe wound he had received in the head during the heat of the attack.

At this time it appeared that victory had already declared itself in our favour; for although *L'Orient*, *L'Heureux*, and *Tonnant* were not taken possession of, they were considered as completely in our power, which pleasing intelligence Captain Berry had likewise the satisfaction of communicating in person to the admiral.

A few minutes after nine a fire was observed to have

broken out in the cabin of *L'Orient;* to that point Captain Hallowell ordered as many guns as could be spared from firing on the *Franklin* to be directed, and that Captain Allen of the marines should throw in the whole fire of his musketry on the enemy's quarter, while the *Alexander* on the other side was keeping up an incessant shower of shot on the same point. The conflagration now began to rage with dreadful fury; still the French admiral sustained the honour of his flag with heroic firmness; but at length a period was put to his exertions by a cannon ball, which cut him asunder. He had before received three desperate wounds, one on his head, and two on his body, but could not be prevailed upon to quit his station on the arm-chest. His captain, Casa Bianca, fell by his side. Several of the officers and men seeing the impracticability of extinguishing the fire, which had now extended itself along the upper decks, and was flaming up the masts, jumped overboard; some supporting themselves on spars and pieces of wreck, others swimming with all their might to escape the dreadful catastrophe. Shot flying in all directions dashed many of them to pieces; others were picked up by the boats of the fleet, or dragged into the lower part of the nearest ships. The British sailors stretched forth their hands to save an enemy, though the battle at that moment raged with uncontrolled fury. The *Swiftsure*, anchoring within half pistol shot of the larboard bow of the *L'Orient*, saved the lives of the commissary, first lieutenant, and ten men, drawn out of the water through the lower-deck ports during the hottest part of the action. The situation of the *Alexander* and *Swiftsure* now became perilous in the extreme. The expected explosion of such a ship as *L'Orient* was to be dreaded as involving all around in certain destruction. Captain Hallowell, however, determined not to move from his devoted station, though repeatedly urged to do so. He perceived the advantage he possessed in being to windward of the burning ship. Captain Ball was not so fortunate: twice he had the mortification to perceive that the fire of the enemy had communicated to the

Alexander. He was, therefore, under the necessity of changing his berth, and moving to a greater distance.

The admiral was informed, by Captain Berry, of the situation of the enemy. Forgetting his own sufferings, he hastened on deck; the first consideration that struck his feeling mind, was, concern for the danger of such a number of lives. To save as many of them as possible, he ordered Captain Berry to make every exertion in his power. The only boat that could swim was despatched from the *Vanguard;* the other ships immediately followed the example, and above seventy drowning wretches were preserved by those lately employed in their destruction.

The van of the English fleet, having for the present finished their part in the glorious contest, now enjoyed a sublime view of the two lines illumined by the fire of the ill-fated foe ; the colours of the contending vessels being plainly distinguished. The moon, which had by this time risen, opposing her cold light to the warm glow of the fire beneath, added to the grandeur and solemnity of the picture. The flames had now made such progress that an explosion was instantly expected, yet the enemy on the lower deck, either insensible to the danger that threatened them, or impelled by the last paroxysms of despair and vengeance, continued to fire.

At thirty-seven minutes past nine the fatal explosion happened. The first communicated to the magazine, and *L'Orient* blew up with a crashing sound that deafened all around her. The tremendous motion, felt to the very bottom of each ship, was like that of an earthquake. An awful pause and deathlike silence of about three minutes ensued before the fragments driven to a vast height into the air could descend ; and then the greatest apprehension was formed, from the volumes of burning matter which threatened to fall on the decks and rigging of the surrounding ships. Fortunately, however, no great damage occurred. A port fire fell into the main-royal of the *Alexander*, and she was once more in danger of sharing the fate of the enemy; but by the exertions of Captain Ball, the flames were soon extinguished. Two large pieces of the wreck likewise dropped into the main and foretops of the *Swiftsure*, from which the men had fortunately withdrawn.

An awful silence now reigned, of several minutes, as if the contending squadrons, struck with horror at the dreadful event, which in an instant had hurried so many brave men into eternity, had forgotten their hostile rage, in pity for the sufferers. But short was the pause of death; vengeance soon roused the drooping spirits of the enemy. The *Franklin*, which now bore the French commander's flag, opened her fire with redoubled fury on the *Defence* and *Swiftsure*, and made the signal for renewed hostilities. The *Swiftsure*, being disengaged from her late formidable adversary, had leisure to direct her whole fire into the quarter of the foe who had thus presumed to break the solemn silence; and in a very short time, by the well-directed and steady fire of these two ships, and the *Leander* on her bows, the *Franklin* was compelled to call for quarter, and struck to a superior force.

The *Alexander*, the *Majestic*, and occasionally the *Swiftsure* were now the only British ships engaged; but the commander of the latter, finding that he could not direct his guns clear of the *Alexander*, which had dropped between him and the *Tonnant*, and fearful lest he should fire into a friend, desisted, although he was severely annoyed by the shot of the *Tonnant*, which was falling thick about him. Most of the English ships were so cut up in their masts and rigging, that they were unable to set any sail, or to move from their stations. The firing ceased entirely about three in the morning of the 2nd of August; but at four, just as the day began to dawn, the *Alexander* and *Majestic* recommenced the action with the *Tonnant, Guillaume Tell, Genereux*, and *Timoleon*. *Heureux* and *Mercure* had fallen out of the line, and anchored a considerable distance to leeward.

Captain Miller, perceiving the unequal contest, bore down to assist his friends, and began a furious cannonade on the

The Battle of the Nile. 173

enemy. The *Theseus* had as yet fortunately received but little damage in her masts and rigging, and that little had been repaired by the active exertions of her commander, as soon as the first part of the action in the van had terminated in favour of the British arms. *L'Artemise* frigate, stationed on the left of the centre of the French line, fired a broadside at the *Theseus*, and then struck her colours. Captain Miller dispatched an officer to take possession of her, but when the boat had arrived within a short distance, she burst into a flame, and blew up. This unofficer-like and treacherous conduct reflects disgrace on the name of Estandlet, who commanded her. After having surrendered his ship by striking her ensign and pendant, conscious that he was then secure from immediate danger, he set fire to her, and most of his crew escaped to the shore.

At six o'clock, the *Leander* having as yet received but little damage, was ordered by signal from the admiral to assist the ships engaged, which was accordingly obeyed. At this time the action between the three British ships, *Alexander*, *Majestic*, and *Theseus*, and the *Guillaume Tell*, *Genereux*, *Tonnant*, and *Timoleon*, had become very distant, as the latter continued imperceptibly to drop to leeward, and the *Theseus* was obliged to veer on two cables to keep within reach of them.

At 8 A.M. the *Goliath* bore down and anchored near the *Theseus*, the French ships having brought to again. The fire of the British was now chiefly turned against the *Heureux* and *Mercure*, which were soon obliged to surrender. The *Timoleon* was ashore, and the *Tonnant* was rendered a complete wreck. Under these circumstances Rear-Admiral Villeneuve, in the *Guillaume Tell*, of 80 guns, perceiving that few, if any, of our ships were in condition to make sail, resolved to lose no time in escaping from the inevitable fate that would otherwise have awaited him. About 7 o'clock he cut his cable and got under weigh, and his example was followed by the *Genereux*, with two frigates, *La Justice* and *La Diane*.

Perceiving their intention, the British admiral, by signal,

ordered the *Zealous* to intercept them. Unfortunately none of the windward ships were in a condition to second his attempt to stop the fugitives. Captain Hood did all that could be done : as they passed by him, he received and returned the fire of each in succession. The damage he sustained prevented him from tacking, and the admiral, with his usual judgment, gave the signal of recall.

The whole day of the 2nd was employed by the British admiral, his officers and men, in securing the ships that had struck, and repairing the damages their own had sustained. Though this was fully sufficient to occupy their attention, yet the mind of the victorious commander was too deeply impressed with the most pious gratitude to the Supreme Being, for the success which had crowned his endeavours in the cause of his country, to delay returning his public acknowledgments for the Divine favour. On the morning of the 2nd he therefore issued the following memorandum to the different captains of his squadron :

Vanguard, off the Mouth of the Nile,
2nd day of August, 1798.

Almighty God having blessed His Majesty's arms with victory, the admiral intends returning public thanksgiving for the same at two o'clock this day, and he recommends every ship doing the same as soon as convenient.

To the respective captains of the squadron.

Accordingly, at two o'clock public service was performed on the quarter deck of the *Vanguard*, by the Rev. Mr. Comyn, the other ships following the example of the admiral, though perhaps not all at the same time. The solemn act of gratitude to Heaven seemed to make a deep impression on many of the prisoners, and some of them even remarked, " that it was no wonder the English officers could maintain such discipline and order, when it was possible to impress the minds of their men with such sentiments, after a victory so great, and at a moment of such seeming confusion."

The same day the following memorandum, expressive of the admiral's sentiments of the noble exertions of the different officers and men of his squadron, was sent round to all the ships :

Vanguard, off the Mouth of the Nile,
2nd day of August, 1798.

The admiral most heartily congratulates the captains, officers, seamen, and marines of the squadron he has the honour to command, on the event of the late action ; and he desires they will accept his most sincere and cordial thanks for their very gallant behaviour in this glorious battle. It must strike forcibly every British seaman, how superior their conduct is, when in discipline and good order, to the riotous behaviour of lawless Frenchmen.

The squadron may be assured the admiral will not fail with his dispatches to represent their truly meritorious conduct in the strongest terms to the commander-in-chief.

To the captains of the ships of the squadron.

The Arabs and Mamelukes, who had lined the shores of the bay, beheld with transport that victory had declared itself in favour of the English. Their exultation was almost equal to that of the conquerors, and for the three following nights the whole coast was illumined in celebration of the victory.

THE BATTLE OF TRAFALGAR.

ON the 19th of October, 1805, the combined fleets, French and Spanish, put to sea, and on the 21st Lord Nelson intercepted them off Cape Trafalgar, and sixty miles eastward of Cadiz. When his lordship found that by his manœuvres he had placed the enemy in such a situation that they could not avoid an engagement, he displayed the utmost animation, and his usual confidence of victory. "Now," said he, to Captain Hardy and the other officers, "they cannot escape us; I think we shall at least make sure of twenty of them. I shall probably lose a leg, but that will be purchasing a victory cheaply."

The following is transcribed from Lord Nelson's private memorandum of that day, for which we are indebted to Mr. Harrison's "Life of Nelson": " We were between Trafalgar and Cape Spartel. The frigates made the signal, nine sail outside the harbour. I gave the frigates instructions for their guidance, and placed *Defence, Colossus,* and *Mars* between me and the frigates. At noon, fresh gales and heavy rain—Cadiz north-east, nine leagues. In the afternoon Captain Blackwood telegraphed that the enemy seemed determined to go to the westward—and that they shall not do, if in the power of Nelson and Bronte to prevent them! At five, telegraphed Captain Blackwood that I relied on his keeping sight of the enemy. At five o'clock, *Naiad* made the signal for thirty-one sail of the enemy north-north-east. The frigates and look-out ships kept sight of the enemy most admirably all night; and told me, by signals, which tack they were upon. At eight we wore, and stood for the south-west; and at 4 A.M. wore, and stood to the north-east.

"Monday, October 21st, 1805. At daylight, saw the enemy's combined fleet, from east to east-south-east. Bore away; made signal for order of sailing, and to prepare for battle; the enemy with their heads to the southward. At seven, the enemy wearing in succession." And then follows his lordship's appeal to heaven for success, which were probably the last words written by this great and brave commander :—

" May the great God, whom I worship, grant to my country, and for the benefit of Europe in general, a great and glorious victory! and may no misconduct in any one tarnish it: and may humanity after victory be the predominant feature in the British fleet! For myself, individually, I commend my life to Him who made me; and may His blessing light upon my

The Battle of Trafalgar.

endeavours for serving my country faithfully! To Him I resign myself, and the just cause which is entrusted to me to defend. "Amen! Amen! Amen!"

About twelve at noon the action began, and the last signal before it commenced was a private one by telegraph—a signal too emphatic ever to be forgotten—" ENGLAND EXPECTS EVERY MAN TO DO HIS DUTY."

While the *Victory* was going into action, his lordship walked the deck very quickly, and exclaimed, "This is the happiest day of my life—and it is a happy day, too, for Burnham Thorpe (the place of his nativity), for it is the day of their fair." He then went over the different decks, saw and conversed with the seamen, encouraged them with his usual affability, and was much pleased at the manner in which they had barricadoed the hawser-holes of the ship. All was perfect death-like silence, till just before the action began. Three cheers were given his lordship as he ascended the quarter-deck ladder. He had been particular in recommending cool, steady firing, in preference to a hurrying fire without aim or precision, and the event justified his lordship's advice, as the masts of his opponents came tumbling down on their decks, and over their sides, within half an hour after the battle began to rage in its full fury.

The conduct of their leader was fully adequate to rouse the British officers to deeds of hardy enterprise. It was his intention to have begun the action by passing ahead of the *Bucentaure*, the flagship of Admiral Villeneuve, that the *Victory* might be ahead of that ship, and astern of the *Santissima Trinidada;* but the *Bucentaure* shooting ahead, his lordship was obliged to go under her stern, raked her, and luffed up on her starboard side. The *Bucentaure* fired broadsides at the *Victory*, before his lordship ordered the ports to be opened, when the whole broadside, which was double-shotted, was fired into her, and the discharge made such a tremendous crash that the *Bucentaur* was seen to heel. The number of her men killed proved to be three hundred and sixty-five; wounded, two hundred and nineteen. The flag of the *Bucentaure* was then struck, as she was dismasted and quite unmanageable.

Lord Nelson now shot ahead to the Spanish admiral's ship, the *Santissima Trinidada*. He had already gained the highest honour in grappling with this ship during the action off Cape St. Vincent, in 1797. She was the largest ship in the world, carried 136 guns, and had four decks. The hero ordered the *Victory* alongside his old acquaintance as he called her, and to be lashed to his tremendous opponent. The conflict was horrible; the enemy were engaged at the muzzle of their guns. A dreadful carnage was made in the Spanish ships, which were full of men. The *Santissima Trinidada* had on board sixteen hundred, including a corps of troops, among whom were some sharp-shooters.

The royal marines on the poop of the *Victory*, as well as the officers, seamen, and marines on the quarter-deck, soon felt the effects of the system of sharp-shooting. The men began to drop fast; and, as Captain Adair, of the marines, wishing to counteract the destructive fire, went up the shrouds with a party, he fell quite dead on the poop, perforated with near twenty balls from those marksmen. The action then became very hot, and Lord Nelson was advised not to appear so conspicuously, in full uniform, to the mark of the topmen of the enemy. His answer was, "No, whatever may be the consequences, the insignia of the honours I now wear I gained by the exertions of British seamen under my command in various parts of the world, and in the hour of danger I am proud to show them and the enemies of old England that I will never part with them; if it please God I am to fall, I will expire with these trophies entwined round my heart."

Amidst the conflict of cannon, fired muzzle to muzzle, showers of bullets were directed on the quarter-deck, where the gallant hero stood, fearlessly giving his orders, and cheerfully abiding every peril. His heart was animated, and his spirits gay. The stump of his right arm, which he always

The Battle of Trafalgar. 179

facetiously denominated his fin, moved the shoulder of his sleeve up and down with the utmost rapidity, as was customary when he felt greatly pleased. Captain Hardy observing from the manner in which the sharp-shooters fired that it was their object to single out the officers, repeatedly requested Lord Nelson to change his coat, or to put on a great coat over it. The undaunted admiral answered he had not time. Too soon were Captain Hardy's apprehensions verified. A shot from the main-top of the enemy carried away part of the epaulette, and penetrating through the star, entered his left breast, and took a direction through the vital parts. He fell on the deck. Captain Hardy ran to him, and said, " I hope it is not mortal, my lord." He replied, " They have caught me at last." He was then taken below by Mr. Bourke, the purser of the *Victory*, who carried him in his arms, and laid him on a bed. His lordship said, " Bourke, my back is broke." The surgeon (Mr. Beatty) soon came and examined the wound. He said, " Doctor, you can be of no use to me; go and assist those to whom you can be of service, as I have but a few moments to live." He repeatedly asked for Captain Hardy, of whom his lordship inquired "how they went on ? " Captain Hardy replied that ten ships had struck; and his lordship said, " I hope none of ours have struck;" to which Captain Hardy replied "There is no fear of that.' He then returned to the deck. After the *Victory* had ceased firing, Captain Hardy again went to his lordship, who took him by the hand, and said, " I am now happy." Captain Hardy now told him the number of the enemy that had struck, and his lordship said, " Hardy, bring the fleet to an anchor," and that was the last order his lordship gave. Captain Hardy again returned to the deck; his lordship previously said, " I shall be dead before you return, take my body home." A short time after he said to Mr. Bourke (and these were his last words), " I have done my duty—I praise God for it!" and in a few moments he expired without a groan.

It was known on board the *Trinidada* that the British

admiral had been wounded, and the moment he fell there was a general shout on board the Spanish ship. Short, however, was the exultation of her crew, who were soon obliged to strike to the irresistible prowess of the British tars. After this conquest, the *Victory* subdued a third ship, which closed her part in the engagement.

The following particulars of Nelson's last moments are related by Mr. Beatty, the surgeon, and Mr. Bourke, the purser :—

About the middle of the action with the combined fleets, on the 21st of October, Lord Nelson was upon the quarter-deck, where he had resolved to take his station during the whole of the battle. A few minutes before he was wounded, Mr. Bourke was near him ; he looked steadfastly at him, and said, " Bourke, I expect every man to be upon his station." Mr. Bourke took the hint, and went to his proper situation in the cockpit.

At this time his lordship's secretary, Mr. Scott, who was not, as has been represented, either receiving directions from him, or standing by him, but was communicating some orders to an officer at a distant part of the quarter-deck, was cut almost in two by a cannon shot. He expired on the instant, and was thrown overboard.

Lord Nelson observed the act of throwing his secretary overboard, and said, as if doubtful, to a midshipman who was near him, " Was that Scott ? " The midshipman replied he believed it was. He exclaimed, " Poor fellow ! "

He was now walking the quarter-deck, and about three yards from the stern, the space he generally walked before he turned back. His lordship was in the act of turning on the quarter-deck, with his face towards the enemy, when he was mortally wounded in the left breast by a musket ball, supposed to have been fired from the mizen-top of the *Redoubtable*, French ship of the line, which the *Victory* had attacked early in the battle.

He instantly fell. He was not, as has been related, picked

The Battle of Trafalgar.

up by Captain Hardy. In the hurry of the battle, which was then raging in its greatest violence, even the fall of their beloved commander did not interrupt the business of the quarter-deck. The sailors, however, who were near his lordship, raised him in their arms, and carried him to the cockpit. He was immediately laid upon a bed, and the following is the substance of the conversation which really took place in the cockpit, between his lordship, Captain Hardy, Mr. Bourke, and Mr. Beatty.

Upon seeing him brought down, Mr. Bourke immediately ran to him. "I fear," he said, "your lordship is wounded." "Mortally, mortally." "I hope not, my dear lord; let Mr. Beatty examine your wounds." "It is of no use," exclaimed the dying Nelson; "he had better attend to others."

When Bourke returned into the cockpit with Captain Hardy, Lord Nelson told the latter to come near him. "Kiss me, Hardy," he exclaimed. Captain Hardy kissed his cheek. "I hope your lordship," he said, "will live to enjoy your triumph." "Never, Hardy," he exclaimed; "I am dying! I am a dead man all over, Beatty will tell you so. Bring the fleet to anchor; you have all done your duty. God bless you." Captain Hardy now said, "I suppose Collingwood, my dear lord, is to command the fleet?" "*Never*," exclaimed he—"*whilst I live.*" Meaning, doubtless, that so long as his gallant spirit survived, he would never desert his duty.

What passed after this was merely casual; his lordship's last words were to Mr. Beatty, whilst he was expiring in his arms, "I could have wished to have lived to enjoy this, but God's will be done." "My lord," exclaimed Hardy, "you die in the midst of triumph." "Do I, Hardy?" he smiled faintly. "God be praised!" These were his last words before he expired.

The day after the victory, Admiral Collingwood issued the following general order:—

Euryalus, October 22nd, 1805.

The ever-to-be-lamented death of Lord Viscount Nelson, Duke of Bronte, the commander-in-chief, who fell in the action on the 21st, in the arms of victory, covered with glory, whose memory will ever be dear to the British navy and the British nation, whose zeal for the honour of his king and for the interests of his country will be ever held up as a shining example for a British seaman, leaves to me a duty to return my thanks to the Right Honourable Rear-admiral, the captains, officers, seamen, and detachments of royal marines, serving on board His Majesty's squadron now under my command, for their conduct on that day: but where can I find language to express my sentiments of the valour and skill which were displayed by the officers, the seamen, and marines, in the battle with the enemy, where every individual appeared a hero, on whom the glory of his country depended; the attack was irresistible, and the issue of it adds to the page of our naval annals a brilliant instance of what Britons can do, when the king and country need their service.

To the Right Honourable Rear-admiral the Earl of Northesk, to the captains, officers, and seamen, and to the officers, non-commissioned officers, and privates of the royal marines, I beg to give my sincere and hearty thanks, for their highly meritorious conduct, both in the action, and in their zeal and activity in bringing the captured ships out from their perilous situation in which they were, after their surrender, among the shoals of Trafalgar, in boisterous weather.

And I desire that the respective captains will be pleased to communicate to the officers, seamen, and royal marines, this public testimony of my high approbation of their conduct, and my thanks for it.

C. COLLINGWOOD.

To the Right Honourable Rear-Admiral the Earl of Northesk, and the respective captains and commanders.

The Battle of Trafalgar.

General Order.

The Almighty God, whose arm is strength, having of His great mercy been pleased to crown the exertion of His Majesty's fleet with success, in giving them a complete victory over their enemies, on the 21st of this month ; and that all praise and thanksgiving may be offered up to the throne of grace for the great benefits to our country and to mankind :

I have thought proper that a day should be appointed of general humiliation before God, and thanksgiving for this His merciful goodness, imploring forgiveness of sins, a continuation of His divine mercy, and His constant aid to us, in the defence of our country's liberties and laws, without which the utmost efforts of man are nought, and I direct, therefore, that a day be appointed for this purpose.

Given on board the *Euryalus*, off Cape Trafalgar, 22nd October, 1805.

C. COLLINGWOOD.

When the news of the victory arrived in England, addresses to the throne poured in from every part of the country. The city of London as usual took the lead, and the Court and Common Council waited on His Majesty at St. James's, with an address of congratulation.

To this address His Majesty George III. was pleased to return this most gracious answer :—

" I receive with peculiar satisfaction the congratulations of my loyal city of London on the late glorious and decisive victory, obtained, under the blessing of *God, by my fleet commanded by the late Lord Viscount Nelson, over the combined force of France and Spain. The skill and intrepidity of my officers and seamen were never more conspicuous than on this important occasion. The loss of the distinguished commander under whom this great victory has been achieved, I most sincerely and deeply lament ; his transcendent and heroic services will, I am persuaded, exist for ever in the recollection of my people, and whilst they tend to stimulate those who come after him to similar exertions, they will prove a lasting source of strength, security, and glory to my dominions."

LUTHER BEFORE THE EMPEROR,

LUTHER standing alone before the Emperor Charles V., and the Imperial assembly at the Diet of Worms, is one of the grandest scenes in the history of the world. Apart from the religious aspect of the event, as bearing on the cause of the Reformation, there never was a more noble instance of personal courage and heroism, and nothing could have sustained the humble solitary monk in such a contest, save his living faith in Divine power and help.

It was with great reluctance, and after many efforts at obtaining internal reform, that Luther at last resolved to break into the Roman Catholic Church. When cited to Rome, in 1519, he still professed readiness to submit himself : "I am willing to be silent," he said, "if they will not attempt to silence the gospel." When the scandalous sale of pardons by Tetzel, the papal envoy, roused his indignation, and he published his theses against indulgences, the Pope replied by sending a bull of excommunication.

It was on December 10th, 1520, that he burned publicly the Pope's decretal against him, the students and the people of Wittenberg witnessing the scene, amidst great excitement. This was at length an open rupture with Rome, and a deed of defiance from which there could be no retreat.

In less than a fortnight after the burning of the papal bull, Luther heard of a citation to appear before the new Emperor, Charles V. It was as yet doubtful what part the German nation, represented by its chief and princes, would take in a conflict with Rome. The Emperor paid great deference to the Elector, Frederic the Wise, and it was by his advice that he refused to obey blindly the papal commands, but decided first to examine into the matters at issue. Hence the citation of

Luther before the Emperor. 185

the German monk to appear before the Diet summoned to assemble at Worms. The citation was put into his hands on March 26th by the Imperial Herald, Caspar Sturm, who appeared at Wittenberg to escort him, bearing a safe-conduct. In the beginning of April they set out, and arrived on the 16th, a journey which can now be made by rail in a few hours.

Some of the crowd who accompanied him in the outset of his journey, said, "There are many cardinals and prelates at Worms! You will be burnt alive, and your body be reduced to ashes, as they did with John Huss." "Though they should kindle a fire," he replied, "whose flames should reach from Worms to Wittenberg and rise up to heaven, I would go through it in the name of the Lord, and stand before them."

One day, when he had entered into an inn, and the crowd was as usual pressing to see him, an officer made his way through, and thus addressed him, "Are you the man who has taken in hand to reform the papacy? How can you expect to succeed?" "Yes," said Luther, "I am the man. I place my dependence upon the Almighty God, whose word and commandment are before me." The officer, deeply affected, gazed on him with a look of kindly sympathy, and said, "Dear friend, there is much in what you say. I am a servant of the Emperor Charles, but your Master is greater than mine. He will help and protect you."

At Naumberg Luther met a priest, said to have been J. Langor, a man of stern zeal, who kept hung up in his study a portrait of Jerome Savonarola, of Ferrara, who perished in the flames at Florence in the year 1498, by order of Pope Alexander VI., a martyr for liberty and morals rather than an enlightened confessor of the Gospel. Taking down the portrait, the priest held it forth in silence as he approached Luther, who saw the import of his solemn and silent action. But his intrepid spirit was unmoved. "It is Satan," he remarked, "who seeks by these terrors to hinder the confession of the truth in the assembly of the princes, for he foresees the effect it will have on his kingdom." "Stand fast in the truth thou hast professed," replied the austere but honest and friendly priest, "and thy God will never forsake thee."

From Frankfort he wrote to Spalatin, "I am arrived here, although Satan has sought to stop me on my way by sickness. From Eisenach to this place I have been suffering, and I am at this moment in worse condition than ever. I find that Charles has issued an edict to terrify me; but Christ lives, and we shall enter Worms in spite of all the councils of hell, and all the powers of the air. Therefore engage a lodging for me."

Spalatin soon became alarmed; and when Luther was approaching the city he sent a message by a servant, who said, "Abstain from entering Worms." This was at Oppenheim, a few miles from the city, now the last station on the railway between Mayence and Worms. Luther, still undaunted, turned his eyes on Spalatin's messenger, and answered, "Go, tell your master that though there should be as many devils at Worms as there are tiles on its roofs, I would enter it."

Not long before his death, Luther was reminded of this, when he said, "I feared nothing. God can give this boldness to man. I know not whether now I should have so much liberty and joy."

When Luther was in the hall, about to be ushered into the presence of the assembly, a veteran knight, George Freundsborg, commander of the guard, touched him on the shoulder, and said kindly, "My poor monk, my poor monk, thou hast a march and a struggle to go through, such as neither I nor many other captains have seen the like of in our worst campaigns. But if thy cause be just, and thou art sure of it, go forward, in God's name, and fear nothing! He will not forsake thee!" A noble tribute from a brave soldier to the courage of the soul!

After Luther made his first appearance before the Diet, and had delivered the addresses prepared by him in defence of himself against the charges made, he was required to retire. He went to his inn, a few of his friends accompanying him, and a great crowd filling the streets, and struggling to catch a sight

Luther before the Emperor.

of the man about whom so much stir was being made. He sought the quiet of his chamber, and there he wrote a letter to the Councillor Caspianus in these words, "I am writing to you from the very midst of a tempest" (alluding probably to the noise outside the inn, and the excitement in the town). "An hour ago I appeared before the Emperor and his brother. I avowed myself the author of my books, and I have promised to give my answer to-morrow as to recantation. By the help of Jesus Christ, I will not retract a single letter of my writings." He had already in prayer sought and found the strength which made him firm as a rock.

Luther mentions in his letter that he had appeared before the Emperor and his brother, the Archduke Ferdinand. But in truth there had seldom if ever been seen so great and august an assembly. The six Electors of the Empire, whose descendants almost all became kings; eighty dukes, rulers of large territories; thirty archbishops and other Romish prelates; many princes, barons, counts, and knights of good estate; seven ambassadors, including those of France and England; the Pope's nuncios; in all above 200 notables; such was the imposing Court before which "the solitary monk" appeared.

On the morrow, when ushered into the presence of the Emperor and the assembly, when the question was put to him, "Will you, or will you not, recant?" Luther answered unhesitatingly, "Since your Most Serene Majesty and your High Mightinesses require of me a simple, clear, and direct answer, I will give one, and it is this: I cannot submit my faith either to the Pope or to the Councils, because it is clear as noonday that they have often fallen into error, and even into glaring inconsistency with themselves. If, then, I am not convinced by proof from Holy Scripture, or by cogent reasons, if I am not satisfied by the very texts I have cited, and if my judgment is not in this way brought into subjection to God's Word, I neither can nor will retract anything, for it cannot be right for a Christian to speak against his conscience."

Then turning a look on that assembly before whom he stood,

and which held in its hand life or death, he said, "HERE I STAND. I CANNOT DO OTHERWISE, GOD HELP ME! AMEN."

The assembly for a time was motionless with astonishment. Luther's friends were proud of their champion, yet felt painful anxiety as to the result. Several of the princes present could scarcely conceal their admiration. The Emperor, who had the day before listened to Luther with marked attention and interest, on recovering from the first impression made by this declaration of firmness, exclaimed, "The monk speaks with an intrepid heart and unshaken courage."

"If you do not retract," resumed the Chancellor, the assembly being recalled to attention, "the Emperor and the States of the Empire will proceed to consider how to deal with an obstinate heretic." At these words Luther's friends trembled, but the monk repeated, "May God be my helper, for I can retract nothing!" Luther was conducted out of the hall during the deliberation, and on being again called in, the Chancellor then addressed him: "Martin, you have not spoken with that humility which befits your condition. The distinction which you have drawn as to your works was needless, for if you retracted such as contained errors the Emperor would not allow the rest to be burnt. It is absurd to require to be refuted by Scripture, when you are reviving heresies condemned by the General Council of Constance. The Emperor, therefore, commands you to say simply 'Yes' or No,' whether you mean to affirm what you have advanced, or whether you retract any part thereof."

"I have no other answer to give than that which I have already given," said Luther, quietly but firmly.

The Elector Frederic had expected that possibly Luther's courage would have failed him in the Emperor's presence; however, he was the more deeply affected by the Reformer's firmness. He felt proud of having taken such a man under his protection. He said afterwards to Spalatin, "Oh! how Luther spoke before the Emperor and all the States of the Empire: all I feared was that he might go too far."

Well may it be said that this was the grandest scene in the history of the Reformation, one of the grandest scenes in all history.

JUGGERNAUT IN 1806.

MUCH has been written about the Hindoo idol Juggernaut, not only in missionary records, but also in books of travel and history. The horrible scenes formerly witnessed during the festivals have been checked by the interference of the British Government, and especially the sacrifice of human life is prevented by the authority of the law, and the regulations of the police. Before long it is to be hoped that Christian influence and educational enlightenment will put an end to what still prevails of heathen idolatry and superstition. The following account of the festival, during the times when priestcraft and fanaticism were as yet unchecked, is from the journal of an eye-witness, Dr. Claudius Buchanan, an enterprising traveller, and a man distinguished for his learning and piety.

The idol called Juggernaut, says Dr. Buchanan, has been considered as the Moloch of the East, and he is justly so named, for the sacrifices offered up to him by devotees are not less criminal, perhaps not less numerous, than those recorded of the Moloch of Canaan.

Two other idols accompany Juggernaut—namely, Bolovam and Shubudra, his brother and sister; for there are three deities worshipped here. They receive equal adoration, and sit on thrones of nearly equal height. The temple is a stupendous fabric, truly commensurate with the extensive sway of the " horrid king."

On the 18th June, 1806, I witnessed a scene which I shall never forget. It was the great day of the Feast, and at twelve o'clock the Moloch of Hindostan was brought out of his temple, amid the acclamations of hundreds of thousands of his worshippers. When the idol was placed upon his throne, a shout was raised by the multitude, such as I had never heard before. It continued equable for a few minutes, then gradually died away.

After a short interval of silence, a murmur was heard in the distance. All eyes were turned to the place, and beheld a grove advancing. A body of men, having green branches or palms in their hands, approached with great celerity. The people opened a way for them, and when they had come up to the throne, they fell down before him that sat thereon, and worshipped. And the multitude again sent forth a voice "like the sound of a great thunder." But the voices I now heard were not those of melody or of joyful acclamation. Their number indeed brought to my mind the countless multitude of the Revelation, but their voices gave no tuneful hosanna or hallelujah—it was rather a yell of approbation.

The throne of the idol was placed on a stupendous car, about sixty feet in height, resting on wheels, which indented the ground deeply as they turned slowly under the ponderous machine. Attached to it were six cables, by which the people drew it along. Upon the tower were the priests and satellites of the idol, surrounding his throne. The idol is a block of wood, having a frightful visage, painted black, with a distended mouth of bloody colour; his arms are of gold, and he is dressed in gorgeous apparel. The other two idols are of a white and yellow colour. Five elephants preceded the three towers, bearing lofty flags, dressed in crimson caparisons, and having bells hanging thereto, which sounded musically as they moved.

I went on in the procession, close by the tower of Moloch, which, as it was drawn with difficulty, grated on its wheels harshly. After the tower had proceeded some way, a pilgrim announced that he was ready to offer himself a sacrifice to the idol. He laid himself down in the road before the tower, as it was moving along, lying on his face, with his arms stretched forward. The multitude passed round him, leaving the space clear, and he was crushed to death by the wheels of the car. A shout of joy was raised to the god, and the people threw cowries, or small money, on the body of the victim, in approbation of the deed. He was left to view a considerable time, and was then carried by the *hurries* to the Golgotha. A woman next devoted herself to the idol. She laid herself down in the road obliquely, so that the wheels did not kill her instantaneously, as is generally the case, but she died in a few hours. Next morning, as I passed the place where she had been taken, nothing of her remained but the bones.

And this, thought I, is the religion of the Brahmins of Hindostan, and their worship in its highest degree! What, then, shall we think of their private manners and moral principles? For it is equally true of India as of Europe, if you would know the state of the people look at the state of the temple.

The idolatrous processions continue some days longer, but my spirits, adds Dr. Buchanan in his journal, are so exhausted by the constant view of these enormities, that I mean to hasten away from Juggernaut sooner than I at first intended.

As to the number of worshippers assembled here at this time no accurate calculation can be made. The natives themselves, when speaking of the number at particular festivals, usually say that a lac (100,000) of people would not be missed. I asked a Brahmin how many he supposed were present at the most numerous festival he had ever witnessed. "How can I tell," said he; "how many grains are there in a handful of sand?"

LIFE-BOAT SERVICES.

EVERY year, all round the coasts of the British Islands there are deeds of daring and of endurance done by the men of the Life-Boat Service, worthy of record among the noblest histories of heroism. It is but rarely that there are eyes to bear public witness, or pens to chronicle these heroic deeds. A bare report of the fact of a boat going out, and of so many men saved from a watery grave, is all that is usually heard of. Now and then some shipwreck of unwonted magnitude, or rescue services of special gallantry, attract attention, and medals and honours from the Royal National Life-Boat Institution reward the crew. But there is no need of such inducements to prompt to efforts for saving life. The sense of duty and the feeling of benevolence suffice to bring volunteers for the service. At the same time, it makes a great difference to a poor sailor or boatman, when he knows that those dependent on him will not be forgotten if he risks his life. It is to be desired, therefore, that ample funds be at the disposal of the managers of the Institution we have named, and of other societies for kindred objects, not merely to support the service in efficiency, but to help the widows and orphans of those that perish in the good cause.

Of the importance of the Life-Boat work some idea may be formed by the statement that in one single year 1,200 lives were saved through its means; since the beginning of the Institution about 35,000 have been saved. The expenditure every year is now not far from £40,000, figures which show the magnitude to which the work has attained. The number of boats is now about 280. It is pleasant to record that amongst the latest additions to this great fleet of mercy are two boats subscribed for by readers of the *Boys' Own Paper*. One of these boats, almost immediately after it was placed on its station, at Poole, in Dorsetshire, had the good fortune to rescue the crew of a foreign ship. The subscriptions for these two boats was mostly in small sums, collected by boys themselves in every part of the kingdom, giving good hope and happy augury that the work will be maintained and extended in future years.

Kindred in purpose and spirit, is the work of the Rocket and Mortar Apparatus, under the direction of the Board of Trade, and the management of the Coast-Guard. To the exertions of Captain Manby the nation is mainly indebted for the establishment and thorough organization of this important service. There are many parts of the coast where, from the rocky nature of the shore, the deep water running up to steep cliffs, the absence of a sufficient population from which to draw a crew, and other reasons, life-boats would be either useless, or could not be maintained in a state of efficiency. On such coasts the rocket apparatus is the ship-wrecked sailor's only hope. Many thousands of lives have been saved. In one year there were above 500 men thus rescued. Information about these and other services for the benefit of sailors will be found in Dr. Macaulay's book of "Sea Pictures" (Religious Tract Society). Of the Life-Boat Service a full account is given in "The History of the Life-Boat and its Work," by the late Mr. R. Lewis, Secretary of the Institution; and also in the periodical the *Life-Boat Journal.* From that Journal we extract a remarkable narrative, not because of special gallantry in the men, nor unusual peril in the service, but because we happen to have a more clear and detailed account of the wreck and the rescue, than in most other recent cases. But in turning over the pages of the *Life-Boat Journal* we meet with many brave and noble deeds, as worthy of public recognition as those of any of the gallant men who have gained the Victoria Cross. The Albert medal is occasionally given for such services.

Before quoting, however, the account of the "Wreck of the *Indian Chief*," let us, very briefly, refer to two or three other recent cases, which show the variety and extent of work, and the readiness of resource, and the hard labour, sometimes necessary before the oars can be put into the water, or the sail hoisted.

The first case is on an Irish station, the boatmen of the Sister Island not being deficient in the qualities most required in the service.

I. At Ballywalter, County Down.—A messenger having brought information at 1.30 P.M. on the 6th February, 1883, that a vessel was ashore on the north end of the Long Rock, the crew of the *Admiral Henry Meynell* Life-boat at once assembled, and crowds of the villagers dragged the boat by road to the scene of the wreck, much difficulty being experienced in getting her to the shore, on account of there being two ditches on the way. The boat was at last launched, but notwithstanding the noble exertions of her crew to battle with the fierce gale blowing from the E.S.E., she was driven ashore with great violence, three of her oars being broken. Owing to the strength of the gale and the violence of the surf great difficulty was experienced in saving the boat. After renewed exertions, however, she was again launched at 3 A.M., and succeeded in rescuing the crew of the vessel, consisting of six men, who had been all night in the rigging. The vessel was the brig *Euphemia Fullerton*, of Londonderry, bound to that port from Maryport with a cargo of coal. She became a total wreck.

II. At Holy Island, Northumberland.—We are glad to meet with the honoured name of *Grace Darling*, more than one boat being called after her on the coast where she gained her renown. The ketch *Mary Tweedie*, of Berwick, was seen running before the wind, under bare poles, at 3 P.M., on the 6th March, 1883, during a fearful gale of wind from N. to N.E. and a very heavy sea, the whole bar and the sea as far as the eye could reach being one mass of broken water. The No. 1 Life-boat, *Grace Darling*, was launched, and was more than three hours in reaching the vessel. The crew pulled bravely until almost exhausted; but every time they seemed to be near enough to throw a line on board, a huge wave washed them about a

Life-Boat Services. 195

hundred yards astern. This was repeated ten or twelve times before the life-boat men were able to get a rope fast to the vessel, after which they took two men into the boat, by means of the life-buoy, in a very exhausted and numbed condition. One of the crew had received a blow on the head from a falling spar, and had died soon afterwards.

III. The next rescue is on the coast of North Wales. On the morning of the 30th March, 1883, it was reported that a barque was ashore on Cymeran Beach, with all hands in the fore rigging, the vessel having sunk, and her mainmast having been carried away during a heavy S.S.W. gale. The Rhosneigir Life-boat went to her assistance, but being disabled by the breaking of several rowing crutches, was compelled to return to the shore, one of the boat's crew being also washed overboard by a heavy sea, and rescued with some difficulty. The Holyhead Life-boat was then launched, and at about 11 o'clock was taken in tow by the s.s. *George Eliot* to the N.W. of the South Stack. Here the life-boat was cast off, and proceeded under canvas until about 12.30, when she fell in with the steam-tug *Challenger*, by which she was towed in the direction of the stranded vessel. Owing, however, to the heavy sea, the tug could not go within a mile of the wreck, and the life-boat, being obliged to continue her course under oars, made three fruitless attempts to reach the vessel, owing to the broken water and the heavy surf. As the wind was rising, and there was no place to breach the boat, it was obliged to return to Holyhead. Other unsuccessful attempts to reach the vessel were subsequently made by the Rhosneigir Life-boat, but they failed, and endeavours to rescue the shipwrecked men by means of the rocket apparatus also proved unavailing. As the Rhosneigir men were reported to be exhausted by their exertions, it was suggested that the Holyhead crew should proceed to Rhosneigir and try to get to the vessel in that life-boat. An application was accordingly made to the railway authorities for a special engine, which was at once granted, and the Holyhead crew were thus conveyed to the spot nearest to the wreck. It was now quite dark, and the men had scarcely any knowledge of the position of hidden rocks on that coast, but they nevertheless gallantly took the boat out, succeeded in reaching the wrecked vessel, and in rescuing the twenty men who were on board.

The Silver Medal of the Institution was presented to Mr. T. Roberts, coxswain of the Holyhead Life-boat, and the thanks of the Institution, inscribed on vellum, with an extra pecuniary reward to each of his crew, in consideration of their heroic exertions.

IV. At Seaton Carew, County Durham.—On the 11th March, 1883, at about 8.30 P.M., during a violent gale from the N.E., accompanied by thick snow-showers and a very heavy sea, signals of distress were exhibited from the Long Scar Rocks off this place. The Seaton Carew Life-boat was at once launched, and proceeded in the direction indicated, but no trace of any wreck could be found. Henry Hood, the coxswain of the Life-boat, and one of the crew named John Franklin, then determined to land on the reef and make a thorough search for it, as it was impossible to take the Life-boat among the rocks in the darkness. With much difficulty and danger, the sea breaking heavily over them, and the coxswain on one occasion being washed off the rocks, they at last discovered the wreck, and being afterwards joined by another of the life-boat men, Matthew Franklin, they, after many ineffectual attempts, succeeded in throwing the heaving line over the stern. Just as this was accomplished, Hood heard a voice, and seeing some dark object in the surf, he rushed into the sea, and, with the aid of his companions, rescued a man, who proved to be the mate of the vessel, in a most exhausted condition. They then hailed the wreck, and the remaining four men, by means of the communicating line, were got on to the rocks. The rescuers and the rescued now made for the life-boat; after a perilous journey across the rocks, which were being swept by the sea, they at last reached it, and pulled for the shore, which was made in safety about half an hour after midnight. The wrecked vessel was the schooner *Atlas*, of Drammen, bound thence to Sunderland. She broke up very soon after the crew had been rescued.

Her Majesty the Queen subsequently conferred the decoration of the Albert Medal of the Second Class on Henry Hood, in recognition of his most gallant conduct on this occasion, and the Institution also awarded its Silver Medal to him, and to the two Franklins.

V. We give one other case, which shows the labour often necessary in reaching the scene of action. On Sunday, the 25th November, 1883, intelligence was received that a large foreign barque was riding at her anchors off Beachy Head Lighthouse, in a very dangerous position, with a signal of distress flying. With as little delay as possible, the crew of the *William and Mary* Life-boat were mustered, and the boat, mounted on its transporting carriage, started for Birling Gap, drawn by seven horses. The route taken was through Meads, where three additional horses were procured, and with this extra power, she speedily mounted the hill, and crossed the downs to Birling Gap, a distance altogether of five miles. There the boat was obliged to be taken off her carriage, as the Gap had to be widened to admit even of the passage of the boat, and the incline was very sharp. The lower part of the Gap had been washed away by the sea, but this difficulty was overcome by using some long pieces of timber which were fortunately on the spot. Under the superintendence of the coxswain, the boat was by great exertions got safely down to the beach, and was launched at 1.15. The wind was blowing a gale from the S.S.W., and a tremendous sea was rolling in. At about 2 o'clock, after a very hard struggle against the head sea, the midship oars being double-banked, the vessel was reached; she was then opposite the Gap, about a mile from shore, labouring heavily in the seas with two anchors down, sails torn, and spars carried away. A storm of rain then came on, and the vessel and life-boat were hidden from the view of the spectators who lined the cliffs. After a period of suspense, the life-boat was seen making for the shore, and in gallant style she took the beach almost close to the spot from whence she had started, and landed the rescued crew of eleven men. The life-boat had anchored as close as possible to the vessel, and the crew were then hauled into her. The poor fellows, who were in a very exhausted state, one of them having sustained a fracture of the ribs, were taken to the Coastguard Station, where they received every attention from the Chief Officer and the Coastguardmen. The life-boat was got up the Gap with considerable difficulty, and arrived back at her station about 7.30. The distressed vessel was the barque *New Brunswick*, of Brevig, 480 tons, bound from Quebec to West Hartlepool with a cargo of timber.

WRECK OF THE "INDIAN CHIEF," AND GALLANT RESCUE-SERVICES OF THE RAMSGATE LIFE-BOAT, THE " BRADFORD."

In the *Life-Boat Journal* for February 1881, we find a full report of the wreck of the *Indian Chief*, and of the rescue of the survivors of the crew by the Ramsgate Life-boat, the *Bradford*. This report seems to have been chiefly gathered from the mate of the wrecked ship, and from the coxswain of the Life-boat, by the correspondent of the *Daily Telegraph*, who visited the place soon after the events narrated. It is not the first time that the gallant services of the Ramsgate boatmen have been conspicuous. Their station is one of the most important on all our coasts, and the wreck-chart shows how often help is needed in that region of the northern seas. In a letter from Mr. Braine, the harbour-master, special testimony is borne to their services on the present occasion. He says :—

" Of all the meritorious services performed by the Ramsgate tug and life-boat, I consider this one of the best. The decision the coxswain and crew arrived at to remain till daylight, which was in effect to continue for fourteen hours cruising about with the sea continually breaking over them in a heavy gale and tremendous sea, proves, I consider, their gallantry and determination to do their duty.

WRECK OF THE "INDIAN CHIEF," AND SERVICES OF THE RAMSGATE LIFEBOAT. [*page* 193

"The coxswain and crew of the life-boat speak in the highest terms of her good qualities; they state that when sailing across the 'Long Sand,' after leaving the wreck, the seas were tremendous, and the boat behaved most admirably. Some of the shipwrecked crew have since stated that they were fearful, on seeing the frightful-looking seas they were passing through, that they were in more danger in the life-boat than when lashed to the mast of their sunken ship, as they thought it impossible for any boat to live through such a sea."

It was during the night of the 5th January, 1881, that the tidings reached Ramsgate that a large ship had gone ashore on the Long Sand. From Aldborough, in Suffolk, from Clacton and from Harwich in Essex, where signals or messages had also reached, the life-boats put off to the scene of danger, but none of these succeeded in reaching the wreck. Happily the *Bradford* boat, of Ramsgate, persevered amidst difficulties, hardships, and dangers, rarely surpassed in the service, and had the reward of saving eleven of the crew, who were nearly perishing, after exposure for nearly thirty hours, in bitterly cold weather. The following is the account given by Mr. W. Meldrum Lloyd, the second officer of the ship. The captain and sixteen of the crew perished that night.

THE MATE'S ACCOUNT.

Our ship was the *Indian Chief*, of 1,238 tons register; our skipper's name was Fraser, and we were bound, with a general cargo, to Yokohama, in Japan. There were twenty-nine souls on board, counting the North-country pilot. We were four days out from Middlesborough, but it had been thick weather ever since the afternoon of the Sunday on which we sailed. All had gone well with us, however, so far, and on Wednesday morning, at half-past two, we made the Knock Light. The water is here just a network of shoals; for to the southward lies the Knock, and close over against it stretches the Long Sand, and beyond, down to the westward, is the Sunk Sand.

Shortly after the Knock Light had hove in sight, the wind shifted to the eastward and brought a squall of rain. We were under all plain sail at the time, with the exception of the royals, which were furled, and the mainsail that hung in the buntlines. The Long Sand was to leeward, and finding that we were drifting that way the order was given to put the ship about. It was very dark, the wind breezing up sharper and sharper, and cold as death. The helm was put down, but the main braces fouled, and before they could be cleared the vessel had missed stays and was in irons. We then went to work to wear the ship, but there was much confusion, the vessel heeling over, and all of us knew that the Sands were close aboard. The ship paid off, but at a critical moment, the spanker-boom sheet fouled the wheel; still, we managed to get the vessel round, but scarcely were the braces belayed and the ship on the starboard tack, when she struck the ground broadside on. She was a soft-wood built ship, and she trembled, as though she would go to pieces at once like a pack of cards. Sheets and halliards were let go, but no man durst venture aloft. Every moment threatened to bring the spars crushing about us, and the thundering and beating of the canvas made the masts buckle and jump like fishing-rods.

We then kindled a great flare and sent up rockets, and our signals were answered by the Sunk Lightship and the Knock. We could see one another's faces in the light of the big blaze, and sung out cheerily to keep our hearts up; and, indeed, although we all knew that our ship was hard and fast and likely to leave her bones on that sand, we none of us reckoned upon dying. The sky had cleared, the easterly wind made the stars sharp and bright, and it was comforting to watch the lightships' rockets rushing up and bursting into smoke and sparks over our heads, for they made us see that our position was known, and they were as good as an assurance that help would come along soon, and that we need not lose heart. But all this while the wind was gradually sweeping up into a gale—and oh, the bitter cold of that wind!

It seemed as long as a month before the morning broke, and just before the grey grew broad in the sky, one of the men yelled out something, and then came sprawling and splashing aft to tell us that he had caught sight of the sail of a life-boat dodging among the heavy seas. It was not a life-boat, but a fishing-smack, which after vain efforts to come near us, probably took the news to Harwich. She was a good distance away, and she stood on and off, on and off, never coming closer, and evidently shirking the huge seas which were now boiling around us. At last she hauled her sheet aft, put her helm over, and went away. One of our crew groaned, but no other man uttered a sound, and we returned to the shelter of the deckhouses.

Though the gale was not at its height when the sun rose, it was not far from it. We plucked up spirits again when the sun shot out of the raging sea, but as we lay broadside on to the waves, the sheets of flying water soon made the sloping decks a dangerous place for a man to stand on, and the crew and officers kept the shelter of the deck-cabins, though the captain and his brother and I were constantly going out to see if any help was coming. But now the flood was making, and this was a fresh and fearful danger, as we all knew, for at sunrise the water had been too low to knock the ship out of her sandy bed, but as the tide rose it lifted the vessel, bumping and straining her frightfully. The pilot advised the skipper to let go the starboard anchor, hoping that the set of the tide would slue the ship's stern round, and make her lie head on to the seas; so the anchor was dropped, but it did not alter the position of the ship.

To know what the cracking and straining of that vessel was like, as bit by bit she slowly went to pieces, you must have been aboard of her. When she broke her back a sort of panic seized many of us, and the captain roared out to the men to get the boats over, and see if any use could be made of them. Three boats were launched, but the second boat, with two hands in her, went adrift, and was instantly engulphed, and the poor fellows in her vanished just as you might blow out a light. The other boats filled as soon as they touched the water. There was no help for us in that way, and again we withdrew to the cabins. A little before five o'clock in the afternoon a huge sea swept over the vessel, clearing the decks fore and aft, and leaving little but the uprights of the deck-houses standing. It was a dreadful sea, but we knew worse was behind it, and that we must climb the rigging if we wanted to prolong our lives. The hold was already full of water, and portions of the deck had been blown out, so that everywhere great yawning gulfs met the eye, with the black water washing almost flush. Some of the men made for the fore-rigging, but the captain shouted to all hands to take to the mizenmast, as that one, in his opinion, was the securest. A number of the men who were scrambling forward returned on hearing the captain sing out, but the rest held on and gained the foretop. Seventeen of us got over the mizentop, and with our knives fell to hacking away at such running gear as we could come at to serve as lashings. None of us touched the mainmast, for we all knew, now the ship had broken her back, that that spar was doomed, and the reason why the captain had called to the men to come aft was because he was afraid that when the mainmast went it would drag the foremast, that rocked in its step with every move, with it.

I was next the captain in the mizentop, and near him was his brother, a stout-built, handsome young fellow, twenty-two years old, as fine a specimen of the English sailor as ever I was shipmate with. He was calling about him cheerfully, bidding us not to be down-hearted, and telling us to look sharply around for the life-boats. He helped several of the benumbed men to lash themselves, saying encouraging things to them as he made them fast. As the sun sank the wind grew more freezing, and I saw the strength of some of the men leaving them fast. The captain shook hands with me, and, on the chance of my being saved, gave me some messages to take home. He likewise handed me his watch and chain, and I put them in my pocket. The canvas streamed in ribbons from the yards, and the noise was like a continuous roll of thunder overhead. It was dreadful to look down and watch the decks ripping up, and notice how every sea that rolled over the wreck left less of her than it found.

The moon went quickly away—it was a young moon with little power—but the white water and the starlight kept the night from being black, and the frame of the vessel stood out like a sketch done in ink every time the dark seas ran clear of her and left her visible upon the foam. There was no talking, no calling to one another; the men hung in the topmast rigging like corpses, and I noticed the second mate to windward of his brother in the top, sheltering him, as best he could, poor fellow, with his body from the wind that went through our skins like showers of arrows. On a sudden I took it into my head to fancy that the mizenmast wasn't so secure as the foremast. It came into my mind like a fright, and I called to the captain that I meant to make for the foretop. I don't know whether he heard me or whether he made any answer. Maybe it was a sort of craze of mine for the moment, but I was wild with eagerness to leave that mast as soon as ever I began to fear for it. I cast my lashings adrift and gave a look at the deck, and saw that I must not go that way if I did not want to be drowned. So I climbed into the crosstrees, and swung myself on to the stay, so reaching the maintop, and then I scrambled on to the main topmast crosstrees, and went hand over hand down the topmast stay into the foretop. Had I reflected before I left the mizentop, I should not have believed that I had the strength to work my way for'rards like that; my hands felt as if they were skinned and my finger-joints appeared to have no use in them. There were nine or ten men in the foretop, all lashed and huddled together. The mast rocked sharply, and the throbbing of it to the blowing of the great tatters of canvas was a horrible sensation.

From time to time they sent up rockets from the Sunk lightship—once every hour, I think—but we had long since ceased to notice those signals. There was not a man but thought his time was come, and, though death seemed terrible when I looked down upon the boiling waters below, yet the anguish of the cold almost killed the craving for life. It was now about three o'clock on Thursday morning; the air was full of the strange, dim light of the foam and the stars, and I could very plainly see the black swarm of men in the top and rigging of the mizenmast. I was looking that way, when a great sea fell upon the hull of the ship with a fearful crash; a moment after, the mainmast went. It fell quickly, and, as it fell, it bore down the mizenmast. There was a horrible noise of splintering wood and some piercing cries, and then another great sea swept over the after-deck, and we who were in the foretop looked and saw the stumps of the two masts sticking up from the bottom of the hold, the mizenmast slanting over the bulwarks into the water, and the men lashed to it drowning. There never was a more shocking sight, and the wonder is that some of us who saw it did not go raving mad. The foremast still stood, complete to the royal mast and all the yards across, but every instant I expected to find myself hurling through the air. By this time the ship was completely gutted, the upper part of her a mere frame of ribs, and the gale still blew furiously; indeed, I gave up hope when the mizenmast fell, and I saw my shipmates drowning on it.

It was half an hour after this that a man, who was jammed close against me, pointed out into the darkness and cried in a wild hoarse voice, "Isn't that a steamer's light?" I looked, but what with grief and suffering and cold, I was nearly blinded and could see nothing. But presently another man called out that he could see a light, and this was echoed by yet another; so I told them to keep their eyes upon it and watch if it moved. They said by-and-by that it was stationary; and though we could not guess that it meant anything good for us, yet this light heaving in sight and our talking of it gave us some comfort. When the dawn broke we saw the smoke of a steamer, and agreed it was her light we had seen; but I made nothing of that smoke, and was looking heart-brokenly at the mizenmast and the cluster of drowned men washing about it, when a loud cry made me turn my head, and then I saw a life-boat under a reefed foresail heading direct for us. It was a sight, sir, to make one crazy with joy, and it put the strength of ten men into every one of us. A man named Gillmore stood up and waved a long strip of canvas. But I believe they had seen there were living men aboard us before that signal was made.

The boat had to cross the broken water to fetch us, and in my agony of mind I cried out, " She'll never face it ! She'll leave us when she sees that water ! " for the sea was frightful all to windward of the Sand and over it, a tremendous play of broken waters, raging one with another, and making the whole surface resemble a boiling cauldron. Yet they never swerved a hair's breadth. Oh, sir, she was a noble boat ! We could see her crew—twelve of them—sitting on the thwarts, all looking our way, motionless as carved figures, and there was not a stir among them as, in an instant, the boat leapt from the crest of a towering sea right into the monstrous broken tumble. The peril of these men, who were risking their lives for ours, made us forget our own situation. Over and over again the boat was buried, but as regularly did she emerge, with her crew fixedly looking our way, and their oilskins and the light-coloured side of the boat sparkling in the sunshine, while the coxswain, leaning forward from the helm, watched our ship with a face of iron. By this time we knew that this boat was here to save us, and that she *would* save us, and, with wildly beating hearts, we unlashed ourselves, and dropped over the top into the rigging. We were all sailors, you see, and knew what the life-boat men wanted, and what was to be done. Swift as thought we had bent a number of ropes' ends together, and securing a piece of wood to this line, threw it overboard, and let it drift to the boat. It was seized, a hawser made fast, and we dragged the great rope on board. By means of this hawser the life-boat men hauled their craft under our quarter, clear of the raffle. But there was no such rush made for her as might be thought. No! I owe it to my shipmates to say this. Two of them shinned out upon the mizenmast to the body of the second mate, that was lashed eight or nine feet away over the side, and got him into the boat before they entered it themselves. I heard the coxswain of the boat—Charles Fish by name, the fittest man in the world for that berth and this work—cry out, "Take that poor fellow in there!" and he pointed to the body of the captain, who was lashed in the top with his arms over the mast, and his head erect and his eyes wide open. But one of our crew called out, "He's been dead four hours, sir," and then the rest of us scrambled into the boat, looking away from the dreadful group of drowned men that lay in a cluster round the prostrate mast. The second mate was still alive, but a maniac; it was heartbreaking to hear his broken, feeble cries for his brother, but he lay quiet after a bit, and died in half an hour, though we chafed his feet and poured rum into his mouth, and did what men in our miserable plight could for a fellow-sufferer. Nor were we out of danger yet, for the broken water was enough to turn a man's hair grey to look at. It was a fearful sea for us men to find ourselves in the midst of, after having looked at it from a great height, and I felt at the beginning almost as though I should have been safer on the wreck than in that boat. Never could I have believed that so small a vessel could meet such a sea and live. Yet she rose like a duck to the great roaring waves which followed her, draining every drop of water from her bottom as she was hove up, and falling with terrible suddenness into a hollow, only to bound like a living thing to the summit of the next gigantic crest.

When I looked at the life-boat's crew and thought of our situation a short while since, and our safety now, and how to rescue us these great-hearted men had imperilled their own lives, I was unmanned; I could not thank them, I could not trust myself to speak. They told us they had left Ramsgate harbour early on the preceding afternoon, and had fetched the Knock at dusk, and not seeing our wreck had lain to in that raging sea, suffering almost as severely as ourselves, all through the piercing tempestuous night. What do you think of such a service, sir? How can such devoted heroism be written of, so that every man who can read shall know how great and beautiful it is? Our own sufferings came to us as a part of our calling as seamen. But theirs was bravely courted and endured for the sake of their fellow-creatures. Believe me, sir, it was a splendid piece of service; nothing grander in its way was ever done before, even by Englishmen. I am a plain seaman, and can say no more about it all than this. But when I think of what must have come to us eleven men before another hour had passed, if the life-boat crew had not run down to us, I feel like a little child, sir, and my heart grows too full for my eyes.

The facts of the foregoing statement were no doubt given in detail by the mate, but the narrative owes much of its graphic power to the newspaper writer, from whose report of the work done by the life-boat we add some extracts :

Two days had elapsed (continues the writer in the *Daily Telegraph*) since the rescue of the survivors of the crew of the *Indian Chief*, and I was gazing with much interest at the victorious life-boat as she lay motionless upon the water of the harbour. It was a very calm day, the sea stretching from the pier-sides as smooth as a piece of green silk, and growing vague in the wintry haze of the horizon, while the white cliffs were brilliant with the silver sunshine. It filled the mind with strange and moving thoughts to look at that sleeping life-boat, with her image as sharp as a coloured photograph shining in the clear water under her, and then reflect upon the furious conflict she had been concerned in only two nights before, the freight of half-drowned men that had loaded her, the dead body on her thwart, the bitter cold of the howling gale, the deadly peril that had attended every heave of the huge black seas. Within a few hundred yards of her lay the tug, the sturdy steamer that had towed her to the Long Sand, that had held her astern all night, and brought her back safe on the following afternoon. The tug had suffered much from the frightful tossing she had received, and her injuries had not yet been dealt with; she had lost her sponsons, her starboard side-house was gone, the port side of her bridge had been started, and the iron railing warped, her decks still seemed dank from the remorseless washing, her funnel was browned with rust, and the tough craft looked a hundred years old. Remembering what these vessels had gone through, how they had but two days since topped a long series of merciful and dangerous errands by as brilliant an act of heroism and humanity as any on record, it was difficult to behold them without a quickened pulse. I recalled the coming ashore of their crews, the life-boatmen with their great cork jackets around them, the steamer's men in streaming oilskins, the faces of many of them livid with the cold, their eyes dim with the bitter vigil they had kept, and the furious blowing of the spray; and I remembered the bright smile that here and there lighted up the weary faces, as first one and then another caught sight of a wife or a sister in the crowd waiting to greet and accompany the brave hearts to the warmth of their humble homes. I felt that while these crews' sufferings and the courage and resolution they had shown remained unwritten, only half of a very stirring and manful story had been recorded. The narrative by the coxswain of the life-boat, Charles Fish, is given with great detail in the same number of the *Life-Boat Journal*, but we have space only for the concluding paragraphs.

We lay to all night, despite the bitter cold and fierce seas, that we might be at hand when the dawn would show where she was. The morning had only just broke, and the light was grey and dim, and down in the west it still seemed to be night; the air was full of spray, and scarcely were we a-top of a sea than we were rushing like an arrow into the hollow

Wreck of the "Indian Chief." 209

again, when young Tom Cooper bawled out, "There she is!" pointing with his hand. The moment he sung out and pointed, all hands cried out, "There she is!" But what was it, sir? Only a mast about three miles off—just one single mast sticking up out of the white water. Yet that was the ship we had been waiting all night to see. There she was, and my heart thumped in my ears the moment my eye fell on that mast. "Up foresail," I shouted, and two minutes after we had sighted that mast we were dead before the wind, our storm foresail taut as a drum-skin, our boat's stem heading full for the broken seas and the lonely stranded vessel in the midst of them. It was well that there was something in front of us to keep our eyes that way, and that none of us thought of looking astern, or the sight of the high and frightful seas which raged after us might have unnerved the stoutest hearts. Some of them came with such force that they leapt right over the boat, and the air was dark with water flying a dozen yards high over us in broad solid sheets, which fell with a roar. But we took no notice of these seas even when we were in the thick of the broken waters, and all the hands holding on to the thwarts for dear life. Every thought was upon the mast that was growing bigger and clearer, and sometimes when a sea hove us high we could just see the hull, with the water as white as milk flying over it. The mast was what they called "bright," that is scraped and varnished, and we knew that if there was anything living aboard that doomed ship we should find it on that mast; and we strained our eyes with all our might, but could see nothing that looked like a man.

But on a sudden I caught sight of a length of canvas streaming out of the top, and all of us seeing it we raised a shout, and a few minutes after we saw the men. They were all dressed in yellow oilskins, and the mast being of that colour was the reason why we did not see them sooner. They looked a whole mob of people, and one of us roared out, "All hands are there, men!" and I answered, "Aye, the whole ship's company, and we'll have them all!" for though, as we afterwards knew, there were only eleven of them, yet, as I have said, they looked a great number huddled together in that top, and I made sure the whole ship's company were there. By this time we were pretty close to the ship, and a fearful wreck she looked, with her mainmast and mizenmast gone, and her bulwarks washed away, and great lumps of timber and planking ripping out of her and going overboard with every pour of the seas. We let go our anchor fifteen fathoms to windward of her, and as we did so we saw the poor fellows unlashing themselves and dropping one by one over the top into the lee rigging. As we veered out cable and drove down under her stern, I shouted to the men on the wreck to bend a piece of wood on to a line and throw it overboard for us to lay hold of. They did this, but they had to get aft first, and I feared for the poor half-perished creatures again and again as I saw them scrambling along the lee rail, stopping and holding on as the mountainous seas swept over the hull, and then creeping a bit further aft in the pause. There was a horrible muddle of spars and torn canvas and rigging under her lee, but we could not guess what a fearful sight was there until our hawser having been made fast to the wreck, we had hauled the life-boat close under her quarter. There looked to be a whole score of dead bodies knocking about among the spars. It stunned me for a moment, for I had thought all hands were in the foretop, and never dreamt of so many lives having been lost. Seventeen were drowned, and there they were, most of them, and the body of the captain lashed to the head of the mizenmast, so as to look as if he were leaning over it, his head stiff upright and his eyes watching us, and the stir of the seas made him appear to be struggling to get to us. I thought he was alive, and cried to the men to hand him in, but someone said he was killed when the mizenmast fell, and had been dead four or five hours.

Well, sir, the rest of this lamentable story has been told by the mate of the vessel, and I don't know that I could add anything to it. We saved the eleven men, and I have since heard that all of them are doing well. If I may speak, as coxswain of the life-boat, I would like to say that all hands concerned in this rescue, them in the tug as well as the crew of the boat, did what might be expected of English sailors—for such they are, whether you call some of them boatmen or not ; and I know in my heart, and say it without fear, that from the hour of leaving Ramsgate Harbour to the moment when we sighted the wreck's mast, there was only one thought in all of us, and that was that the Almighty would give us the strength and direct us how to save the lives of the poor fellows to whose assistance we had been sent.

THE TALKING WOOD CHIP.

AN INCIDENT OF EARLY MISSIONARY DAYS IN RAROTONGA.

AMONG the islands of the Pacific Ocean there is no one which has been more wonderfully transformed, by the influence of Christian missions, than Rarotonga, in the Hervey Island group. This group was formerly called Cook's Islands, having been first brought to notice by the great navigator, who arrived at the adjoining island of Mangaia in March 1777. Rarotonga was not known till long afterwards, and the first missionary who planted the gospel there was John Williams, " the martyr of Erromango."

We have heard much of these Hervey Islands in recent times from the letters and books of the Rev. W. Wyatt Gill, one of the most accomplished as well as devoted of the many noble missionaries who have spent their lives in spreading peace and true happiness in these distant isles of the sea. In the Hervey group, pagan idolatry, with all its horrible crimes and cruelties, has long ceased to exist. The savage is now completely civilized. The bulk of the population read the word of God intelligently in their own tongue. A large number are members of churches, the young are taught in schools, and the natives help, by their industry and trade, to send the gospel to islands less favoured. Such is the result of the good work of which the Rev. John Williams was the pioneer.

From the "Narrative of a Missionary Enterprise in the South Sea Islands," the book in which Williams first published a record of his work in connection with the London Missionary Society, we give a description of some of his early experiences in Rarotonga. After a period of absence, native teachers having been left in charge of the converts, he returned to visit the station.

We found, he says, the teachers and people just about to abandon the old settlement, a new one having been formed on the eastern side of the island. As the Thursday after our arrival was the day appointed for the removal, we determined not to interfere with this or any other arrangement, until, by a more accurate acquaintance with the affairs of the station, we should be enabled to take the arrangement of the Mission into our own hands. On Wednesday afternoon we attended service, when one of the teachers addressed the assembly; after which, the multitude gave us a welcome by a hearty shake of the hand. As there were between two and three thousand of them, and they considering that the sincerity of their affection was to be expressed by the severity of the squeeze, and the violence of the shake, we were not sorry when the ceremony was over, for our arms ached severely for hours after. Early the following morning, with nearly the whole of the inhabitants of the island, we proceeded to the new station, to which we found but little difficulty in getting our things conveyed, as every person was desirous of carrying some part of our property. One took the tea-kettle, another the frying-pan; some obtained a box, others a bedpost; even the chief himself felt honoured in rendering assistance, and during the journey he ceased not to manifest his admiration of the devices printed upon the articles of earthenware with which he was entrusted, and to exhibit them to the crowd that surrounded him.

A heavy fall of rain had rendered the ordinary road unfit for travelling, or otherwise the walk would have been delight-

The Talking Wood Chip. 213

ful; but as the kind people conveyed goods, wives and children, upon their Herculean shoulders, all delighted with their occupation, the journey was by no means unpleasant.

On our arrival, we found that the teachers had very comfortable houses, one of which they most cheerfully gave up to us. A day or two afterwards, they requested us to take our seat outside the door; and on doing so, we observed a large concourse of people coming towards us, bearing heavy burdens. They walked in procession, and dropped at our feet fourteen immense idols, the smallest of which was about five yards in length. Each of these was composed of a piece of aito, or iron wood, about four inches in diameter, carved with rude imitations of the human head at one end, and with an obscene figure at the other, wrapped round with native cloth, until it became two or three yards in circumference. Near the wood were red feathers, and a string of small pieces of polished pearl shells, which were said to be the manava, or soul of the god. Some of these idols were torn to pieces before our eyes; others were reserved to decorate the rafters of the chapel we proposed to erect; and one was kept to be sent to England, which is now in the Missionary Museum. It is not, however, so respectable in appearance as when in its own country; for the Custom House officers in London, fearing lest the god should be made a vehicle for defrauding the revenue, very unceremoniously took it to pieces; and not being so well skilled in making gods as in protecting the revenue, they have not made it so handsome as when it was an object of veneration to the deluded Rarotongans. An idol was placed upon the fore part of every fishing canoe; and when the natives were going on a fishing excursion, prior to setting off, they invariably presented offerings to the god, and invoked him to grant them success. Surely professing Christians may learn a lesson from this practice. Here we see pagans of the lowest order imploring the blessing of their gods upon their ordinary occupations,—a lesson to Christians to do likewise.

On the following Sabbath, a congregation of about four thousand assembled; but as the house was a temporary building, and would not accommodate half the people, they took their seats outside. This induced us to determine to erect immediately a place of worship. With this view the chiefs and people were convened, and arrangements made for commencing the building; and so great was the diligence with which the people laboured, that although ill supplied with tools, the house was thoroughly completed in two months. It was one hundred and fifty feet in length, and sixty wide; well plastered, and fitted up throughout with seats. It had six large folding-doors. The front windows were made in imitation of sashes, whilst those in the back resembled Venetian blinds. It was a large, respectable, and substantial building; and the whole was completed without a single nail, or any iron-work whatever. It will accommodate nearly three thousand persons.

In the erection of this chapel, a circumstance occurred which will give a striking idea of the feelings of an untaught people, when observing for the first time the effects of written communications. As I had come to the work one morning without my square, I took up a chip, and with a piece of charcoal wrote upon it a request that Mrs. Williams would send me that article. I called a chief who was superintending his portion of the work, and said to him, "Friend, take this; go to our house, and give it to Mrs. Williams." He was a singular-looking man, remarkably quick in his movements, and had been a great warrior: but, in one of the numerous battles he had fought, had lost an eye, and giving me an inexpressible look with the other, he said, "Take that! she will call me a fool and scold me, if I carry a chip to her." "No," I replied, "she will not, take it, and go immediately; I am in haste." Perceiving me to be in earnest, he took it, and asked, "What must I say?" I replied, "You have nothing to say, the chip will say all I wish." With a look of astonishment and contempt, he held up the piece of wood, and said, "How can this speak? Has this a mouth?" I desired him to take it immediately, and not spend so much time in talking about it.

On arriving at the house, he gave the chip to Mrs. Williams, who read it, threw it down, and went to the tool-chest; whither the chief, resolving to see the result of this mysterious proceeding, followed her closely. On receiving the square from her, he said, "Stay, daughter, how do you know that this is what Mr. Williams wants?" "Why," she replied, "did you not bring me a chip just now?" "Yes," said the astonished warrior, "but I did not hear it say anything." "If you did not, I did," was the reply, "for it made known to me what he wanted, and all you have to do is to return with it as quickly as possible." With this the chief leaped out of the house; and catching up the mysterious piece of wood, he ran through the settlement with the chip in one hand and the square in the other, holding them up as high as his arms would reach, and shouting as he went, "See the wisdom of these English people; they can make chips talk! They can make chips talk!" On giving me the square, he wished to know how it was possible thus to converse with persons at a distance. I gave him all the explanation in my power; but it was a circumstance involved in so much mystery, that he actually tied a string to the chip, hung it round his neck, and wore it for some time. During several following days, we frequently saw him surrounded by a crowd, who were listening with intense interest while he narrated the wonders which this chip had performed.

EUSTACHE, THE NEGRO SLAVE.

EUSTACHE was born in the year 1778, on the estate of M. Belin de Villeneuve, a planter in the northern district of the island of St. Domingo, now known as the Republic of Hayti. During his childhood he seemed indifferent to the society of the young negroes, and eagerly sought that of the whites. This did not proceed from any servility of disposition,

Eustache, the Negro Slave.

but evidently from the desire to avail himself of the advantage to be gained from intercourse with those above him in intelligence. His shrewdness and integrity induced his master to place him in the service of the overseers employed in the sugar-house, where he conducted himself in so unexceptionable a manner, that never was it found necessary to inflict even the slightest punishment on him; and while he gained the regards of his master by his good behaviour, he also contrived to acquire daily that influence which is the result of superior intelligence over the negroes of his own, as well as the adjoining plantations.

During the time M. Belin was travelling in Europe, symptoms of revolution began to be exhibited in St. Domingo. Eustache was at this time about nineteen years old, and then did he commence that course of noble disinterestedness which became a habit with him through life. Even at this early period of his life, the negroes who had revolted possessed such unbounded confidence in him, as to reveal to him their projects, and admit him into all their councils. He made a point of turning to good account the information he thus received, and by his address on one occasion, saved the lives of four hundred whites from being massacred by his infuriated countrymen.

About this time of tumult, M. Belin returned to St. Domingo. His faithful negro received him with joy, and advised him to take up his abode for safety near the sugar-work, where he had taken the precaution of providing provisions, at his own cost, with the knowledge of those blacks in whom he could repose confidence. Thus through the fidelity of Eustache, his master enjoyed a security and comfort unknown to the other proprietors in those troubled times.

At length a favourable occasion seemed to offer of obtaining deliverance from these dangers. An American vessel touched at the neighbouring coast, and after a consultation with his master, Eustache lost no time in agreeing with the captain to receive M. Belin on board during night. Another preliminary required to be settled: none of his master's property could at the moment be converted into money, and he could not leave home a beggar. Here the ingenuity of his faithful slave supplied a remedy for the evil : he collected the negroes of the estate, and appealed in the most feeling manner to their humanity; he succeeded beyond expectation, and, out of five hundred who were present, three hundred and sixty-five agreed to contribute a supply of white sugar : so that in a short time M. Belin was owner of a good cargo. While tears of gratitude flowed down the master's cheek, and he in vain tried to express his gratitude, his faithful friend declared that the only return he asked was permission to accompany him, and to share, if he could not alleviate, the sorrows that might await him.

The plan seemed to prosper; but, alas! they had scarcely been two days on board, when their vessel was seized by English privateers. How shall we describe the anguish of Eustache,—his master a prisoner, and deprived of all the resources it had cost him so much trouble to collect! But his motto seemed to be, " Never Despair." Difficulty seemed but to call forth his energies the more. Happily for him, he was a proficient in cookery, and it occurred to him, that he might turn this to account in gaining the good graces of the captains of the vessels. He succeeded beyond his expectation. Every day he produced some new dish, which seemed more relished than the last; and by-and-by he became such a favourite that they were almost disposed to prolong their voyage, so much did they enjoy feasting on the good things provided by the skilful Eustache.

They went on thus for some time, when an opportunity occurred too favourable not to be embraced for effecting their escape. It was agreed betwixt the American captain and Eustache, that an attempt should be made to regain their liberty by seizing the privateering ships, which were not strongly manned. Accordingly, one afternoon when they had feasted and drank in abundance, and were probably drinking Eustache's health, with three times three, the signal for a general movement on the part of the American seamen was made. The brave Eustache was foremost in the fray; he attacked them sword in hand. The captain also distinguished himself by his valour. Little resistance was made; and in a short time the English sailors were overpowered and made prisoners. The captain resumed the command of his own vessel, proceeded to Baltimore, his original place of destination, carrying along with him the ships which they had so gallantly captured.

Here M. Belin and his deliverer found many of the wretched inhabitants of St. Domingo, who had formerly been in opulent circumstances, reduced to the utmost necessity. The witnessing such scenes by the benevolent slave, took away from the pleasure he would otherwise have enjoyed in the improved situation of his master. The sugar had been sold to advantage, and the proceeds were a little fortune to them. Eustache engaged in a little commercial undertaking for the benefit of the necessitous friends of his master; and never did a day pass over his head in which the little produce of his labours did not help to relieve the sorrows of the poor and destitute.

The state of St. Domingo seemed to become more tranquil, and the fugitives ventured home. Scarcely, however, had they arrived, when a new insurrection arose, and a massacre of five hundred whites took place at one time. M. Belin was of the number of those who barely escaped with their lives; he was separated from his friend, and owed his safety to the protection of a Spanish captain, who happened to recognise him. Eustache anxiously sought his master, but without success; he continued to hope that Providence would some time throw them together; and in the meantime, in order to secure his trunks and a valuable chest of silver plate, he gave them into the custody of the wife of Jean Francois, a negro who stood high in the esteem of his companion. After placing the goods in safety, he went to the scene of carnage, and made a search for his beloved master's body, trembling lest he should discover him among the slain. He soon after learned at the Spanish fort, that M. Belin had been seen embarking in a sloop for the Mole of St. Nicholas, then occupied by the English. He determined immediately to rejoin him; but made the disagreeable discovery that the lady

Eustache, the Negro Slave. 219

to whom M. Belin's effects had been consigned was rather indisposed to part with them. Here a new exercise of ingenuity was requisite : he engaged himself as a sick nurse during an illness she had, waited on her for some time with the utmost assiduity, and one night, when she was sound asleep, assisted by some friendly negroes, he succeeded in carrying off what now constituted all his master's worldly wealth.

The arrival of Eustache at the Mole was celebrated like a fête. M. Belin had spread the report of his heroic devotedness ; and such was the public estimation in which he was held, that he was borne into the town as the hero of a triumphal procession, in honour of his noble and disinterested conduct.

M. Belin soon after went to Port-au-Prince, where he was appointed president of the privy council. Here Eustache, restored to domestic life, engaged himself in providing a mansion suited to his master's new dignity ; and little was that master aware that the luxuries and comforts he enjoyed in such profusion were the fruits of Eustache's daily labour. His freedom was at this time bestowed on him ; but in this case freedom and slavery were but names ; he remained the same faithful servant as ever.

Some time after, M. Belin was afflicted with sleeplessness and weakness of the eyes ; and he one day incidentally expressed a regret that Eustache had not been taught to read in his youth, as it would have been an agreeable way of beguiling the time to have him to read aloud occasionally. Without saying a word to his master, he immediately went and hired an instructor ; and, to prevent his lessons interfering with his other duties, he fixed four in the morning as his hour for study. Three months after, he approached his master with a newspaper in his hand, and, to his surprise and delight, began to read with the utmost fluency. What a remarkable instance of willingness and perseverance, and at the same time, of that delicate attention to the wishes of another, which one would think the refinement of woman alone could have suggested !

By a change in the government of St. Domingo, M. Belin had

his property once more restored to him. The arrival of General Leclerc, however, again excited the indignation of the blacks, and a scene of tumult ensued, when Eustache once more saved the life of his master. He had by this time become blind and very feeble, and the care of his faithful domestic could not ward off the stroke of the last enemy. He expired in the arms of one who had shown to him more than a father or a brother's love.

That M. Belin was not unmindful of his fidelity and regard, he proved, by leaving his property, in money as well as moveables, to his most faithful friend.

Though deeply afflicted, the benevolent mind of Eustache did not allow him to sink into that state of inactivity which sometimes follows intense grief. He found comfort in the performance of acts of charity to his fellow-men. To some he gave liberally of his money, to others he dispensed clothes and other necessaries. Was money required to send a poor forsaken infant out to nurse; was a soldier disappointed of his pay? in short, was there any exercise of liberality requisite; only let it be made known to Eustache, and his heart and his purse were opened, with a readiness that showed how much more blessed he thought it was to *give* than to *receive*. He at length so impoverished himself, that he found it necessary to engage himself in the service of General Rochambeau, whom he accompanied to England, and afterwards to France. We need not be apprehensive of lessening the admiration of our readers, by following out the history of Eustache to the day of his death.

From this period not a day passed unmarked by some act of humanity. It was justly remarked by a friend, that to him the exercise of benevolence was as natural as it was to others to inhale the air they breathed. One instance, among many, we quote.

He learned that a young female who had recently come from the country, had been deprived of her husband by death, and left totally unprovided for with four helpless children. He immediately went in search of her, clothed and fed her children, placed the oldest in a respectable apprenticeship at his own expense,—not forgetting to provide for him the tools necessary for practising his trade. Some time after, he had the reward of seeing that child grow up an active tradesman, and in the way of providing for the remainder of the family. On another occasion, being aware that an old friend of his master's had fallen into sickness and poverty, and that his master was unable to give the assistance his inclination would have suggested, he secretly devoted for a twelvemonth all the money he gained to the relief of this object of his solicitude. He delicately let it be understood that the charity bestowed was from his master; and it was not till the poor man came to express his gratitude to his benefactor that the disclosure was made, that that benefactor was no other than Eustache.

Eustache died 15th March, 1835, at the age of sixty-two. Had he lived in a country where virtue is as highly esteemed as genius or valour, a monument would have honoured his name.

In 1832 the French Academy had bestowed on him the first "Montyon Prize" for virtuous conduct. Never was that honourable distinction more worthily bestowed, although many a noble and generous life has been made known by this award, of which our next article gives some account.

THE MONTYON PRIZE OF VIRTUE.

THERE is published every year by the French Academy, that select and illustrious body to which the greatest men in science and literature aspire to belong, a programme of prizes, of which they are the trustees and awarders. Some of these prizes are for discoveries in science, or improvements in arts and manufactures; others for distinguished works in history or poetry, and various results of intellectual power and genius. But there are also some prizes for the encouragement of moral excellence, and among these the best known is tha called the Montyon Prize, given either in one award, or divided among several recipients, for virtuous conduct. There are some other prizes of a similar kind, but this is so conspicuous above all, that it is always spoken of as *the Prix de Vertu*. What was its origin ? and what are the deeds thus crowned with reward and honour ?

Before the great Revolution, there lived in Paris a lawyer, named M. Montyon, about whom little is known except that he was wealthy and beneficent. Much was heard in those days about " the *rights* of man "; this good citizen often told his friends that they ought to hear more about the *duties* of man. One of the first of these duties was to help the helpless, to relieve the destitute, to encourage charity, and good deeds. He thought that one way of promoting this true fraternity would be to award public prizes for acts of virtue and kindness, wherever they were found. Some remarkable cases were made known, but before long the storms of the revolutionary epoch broke out, followed by the military despotism of Napoleon, and the peaceful proposal of M. Montyon was neglected and forgotten.

After the fall of Napoleon, and the restoration of peace to France, M. Montyon, who had emigrated and lived in exile, returned to France. He resumed his work as a solicitor, and anonymously—so retiring and modest was he in his beneficence —he sent money to revive and enlarge the fund for the *Prix de Vertu*, which he had founded thirty years before. It does not appear that the donor was publicly known, but after his death, in 1820, he bequeathed four sums of ten thousand francs each, for these four good objects ; a prize for the book adjudged by the Academy to be most beneficial to morals ; a prize for the greatest improvement in the healing art, medical or surgical ; a prize for the discovery of lessening the danger or unhealthiness of any art or trade ; and lastly, a prize for the most virtuous action ; and this is the world-famed Prize of Virtue.

I have before me the official rules and conditions for this prize, and they show clearly the sorts of action to be recognized, and also the conscientious care in carrying out the worthy founder's good object. I ought to have said that before his death we find him bearing the title of Baron de Montyon, so that some one capable of judging, had discovered and honoured his character and merit. Well, the rules require that an account, in full detail, must be sent, signed by the Préfet, or Maire, or other responsible public functionary, and attested by neighbours and others in good position to witness the deeds reported to the Academy. These reports may come from any part of the French dominion; and one useful regulation is that the life of the candidate must have been known for at least two years previously. This excludes any award for sudden or single acts of courage, for which other rewards are always ready to be given, and shows that the Montyon award is intended rather for the encouragement of "patient continuance in well-doing," a much higher and more difficult virtue than a daring act which may be the result only of momentary impulse. The word "candidate" was used, but the cases are not competitive; in most of them the recipients are utterly unconscious of their deeds being observed, and are often greatly surprised when they hear of the awards.

On the day of the prize or prizes being given, the receiver appears either in person, or by proxy, and one of the members of the Academy delivers a discourse on virtue in general, and on the particular good deed or good conduct now to be specially recognised. All this seems to us rather "French" in idea and in style, and most of the English folk who might be worthy of such distinction would prefer letting their virtue "blush unseen," and not be blazoned by an eloquent Academician. However, it is "the way" in France, and the published reports or *éloges* of the Montyon orators form a most interesting and instructive record of noble and generous deeds, of which we have told one in the story of the Haytian negro Eustache; of a few others we give merely a brief mention.

Some of the instances have very little romance in them, so far as narrative goes, yet imply long and unwearying service made light by love. Such are histories of children toiling to support aged or disabled parents; nurses devoting themselves to the unpaid tending of the sick and suffering; a daughter who accompanied her mother to prison, and was allowed to remain with her; a young labourer who gave the earnings of years, to purchase the release of a conscript, the sorrow of whose mother he could not bear to witness; a young lady who refused a splendid offer of marriage, because she preferred being wedded to the poor among whom she toiled; a young graduate who surrendered his prospects, and went to a provincial town to take employment as a porter, in order to secure support for his parents suddenly reduced to poverty; and many such instances of humble devotion and self-denial.

"Unromantic," we said, but sometimes a gleam of romance meets us, as when we read of Alexandre Martin, the servant of the Marquis d'Aubespine, the descendant and representative of the great statesman, the Duc de Sully. After some generations the name of Sully became extinct in the male line, but a daughter of the family had carried the property and the ancestral domains to the house of Aubespine. At the time of the Revolution, the then marquis had to sell the castle of Villebon, and all that remained of the property of the great Sully. Out of the price he could only save enough to purchase for himself a life annuity of six thousand francs, another of two thousand four hundred francs for his son, and another of four hundred francs, for his faithful attendant, Martin, who had served him for thirty-five years. Soon after, the old Marquis died, and being in debt, the creditors, we do not know how, but unjustly as it seems to us, seized the annuity not only of the old man, but of his son and of Alexandre Martin. No redress could be obtained, and Martin went back to his native village, Champond-en-Gatinais, and worked as a carpenter, having learned the trade at the expense of the Marquis, before becoming his servant.

One day, in June 1830, his old master's son, the Count d'Aubespine, came to Martin's cottage, with his three children.

He told him that they had been left motherless; that he had lost all his property, and was leaving France for a time; and that he knew no one whom he could entrust with the care of his children, except Martin. Nothing was said about paying their expenses, and probably Martin guessed at once that the Count had no means of paying. Yet he hesitated not a moment, and gladly undertook the charge, for the sake of his old master, although he had three children of his own to provide for.

Martin's eldest daughter was able to earn a trifling sum, when not required for looking after the younger children, and his wife also gained a little by going out to work. His own earnings averaged only about thirty sous a day, and the whole household had to live on less than sixty sous a day. Nevertheless the Count's children were well cared for, and were treated with the utmost respect and consideration. They were served as if they were well-paying lodgers, the family living in the most frugal way, that the guests might feel no want. They ate brown bread that the little Aubespines might always have white, and old clothes had to be worn threadbare that they might be well clad. Something was even paid to the village curé for their education. The father never sent any money, nor indeed was he ever heard of, till news came of his death, six years after. The tidings became known in the neighbourhood, and inquiries began to be made about the guests in the carpenter's home. Some ladies at Chartres then offered to take charge of the two girls, and Martin's wife, with much regret, allowed them to go, well pleased that they would now be brought up as ladies, as the descendants of Sully ought to be. The third child, a son, was sent to a charitable foundation endowed by his great ancestor, and then, as Miss Yonge says, who tells the story in her book of "Golden Deeds" (Macmillan), "thus, the only portion of the wealth of Sully that ever reached his own descendants, was that which had been laid up in the true treasure house of Charity."

After a time, the rumour of what had been done reached

Paris, and came to the ears of the King, Louis Philippe, by whom a presentation was given for young Aubespine to the College of Henri IV., for completing his education. What his subsequent career was I do not know, but what concerns us now is that he was present, along with his generous benefactor, Alexandre Martin, at the annual meeting of the French Academy in 1838, when the Montyon prizes were awarded. The customary discourse was delivered by M. Salvandi, part of which deserves to be recorded: "Martin, your task is accomplished, you have deserved well of your country and of all good men. You have shown our age, what is too seldom seen, an example of gratitude, fidelity, honour. The Academy awards to your virtue the prize of 3,000 francs. And you, Louis d'Aubespine, as you are present at this solemn ceremony, may it make a deep and lasting impression on your young heart. You are entering life, as persons are sometimes forced to appear at maturer age, with all eyes upon you. Learn that the first of earthly blessings is to be honoured by one's country, and pray to God, who has watched over your infancy, to enable you to use that blessing that depends on our own efforts, and that no event can rob us of. One day you will be told that illustrious blood flows in your veins, but never forget that you must trace your line as far back as to the great Sully, before you can find a name worthy to stand beside that of Alexandre Martin. Grow up then to show yourself worthy of the memory of your ancestor, the devotion of your benefactor, and the patronage of the king."

Many similar cases of gratitude, fidelity, and exertion, on the part of servants and dependents, appear in the records of the Montyon awards. There is one in which a woman-servant named Rose Pasquer, at Nantes, entirely supported her master and mistress, who were reduced to penury by the loss of their West Indian estates. She had been eighty years in the service of the same family, and she was herself in her hundredth year when she received a prize, in 1856. Another woman, Madeleine Blanchet, had saved her mistress at the hazard of her own life during a time of revolutionary riot, and rescued some of the property from the plunderers. This was at Buzancais, in the Department Indre-et-Loire. When order was restored, and the rioters were tried for their atrocities, Madeleine was called as a witness. She told what she had seen, but said nothing as to the part she had taken. The judge said that witnesses had described her as covering her mistress with her own body, and being heard to declare that they should kill her before they injured her mistress. Was this true? "Yes, sir," she replied, and without appearing as if she had done anything out of the way. "If," said the President of the Court, after hearing all the evidence, "if there had been only twenty men in Buzancais with the heart of that woman, none of the disasters we deplore would have taken place." She received a gold medal, and an extra reward of 5,000 francs for her courage and devotion.

Another poor woman, the wife of Jacqnemin, a water-carrier in Paris, who had to support three children, one of them dumb and infirm, interested herself in seeking relief for a poor woman, reduced from better circumstances. In seeking help for her, the curate of the parish learned the poverty of this petitioner on behalf of others. He gave her ten francs, meaning it for herself, but with tears of gratitude she said, "Oh, how happy this will make Madam Petrel!" The worthy curate was the more interested by this incident, so expressive of charitable feeling. He inquired, and learned all the details of the poor water-carrier's self-denial and labour. He got friends to provide for the poor widow Petrel, and made known the circumstances of the Jacqnemins, and the mother received a Montyon award.

The cases last mentioned are those of women, and it is perhaps only what we might expect, that the majority of those rewarded should be of the gentler sex. In thirty-five years the proportion of those receiving prizes, including lesser awards, was 565 women to 211 men. As one of the orators said in announcing this fact, "Such is the *rôle* of the sexes respectively;

we make the laws, they form the manners and character. *Continuez à faire les lois, Messieurs, laissez les femmes faire les mœurs."* Although the examples cited have been chiefly those of the virtuous poor, the prizes are not restricted to humble life, nor to any class of the community. Some men of good social position have been as proud to receive the honour, as the poorest recipients have been grateful for the money. The prize has been also awarded to persons of all creeds and callings—to Roman Catholic sisters of mercy, for instance, and to the venerated Jean Bost, the founder and patient administrator of the Asylums of La Force, which are still superintended by members of his family.

Amidst all the future political or social changes of France, long may the French Academy continue its honourable and useful services, among which few have greater interest for us than the administration of the Montyon Prizes.

REMARKABLE ESCAPE FROM THE MASSACRE AT CAWNPORE.

ON a previous page (see p. 52) will be found a brief account of the origin of the Indian Mutiny. One of the most fearful episodes of that revolt of the Sepoy Army was the massacre of the English garrison and residents at Cawnpore. The details of that scene of carnage are given in the histories of the time, and can be read only with pain and horror. The following narrative of a wonderful escape is from the pen of Lieutenant Thompson, one of the very few survivors of that tragic event :

We had plenty of warning, he says, of what was to happen at our station, by the example that was set to our troops by those that were stationed at Meerut and Delhi. At Cawnpore we had the 2nd Light Cavalry, the 1st Regiment N.I., the 53rd

the Massacre at Cawnpore. 229

Regiment N.I., and the 56th N.I. The European part of the garrison consisted of the invalid depôt of H.M.'s 32nd Regiment, in all about 80 men, about 50 men of the Queen's 84th, 15 men of the 1st Fusiliers, and a company of European Artillery, 59 men; total, 204 fighting men. There were also a great many private individuals, such as civil engineers, tradesmen, writers in offices, etc.; in all, together with the soldiers, about 300 men. The ladies, women, and children, I am afraid to mention—certainly not less than 450.

It must have been about the 15th of May that rumours first began to spread that the 2nd Cavalry were ripe for mutiny, but this their officers declared was absurd, and if any one hinted at the idea of their mutinying they were quite offended. Things went on in this state until the 20th, when a fire broke out in the 1st lines; then the guns belonging to the artillery were sent down to the barracks occupied by the sick of the 32nd Foot, which was the site fixed upon for our position. There we were to make our stand if attacked by the rebels. A worse position could not have been chosen, as on the northwest side of the building there were several houses which quite commanded the wretched trenches which were thrown up around the barracks. You can imagine the consistency of the earthwork when I tell you it was hardly bullet-proof. In the next place, one of the barracks was thatched; but of course the rebels would not set fire to it! The magazine, alas! was hardly given a thought to; everybody said there was nothing in it. So the magazine was left alone.

To make matters worse, the Nana Sahib about this time came into Cawnpore, and offered our collector his assistance in protecting the treasury, in case the troops should rise. His offer was accepted; so he sent 400 infantry, 200 cavalry, and two small guns into Cawnpore for the treasury guard. Fancy married men, when these preparations for defence were being made, not sending their wives away to Calcutta out of danger! Many and many a time did I beg of the ladies I knew at all intimately to go away; but no, they said, "Why should we go ? The General keeps his family here ; surely there can be no danger for us ! " Poor creatures, how little did they know what was in store for them ! Provisions were laid in for a month, in case the place should be invested. Still no one thought of sending their families away.

Things went on in this unsettled way until the night of the 5th, or rather the morning of the 6th of June, when the cavalry went off towards the treasury, followed by the 1st N.I. The 53rd and 56th both remained under arms until daylight, when they were dismissed and sent to their lines. It was supposed that these regiments were staunch ; but about nine o'clock the 56th ran away, taking their colours with them, and they were immediately followed by our regiment. All made for the treasury, where they plundered nine lacs of rupees. The Nana's forces, which had come to protect us, of course never drew a sword in our favour. The regular troops, after getting all the money they could, were setting off for Delhi, and had actually gone some distance on the road, when they were sent for by the Nana, and told they had much better come back and murder the Feringhees, which could be very easily accomplished, as the magazine was well furnished with guns of all calibre, and ammunition enough to last for a twelvemonth. You see he knew better what was in our magazine than we did.

When the troops consented to return, the Nana sent a letter to the General to say he intended to attack his position the next morning (the 7th of June), and, true to his word, he commenced the attack by opening a 9-pounder gun on us. This was the beginning of a cannonade which lasted for twenty-two days, the equal to which I suppose is hardly known in history ; for we had pounding into us fourteen guns —viz., three 24-pounders, two 18-pounders, two 6-pounders, and seven 9-pounders. These, together with some 3,000 infantry, kept up an incessant fire all day, and at night they had three mortars playing on us, which very effectually kept us from getting rest.

the Massacre at Cawnpore. 231

How thankful I was when once their firing commenced that I had no relations in the entrenchments! Then it was that one heard husbands and fathers cursing their stupidity for not sending away their families; but of what avail was their only now having their eyes opened to their folly? It was too late. Wives saw their husbands' bodies mutilated in the most awful manner with round shot, and husbands saw their wives suffering the most excruciating agonies from wounds which they were unable to heal. Then there was the screaming of children after their dead parents. Poor little things, how it unnerved one to see them! but at last one got accustomed to the horrible scenes which were going on around, till at last they hardly made any impression.

One scene I can never forget. A poor woman of the name of White was walking along the trenches with her husband, and nursing her children (twins) in her arms; some fiend fired at them, killed the man, and broke both the poor woman's arms. The children fell to the ground, one of them wounded. Then followed a scene which can only be imagined. Fancy the poor woman throwing herself down beside her children and not being able to assist them on account of the wounds she had received! Another woman, who was in a wretched state, bordering on starvation, was seen to go out of the protection of the trenches with a child in each hand, and stand where the fire was heaviest, hoping that some bullet might relieve her and her little ones from the troubles they were enduring. But she was brought back, poor thing, to die a more tedious death than she had intended for herself. Here you saw poor Mrs. W. hit by a ball in the face, passing through the palate of the mouth; and by her side you saw her daughter who, although she was badly wounded in her shoulder, was doing all she could to alleviate the sufferings of her unfortunate mother. Poor creatures, they both died from their wounds! Then you saw an unfortunate native servant, who had remained faithful to her mistress, and was nursing her infant under the protection of the walls of the barrack, as she imagined; but all of a sudden you saw her knocked over, and the child hurled out of her arms, and on examination you found both her legs cut clean off by a round shot, but the child was picked up uninjured. Many other such horrid scenes could I describe, but, judging from my own feelings on the subject I know that I shall only be stirring up in the minds of those who may see this letter a feeling for revenge which can never be properly accomplished on the right objects of justice.

On the evening of the 9th of June the thatched barrack which I mentioned above was set fire to by the rebels. No arrangements had been made in anticipation of such an occurrence, so those who were able to get into the trenches were saved from the flames, but many a poor wounded man, who was unable to move, was burnt alive. All the medicine chests and surgical instruments were destroyed, so that all who were wounded or fell sick after this date were unable to be attended to.

During the time that the barrack was burning, we all expected the rebels to come down upon us, and if they had had the courage of anything in them except that of an Asiatic, they would certainly have made an attempt. But the wretches had not the heart to come nearer than 200 yards from the trenches. After this the cannonading continued, I must say, without intermission, until the 23rd of June (anniversary of the Battle of Plassey), committing frightful havoc amongst our little but heroic garrison, but still they were willing to hold out till the last, as they were told by General Wheeler that relief must come.

On the 23rd of June the rebels showed in great force around us, and made attempts on every quarter to get into our entrenchments. But all their endeavours were useless, as when the main body charged, a few were knocked over, and this intimidated the rest, and back they went with greater speed than they advanced. The rebel chieftain, finding he could not dislodge us by fair means, thought it wiser to adopt another plan, as I suppose he had heard some news of a force leaving Allahabad for our relief. Any way, he sent a woman, whom he had taken a prisoner, over to us with a letter to this effect:—

"TO THE SOLDIERS AND SUBJECTS OF HER MOST GRACIOUS MAJESTY QUEEN VICTORIA.

"All men who have in no way been connected with the Act of Lord Dalhousie, and are willing to lay down their arms, shall have permission and protection to proceed to Allahabad."

This artfully-worded letter, I am sorry to say, had its desired effect, and a brave officer, Captain Moore, who had always had the management and carrying out of any little enterprise which was set on foot, such as the spiking of the enemy's guns, or charging the rascals when they congregated in the building near us—this man, who seemed to be the very life of our garrison, was immediately for making a treaty with the enemy. We all expected he would be the last to give in. He did not know with whom he wished to treat. Poor fellow, he had a wife in the trenches, and this must have biassed him in a great measure. He saw that in making a treaty there was some chance of escape for the women and children, but unless relief came for us he knew we must give in at last, as provisions were running short, and then I suppose he thought something more awful would happen. Poor M. had not been long in the country, or he would never have attempted to treat with a native of India, especially a Mahratta.

General Wheeler, although not wishing to treat with the Nana, told Captain M. that he might do what he thought proper. Accordingly, a treaty was signed that very evening, 26th of June, 1857. The following were the conditions of the treaty :—" That the garrison should give up their guns, ammunition, and treasure; should be allowed to carry their muskets and sixty rounds of cartridges with them; that the Nana should provide carriages for the sick, wounded, women, and children, to the river's bank, where boats should be in readiness to convey all to Allahabad." This seemed to promise a speedy release from our troubles; but many an one seemed to doubt the fulfilment of the same. A committee was sent down to the boats to see all was in preparation for our departure the following morning, and nothing was found wanting. The morning broke and found everyone getting ready for our departure. The carriages came down at sunrise for our wounded, etc., etc.; and, after making over all our military stores, as agreed upon, we marched off for the boats. We reached them in safety, and everybody who left the trenches on the memorable morning of the 27th of June, 1857, got on board safely. But immediately we began to shove off from the shore, at a given signal from the rebels, all our boatmen deserted us, leaving fire in the thatches of the boats; the consequence was, they were all in a blaze very quickly. The guns opened on us from the Cawnpore side of the river, with a frightfully heavy fire of musketry.

I must now come to the egotistical part of my narrative, as it is impossible for me to describe what became of the rest of our unfortunate garrison except those with whom I came in personal contact. When the boat I first took shelter in was fired, I jumped out with the rest into the water, and tried to drag her off the sand-bank, but to no purpose; so I deserted her, and made across the river to the Oude side, where I saw two of our boats. It was an awful swim that! Grape-shot and bullets came whizzing along the water after my more unfortunate companions, several of whom I saw perish close beside me; but still I persevered in my object to gain the boats, which at last I succeeded in doing. It was a hard struggle, I can assure you, as I was rather heavily clothed for so long a swim. How I thanked God for having learned to swim! I had on a regimental pair of cloth trousers and a flannel shirt, so you can imagine the weight of them when they got thoroughly saturated. When I arrived at the boat I was so much exhausted that I was obliged regularly to be pulled on board.

The two boats managed to keep together for about a mile down the river, when a round shot went through the rearmost one, and rendered it useless, so we took all her passengers on board our boat. [There were now in this boat more than fifty persons, including women and children; there were a large number of officers.] With this boat-load we managed to get ahead five or six miles down the river; but as the rebels continued to follow us on the Oude side, with two guns and about 2,000 infantry and cavalry, who kept up an incessant fire, you may suppose our numbers were considerably thinned. The first day we lost Captain Moore, Captain Ashe, Lieutenant-Colonel Wiggins, Lieutenants Burney, Glanville, Satchwell, and Bassilico; wounded, Major Vibart, Captain A. Turner, Lieutenants Fagan, Mainwaring, Master Henderson, and myself. I received a severe wound on the head with a bullet. I was hit in two other places, merely contusions, but still unpleasant.

We remained where the boat grounded until nightfall, when we managed to get once more afloat, and, will you believe it, the rascals followed us down the river with torches and lighted arrows in their hands, doing all they could to fire our boat, so we were obliged to throw overboard the thatched covering we had to protect us from the sun and rain. We sailed on after this for some hours in peace; but when we arrived at Nuzzuffghur, some distance down the Ganges, we again got aground, and again fell in with the enemy, who brought a gun to bear upon us, with which, through God's mercy, they were unable to do us any harm.

Our numbers were again thinned by the musketry. As the enemy came by mistake nearer to us than they intended, we beat them off with severe loss on their side, and they returned to Cawnpore to tell the Nana that they could do nothing with us; so the fiend sent two fresh companies of sepoys after us. During the time we were aground at Nuzzuffghur we lost Captain Whiting, Lieutenant Harrison, and several privates killed. Captain A. Turner again wounded, Captain Seppings and his poor wife, and Lieutenants Daniel and Quin wounded.

A tremendous storm coming on now freed us from this awful position, and we floated down the river till dawn, when we again stuck at a place called Soorajpore, and daylight revealed our position. We were immediately attacked by the sepoys belonging to a hostile zemindar; so I was sent on shore with Delafosse, a sergeant named O'Grady, 84th Foot, and eleven men, to beat off the rebels, whilst the rest of the survivors endeavoured to get off the boat. On our part we succeeded only too well; we drove off the scoundrels until they surrounded us on all sides, so we were obliged to try a retreat, which we partially effected—that is to say, we took shelter in a temple on the river bank, having only lost one of our number, the poor sergeant, who was hit in the eye by a bullet. I attempted to parley with the rascals, but was answered by a shower of bullets. The rebels tried all in their power to get us out of the temple; they brought a small gun to bear upon it, they tried to undermine the foundations, but all in vain. We still remained in possession, and still continued to knock them over, until at last they hit upon the idea of burning us out. After heaping the brushwood before the door (we could not help their doing this, as the temple was round, and had only one entrance), it was lighted, and we waited to see the result, and by God's blessing, the wind was blowing from such a quarter that it did us no harm—not a particle of smoke came inside. Again they piled the brushwood, and this time they threw powder into the fire, and the smoke came in in volumes; and, almost suffocated, we resolved, when the fire consumed itself, to make one rush for the river.

We waited our time, and, with a regular British cheer, out we went. Our enemies, although their numbers must have been forty to one against us, ran in all directions. Six of our poor fellows, who could not swim, charged home into the crowd, and met the death they sought. The remaining seven of us got into the river; two more were shot before they could make many strokes from the bank; but Delafosse, myself, privates Murphy, Sullivan, and Ryan, swam some distance down the Ganges, followed all the time by the mutineers, who continued firing at us, when Ryan (I suppose from

the Massacre at Cawnpore. 237

exhaustion), made for the shore, and was killed by three ruffians who previously had offered to protect Delafosse and Murphy, if they would give themselves up. But when their offers were rejected, they made a rush at their intended victims, but were baulked of their prey by the fugitives diving. Murphy received a severe rap on his head from one of their clubs. After this we swam on for some distance undisturbed ; so we thought, the coast being clear, we would take a rest.

I had hardly got into my depth, where I was sitting up to my neck in water, when looking behind me, I saw three men, armed, running along the shore, evidently making for us. I gave the alarm, and we were all off into the stream in a minute. When these natives came abreast of us they addressed me in a very respectful manner, and begged I would entrust myself to their charge, as they meant me no harm. Their Rajah, they said, was friendly to our Government, and if we would avail ourselves of his protection, he would send us safely to Allahabad. From the moment they addressed me I felt there was no treachery, so I went on shore, and was kindly received. The others at first hesitated, but at last yielded to my persuasion. These three men (sepoys in the service of the Rajah) took us to their village, and gave us a capital meal of dhâl and chupatties, which we devoured most eagerly, not having tasted food since we left Cawnpore. I cannot understand how our strength was kept up after so long a fast. We swam six miles down the river, which is a great feat to accomplish at any time, but after a three days' fast it really must sound very like an impossibility. Nevertheless, it is true. Our party remained a month with the old Rajah, and we were treated during our stay with all the kindness a native could show.

The Nana sent down for us twice (according to the records found at Cawnpore), but the Rajah refused to give us up, and immediately sent us across the river to a friendly zemindar, who supplied us with carriage for our trip to Allahabad, and an escort of a few men. We had, however, only to travel a few miles with this retinue, as we met a detachment of ours on its road to Cawnpore, so we determined to retrace our steps, and I joined General Havelock's force.

THE SIEGE OF JERUSALEM BY TITUS.

THE destruction of the city and temple of Jerusalem by the Romans, while one of the most memorable events in the history of the world, has also a special interest as a fulfilment of sacred prophecy. The woes predicted against the doomed city and its inhabitants were terribly carried into execution, and one of the Jewish nation has been the instrument used to tell the tragic tale. Josephus, in his books of the wars of the Jews, gives a detailed narrative of the siege and capture of the city by the Roman General, Titus, in whose camp and near whose presence he was during all the events which he describes. From his pages has been compiled* the following narrative. While we know that the "accursed nation" brought upon itself the terrible judgment of that time, we cannot refrain from a feeling of admiration at the courageous and determined resistance offered to the conquering Romans, and at the last efforts of Jewish patriotism.

When Titus had collected and arranged his forces, he proceeded to within three miles and three-quarters of the city, where he encamped at a place called the Valley of Thorns. Having selected six hundred choice horsemen he proceeded to survey the city, with the hope that the Jews would surrender;

* "The Judgment of Jerusalem," by the Rev. D. Patton, of New York, published by the Religious Tract Society, contains a complete view of the events predicted in Scripture, and fulfilled in history in these times. Many other books contain accounts of the siege, but all of them founded on the history of Josephus.

for he had heard that the citizens were desirous of peace, being sorely oppressed with the robbers. So long as he rode along the straight road, which led to the wall of the city, nobody appeared out of the gates; but when he went out of that road, and declined towards the tower of Psephinus, and led the band of horsemen obliquely, an immense number of the Jews leaped out suddenly through the gate, and intercepted his horse, and cut him and a few others off from the main body of his horsemen. By surprising personal courage he cut his way through the masses; and though several of his men were killed, and many darts thrown at him, still, shielded by the providence of God, he escaped unhurt, notwithstanding he had on neither his headpiece nor his breastplate.

Titus now divided his army into three portions. He stationed two legions in a fortified camp at the north, at a place called Scopus, less than a mile from the city. The fifth legion was stationed half a mile from them. The tenth legion he stationed on the Mount of Olives,—on the east side, about three-quarters of a mile from the city.

Seeing these determined preparations, the factions within the city were now compelled to cease their strifes, and unite for the common defence. They immediately put on their armour, and ran out upon the tenth legion, who were fortifying their camp, and fell upon them with eagerness. The Romans, having laid aside their arms in order to perform their work, were taken at disadvantage and in different parties, and were consequently thrown into great confusion. The success of this onset drew larger numbers from the city, who so pressed upon the tenth legion that they were driven back.

Titus now ordered that the space between Scopus and the wall of the city should be levelled. In four days they finished the work, cutting down the hedges and the trees, filling up the hollow places, and demolishing the rocky precipices, thus making a level place suitable for an encampment. Titus with the strongest part of his army encamped over against the wall on the north and western quarter, near the tower of

Psephinus. Another portion fortified itself near the tower of Hippicus; whilst the tenth legion still continued on the Mount of Olives.

Titus, in company with a few chosen men, made another survey of the walls, to fix upon the points of attack. In the valleys the walls were inaccessible for the engines. The first, or old wall round Zion, appeared too strong to be shaken. The place he finally fixed upon was where there was a gap, the first fortification being lower than the second, and not joined to it, the builders neglecting to build the wall strong where the new city was not much inhabited.

Before making the attack he determined again to propose terms of peace. In company with Josephus and Nicanor, he approached near the wall. Instead of listening to proposals, they hurled darts at the messengers, and severely wounded Nicanor in his left shoulder. This so incensed Titus, that he gave orders to set fire to the suburbs, also to bring forward timber to raise the banks or platforms, and to set the engines against the wall. This they did with great despatch, but not without serious annoyance from the Jews, who made frequent sallies both by night and by day, and did much injury to the Romans. The banks, however, were prepared, and the engines, seventy-five feet high, placed thereon, and brought to the wall. For awhile they plied their battering-rams without any serious hindrance from the Jews. Suddenly the Jews sallied forth, through an obscure gate at the tower of Hippicus, for the purpose of burning the engines and destroying the banks; and, with the courage of desperation, they went up to the very fortifications of the Romans. The conflict was fearful, —the Romans were driven back, and fire was applied to the engines and the banks. But as fresh legions, led on by Titus in person, came up, the Jews were forced to retreat within their walls. On the fifteenth day the Romans, by the incessant application of their battering-rams, succeeded in making a breach in the wall of the city at Bezetha. The troops immediately mounted this breach, and poured into the

The Siege of Jerusalem by Titus.

narrow and crowded streets. They were attacked from the roofs and side alleys with such fury, that with considerable loss they were compelled to retreat without the wall. It was some days before Titus could regain what he had thus lost, and again enter the streets of Bezetha. When he did return, the Jews fled from the outer wall, and entrenched themselves within the second one, which enclosed Acra. There being no armed force to resist, the gates were thrown open, when the army entered and demolished the wall and a large portion of the city.

Titus, having now removed his camp within the city, immediately commenced his attacks upon the second wall around Acra. The Jews divided themselves into several bodies, and in the most courageous manner defended this wall. John and his troops occupied the tower of Antonia and the northern cloisters of the temple. Simon, to whom was committed the defence of the wall, placed himself near the tower of Hippicus. The Jews made many violent sallies from the walls, and with the most determined boldness attacked the Romans. "Nor did either side grow weary," says Josephus, "but all day long there were attacks and fightings on the wall, and perpetual sallies from the gates. And the night had much ado to part them, when they began to fight in the morning. The night was passed without sleep on both sides, and was more uneasy than the day to them. The one was afraid lest the wall should be taken, and the other lest the Jews should make sallies upon their camps. Both sides lay in their armour, and were ready at the first appearance of light to go to the battle."

This continued for several days. Twice the Romans were driven back after effecting an entrance, and the breaches in the wall were repaired. But at length the Jews were compelled to take refuge in the temple and in Zion, or the upper city. Thus Titus regained possession of this second wall, which he immediately and entirely destroyed. He put garrisons in the towers on the south part of the city, and then devised his plan for the assault on the third wall.

Having gained the control of Acra, or the lower city, he decided not to proceed immediately, but to relax the siege a little, to allow the citizens time for consideration, supposing that his successes and demonstrations of power would decide them to surrender. To impress their minds the more deeply, he had his whole army drawn up in battle array in the face of the enemy, and for four days publicly distributed subsistence money among them. The historian adds, "The whole old wall and the north side of the temple was full of spectators; nor was there any part of the city which was not covered over with their multitudes, nay, a very great consternation seized upon the hardest of the Jews themselves, when they saw all the army in the same place, together with the fineness of their arms, and the good order of their men. And I cannot but think that the seditious would have changed their minds at that sight, unless the crimes they had committed against the people had been so horrid that they despaired of forgiveness from the Romans; but as they believed death with torments must be their punishment if they did not go on in the defence of the city, they thought it much better to die in the war."

This interval lasted four days. "But on the fifth, when no signs of peace came from the Jews, Titus divided his legions, and began to raise banks both at the tower of Antonia and at John's monument. His design was to take Zion, or the upper city, at that monument, and the temple at the tower of Antonia; for if the temple were not taken it would be dangerous to keep the city itself. So, at each of these parts, he raised his banks, each legion raising one." The conflict at these two points was exceedingly sanguinary, and for a time proved too much for the Romans. The determination of Titus to conquer became more settled and firm. Before proceeding to more extreme measures, he sent Josephus again to exhort the people to surrender. The Jews only ridiculed his exhortation, and by throwing stones and darts defied the utmost power of the Romans. Josephus was struck on the head with a missile, and carried to the camp insensible. At this time

The Siege of Jerusalem by Titus. 243

many of the people endeavoured to escape from the city, but they were either killed by the seditious, or destroyed by the Roman soldiers for the sake of the gold which they were said to have swallowed.

In order to bring the battering-rams and other engines to bear upon the walls, it became necessary, by means of timber and other materials, to erect new mounds. For the wall on the brow of Zion was on a precipice thirty feet high, whilst a deep trench defended the tower of Antonia. For seventeen days they were employed in raising these banks. There were now four great mounds. One at the tower of Antonia, raised by the fifth legion. Another, cast up by the twelfth legion, at the distance of about thirty feet from the first. The third, erected by the tenth legion, was on the north quarter of the old wall. The fourth, built by the fifteenth legion, was about thirty feet from the third. On all these banks immensely powerful battering-rams were placed.

John, who had possession of Antonia, carefully watched the operations of Titus, and was busy in excavating from within the wall at Antonia, so as to undermine and destroy the foundations upon which the engines of the Romans rested. Having supported the excavated ground, under the engines, with beams laid across, he brought in the most combustible materials, which he set on fire. So that while the Romans were working the engines, the materials beneath were burning, until the beams were burnt through, when the engines suddenly fell into the mine, and with many men were destroyed. This happened just as the Romans were in hopes of forcing the wall, and it very much cooled their ardour.

Two days after this, Simon made an attempt to destroy the other banks on the north side of Zion, for the Romans had begun to make the wall shake. They ran out suddenly, with lighted torches, and violently rushing through those who were working the engines, set these machines on fire. Although assaulted on every side with darts and swords, yet did they not give way, but caught hold of the machines. When the

Romans saw the flames, multitudes hurried from the camp to save their engines. Then the Jews fought with those who endeavoured to quench the fires. When the Romans endeavoured to pull the battering-rams out of the fire, the Jews caught hold of them through the flames, grappling them fast, although the iron upon them became red hot. The flames extended also to the banks. Many more rushed out from the city, and the Jews becoming still more bold drove back the Romans, pursuing them to the very fortifications of their camp, and there fought most desperately. This assault was concluded by Titus, with a body of troops, attacking the Jews in the rear. They immediately wheeled about, and attacked the new enemy. After a fierce conflict, the Jews were driven into the city, but the Romans lost their banks and battering-rams.

The Romans spent twenty-one days in reconstructing new mounds, when they again brought forward their engines. Those in the city felt that unless they could succeed in burning these also, it would be impossible longer to resist. The Romans felt that if these were destroyed it would be exceedingly difficult to construct others, as materials had become very scarce, owing to the fact that the trees about the city had already been cut down within a circuit of more than twelve miles.

The attack on Antonia was renewed, and the conflict continued with the utmost desperation on both sides. The engines were worked with wonderful power. The resistance and strategies of the Jews were perplexing and distressing to the army of Titus. The wall by night was so shaken by the battering-rams, in the place where John had undermined it for the purpose of burning the banks, as already stated, that it gave way and fell suddenly. This encouraged the Romans. But the Jews felt confident, as the tower of Antonia still stood. The Romans pressed on through this breach; but they found another wall within, which John had built up to protect the spot weakened by his own excavations. This, however, was more easily thrown down than the other. Titus encouraged his soldiers to advance, and take the tower of Antonia, saying,

The Siege of Jerusalem by Titus. 245

" If we go up to this tower of Antonia, we gain the city." The attack was renewed on the third day, and continued for fourteen days, when it was carried by the following bold stratagem. Twelve of the Roman guards upon the banks called to them the standard-bearer of the fifth legion and two others of a troop of horsemen and one trumpeter. These went, without noise, about the ninth hour of the night (*i.e.*, about three o'clock in the morning), through the ruins to the tower of Antonia ; and when they had killed the first guards of the place, as they were asleep, they got possession of the wall, and ordered the trumpeter to sound his trumpet. Upon this the rest of the Jewish guards fled, before anybody could see how many had entered, for they imagined that the number of the enemy must be great. Titus, hearing the signal trumpet, crowded forward his men, and entered through the breach. John and Simon rallied their forces, and attacked the Romans with the most determined courage and zeal ; " for they esteemed themselves entirely ruined if once the Romans got into the temple, as did the Romans look upon the same thing as the beginning of their entire conquest. A terrible battle was fought at the very entrance of the temple, and great slaughter was made on both sides. The contending forces had alternate success and defeat. At length the Jews' violent zeal was too much for the Romans' skill, and the battle already inclined entirely that way ; for the fight had lasted from the ninth hour of the night (*i.e.*, 3 a.m.), till the seventh hour of the day (*i.e.*, 1 p.m.) ; ten full hours.

Here occurred one of the most extraordinary displays of valour of the whole siege. " For there was one Julian, a centurion, famed for his skill in arms, bodily strength, and courage of soul, seeing the Romans giving ground and in a sad condition, leaped out, and of himself alone put the Jews to flight, when they were already conquerors, and made them retire as far as the corner of the inner court of the temple. From him the multitude fled away in crowds, supposing that neither his strength nor his violent attacks were those of a mere man.

He rushed through the midst of them, killing those whom he caught. As he ran he slipped upon the bloody pavement of the court, and fell upon his back. Immediately the Jews surrounded him, striking at him with their spears and swords. For a considerable time he defended himself with his shield, but being overpowered by the multitude, he cut his own throat and died." The Jews caught up his dead body, bore it with them as a trophy, put the Romans to flight, driving them from the temple area, and shut them up in the tower of Antonia, which they had gained by stratagem, and at a vast expense of time, and labour, and life.

Titus now gave orders to his soldiers to make a breach in the foundations of Antonia, except such portions as were needed for the garrison, and to make a ready passage for his army to come up. While these orders were being executed, he made one more effort to save the city and temple, sending Josephus as before. Josephus, speaking in the Hebrew language, urged upon the people a variety of considerations why they should, without any further shedding of blood, submit, and throw themselves upon the clemency of Titus. His manner was very earnest and sorrowful, speaking with groans and sobs which interrupted his words. This moved the people; but John cast reproaches and imprecations upon Josephus, and defied the power of the Romans, because this was God's city, and He would take care of it.

Having failed to make any arrangement with the Jews, Titus prepared his forces for an attack upon the temple. As he could not bring all his army into action, the place being so narrow, he chose thirty soldiers of the most valiant out of every hundred, and committing one thousand to each tribune, he ordered them to attack the guards of the temple about the ninth hour of the night (*i.e.*, 3 a.m.). They did not find the guards asleep, as they hoped, but were compelled to fight with them hand to hand, as with shoutings and great violence they rushed upon them. Those in the temple ran to the help of the guards. By reason of the darkness there was great confusion,

The Siege of Jerusalem by Titus. 247

and many of the Jews were slain by mistake by their own friends. The fight continued from 3 a.m. until 11 a.m. in the same place where it began, for neither party could say that they had made the other retire, so neither could claim the victory.

For the next seven days the Roman army was employed in throwing down some of the walls of Antonia, that a ready and a broad way might be made to the temple, that thus a much larger force might be brought into action. When this was accomplished, then the legions came near the first court, or court of the Gentiles. Seeing the enemy advancing to the holy house itself, in their desperation they set fire to the northwest cloister, which was joined to the tower of Antonia, and thus broke off thirty feet of that cloister, and thereby made a beginning in burning the sanctuary. Two days after this, on the twenty-fourth of Panemus, the Romans set fire to the cloister that joined to the other, when the fire went twenty-two and a half feet farther. Nor was the work of destruction in this quarter ended until the tower of Antonia was parted from the temple, even though it was in the power of the Jews to have stopped the fire.

When two of the legions had completed their banks, Titus gave orders that the battering-rams should be brought and set over against the western edifice of the inner temple; for before these were brought, the most powerful of all the other engines had battered the wall for six days together without ceasing, without making any impression upon it; the largeness of the stones and strong masonry of the walls was superior to the power of the engines. Others undermined the foundation of the northern gate, and after a world of pains removed the outermost stones; yet was the gate upheld by the inner stones, and stood still unhurt. The soldiers now brought their ladders to the walls to scale the place; but the Jews fell upon them, threw them back headlong, and got possession of the engines and destroyed them.

Titus the next day ordered the soldiers to quench the fire,

whilst he called a council of his generals to decide what should be done with the holy house. Some were for demolishing it; others would preserve it if the Jews would surrender, if not then to burn it. But Titus said "that he was not, in any case, for burning down so vast a work as that was,—it would be an ornament to the Roman empire; and that it should be spared, even though the Jews should fight from it." But the historian adds, "God had for certain long ago doomed it to the fire, and now that fatal day had come."

The consultation having ended, "Titus retired into the tower of Antonia, resolved to storm the temple the next day early in the morning." The more effectually to succeed, he determined to bring his whole army and encamp round about the holy house. When Titus thus retired, the seditious for a little while lay still; then suddenly they attacked the Romans who were quenching the fire, which had reached and was burning the inner court of the temple. But the Jews "were put to flight, and the Romans proceeded as far as the holy house itself; at which time one of the soldiers, without staying for any orders, and without any concern or dread upon him at so great an undertaking, and being hurried on by a certain divine fury, snatched somewhat out of the materials that were on fire, and being lifted up by another soldier, he threw a burning brand through a window into the rooms that were round about the holy house on the north side of it."

It will be remembered that the interior of the temple was richly furnished with the choicest woods, that the floors were of cedar, covered with fir; consequently the flames spread with great rapidity. "As the flames went upward, the Jews made a great clamour, . . . and ran together to prevent it; and now they spared not their lives any longer, nor suffered anything to restrain their force, since the holy house was perishing." A messenger ran to the tent of Titus, who was resting himself after the last battle, and told him, "whereupon he rose up in great haste, and as he was ran to the holy house in order to have a stop put to the fire. After him followed all

The Siege of Jerusalem by Titus. 249

his commanders and several legions. Then, both by calling with a loud voice to the soldiers, who were fighting, and by giving a signal to them with his right hand, he ordered them to quench the fire. But they did not hear what he said, having their ears dinned by the greater noise another way; nor did they attend to the signal he made with his hand. But as for the legions that came running thither, neither any persuasions nor any threatenings could restrain their violence; but each one's own passion was his commander at this time; and as they were crowding into the temple, many of them were trampled to death, whilst a great number fell among the ruins of the cloisters, which were still hot and smoking, and were destroyed: and those who came near the holy house made as if they did not hear Titus' orders, but encouraged those who were before them to set it on fire."

As Titus was unable to restrain the mad fury of the soldiers, and as the fire spread yet more and more, he went, with his commanders, into the Holy of Holies, and saw what was in it— viz., the golden censer, the ark of the covenant overlaid round about with gold, and the tables of the covenant, and over it the cherubim of glory shadowing the mercy-seat. The sight he found to be far superior to what he had previously heard. " As the flames had not yet reached to its inward parts, but were consuming the rooms about the holy house, supposing that the house itself might yet be saved, he came up in haste, and endeavoured to persuade the soldiers to quench the fire. He ordered the refractory to be beaten and restrained; yet were their passions too fierce for their regard for Titus, or their dread for those who forbade them. The hope of plunder induced many to go on, as having this opinion that all the places within were full of money, and as seeing that all round about it was made of gold." One of those who went into the place prevented Titus, when he ran out so hastily to restrain the soldiers, and soon the flames burst out from within the holy house itself, consuming the remains of the cloisters and the gates, also the treasury chamber, in which there was an immense quantity of money, garments, and precious goods. Thus total and thorough was the destruction by fire.

How signal the overruling providence of God! How marked the destruction! It was accomplished notwithstanding the strong desires of the Jews and their enemies to preserve it. The Jews themselves, and Titus through his soldiers, were the instruments employed for carrying out all that the prophets had written, and all that Jesus Christ had spoken concerning the overthrow and utter ruin of the city and the temple.

The new city Bezetha, the lower city Acra, and the temple on Moriah being in utter ruin, the only remaining portion of Jerusalem was Mount Zion, the upper city, or the city of David. This was connected with the temple by a bridge already described, which spanned the Tyropœon valley. Before proceeding against Zion, Titus made one more attempt to end the war by inducing the Jews to surrender. Standing upon the bridge he, through an interpreter, addressed the people, who were under the command of Simon and John.

The only reply was to require that they, with their wives and children, might go through the wall he had made about them into the desert, and leave the city to him. Titus was indignant that those whom he had conquered should make their own terms as if they were the conquerors. He told them " that they should no more come out to him as deserters, nor hope for any further security; for that he would henceforth spare nobody, but fight them with his whole army; and that they must save themselves as well as they could, for that he would from henceforth treat them according to the laws of war."

Now when Titus perceived that Zion, or the upper city, was so steep that it could not be taken without raising banks against it, he distributed the work among his army. The carriage of the materials was difficult, since all the trees within a distance of twelve miles had been cut down to make the former banks. The banks of the four legions, however, were raised on the west side of the city, over against the royal

The Siege of Jerusalem by Titus. 251

palace. The banks erected by the other troops were at the Xystus, an immense open place on the extreme east, surrounded by a covered colonnade, where the people often assembled, and from whence they reached the bridge. Whilst these preparations were advancing, the commanders of the Idumeans, whom the people had formerly received into the city to defend them against the seditious, surrendered themselves. They were received as prisoners by Titus, and were sold into slavery by his soldiers.

In eighteen days the banks were finished, and the battering-rams brought against the wall. Despairing of saving the city, many of the Jews fled from the wall, and took refuge in the citadel; whilst others went down into the subterranean vaults. Still a great many defended themselves against those who brought the engines. The numbers of the Romans prevailed. As soon as a part of the wall was battered down, and certain of the towers yielded, a great terror fell upon the Jews; and before the Romans got over the breach they had made, they betook themselves to flight.

Thus becoming master of the wall, Titus placed his ensigns upon the towers, and made joyful acclamation for the victory they had gained, as having found the end of the war much lighter than its beginning. For when they had possession the last wall without any bloodshed, they could hardly believe what they found to be true. Seeing nobody to oppose them, they stood in doubt as to what it meant. But when they went in numbers into the lanes of the city, with their swords drawn, they slew those whom they overtook without mercy, and set fire to the houses whither the Jews were fled, and burnt every soul in them. And when they entered the houses to plunder them, they found in them entire families of dead men, and the upper rooms full of corpses of those who died by famine.

"When Titus saw the solid altitude and the largeness of the several stones, and the exactness of their joints, as also how great was their breadth, and how extensive their length, he said, 'We have certainly had God for our assistant in this war, and it was no other than God who ejected the Jews out of these fortifications, for what could the hands of man, or any machines, do towards overthrowing these towers?'" He gave orders that they should now demolish the entire city, leaving the towers of Phasaelis, Hippicus, and Mariamne, and so much of the wall as enclosed the city on the west side. This wall was spared to afford an encampment for those who were to remain in garrison, and the towers to demonstrate to posterity what kind of a city it was, and how well fortified, which the Roman valour had subdued. All the rest of the wall was so thoroughly laid even with the ground that there was left nothing to make those who came thither believe it had ever been inhabited. "This," adds the historian, "was the end to which Jerusalem came,—a city of great magnificence and of mighty fame among all mankind.

To commemorate this victory of Titus, the Roman senate, after his death, erected a magnificent triumphal arch, which to this day stands on the highest point of the Via Sacra, not far from the Colosseum. The two carved tablets are the best known of all Roman remains. One represents Titus on a triumphal car; the other the Jewish captives; the golden table, the seven-branched golden candlestick, silver trumpets, and other spoils from the temple. Whilst the Colosseum, the Forum, and the palaces of the Cæsars are in ruins, this arch stands as a monumental record of the destruction of Jerusalem by the Romans.

CAPTURE OF A SPANISH SLAVE SHIP.

THE time is not very remote when the traffic in human beings for slavery was openly defended in the British Parliament. A great advance in the annals of humanity was made, when the slave trade, through the exertions of Clarkson, Wilberforce, and other Christian men, was denounced, and slave traders ordered to be treated as pirates and robbers of the worst class. Although this resolution was assented to by other civilized nations, it is England which has mainly laboured, at much expenditure of life and treasure, to put down the nefarious traffic. We would not now refer to the crimes and cruelties of former days, were it not that voices are again being heard, not exactly defending the slave trade, but objecting to the employment of British ships and men in this humane service. There is danger, in fact, of the national conscience being deadened, and the national efforts relaxed in this matter. If our cruisers were withdrawn, there is every likelihood of the trade being revived, for there are still countries where slavery flourishes. Many travellers in Africa have described the fearful scenes connected with what Dr. Livingstone called "this plague spot of the world." Even worse than the fatal journeys of the slave gangs towards the coast are "the horrors of the middle passage." To show what these were, and may still be, we give part of the narrative of the capture of a Spanish slaver by a British ship, the *North Star.* The capture was witnessed by Dr. Walsh, a physician on board returning to England from Brazil.

The Spanish ship had taken on board 562 slaves, and had been out seventeen days, during which she had thrown overboard fifty-five dead bodies. On being sighted she made all sail, but the British ship gained on her, and after a chase of thirty hours, got within gun-shot and made her heave to.

The slaves were all enclosed under grated hatchways, between decks. The space was so low, that they sat between each other's legs, and stowed so close together, that there was no possibility of their lying down, or at all changing their position, by night or day. As they belonged to, and were shipped on account of, different individuals, they were all branded like sheep, with the owners' marks of different forms. These were impressed under their breasts, or on their arms, and, as the mate informed me, with perfect indifference, "burnt with the red-hot iron."

As soon as the poor creatures saw us looking down at them, their dark and melancholy visages brightened up. They perceived something of sympathy and kindness in our looks, which they had not been accustomed to, and feeling instinctively that we were friends, they immediately began to shout and clap their hands.

Some, however, hung down their heads in apparently hopeless dejection; some were greatly emaciated, and some, particularly children, seemed dying. But the circumstance which struck us most forcibly was, how it was possible for such a number of human beings to exist, packed up and wedged together as tight as they could cram, in low cells, three feet high, the greater part of which, except those immediately under the grated hatchways, were shut out from light and air, and this, when the thermometer, exposed to the open sky, was standing in the shade at 89°. The space between decks was divided into two compartments, 3 feet 3 inches high; the size of one was 16 feet by 18, and of the other 40 by 21; into the first were crammed the women and girls; into the second the men and boys; 226 fellow-creatures were thus thrust into one space 288 feet square, and 336 into another space 800 feet square. We also found manacles and fetters of different kinds; but it appears that they had all been taken off before we boarded. The heat of these horrid places was so great, and the odour so offensive, that it was quite impossible to enter them, even had there been room. They were measured as above when the slaves had left them, the officers insisting that the poor suffering creatures should be brought on deck to get air and water. It was then that the extent of their sufferings was exposed in a fearful manner. They all rushed like maniacs to the water. No entreaties, or threats, or blows could restrain them; they shrieked and struggled, and fought with one another, for a drop of this precious liquid, as if they grew rabid at the sight of it. There is nothing which slaves, in the mid-passage, suffer from so much as want of water. It is sometimes usual to take out casks filled with sea-water as ballast; and when the slaves are received on board, to start the casks, and re-fill them with fresh. On one occasion, a ship from Bahia neglected to change the contents of the casks, and, on the mid-passage, found, to their horror, that they were filled with nothing but salt-water. All the slaves on board perished.

I was informed by my friends, who had passed so long a time on the coast of Africa, and visited many ships, that this was one of the best they had seen. The height sometimes between decks was only eighteen inches; so that the unfortunate beings could not turn round, or even on their sides, the elevation being less than the breadth of their shoulders; and here they are usually chained to the decks by the neck and legs. In such a place the sense of misery and suffocation is so great, that the negroes, like the English in the Black Hole at Calcutta, are driven to frenzy. They had, on one occasion, taken a slave vessel in the river Bonny; the slaves were stowed in the narrow space between decks, and chained together. They heard a horrid din and tumult among them, and could not imagine from what cause it proceeded. They opened the hatches, and turned them up on deck. They were manacled together in twos and threes. Their horror may be well conceived, when they found a number of them in different stages of suffocation; many of them were foaming at the mouth, and in the last agonies,—many were dead. A living man was sometimes dragged up, and his companion was a dead body; sometimes, of the three attached to the same chain, one was dying and another dead. The tumult they had heard was the frenzy of these suffocating wretches in the last state of fury and desperation, struggling to extricate themselves. When they were all dragged up, nineteen were irrevocably dead. Many destroyed one another in the hopes of getting room to breathe; men strangled those next them, and women drove nails into each other's brains. Many unfortunate creatures, on other occasions, took the first opportunity of leaping overboard, and getting rid, in this way, of an intolerable life. Sometimes a mortal malady had struck them from which they never could recover. They used to lie down in the water of the lee-scuppers, and notwithstanding every care, pined away to skin and bone, wasted with fever and dysentery; and when at length they were consigned to the deep, they were mere skeletons.

It is an honour to England to lead the way in putting down the slave trade, and instead of withdrawing our cruisers, these ought to be the swiftest and strongest steamers that can be obtained. All success to them in their service! And still better, may the noble efforts of men like Livingstone and Gordon, and other Christian Englishmen in Africa, avail to put an end to this inhuman traffic!

SAVED FROM A FLOATING SEPULCHRE.

IN the month of April 1884, one of the great transatlantic steamers, the *State of Florida*, was lost through collision with a barque. Both vessels soon sank, and only a few of those on board either ship were saved. One of the survivors had a wonderful escape. Most of the boats foundered. A passing ship next day picked up several sailors, clinging to the keel of a capsized boat, in a state of extreme exhaustion. Singular to say, one man was underneath the capsized boat throughout the night, having managed to secure himself above the bars. His comrades heard him beneath them, but could do nothing to relieve him. In the morning, when they were picked up, the bottom of the boat had to be broken through to get him out. He had swooned or become unconscious, probably from the exhausted air, which yet buoyed up the boat. With great difficulty he recovered.

The adventure was so remarkable that it recalled a still more strange escape, not from a capsized boat, but from a capsized ship. The men were inside the hull when the ship turned over, and had no chance of escape by boats or by swimming. Most of the crew perished, but some escaped in the remarkable way which we are about to narrate, from the account given in the *Times*, to which is appended the certified report of Lloyd's agent, who took down the statements and depositions of the survivors. The escape took place many years ago, but is curious enough to be worth telling anew.

The brig *Nerina*, of Dunkirk, sailed thence on Saturday, October 31st, 1840, under the command of Captain Pierre Everard, with a cargo of oil and canvas for Marseilles. Her burthen was about 114 tons, and her crew consisted of seven persons, including the captain and his nephew, fourteen years old.

At three in the afternoon of Monday, November 16th, they were forced to heave to in a gale of wind, about ten or twelve leagues south-west of the Scilly Islands. At seven the same evening, still laying to under close-reefed maintopsail and balanced reefed mainsail, a heavy sea struck the vessel, and she suddenly capsized, turning completely bottom up.

The only man on deck at the time was named Boumelard, who was instantly engulfed in the ocean. In the forecastle were three seamen, named Vincent, Vantaure, and Jean Marie. The two former, by seizing hold of the windlass bits, succeeded in getting up close to the keelson, and so kept their heads above water. Poor Jean Marie was not so fortunate. He must have been in some measure entangled, as after convulsively grasping the heel of Vantaure for a few seconds, he let go his hold and was drowned. His body was never seen afterwards. The other two, finding that the shock of the upset had started the bulkhead between the forecastle and the hold, and that the cargo itself had fallen down on the deck, contrived to draw themselves on their faces close alongside the keelson (it could not be called on their hands and knees for want of height, towards the stern of the ship, from whence they thought they heard some voices.

At the time of the accident the captain, the mate, Jean Gallo, and the boy Nicolas were in the cabin. The captain caught the boy in his arms, under the full impression that their last moment had arrived. The mate succeeded in wrenching open the trap-hatch in the cabin deck, and in clearing out some casks, which were jammed in the lazaretto (a sort of small triangular space between cabin floor and keelson where stores are generally stowed away). Having effected this he scrambled up into the vacant space and took the boy from the hands of the captain, whom he then assisted to follow them. In about an hour they were joined by Vincent and Vantaure from the forecastle.

They were then five individuals closely cooped together. As they sat they were obliged to bend their bodies from want of height above them, while the water reached as high as their waists, from which irksome position one at a time obtained some relief by stretching at full length on the barrels in the hold, squeezing himself up close to the keelson. They were able to distinguish between day and night by the light striking from above into the sea, and being reflected up through the cabin skylight and then into the lazaretto through the tophatch in the cabin floor.

The day and night of Tuesday the 17th, and the day of Wednesday the 18th, passed without food, without relief, and almost without hope; but still each encouraged the others when no one could really entertain hope for himself. They endeavoured to assuage the pangs of hunger by chewing the bark stripped off from the hoops of the casks. Want of fresh air threatening them with death by suffocation, the mate worked almost incessantly for two days and one night in endeavouring with his knife to cut a hole through the hull. Happily the knife broke before he had succeeded in accomplishing his object, the result of which must have proved fatal, as the confined air alone preserved the vessel in a sufficiently buoyant state.

In the dead of the night of Wednesday, the 18th, the vessel suddenly struck heavily. On the third blow the stern dropped so much that all hands were obliged to make the best of their way, one by one, further forward towards the bows, in attempting which poor Vincent was caught by the water and drowned, falling down through the cabin floor and skylight.

After the lapse of an hour or two, finding the water to ebb, Gallo got down into the cabin, and while seeking for the hatchet which was usually kept there was forced to rush again into the lazaretto to avoid being drowned by the sea, which rose on him with fearful rapidity. Another hour or two of long suffering succeeded, when they were rejoiced to see by the dawning of the day of Thursday, the 19th, that the vessel was fast on rocks, one of which projected up through the skylight. The captain then went down into the cabin and found that the quarter of the ship was stoved, and looking through the opening he called out to his companions, "Grace à Dieu, mes enfans, nous sommes sauvés; je vois un homme à terre." Immediately after this the man approached and put in his hand, which the captain seized, almost as much to the terror of the poor man as to the intense delight of the captain. Several people of the neighbourhood were soon assembled, the side of the ship was cut open, and the four poor fellows were liberated from a floating sepulchre, after an entombment of three days and three nights in the mighty deep. The spot where the vessel struck is called Porthelick, in the island of St. Mary's, Scilly. She must have been driven on the rocks soon after midnight, at about the period of high water, and was discovered lying dry at about seven o'clock on Thursday morning by a man accidentally passing along the cliffs. In another half hour the returning tide would have sealed their fate. The body of Vincent was thrown on the rocks at a short distance from the wreck, and was interred in the burial ground of St. Mary's with the usual rites of the Established Church.

Not the least remarkable part of the narrative is that in the afternoon of Wednesday, the 18th, the wreck, floating bottom upwards, was fallen in with at about a league and a-half distant from the island by two pilot boats, which took her in tow for about an hour, but, their tow ropes breaking and night approaching, with a heavy sea running and every appearance of bad weather, they abandoned her, not having the least suspicion that there were human beings alive, in the hold of the vessel, which was floating with little more than her keel above water, while had the vessel not been so taken in tow the set of the current would have drifted her clear of the island into the vast Atlantic. The hull was, of course, a complete wreck, and soon went to pieces, and only a small portion of the cargo was saved.

The survivors experienced at the hands of the inhabitants the utmost kindness and hospitality, which they acknowledged with gratitude. Then follows the certificate of Lloyd's agent

"I, the undersigned, Richard Pearce, French Consular Agen and Agent to Lloyd's at Penzance, having personally taker the depositions of the survivors, and having also conversed with several of the inhabitants of the island (among other Augustus Smith, Esq.), some of whom actually assisted at the towing of the *Nerina*, while others assisted at the liberation or the 19th, hereby certify the accuracy of the foregoing state ment.

"RICHARD PEARCE.

"*Penzance, December* 24*th*,·1840."

THE ORIGINAL ROBINSON CRUSOE.

IT is usually stated, and commonly believed, that the world-renowned romance of Robinson Crusoe, by Defoe, was suggested by the story of the sojourn of a Scottish sailor, Alexander Selkirk, on the island of Juan Fernandez. In the book "All True" will be found the authentic narrative of Selkirk's adventures, as reported by Captain Woodes Rogers, of the *Duke* frigate, who found him on the island, and received the relation from his own lips. Selkirk had been master of the *Cinque Ports*, commanded by Captain Stradling, a ship that came to Juan Fernandez with Captain Dampier in 1703. On the recommendation of Dampier, Selkirk was made second mate of the *Duke*, an honourable recompense for his cruel abandonment on the island by his former chief, Captain Stradling. This ship was one of two privateers fitted out by Bristol merchants, the *Duke* commanded by Captain Woodes Rogers, and the *Duchess* by a Captain Cook. The celebrated navigator, Captain Dampier, accompanied this expedition merely as pilot, although during the voyage, which was one round the world, the skill and experience of the veteran seaman often proved of vast use to the younger and inferior captains. Thus at Guayaquil, where plunder was secured to the value of £21,000, with 27,000 dollars as ransom of the town from bombardment, Dampier was in command of the artillery. He was mainly conducive to the capture of a rich Manilla ship off Cape Lucas, and other rich prizes; and after many adventures piloted the privateers safely up the Thames to Gravesend, in October 1711, laden with booty in money and merchandize valued at £150,000. It was some years before this prize money was divided, and it is not certain whether Dampier lived to get his share of the awards.

It is to the discredit of Captain Woodes Rogers that in the narrative of his voyage he seldom names Captain Dampier, and attributes to him little of the success of the expedition.

In all matters of difficulty or doubt, however, we know that Dampier's advice was sought and followed, as might well be the case when the old pilot had forty years' experience of peril and adventure. It seems hard that at the end of his long life he was obliged to take service as pilot, when he had formerly so many opportunities of enriching himself. But his ambition was more for seeing the world, and describing its wonders, than for personal gain. Humboldt, the illustrious man of science, and Malte Brun, the distinguished geographer, both speak with the utmost respect of Dampier, and say that none of the old navigators have left records so valuable and trustworthy as are found in his books of travel.

I have now before me an old copy of one of his books, the title-page of which is worth transcribing, as from it some idea may be formed of the nature and extent of Dampier's researches. It is as follows: "A NEW VOYAGE ROUND THE WORLD, describing particularly the Isthmus of America, several coasts and islands in the West Indies, the Isles of Cape Verd, the passage by Terra del Fuego, the South Sea coasts of Chili, Peru, and Mexico; the Isle of Guam, one of the Ladrones, Mindando, and other Philippine and East-India Islands near Cambodia, China, Formosa, Luconia, Celebes, etc., New Holland, Sumatra, Nicobar Isles; the Cape of Good Hope, and Santa Hellena. Their soil, rivers, harbours, plants, fruits, animals, and inhabitants. Their customs, religion, government, trade, etc. Illustrated with particular maps and draughts. By WILLIAM DAMPIER. The second edition, corrected. London, Printed for James Knapton, at the Crown in St. Paul's Church Yard, MDCXCVII."

A brief notice of this book, which contains the narrative of events from 1679 to 1691,—for he was away all these years,—I will presently give, but at present confine attention to the account of a solitary man left on the island of Juan Fernandez, where he remained above three years. He was left there in 1681, and released in 1684, several years before Alexander Selkirk was heard of. The details are perfectly authentic,

The Original Robinson Crusoe. 263

for Dampier was in the ship which left him in 1681, and which found him in 1684; and Dampier, during a later voyage, commanded one of the two ships, the other of which was commanded by Captain Stradling, the tyrannical chief, who left Selkirk on the island in 1704. Dampier was pilot of the *Duke* privateer, Captain Woodes Rogers, which took off Selkirk, after his solitary exile of four years and four months, in 1709. He knew everything about Selkirk's case, but in his earlier voyage he describes a previous abandonment of a solitary man, and his stay for three years on the same island. Here is the narrative as given in his book.

The nineteenth day (March 1683), when we looked out in the morning, we saw a ship to the southward of us, coming with all the sail she could make after us. We lay muzzled, to let her come up with us, for we supposed her to be a Spanish ship, come from Baldivia, bound to Lima, we being now to the northward of Baldivia, and this being the time of the year when ships that trade thence to Baldivia return home. They had the same opinion of us, and therefore made sure to take us, but coming nearer we both found our mistakes. This proved to be one Captain Eaton, in a ship sent purposely from London for the South Seas. We hailed each other, and the Captain came on board, and told us of his actions on the coast of Brazil and in the River Plate. He met Captain Swan (one that came from England to trade here) at the east entrance into the Straits of Magellan, and they accompanied each other through the straits, and were separated, after they were through, by the storm before mentioned. Both we and Captain Eaton being bound for John Fernando's Isle, we kept company, and we spared him bread and beef, and he spared us water, which he took in as he passed through the straits.

March 22nd, 1684, we came in sight of the island, and the next day got in and anchored in a bay at the south end of the island, in twenty-five fathom water, not two cables' lengths from the shore. We presently got out our canoe, and went ashore to see for a Moskito Indian, whom we left here when we were chased hence by three Spanish ships in the year 1681, a little before we went to Arica, Captain Watlin being then our commander, after Captain Sharp was turned out.

This Indian lived here alone above three years, and although he was several times sought after by the Spaniards, who knew he was left on the island, yet they could never find him. He was in the woods, hunting for goats, when Captain Watlin drew off his men, and the ship was under sail before he came back to shore. He had with him his gun and a knife, with a small horn of powder and a few shot, which being spent, he contrived a way, by notching his knife, to saw the barrel of his gun into small pieces, wherewith he made harpoons, lances, hooks, and a long knife, heating the pieces first in the fire, which he struck with his gunflint and a piece of the barrel of his gun which he hardened, having learnt to do that among the English. The hot pieces of iron he would hammer out and bend as he pleased with stones, and saw them with his jagged knife, or grind them to an edge by long labour, and harden them to a good temper, as there was occasion.

All this may seem strange to those that are not acquainted with the sagacity of the Indians; but it is no more than these Moskito men are accustomed to in their own country, where they make their own fishing and striking instruments, without either forge or anvil, though they spend a great deal of time about them. Other wild Indians, who have not the use of iron, which the Moskito men have from the English, make hatchets of a very hard stone, with which they will cut down trees (the cotton tree, especially, which is a soft, tender wood), to build their houses or make canoas; and though in working their canoas hollow, they cannot dig them so neat and thin, yet they will make them fit for their service. This, their digging or hatchet work, they help out by fire, whether for the felling of the trees or for the making the inside their canoas hollow. These contrivances are used particularly by the savage Indians of Blewfields River, described in a former chapter, whose canoas and stone-hatchets I have seen. These stone-hatchets are about ten inches long, four broad, and three inches thick in the middle. They are ground away flat and sharp at both ends; right in the midst and clear round it they make a notch, so wide and deep that a man might place his finger along it, and, taking a stick or withe about four foot long, they bind it round the hatchet-head, in that notch, and so, twisting it hard, use it as a handle or helve, the head being held by it very fast. Nor are other wild Indians less ingenious. Those of Patagonia, particularly, head their arrows with flint cut or ground, which I have seen and admired.

But to return to our Moskito man on the isle of John Fernando. With such instruments as he made in that manner, he got such provision as the island afforded, either goats or fish. He told us that at first he was forced to eat seal, which is very ordinary meat, before he had made hooks; but afterwards he never killed any seals but to make lines, cutting their skins into thongs. He had a little house or hut, half a mile from the sea, which was lined with goat's skin; his couch or barbecu of sticks lying along about two foot distant from the ground, was spread with the same, and was all his bedding. He had no clothes left, having worn out those he brought from Watlin's ship, but only a skin about his waist. He saw our ship the day before we came to an anchor, and did believe we were English, and therefore killed three goats in the morning, before we came to an anchor, and dressed them with cabbage, to treat us when we came ashore. He came then to the seaside to congratulate our safe arrival; and when we landed, a Mosquito Indian, named Robin, first leapt ashore, and, running to his brother Moskito man, threw himself flat on his face at his feet, who, helping him up and embracing him, fell flat with his face on the ground at Robin's feet, and was by him taken up also. We stood with pleasure to behold the surprise and tenderness and solemnity of this interview, which was exceedingly affectionate on both sides; and when their ceremonies of civility were over, we, also, that stood gazing at them, drew near, each of us embracing him we had found here, who was overjoyed to see so many of his old friends come hither, as he thought, purposely to fetch him. He was named Will, as the other was Robin. These were names given them by the English, for they have no names among themselves, and they take it as a great favour to be named by any of us, and will complain for want of it if we do not appoint them some name when they are with us, saying of themselves they are poor men, and have no name.

This island is in latitude 34° 15″, and about 120 leagues from the main. It is about twelve leagues round, full of high hills and small, pleasant valleys, which, if manured, would probably produce anything proper for the climate. The sides of the mountains are part savanahs, part woodland. Savanahs are clear pieces of land without woods, not because more barren than the woodland, for they are frequently spots of as good land as any, and often are intermixed with woodland. In the Bay of Campeachy are very large savanahs, which I have seen full of cattle; but about the River Plate are the largest that ever I heard of—50, 60, or 100 miles in length; and Jamaica, Cuba, and Hispaniola have many savanahs intermixed with woods. Places cleared of wood by art and labour do not go by this name, but those only which are found so in the uninhabited parts of America, such as this isle of John Fernando, or which were originally clear in other parts.

The grass in these savanahs at John Fernando is not a long, flaggy grass, such as is usually in the savanahs in the West Indies, but a sort of kindly grass, both thick and flourishing the biggest part of the year. The woods afford divers sorts of trees, some large and good timber for building, but none fit for masts. The cabbage trees of this isle are but small and low, yet afford a good head, and the cabbage very sweet.

The savanahs are stocked with goats in great herds, but those that live on the east end of the island are not so fat as those on the west end, for though there is much more grass and plenty of water in every valley, nevertheless they thrive not so well here as on the west end, where there is less food, and yet there are found greater flocks, and those, too, fatter and sweeter.

That west end of the island is all high champain ground, without any valley, and but one place to land; there is neither wood nor any fresh water, and the grass short and dry.

Goats were first put on the island by John Fernando, who first discovered it in his voyage from Lima to Baldivia (and discovered also another island about the same bigness, twenty leagues to the westward of this). From those goats these were propagated, and the island hath taken its name from this its first discoverer, who, when he returned to Lima, desired a patent for it, designing to settle here; and it was in his second voyage hither that he set ashore three or four goats, which have since, by their increase, so well stocked the whole island. But he could never get a patent for it, therefore it lies still destitute of inhabitants, though doubtless capable of maintaining four or five hundred families by what may be produced off the land only. I speak much within compass, for the savanahs would at present feed one thousand head of cattle, besides goats; and the land, being cultivated, would properly bear corn or wheat, and good peas, yams, or potatoes, for the land in their valleys and sides of the mountains is of a good, black, fruitful mould. The sea about it is likewise very productive of its inhabitants. Seals swarm as thick about this island as if they had no other place in the world to live in, for there is not a bay nor rock that one can get ashore on but is full of them. Sea lions are here in great companies, and fish, particularly snappers and rock-fish, are so plentiful, that two men, in an hour's time, will take, with hook and line, as many as will serve one hundred men.

* * * * *

There are only two bays in the whole island where ships may anchor; these are both at the east end, and in both of them is a rivolet of good fresh water. Either of these bays may be fortified with little charge, to that degree, that fifty men in each may be able to keep off one thousand; and there is no coming into these bays from the west end, but with great difficulty, over the mountains, where, if three men are placed, they may keep down as many as come against them on any side. This was partly experienced by five Englishmen that Captain Davis left here, who defended themselves against a great body of Spaniards who landed in the bays, and came here to destroy them; and though the second time one of their consorts deserted and fled to the Spaniards, yet the other four kept their ground, and were afterward taken in from hence by Captain Strong, of London.

We remained at John Fernando sixteen days. Our sick men were ashore all the time, and one of Captain Eaton's doctors (for he had four in his ship) tending and feeding them with goat and several herbs, whereof here is plenty growing in the brooks, and their diseases were chiefly scorbutic.

CAPTAIN DAMPIER AND THE BUCCANEERS.

THE name of Captain Dampier has been associated in history with the buccaneers of America. In point of fact he spent a part of his life among them, and the ships which are called privateers in his books were pirates to all intents and purposes. In the time of the great war with Spain, it was common to send out ships as privateers, authorized to attack the enemies of England wherein they could be met with, and to pay their own expenses by the plunder they could take. After peace was restored, this irregular war in foreign parts and at sea was continued, especially by English and French freebooters, the former being known by the name of buccaneers, and the latter as filibustiers. Buccaneer is said to be derived from the word " boucan," which was the name given by the Carib Indians to the dry beef prepared for food; and the huts where the meat was smoked also had the same appellation. The various names of privateers, pirates, freebooters, filibustiers, sea-rovers, and others, were all merged gradually in that of buccaneers. They were a people consisting of adventurers of various nations, many of them criminals and outlaws, leagued together sometimes for common plunder or common defence, but often separated into rival bands of robbers.

One of the current maxims with all buccaneers was, "No peace beyond the Line." The settlements on the American coasts and islands were all originally Spanish; and against these colonial stations the buccaneers waged unceasing war. There was not the same disgrace attached to the cause or to the name of buccaneers, that their cruelty and crimes afterwards fastened upon them. Hence, there appeared among them at first some men, like Dampier, who deemed the service only a continuance of the privateering expeditions of the heroes of the war-time, such as Drake, Raleigh, and Cavendish. Indeed, some of the most noted buccaneers had sailed in early life with these gallant commanders. But a more desperate and ferocious set of leaders soon came to the front, such as the Frenchmen Lolonnois and Montbar, the Dutchman Mansvelt, and the Englishman, or rather Welshman, Morgan.

This Morgan became the most powerful and celebrated of all the buccaneer leaders. At first he served under Mansvelt, on whose death he assumed command of a barque, which had already carried terror and devastation to many a Spanish settlement. By degrees his power grew, his successes attracting numbers of desperate villains, and he had at one time a fleet of fifteen armed ships, and above two thousand men under his command. Some of his enterprises, such as the capture of Porto Bello and of Panama, were deeds of great daring, and brought immense wealth as well as much renown to the captors. But the leader was a cruel, sordid, brutal man—a disgrace not only to the English name but to human nature.

His cruelties often shocked even his lawless followers, as he maintained his authority by fear alone. The atrocities committed after the storming of Panama are too terrible to be described, and the record of them destroys every vestige of the romance that had gathered round some of the earlier exploits of the buccaneers. Sometimes, in our own day, tales appear about them, but they can be read with pleasure only by those who take delight in the lowest kinds of *Police News* or other criminal literature. Morgan acquired so much money that he was able to procure from the venal and profligate King Charles II. the deputy-governorship of Jamaica, and the title of knighthood, so that he figures in the history of those times as Sir Henry Morgan, Knight. He was afterwards removed from his office, and being sent home a prisoner, we believe that he died in obscurity, during the reign of James II.

It does not appear that Dampier ever was with Morgan, but the "privateers" named in his books were most of them buccaneers. Some of the ships in which he sailed were merchantmen, but no mercantile venture in those times on those seas was without expectation of readier and richer prizes than could be got by trading. Captain Eaton, Captain Davis, and notably Captain Swan were famous buccaneers in their day, and with all of them Dampier sailed. He did his part in the fighting, and more than his part in the navigation, but he showed no keenness about the booty. His chief motives were love of adventure and desire for knowledge, and fortunately he always kept a journal, in which he carefully entered his notes and observations. Of some of the countries visited during his long wanderings there are not to this day more valuable descriptions and more exact information. His association with the buccaneers left his name for a time under a cloud, but justice has since been done to his memory. He was a humane and temperate, as well as a brave and intelligent man. He detested the cruelty and loathed the vices of his associates, although he, strangely enough, makes no attempt either to justify or to excuse his own presence among them.

In his old age he seems to have had remorseful feelings as to his earlier career, but at the time he had no compunction as to privateering. The fact of his remaining poor to the last proves that he had no base motive in belonging to such banditti, and his published works attest his zealous and laudable desire for obtaining and imparting knowledge.

His chief work, the "New Voyage Round the World," is dedicated to the Hon. Charles Montague, then President of the Royal Society, and in the dedication, while deprecating criticism of a book written by one of no profession of learning he says, "Yet dare I avow, according to my narrow sphere and poor abilities, a hearty zeal for the promoting of useful knowledge, and of anything that may never so remotely tend to my country's advantage."

In the Introduction, he tells, in the most artless and straightforward way, how he got among the buccaneers. He tells how he sailed, in 1679, in the *Loyal Merchant* bound for Jamaica, as a passenger, "intending to go thence to the Bay of Campeachy, in the Gulf of Mexico, to cut log-wood; where in a former voyage I had spent three years in that employ." Some English goods brought from home, he sold at Port Royal, and stocked himself with such commodities as he knew he could dispose of among the Campeachy log-wood cutters. But a friend at Port Royal, Mr. Hobby, persuaded him to go a short trading voyage to the country of the Moskito Indians. He assented, because he wanted money to complete the purchase of a small estate in Dorsetshire, near his native county of Somerset.

"Soon after our setting out we came to an anchor again in Negril Bay at the west end of Jamaica; but finding there Captain Sawkins, Sharp, and other privateers, Mr. Hobby's men all left him to go with them, upon an expedition they had contrived, leaving not one with him beside myself; and being thus left alone, after three or four days' stay with Mr. Hobby, I was the more easily persuaded to go with them too."

Captain Sawkins was at first the leader, but on his being

slain in an attack on Puebla Nova, the majority wished to make Captain Sharp the commander. A minority disapproved of this, including Dampier, who then started with a band of about fifty men, in a launch or long-boat, and two canoes, or canoas, as he always calls them. There were forty-four whites, a Spanish Indian, two Moskito Indians, expert in spearing fish, turtles, and manatees, or sea-cows; also five negro slaves. After a journey across the Isthmus of Panama, on the North Sea Dampier found quite a fleet of privateers, eight vessels, four English, one Dutch, and three French.

We are not able to give details of the various expeditions and adventures of the years from 1681 to 1685, but one extract in the journal of the latter year contains some interesting personal references, and will serve also as a good specimen of the style of the narrative. It is a description of New Panama, and an incident that occurred there.

Old Panama was formerly a famous place, but it was taken by Sir Henry Morgan about the year 1673, and at that time great part of it was burned to ashes, and it was never reedified since.

New Panama is a very fair city, standing close by the sea, about four miles from the ruins of the old town. It gives name to a large bay, which is famous for a great many navigable rivers, some whereof are very rich in gold. It is also very pleasantly sprinkled with islands, that are not only profitable to their owners, but very delightful to the passengers and seamen that sail by them. New Panama is encompassed on the back side with a pleasant country, which is full of small hills and valleys, beautified with many groves and spots of trees, that appear in the savannahs like so many little islands. This city is encompassed with a high stone wall. The houses are said to be of brick. Their roofs appear higher than the top of the city wall. It is beautified with a great many fair churches and religious houses, besides the president's house and other eminent buildings, which altogether make one of the finest objects that I did ever see,

Captain Dampier and the Buccaneers. 273

in America especially. There are a great many guns on her walls, most of which look toward the land. They had none at all against the sea when I first entered those seas with Captain Sawkins, Captain Coxon, Captain Sharp, and others, for till then they did not fear any enemy by sea, but since then they have planted guns clear round. This is a flourishing city by reason it is a thoroughfare for all imported or exported goods and treasure, to and from all parts of Peru and Chili, whereof their storehouses are never empty. The road, also, is seldom or never without ships. Besides, once in three years, when the Spanish Armada comes to Portobel then the Plate Fleet, also, from Lima, comes hither with the king's treasure, and abundance of merchant ships full of goods and plate. At that time the city is full of merchants and gentlemen, the seamen are busy in landing the treasure and goods, and the carriers or caravan masters employed in carrying it overland on mules, in vast droves every day, to Portobel, and bringing back European goods from thence. Though the city be then so full, yet, during this heat of business, there is no hiring of an ordinary slave under a piece of eight a day. Houses, also chambers, beds, and victuals are then extraordinary dear.

Now I am on this subject, I think it will not be amiss to give the reader an account of the progress of the Armada from Old Spain, which comes thus every three years into the Indies. Its first arrival is at Cartagena, from whence, as I have been told, an express is immediately sent overland to Lima, through the southern continent, and another by sea to Portobel, with two packets of letters, one for the viceroy of Lima, the other for the viceroy of Mexico. I know not which way that of Mexico goes after its arrival at Portobel, whether by land or sea, but I believe by sea to La Vera Cruz. That for Lima is sent by land to Panama, and from thence by sea to Lima.

Upon mention of these packets I shall digress yet a little further, and acquaint my reader, that before my first going over into the South Seas with Captain Sharp, and, indeed, before any privateers, at least, since Drake and Oxenham, had gone that way which we afterwards went, except La Sound, a French captain, who, by Captain Wright's instructions, had ventured as far as Cheapo town with a body of men, but was driven back again. I being then on board Captain Coxon's ship along with three or four more privateers, about four leagues to the east of Portobel, we took the packets bound thither from Cartagena. We opened a great quantity of the merchants' letters, and found the contents of many of them to be very surprising, the merchants of several parts of Old Spain thereby informing their correspondents of Panama and elsewhere of a certain prophecy that went about Spain that year, the tenor of which was, That there would be English privateers that year in the West Indies who would make such great discoveries as to open a door into the South Seas, which they supposed was fastest shut, and the letters were accordingly full of cautions to their friends to be very watchful and careful of their coasts.

This door they spake of we all concluded must be the passage overland through the country of the Indians of Darien, who were, a little before this, become our friends, and had lately fallen out with the Spaniards, breaking off the intercourse which for some time they had with them; and upon calling also to mind the frequent invitations we had from those Indians a little before this time, to pass through their country, and fall upon the Spaniards in the South Seas, we from henceforward began to entertain such thoughts in earnest, and soon came to a resolution to make those attempts which we afterwards did, with Captains Sharp, Coxon, etc. So that the taking these letters gave the first life to those bold undertakings; and we took the advantage of the fears the Spaniards were in from that prophecy, or probable conjecture, or whatever were, for we sealed up most of the letters again, and sent them ashore to Portobel.

The occasion of this our late friendship with those Indians was thus. About fifteen years before this time, Captain

Wright being cruising near that coast, and going in among the Samballoes Isles to strike fish and turtle, took there a young Indian lad as he was paddling about in a canoa. He brought him aboard his ship, and gave him the name of John Gret, clothing him, and intending to breed him among the English. But his Moskito strikers, taking a fancy to the boy, begged him of Captain Wright, and took him with them at their return into their own country, where they taught him their art, and he married a wife among them, and learnt their language, as he had done some broken English while he was with Captain Wright, which he improved among the Moskitoes, who, corresponding so much with us, do all of them smatter English after a sort, but his own language he had almost forgot. Thus he lived among them for many years, till about six or eight months before our taking these letters, Captain Wright being again among the Samballoes, took thence another Indian boy about ten or twelve years old, the son of a man of some account among those Indians; and wanting a striker, he went away to the Moskito's country, where he took in John Gret, who was now very expert at it. John Gret was much pleased to see a lad there of his own country, and it came into his mind to persuade Captain Wright upon this occasion to endeavour a friendship with those Indians, a thing our privateers had long coveted, but never durst attempt, having such dreadful apprehensions of their numbers and fierceness; but John Gret offered the captain that he would go ashore and negotiate the matter, who accordingly sent him in his canoa till he was near the shore, which of a sudden was covered with Indians, standing ready with their bows and arrows. John Gret, who had only a cloth about his middle, as the fashion of the Indians is, leaped then out of the boat, and swam, the boat retiring a little way back; and, the Indians ashore seeing him in that habit, and hearing him call to them in their own tongue, which he had recovered by conversing with the boy lately taken, suffered him quietly to land, and gathered all about to hear how it was with him.

He told them particularly that he was one of their countrymen, and how he had been taken many years ago by the English, who had used him very kindly; that they were mistaken in being so much afraid of that nation, who were not enemies to them, but to the Spaniards. To confirm this, he told them how well the English treated another young lad of theirs they had lately taken, such an one's son, for this he had learnt of the youth, and his father was one of the company that was got together on the shore. He persuaded them, therefore, to make a league with these friendly people, by whose help they might be able to quell the Spaniards, assuring, also, the father of the boy, that if he would but go with him to the ship, which they saw at anchor at an island there,—it was Golden Island, the easternmost of the Samballoes, a place where there is good striking for turtle,— he should have his son restored to him, and they might all expect a very kind reception. Upon these assurances, twenty or thirty of them went off presently, in two or three canoas laden with plantains, bananoes, fowls, etc., and Captain Wright, having treated them on board, went ashore with them, and was entertained by them, and presents were made on each side. Captain Wright gave the boy to his father in a very handsome English dress, which he had caused to be made purposely for him; and an agreement was immediately struck up between the English and these Indians, who invited the English through their country into the South Seas.

Pursuant to this agreement, the English, when they came upon any such design, or for traffic with them, were to give a certain signal which they pitched upon, whereby they migh' be known. But it happened that Mr. La Sound, the French captain, spoken of a little before, being then one of Captain Wright's men, learnt this signal, and staying ashore at Peti Guavres, upon Captain Wright's going thither soon after, who had his commission from thence, he gave the other French there such an account of the agreement before mentioned, and the easiness of entering the South Seas thereupon, that he go at the head of about one hundred and twenty of them, who made that unsuccessful attempt upon Cheapo, as I said, making use of the signal they had learnt for passing the Indians' country, who at that time could not distinguish so well between the several nations of the Europeans as they can since.

From such small beginnings arose those great stirs that have been since made all over the South Seas—viz., from the letters we took, and from the friendship contracted with these Indians by means of John Gret. Yet this friendship had like to have been stifled in its infancy, for within a few months after, an English trading sloop came on this coast from Jamaica, and John Gret, who by this time had advanced himself to be a grandee among these Indians, together with five or six more of that quality, went off to the sloop in their long gowns, as the custom is for such to wear among them. Being received aboard, they expected to find everything friendly, and John Gret talked to them in English; but these Englishmen, having no knowledge at all of what had happened, endeavoured to make them slaves, as is commonly done; for, upon carrying them to Jamaica, they could have sold them for £10 or £12 apiece. But John Gret and the rest perceiving this, leaped all overboard, and were by the others killed, every one of them, in the water. The Indians on shore never came to the knowledge of it; if they had, it would have endangered our correspondence. Several times after, upon our conversing with them, they inquired of us what was become of their countrymen; but we told them we knew not, as, indeed, it was a great while after that we heard this story; so they concluded the Spaniards had met with them, and killed or taken them.

But to return to the account of the progress of the Armada, which we left at Cartagena. After an appointed stay there of about sixty days, as I take it, it goes thence to Portobel, where it lies thirty days, and no longer. Therefore the viceroy of Lima, on notice of the Armada's arrival at Cartagena, immediately sends away the king's treasure to Panama, where it is landed, and lies ready to be sent to Portobel upon the first news of the Armada's arrival there. This is the reason, partly, of their sending expresses so early to Lima, that upon the Armada's first coming to Portobel, the treasure and goods may lie ready at Panama to be sent away upon the mules; and it requires some time for the Lima fleet to unlade, because the ships ride not at Panama, but at Perica, which are three small islands two leagues from thence. The king's treasure is said to amount commonly to about 24,000 of pieces of eight, besides abundance of merchants' money. All this treasure is carried on mules, and there are large stables at both places to lodge them. Sometimes the merchants, to steal the custom, pack up money among goods, and send it to Venta de Cruzes, on the river Chagre, from thence down the river, and afterwards by sea to Portobel, in which passage I have known a whole fleet of periagos and canoas taken.

The merchants who are not ready to sail the thirtieth day after the Armada's arrival, are in danger to be left behind, for the ships all weigh the thirtieth day precisely, and go to the harbour's mouth; yet sometimes, on great importunity, the admiral may stay a week longer, for it is impossible that all the merchants should get ready, for want of men. When the Armada departs from Portobel, it returns again to Cartagena, by which time all the king's revenue which comes out of the country is got ready there. Here, also, meets them again a great ship, called the *Pattache*, one of the Spanish galeons, which, before their first arrival at Cartagena, goes from the rest of the Armada on purpose to gather the tribute of the coast, touching at the Margaritas and other places in her way thence to Cartagena, as Punta de Guaira, Maracaybo, Rio de la Hacha, and Sancta Martha, and at all these places takes in treasure for the king. After the set stay at Cartagena, the Armada goes away to the Havana, in the isle of Cuba, to meet there the flota, which is a small number of Ships that go to La Vera Cruz, and there takes in the effects of the city and country of Mexico, and what is brought thither in the ship which comes thither every year from the Philippine Islands; and, having joined the rest at the Havana, the whole Armada sets sail for Spain, through the Gulf of Florida. The ships in the South Seas lie a great deal longer at Panama before they return to Lima. The merchants and gentlemen which come from Lima stay as little time as they can at Portobel, which is at the best but a sickly place, and at this time is very full of men from all parts. But Panama, as it is not overcharged with men so unreasonably as the other, though very full, so it enjoys a good air, lying open to the sea wind, which riseth commonly about ten or eleven o'clock in the morning, and continues till eight or nine o'clock at night; then the land wind comes, and continues to blow till eight or nine o'clock in the morning.

There are no woods nor marshes near Panama, but a brave, dry, champain land, not subject to fogs nor mists. The wet season begins in the latter end of May, and continues till November. At that time the sea breezes are at S.S.W., and the land winds at N. At the dry season the winds are most betwixt the E.N.E. and the N., yet off in the bay they are commonly at S., but not always. The rains are not so excessive about Panama itself as on either side of the bay, yet in the months of June, July, and August, they are severe enough. Gentlemen that come from Peru to Panama, especially, in these months, cut their hair close, to preserve them from fevers, for the place is sickly to them, because they come out of a country which never hath any rains or fogs, but enjoys a constant serenity; but I am apt to believe this city is healthy enough to any other people. Thus much for Panama.

On reading this account of the Armada, and of the galleons, with the rich treasure for the king of Spain, we can hardly wonder at the keen efforts of the buccaneers to seize their share of the booty. The adventures of Dampier in the years he stayed with them, and afterwards in the islands of the

Eastern seas, are full of varied interest; and we do not know any book of old travel so well worthy of being reprinted than Captain William Dampier's "New Voyage Round the World."*

ARMINIUS VAMBÉRY'S TRAVELS IN ASIA.

ARMINIUS VAMBÉRY, Professor of Languages in the University of Buda-Pesth, is famous as a learned scholar, and is even better known as an adventurous traveller. There are few who have not heard of his going, in the disguise of a Mohammedan Dervish, to visit the Khanates of Khiva and Bokhara, at a time when no European could venture to show himself in those barbarous regions, except at the risk of almost certain death. Bokhara had specially been a place sadly notorious from the death of Stodart and Conolly, of the Indian Service, and from the detention of Dr. Wolff, who bravely volunteered to go to inquire if other Europeans were in danger from the cruel Ameer. Wolff was with difficulty ransomed, after undergoing long and severe imprisonment. It was at this very time that Vambéry ventured to visit Bokhara. In his book of "Travels in Central Asia," published after his return, he writes, "I shuddered when I passed the dungeons of the Ameer, where, perhaps, many who preceded me had been murdered, and where, even at that moment, three wretched

---

* To the last of Dampier's voyages, that in which he went as pilot to Captain Woodes Rogers, in 1708, we have already alluded. It will interest our readers to know that in the *London Gazette* of 18th April, 1703, it is stated that "Captain Dampier, presented by His Royal Highness the Lord High Admiral, had the honour of kissing Her Majesty's (Queen Anne's) hand before departing on a voyage to the West Indies." It was not a successful voyage. One object was to attack the famous Manilla galleon, which was done, but the Spaniards beat off and nearly captured Dampier's ship, the *St. George*.

Europeans were languishing so far from their country and every possible succour."

By his successful disguise Vambéry escaped detection, and his account of his travels, both in his book and at the meetings of the British Association and other Societies, when in England, attracted much attention and curiosity as to these regions, and as to the personal history of the traveller who described them.

In the twenty years that have since passed great changes have taken place. The khanates of Khiva and Bokhara are now subject to Russia, and though Vambéry fosters the British dread of Russian advance in Asia, the truth is that the more rapid the progress of Russia, and the more complete its conquests, the better it is for Asiatic civilization. In these khanates order is now maintained, justice is secured, and slavery abolished. The trade of the Russians with Central Asia had long been greater than with all other foreign countries together. There was, therefore, good reason for their military interference in regions where peaceful commerce needed protection. Asia is wide enough both for English and Russian rule, and alarm for our Indian Empire must not hinder our rejoicing in Russian influence in more barbarous regions. If our rule in India is such as to benefit the people of India, it is sure, in the Providence of God, to be continued. Russian influence can only extend there if we are found unfaithful to our trust. We say this because Vambéry has helped to keep alive the panic about Russian advances.

But we avoid political questions, and confine ourselves to personal matters. Professor Vambéry has lately written a volume of autobiography, a narrative of his life and adventures (T. Fisher Unwin, London) from his earliest recollections to his last visit to England. There are things in this work not in his earlier book of travels, and being confined to personal narrative, the reader's liveliest interest is sustained throughout.

Beginning with the days of his childhood, he enumerates the many difficulties which he had to overcome, and shows how invincible his zeal must have been in the pursuit of knowledge, when he allowed neither poverty nor physical infirmity to interfere with his studies, which from an early period were directed to the attainment of great linguistic capacity. "No one," said the reviewer of the work in the *Spectator*, "can read the details of Professor Vambéry's life without a feeling of mingled sympathy and admiration at the suffering and hardship which he underwent and triumphed over. Yet even in the worst days of his adversity he was always able, not merely to bear up under deprivation, but to look at the bright side of things,—two invaluable qualities for getting through the battle of life under any circumstances, but particularly useful to one whose struggle for existence was long destined to be extremely arduous."

But although Vambéry had to support himself from his childhood—he began work at the age of twelve—and although his resolve to be a savant tied him in his movements, first to the Gymnasium at St. George, and then to the University at Pressburg, he managed to see something of the outside world, and to enjoy his holidays as well as those who were more fortunately situated. He passed his vacation in rambling through the Austrian dominions, and he has no false shame in confessing that he carried on his rambles through the charitable assistance and hospitality of those he came across. We may add, that in those days there was nothing unusual in this, and the closing of the classes at the different Universities always witnessed a great exodus of students, or Wanderburschen, as they were called, over all parts of Germany. These pedestrian trips had a greater significance in the case of Vambéry, for to him they seem to have served as an apprenticeship for his famous journey in Central Asia, in the guise of a dervish.

While he was thus indulging that spirit of liberty which chafed at the restraints of life in a town, Vambéry was sedulously employed in acquiring that intimate acquaintance with foreign languages which has made him one of the most

Arminius Vambéry's Travels in Asia. 283

remarkable linguists of our time. At an early stage of his studies his attention had been attracted to the East. The Hungarians treasure the memory of their Oriental origin, and a long political connection had created something more than a bond of sympathy between them and the Turks. That feeling was revived and strengthened at the time of the Hungarian insurrection, by the protection afforded by the Sultan to those of the Magyar leaders who were so fortunate as to escape the pursuit of the Russians and Austrians. It was only natural, therefore, that Vambéry should as a young man have felt attracted towards the East, and should see in Constantinople the gate through which he might hope to gain access to those hidden treasures which he believed the literature and countries of Asia would be found to contain. His study at the Pressburg University being completed, he went to Constantinople. When he arrived there his small sum of money was exhausted, and only the hospitality of a Hungarian refugee, whom he met by chance, provided him with a lodging. He then gained his livelihood as tutor in a Turkish family, and by bringing out a very useful German-Turkish dictionary first attracted the attention of the learned in his own country. But what was more important towards the realisation of the plan of Asiatic travel, which every day assumed more tangible form in his mind, he acquired during his long residence in the Turkish capital an intimate acquaintance with the language, religion, and social habits of the most orthodox or fanatical Mahomedans.

"I had found," he writes, "in the course of my linguistic researches in the study of Eastern Turkish a field which had been at that time barely cultivated, and devoted to it my full attention. Besides the manuscripts I got hold of in the various libraries, which were of great assistance to me in my studies, I frequented the Tekkes (cloisters) inhabited by the Bokharists, and provided myself, moreover, with a view to attaining to a thorough understanding of these works, with a teacher who was a native of Central Asia. Mollah Khalmurad, as my teacher was called, acquainted me with the customs and modes of thought of Central Asia. I used to hang passionately on his lips when he was relating stories about Bokhara and Samarcand, and told of the Oxus and Jaxartes, for he had travelled a great deal in his own country. He had already made two pilgrimages to the Holy Cities of Arabia, and possessed to a high degree the cunning and clear-sightedness peculiar to every Asiatic, but particularly to the much-travelled Asiatic."

Vambéry had thus qualified himself in every way for his meditated journey, and he tells his readers that he had learnt "to know the whims and foibles of mankind, and had found that man in the rude Asiatic garb was nearly the same as man in the civilised European dress."

Not the least interesting portion of his book is the description of his journey through Armenia, from the port of Trebizonde to the Persian frontier, and he gives an account of the state of that part of the Turkish dominions in the years that followed the close of the Crimean War. Here Vambéry travelled as an effendi, or Turkish official; and while the disturbed condition of the roads showed that there was no security for peaceful traders or ordinary travellers, the respect exhibited towards him personally proved that the Kurd and other marauders had then no wish to come into open collision with the Sultan's Government.

Arrived at Teheran, Vambéry assumed the character of a dervish. He had to resort to much fresh finesse in order to obtain the realisation of his main object, which was to attach himself to some caravan proceeding into the khanates of Central Asia. Success attended his efforts, and in the early months of 1863 he left Teheran with a caravan of dervishes— or, more correctly, of hadji pilgrims—who came for the most part from Khokand or Kashgar. It may be doubted whether he would have met with such complete success, but for the co-operation of the Sultan's Minister at Teheran, who privately informed the hadjis that Reshid Effendi, the name which

Vambéry had assumed, was "the Sultan's civil officer," and consequently a person to be taken care of. Then follows the description of his travels through the frontier provinces of Persia to the Turcoman desert, given with an obvious regard to effect, but still all the same very picturesquely. What could be more graphic than the following account of the caravan leaving Teheran?—

"The caravan numbered twenty-three, besides myself. Those of my friends who could afford to hire a mule or ass to take them to the Persian border were ready, booted and spurred; the former, with pilgrims' staffs in their hands, were waiting, too, for the signal of departure. I observed with astonishment that the shabby garments worn by the party in town had been exchanged for other and far more ragged ones hanging down in a thousand tatters, and fastened by means of a rope across the back; and learned to my great surprise that the miserable dress worn by them in town was their best holiday attire, which was now laid aside in order to save it. But yesterday I fancied myself a beggar in my new costume, to-day I looked fit to be a purple-clad king amidst my companions. Hadji Bilal at last raised his hands for a blessing on our journey, and we had not fairly seized our beards and said our customary Amens, when those of our party who were to walk on foot made a rush towards the gates, in order to get ahead of us who were seated on mules or asses."

At Khiva he was received in personal audience by the Khan, on whom he made so favourable an impression, that he received the useful present of a donkey, to carry him on his further wanderings. He arrived at Bokhara during the Ameer's absence, but he was received by Mozaffur Eddin a few weeks later at Samarcand. His impression of the former city is expressed as follows:—" Although the squalid and rickety buildings, and the streets covered with sand one foot thick did not tend to place 'noble Bokhara' in the most favourable or imposing light, yet upon entering the bazaar, and beholding the thronging multitude animating it, I could not refrain from being intensely interested at the novel sight. The beauty and wealth of the bazaar were not the things that surprised me so much as the immense and multifarious variety in races, dress, and manners which struck the eye everywhere. . . . I was followed by a crowd of curious people, whose embraces and handshaking became very annoying to me. Judging by my gigantic turban and the large Koran suspended from my neck, they evidently took me to be some great Sheikh."

The account of the interview with the dreaded Ameer (or Emir, as Vambéry spells it) we must give in his own words :—

"As we were entering the interior of the city, we were startled to find ourselves stopped by a Mehrem, who gave us to understand that his Badevlet (majesty) wished to see me alone, without my companions. My friends were this time of my opinion, that this message boded ill to me. But what was to be done but to follow the Mehrem to the palace? After being made to wait for about an hour I was conducted into a room where I found the Emir reclining on a mattress of red cloth, amidst books and papers lying about. I recited a short Sura, accompanying it with the usual prayer for the welfare of the governing prince, and after saying amen, to which the Emir responded, I sat down in close vicinity to him, without having first received his invitation to do so. The Emir was struck by my bold behaviour, which was in fact in perfect keeping with the character of a dervish. He fixed his eyes severely on mine as if wishing to embarrass me, and said :—

'Hadji! I hear thou hast come from Roum to visit the graves of Baha-ed-din and the other holy men of Turkestan?'

'Yes, takhsir (sir)! and besides, to be edified by thy blessed beauty.'

'Strange; and hast thou no other object in coming here from such distant lands?'

'No, takhsir! It has ever been the warmest wish of my heart to visit noble Bokhara and enchanting Samarkand, upon whose sacred ground, as is justly observed by Sheikh Djelal, men should walk with their heads rather than their feet. Besides, this is my only vocation, and I having been roaming now through the world for many a day as a *djihangheste*' (a wanderer through the world).

'How is this, a djihangheste with thy lame foot? This is very strange indeed.'

'Let me be thy victim, takhsir!' (This phrase answers our 'I beg your pardon, sir.') 'Thy glorious ancestor Timur (Tamerlane)—may he rest in peace—was afflicted in the same way, and yet he became a *djihanghir*' (a conqueror of the world).

Having bantered me in this preliminary conversation, the Emir inquired what sort of impression Bokhara and Samarkand had made upon me. My answers, which I took occasion to interlard with copious citations of Persian poetry, seemed to make a favourable impression upon the Emir, who was a mollah himself, and spoke Arabic pretty well; but I was not altogether sure yet of my success with him. After the audience had lasted for a quarter of an hour he summoned a servant, and telling him something in a cautious undertone he bade me follow the servant.

I quickly rose from my sitting posture and followed as I had been bid. The servant led me through a number of yards and halls, whilst my mind was at the time cruelly agitated by fears and misgivings as to my fate; my perplexed imagination conjuring up pictures of horror, and seeing myself already travelling on the road to the rack and that dreadful death which was ever present to my mind. My guide showed me, after a good deal of wandering about, into a dark room, conveying to me by a sign that I should expect him here. I stood still, in what state of mind any one can guess. I counted the moments with feverish excitement—when the door opened again. A few seconds yet of suspense and the servant approached at last, and by the light of the opening door I saw him holding in his hand, instead of the frightful instruments of the executioner, a parcel carefully folded up. In it I found a highly ornamental suit of clothing, and an amount of money destined for my onward journey, sent to me as a present by the Emir.

As soon as I obtained possession of the parcel I hastened away to my companions, wild with joy at my escape. They were quite as glad of my success as I myself had been. I subsequently learned that someone had sent the Emir an equivocating report about me, in consequence of which I was received with diffidence at first by the Emir, but succeeded in dissipating his mistrust, thanks to the glibness of my tongue.

None of the decayed cities of Asia made the same impression on Professor Vambéry as Samarcand, which "does in truth excel all the other cities of Central Asia in its ancient monuments, as well as in the splendour of its mosques, its grand tombs, and new structures."

Professor Vambéry returned to Europe through southern Afghanistan and Herat. At Herat, Yakoob Khan, who afterwards became well known in Afghan history, penetrated his disguise for a moment, but was thrown off the scent by the dervish's readiness in quoting a passage from the Koran. With the exception of this incident, the false dervish succeeded in deceiving all his companions and those with whom he came into contact as to his personality. Neither khan nor hadji suspected him of being a European. Suspicion would have led to discovery, and discovery would probably mean certain death. He returned, however, at length in safety to tell Europeans of the strange things he had seen in the lands of Central Asia.

THE FATE OF A GERMAN WATCHMAKER IN BOKHARA.

WHEN Vambéry was in the city of Bokhara, an incident occurred which strikingly illustrates the perils to which all foreigners were exposed in those times. It is not found in his recently published volume, but when in England, shortly after returning from the East, he published the narrative in the *Leisure Hour*, for August 1865.

When near Bokhara I broke the glass of my compass, which was in the shape of a watch, and had often done me essential service on my journey. I call it a compass for my European readers, but, in the eyes of my mendicant fellow-travellers, I carried, as a dervish, a kiblenumah, that is, such an instrument as every devout Mussulman is guided by when travelling, as it indicates the direction in which lie the holy cities of Mecca and Medina, towards which he must kneel to perform his appointed devotions. When we arrived at a station or halting-place, either by night or day, the honour of pointing out the holy sites by the kiblenumah was always accorded to me; but I had so often to consult this instrument, as well on the road as at the stations, to ascertain the right direction, that it behoved me to guard it as the apple of my eye.

Watches are scarce in Bokhara, and it is hardly possible to find a watchmaker; so I began to fear I might have great difficulty in procuring a new glass for my compass. For long I inquired everywhere, till at last some one informed me that, in a certain caravanserai, there was a clever mechanic; but, as such artists were scarce, and his skill was highly prized, it would not be possible for me, a mendicant, to have my work done by him. "If I cannot give much in money," thought I to myself, "I will give an abundance of blessings;" and soon I was on my way to find the workshop of the Tartar mechanic. I wandered long hither and thither ere I found the caravanserai. A long dark passage led to his room. When I opened the door, I was amazed to find myself in a neat apartment, with whitened walls and windows of oiled paper. Such traces of European habits in the midst of the chief town of Tartary astonished me, and I was still further puzzled at perceiving a table and chair, and, seated on the latter, a man in a European dressing-gown and a comfortable cap, who was busy at work, with his back towards me. "Es selam aleikum!" (Peace be to thee!), said I in a loud voice; and I sat down in the greatest bewilderment as to who the mysterious artist could be. After I had uttered the accustomed prayer of a dervish, he turned round, and his Tartar countenance was so marked that I could not be deceived on that point; but my curiosity remained as to his dress and furniture, when the Tartar interrupted his work with the following conversation :—

"Do I understand by your speech that you are from Constantinople? What business has brought you here? There are clever watchmakers in your country. You would have made me happier if you could have brought me springs and wheels, which get broken here."

"Ah," said I, "that is too difficult for such a long journey. But tell me, how have you learned this art, if you have never been in Constantinople?"

"I never was out of Bokhara. I learned this handiwork from a European feringhee (infidel) who dwelt here for three years in the time of the Emir Nasrullah. He was a diligent and excellent workman, and not a bad infidel, whom the pious Emir ordered to be put to death because he tried to return to his native country, though many times forbidden to do so. You know that in Bokhara spies in various disguises are always sent out to watch the feringhees in Bokhara, and, when they return with the needful intelligence, they are taken."

In spite of my eager desire to hear more, I durst not inquire how he was apprehended. I did, however, make an allusion to it, and the Tartar then informed me that his master often

"NO SOONER HAD I TAKEN THE GLASS IN MY HAND THAN I LOOKED TO SEE THE REFLECTION."

did not leave his room for days, and that he read much in a book which the Emir took away after his death.

"Just where you are sitting," continued the watchmaker, "he used to sleep; and when he awoke in the morning, he knelt down before what is written over your head, and performed his devotions."

The words "what is written over your head" filled me at once with the greatest agitation and most painful impatience. For me, as a holy Dervish, to show curiosity might have been dangerous. I recovered myself as well as I could. Without leaving my place or speaking further, I handed him my compass to repair, and asked him to give me a looking-glass, that I might see what caused the painful burning in my eye. No sooner had I taken the ominous glass in my hand than I, trembling, looked in it to see the reflection of the writing over my head. After some research, I did indeed find a line, in small German running-hand, and read the words, "In the name of the Father, Son, and Holy Ghost. Amen." I felt stunned and trembled. The glass was still in my hand, and, in spite of all my efforts, I could not conceal the pallor of my countenance. Within me was a terrible struggle between dread and curiosity, these few words moved me so strongly. Fortunately I was able to control myself, and to quiet my emotion. I continued the conversation. I could not, however, find out much about the poor mechanic, more than that he came hither from Cabul and was killed; that he was a German; and that by his skill he had earned about two thousand tengi, on account of which the greedy tyrant had ordered him to be put to death. I perceived from the words of this man how much he was devoted to his master. To me, who, sitting opposite to him, appeared as a holy man, he was afraid to show his love to the infidel; yet it was evident, not only in his words, but in his care of the furniture and dress, which he had acquired by purchase. Nothing was moved, nothing changed; and, strangest of all, the writing was not obliterated. Perhaps, if I had dared to investigate more narrowly, I might have discovered his name. But how was that possible for me in my character as dervish, and in Bokhara?

For long, long in my distant journeyings, there floated before my eyes the unfortunate destiny and the handwriting of the devout mechanic. When I recalled him to mind, I seemed to see him as he knelt at his devotions, and in the midst of barbaric fanaticism, calling in his mother-tongue on that Spirit who is present to all. How ardent must have been his supplications when carried from this spot to the place of execution! A year afterwards, as I returned through Persia on my way to Europe, I heard in Tabriz, from a German residing there, that the fate of the unhappy watchmaker was not unknown to him, for he had been told of it by some Hadjis from Bokhara. The Italian who met Dr. Wolff in Bokhara had been present at the execution; and a similar fate would probably await any European whose skill might enable him to enrich himself there.

THE GALLANT DEFENCE OF RORKE'S DRIFT.

THERE have been some terrible disasters amidst the glorious successes which have usually brightened the annals of the British army. In recent times no disaster more unexpected and more overwhelming has been recorded, than the almost total destruction of the 24th regiment at Isandhlana, in Zululand. The circumstances may be briefly recalled to mind. The Kaffirs of Zululand, under their king, Cetewayo, were threatening to overrun the territory of Natal, where the white population forms but a small number compared with the natives. It was resolved to carry war into the Zulu territory, as the best way of protecting our own colony. Lord Chelmsford commanded the British force, with native allies,

of Rorke's Drift. 293

employed for this purpose. Entering the Zulu territory, a halt was made at Isandhlana, or Isandula, for the name is variously written. Lord Chelmsford went forward toward the hilly region to reconnoitre, leaving Lieutenant-Colonel Pulleine, with the first battalion of the 24th regiment, under strict orders to defend the camp. Colonel Durnford, in command of the post at Rorke's Drift, was ordered to join Colonel Pulleine, and he arrived with a large number of mounted natives, bringing up the number in camp to about fifteen hundred, more than half of them British troops.

The Zulu forces, who had probably enticed Lord Chelmsford to a distance by retiring as he advanced, now began to concentrate towards the camp at Isandhlana. They numbered over twenty thousand fighting men. They formed an immensely extended semicircle, or line with horns, closing in gradually as they advanced. Durnford, unaware of the force of the Zulus, went out to meet them, instead of strengthening the camp, which could have been made into a fortress by parking or laagering the waggons, and other defensive arrangements. Durnford was driven back, and the whole mass of the enemy closed in upon the camp before preparations to receive them could be made. It was a short and fearful struggle. While ammunition held out the enemy was kept at bay, and many Zulus fell, but before long it was a rout and massacre. A few mounted men managed to reach the river some miles off, but nearly fifteen hundred English and native troops were slaughtered in the camp or during the flight.

Lord Chelmsford was not a dozen miles off, and heard firing, but had no conception of danger till a solitary horseman, Commandant Lonsdale, came up with the startling announcement that the camp was in the possession of the enemy. He knew no details, but having been at some distance from the camp, in the forenoon of the 22nd January, 1879, the day of the disaster, he was surprised to see Zulus dressed in English uniforms, with English weapons as well as their own blood-stained assegais. He could see also the dead lying in heaps.

Not losing his presence of mind, he instantly rode off in the direction where Lord Chelmsford had gone, escaping the shower of bullets sent after him when first observed. His warning came just in time, for the commander-in-chief was leisurely and unsuspectingly returning towards the camp, having of course failed to find the enemy among the hills. Advancing now with great caution, and resting on the march for some hours of the night, the light of the next morning revealed all the horrors of the scene. The victorious Zulus happily did not attack them, and Lord Chelmsford pushed on past the camp, and crossed the river to Rorke's Drift. Here he heard of events equally strange to him, but which stood out in glorious contrast to the gloomy scenes of Isandhlana.

On the same day, the 22nd January, an attack was made by a vast multitude of Zulus, many of them with their hands and weapons red with blood from the slaughtered troops at the camp, on the small outpost at Rorke's Drift. Here were two small houses, or huts, with enclosures, used as a commissariat depôt, and sheltering a few invalids. The post was in charge of Lieutenant Chard, of the Royal Engineers, with a detachment of soldiers, and the keepers of the stores, the whole under his command numbering one hundred and thirty-nine, all told. No danger was thought of, and no rumour of the disaster that had occurred had reached them till the afternoon of that terrible day. Lieutenant Chard was watching at the " ponts " on the river, where a few men were on guard, when two of the fugitives from the camp shouted frantically across. They were at once ferried over, and in hasty broken words told the startling story of that day's tragic work, and that the whole Zulu force would be soon upon them. Hurrying to the post, Lieutenant Chard found that Lieutenant Bromhead, of the company of the 24th left in charge, had already learned the news from an officer of the Native contingent, who had escaped by swimming the river. Bromhead had at once begun to loophole the houses, and to erect barricades with mealie bags. All set to work in right earnest. A rude entrenchment of piled biscuit-boxes, and every sort of material within reach, was arranged for defence. Orders were given clearly to every man as to the particular post he was to occupy, and in little more than an hour all were ready for the fast approaching storm. The invalid soldiers were in one of the huts, the entrances to which were barricaded as strongly as possible, with a guard for their defence.

They had not long to wait in suspense. The Zulus were soon descried, hurrying in swarms towards the post, three thousand of them at the lowest estimate. Rushing forward, they were met by a cool and steadily-aimed volley, which checked their advance. Some sought the cover of the bushes and rocks near, and others swept round to the rear. Whenever an assault in mass was renewed, it was met with the same steady fire as at the first rush. The savages seemed furious at being checked, after their recent triumph over a large British force, and attacked again and again with fearless fury. At times the brave defenders were driven back from their rough outwork, and the Zulus succeeded in setting fire to the house where the invalids were, some of whom perished before they could be moved. The conflict was maintained all through the evening and during the night, and not till four o'clock next morning did the desperate assaults cease. At this time the assailants retired, but with the intention of renewing the attack, reinforced by newly-arriving hosts of Zulus. There was no rest, however, for the holders of the fort, who set to work to strengthen their position for resisting fresh attacks. The bodies of the slain were used, with the mealie bags, and whatever could be found, to form the redoubt, and give shelter for a second line of fire round the post.

It was while thus engaged that Lord Chelmsford arrived on the scene, with his force that had not been engaged, and cheered them by a few words of congratulation and praise, for their "noble efforts and gallant defence." In a general order, issued a few days after, he said: " The odds against them were nearly thirty to one; but taking advantage of the material which lay to hand, and hastily constructing with it such cover as was possible, this heroic little garrison was enabled to resist, during the space of twelve hours, the determined attacks made upon them, and further inflicted heavy loss upon the enemy, the killed alone being more than three times their own number."

The Zulus, perceiving the accession of strength by Lord Chelmsford's arrival, made no further attack, and retired baffled and enraged. The glorious success at Rorke's Drift, when heard of in England, was hailed as the bright episode of a dark and disastrous campaign. Its record places in all the sadder contrast the calamity at Isandhlana, the result of incompetence and misunderstanding painful to remember.

It only remains to present the official report of Lieutenant Chard, the model of what such a report should be, in its modest statement of his own service, and generous recognition of that of his comrades, and affording a graphic sketch of an event which will ever be memorable in the annals of British heroism.

Rorke's Drift, January 25th, 1879.

I have to report that on the 22nd inst. I was left in command at Rorke's Drift, by Major Spalding, who went to Helpmakar in order to hurry forward a company of the 24th Regiment. I was specially ordered to protect the ponts. At 3.15 P.M. that day I was watching at the ponts, when two men came towards us from Zululand at a gallop. They shouted out, and were taken across the river; and I was then informed by one of them—Lieutenant Adendorff, of Commandant Lonsdale's regiment, who afterwards remained to assist in the defence—of the disaster befallen at the Isandula camp, and that the Zulus were advancing on Rorke's Drift. The other, a carbineer, rode on to take the news forward to Helpmakar.

Almost immediately afterwards I received a message from Lieutenant Bromhead, Commander of the company of the 24th Regiment at the post, asking me to come up at once.

GALLANT DEFENCE OF RORKE'S DRIFT. THE MORNING AFTER THE CONFLICT. [*Page* 296.

of Rorke's Drift. 297

I gave instructions to strike tents, and to put all stores into the waggons, while I instantly made my way to the commissariat store, and there found a note that had been received from the Third Column (Lord Chelmsford's), stating that the enemy was advancing in force against our post, which we were to strengthen and hold at all costs. Lieutenant Bromhead was already most actively engaged loopholing and barricading the store building and hospital, and also in connecting the defences of the two buildings by walls, constructed with mealie bags and waggons. I held a hurried consultation with him and Mr. Dalton of the commissariat, who was actively superintending the work of defence, and whom I cannot sufficiently thank for his most valuable services—and I entirely approved all his arrangements. I then went round our position, down to the ponts, and brought up along with their guard (one sergeant and six men) the gear, waggons, etc. I desire to mention, for approval, the offer of these pont guards, Daniels and Sergeant Milne, who, with their comrades, volunteered to moor the ponts out in the middle of the stream, and then to defend them from the decks, with a few men to assist.

We arrived back at our post at 3.30 P.M., and shortly after an officer, with some of Durnford's Horse, came in, and asked orders from me. I requested him to send a detachment to observe the drifts and ponts, and to throw out vedettes in the direction of the enemy, in order to check their advance as much as possible, his men falling back upon the posts when forced to retire, and thereafter to assist in the defence. I next requested Lieutenant Bromhead to station his men, and, having seen every man knew his post, the rest of the work went quickly on.

At 4.20 P.M. the sound of firing was heard behind the hill to the south. The officer of Durnford's Horse returned, reporting that the enemy was now close upon us. His men, he told me, would not obey orders, but were going off towards Helpmakar, and I myself saw them in retreat, apparently about one hundred, going in that direction. About the same time Captain Stephenson's detachment of the Natal Native contingent left us—as did that officer himself.

I saw that our line of defence was too extended for the small number of men now left, and at once commenced an inner entrenchment of biscuit-boxes, out of which we had soon completed a wall two boxes high, when about 4.50 P.M. four or five hundred of the enemy came suddenly in sight round the hill to the south. They advanced at a run towards our south wall, but were met by a well-sustained fire; yet, notwithstanding heavy loss, they continued to advance till within fifty yards of the wall, when their leading men encountered such a hot fire from our front, with a cross fire from the store, that they were checked. Taking advantage, however, of the cover afforded by the cook-house and the ovens, they kept up thence heavy musketry volleys; the greater number, however, without stopping at all, moved on towards the left, round our hospital, and there made a rush upon the north-west wall and our breastwork of mealie bags. After a short but desperate struggle these assailants were driven back, with heavy loss, into the bush round our works.

The main body of the enemy close behind had meantime lined the ledge of rocks, and filled some caves overlooking us, at a distance of one hundred yards to south, from whence they kept up a constant fire. Another body, advancing somewhat more to the left than those who first attacked us, occupied a garden in the hollow of the road, and also the bush beyond it, in great force, taking special advantage of the bush, which we had not had time to cut down. The enemy was thus able to advance close to our works, and in this part soon held one whole side of the wall, while we, on the other, kept back a series of desperate assaults which were made on a line extending from the hospital all along the wall as far as the bush. But each attack was most splendidly met and repulsed by our men with the bayonet, Corporal Scheiss, of the Natal Native contingent, greatly distinguishing himself by conspicuous gallantry. The fire from the rock behind our post, though badly directed, took us completely in reverse, and was so heavy that we suffered very severely, and at 6 P.M. were finally forced to retire behind the entrenchment of biscuit-boxes.

All this time the enemy had been attemping to force the hospital, and shortly afterwards did set fire to the roof. The garrison of the hospital defended the place, room by room, our men bringing out all the sick who could be moved before they retired. Privates Williams, Hook, R. Jones, and W. Jones, of the 24th Regiment, were the last four men to leave, holding the doorway against the Zulus with bayonets, their ammunition being quite expended. From the want of interior accommodation, and the smoke of the burning house, it was found impossible to carry off all the sick, and, with most heartfelt sorrow and regret, we could not save a few poor fellows from a terrible fate. Seeing the hospital burning, and desperate attempts being made by the enemy to fire the roof of our store, we now converted two mealie-bag heaps into a sort of redoubt, which gave a second line of fire all along, Assistant-Commissary Dunn working hard at this, though much exposed, thus rendering most valuable assistance.

Darkness then came on. We were completely surrounded, and after several furious attacks had been gallantly repulsed, we were eventually forced to retire to the middle and then to the inner wall of our kraal, on the east of the position we at first had. We were sustaining throughout all this a desultory fire, and several assaults were attempted, but always repulsed with vigour, the attacks continuing till after midnight, our men firing with the greatest coolness, not wasting a single shot. The light afforded by the burning hospital proved a great advantage. At 4 A.M., on the 23rd of January, firing ceased; and at daybreak the enemy were passing out of sight over the hill to the south-west. We then patrolled the ground, collecting arms from the dead bodies of the Zulus, and we strengthened the position as much as possible. We were still removing thatch from the roof of the store, when about 7 A.M. a large body of the enemy once more appeared upon the hills to the south-west. I now sent a friendly Kaffir, who had come in shortly before, with a note to the officer commanding at Helpmakar asking help. About 8 A.M., however, the British Third Column appeared, and at sight of this the enemy, who had been gradually advancing towards us, commenced falling back, as our troops approached.

I consider the enemy which attacked us to have numbered about three thousand; we killed about three hundred and fifty. Of the steadiness and gallant behaviour of my whole garrison I cannot speak too highly. I wish especially to bring to your notice the conduct of Lieutenant Bromhead, and the splendid behaviour of his Company B. 2, 24th Regiment; of Surgeon Reynolds, in respect of his constant attention to our wounded, under fire, assisting them when they fell; of Acting-Commissary-Officer Dalton, to whose energy much of our defence was due, and who was severely wounded while gallantly assisting in the fight; Assistant-Commissary Dunn, and others.

The following return shows the little number present at Rorke's Drift on January 22nd, 1879—8 officers, 131 non-commissioned officers and men; total 139. The following is the list of killed. (Here follow the names.) Total, 15, and 12 wounded, of whom 2 have since died.

(Signed) JOHN R. M. CHARD, LIEUTENANT, R.E.

HEROES OF THE VICTORIA CROSS.

AFTER the close of the Crimean war, during which the nation was aglow with patriotic feeling, and when the heroic deeds and noble endurance of our soldiers and sailors excited general admiration and sympathy, it was determined to provide a special decoration as a reward of personal valour. Before that time the custom had been to give medals to all who were engaged in any campaign or conflict. There was no

Heroes of the Victoria Cross. 301

discrimination in such awards, and the ordinary service medals might be worn by those who had slight claim to the honour. But a decoration for conspicuous acts of individual valour or devotion was an object of higher ambition, and the Crimean campaign seemed a fit time to institute such an order of merit.

Accordingly, by Royal Warrant, on the 19th January, 1856, the Victoria Cross was instituted. It was not deemed advisable to make the action of the Warrant retrospective, and therefore the Crimean heroes were the first to receive the much-coveted decoration.

Many will long remember the scene in June 1857 when, amidst immense enthusiasm, the Queen fastened with her own hands the plain gun-metal Maltese cross, with the simple legend "FOR VALOUR," on the breasts of about sixty men, of all ranks in both services. Forty-seven were awarded to the army, twelve to the navy, and two to the marines, on that occasion. There are now many hundreds of gallant men who wear the cross, and who are entitled to put the honoured title of V.C. after their names. Every one of these hundreds of names has attached to it a story of stirring interest, and many volumes of the most thrilling adventure could be filled with the records of the deeds that have been thus commemorated. Several books of the sort there are, and they are not only full of interest, but are of practical use in rousing the young military and naval readers of them to emulate the deeds there described. We cannot here give many details, but select only a few cases, as examples of the kind of services which the Victoria Cross seeks to reward and to encourage.

Let four instances suffice from the Crimean War, for valour during which, altogether from first to last, about one hundred and fifty crosses were distributed. Two of them are given from the records of the army, and two from those of the navy.

During the terrible Battle of Inkerman, the result of which depended more upon individual deeds of valour than upon skilful generalship, the Russians at one critical period had gained possession of what was known as the Sandbag Battery, and were pouring from it a deadly fire. Lieutenant-Colonel Sir Charles Russell, of the Grenadier Guards, offered to dislodge them if any of his men would follow him. A sergeant and a number of privates instantly sprang forward. It was a daring venture, against terrific odds. Several of those who made the rush at the battery were shot down, but Sir Charles Russell held his ground, in the midst of a confused *mêlée*. In a letter to his mother after the battle the gallant colonel thus described the critical moment : "There were repeated cries of 'charge,' and some man near me said, 'If any officer will lead us we will charge.' As I was the only one just there, I could not refuse such an appeal, so I jumped into the embrasure, and waving my revolver said, 'Come on, my lads; who will follow me ? I then rushed on." In the desperate struggle that ensued some of the bravest men fell, and the leader was in utmost peril. A private of the Grenadiers, named Palmer, kept close to him, and was one of a small band who saved the colours of the battalion from falling into the hands of the enemy, who were still in overwhelming force. The Russians soon gave way before the desperate valour of their assailants, and the battery was held by the victorious guards. To Sir Charles Russell, and to Palmer, who was promoted next morning to be corporal, the Victoria Cross was presented by Her Majesty.

Now for the two examples of valour in the Royal Navy. We have already referred to the gallant services of Captain William Peel during the Crimean war (*ante*, p. 66), in the story of "A Ride through the Nubian Desert." Captain Peel was in command of H.M.S. *Diamond*, and a naval brigade from that ship formed a battery before Sebastopol, which was named the Diamond Battery. One day some fresh ammunition was brought up from the rear. The enemy were firing briskly, and as the horses were terrified and would not move, it was necessary for some of the men to go into the open, unload the powder-cases from the waggons, and carry them into the battery. While thus engaged a shell came right into their midst. "The fuse is burning!" someone cried out, as he foresaw the awful explosion that seemed imminent. Captain Peel saw the shell with the fuse alight, and without a moment's hesitation leaped over the powder-cases, and lifting the shell threw it over the parapet. It had hardly left his hands when it burst, but now at too great a distance to explode the powder. By this cool heroism, at such terrible risk, a disaster was prevented, and the deed gained for him the Victoria Cross.

A young boatswain's mate of H.M.S. *Rodney* was also serving with the naval brigade on shore. Several times he distinguished himself by daring deeds. It was desirable to plant a flag-staff on a mound behind which a troublesome Russian battery was working. When he gained the height he became a conspicuous mark for the Russian riflemen, but he was cool enough to take observation of the exact position of the Russian guns, and then kneeling down he scraped with his hands a hole for the signal-staff, propping it with stones and earth, after satisfying himself that he was in the line between the brigade guns and the Russian battery which had to be silenced, but of which the exact position could not be seen. For this cool and brave act he received the Victoria Cross; and he obtained also, for other services, French, Sardinian, and Turkish medals.

Within a year and a half of the institution of the order "for valour," the Indian Mutiny broke out, and a new field was opened for daring and heroic deeds. The first exploit honoured by the gift of the Victoria Cross was characteristic of the gallantry and self-devotion which appeared throughout the whole of that fearful time. After the outbreak of the mutiny at Meerut, the native troops made for Delhi. There were, unfortunately,—or rather, let us say by strange mismanagement, —no European regiments in the city of the old Moguls, although it was the most important magazine of military stores in northern India, and the presence of the king was sure to attract the mutinous troops from all directions. On the morning of the 12th May, 1857, Lieutenant Willoughby of the Bengal Artillery, the officer in charge, with two other lieutenants, and the keepers of the military stores, nine in all, were at their usual duties, utterly unaware of what was going on in the city, which was separated from the magazine by the river Jumna. An English resident hastened to inform them that the native regiments were in revolt, and that a strong force was already crossing the bridge to seize the magazine. The natives in the place could not be depended on, and what could nine Englishmen do against the hosts advancing upon them? They determined to defend the post as best they could till succour arrived from Meerut, not knowing of the events that had happened there. If they could not keep the enemy at bay, they resolved to blow up the magazine, being ready to sacrifice their own lives rather than allow the rebels to get possession of the arms and ammunition which they were coming to seize. Guns were posted within the gates, loaded with double charges of grape, to receive the enemy, and in case of the entrance being forced, a train was laid from the magazine, to be lighted as soon as further defence seemed hopeless.

At this time a summons to surrender came from the king, and a message that the gates were to be opened, and the stores delivered up. The summons was treated with indignant contempt. A threat was made that the place would be carried by escalade, and soon the scaling-ladders appeared, and the rebels were swarming over the walls. The native artificers and other attendants had already thrown off their disguise, and fraternized with the rebels. The guns were fired repeatedly, but it was impossible to bring fresh ammunition, and they were exposed to heavy volleys of musketry from the walls. Seeing that resistance was hopeless, the signal was given and the train was fired. Not one of the brave nine expected to escape with life, but Willoughby and three others, though terribly stunned and bruised, managed to make good their retreat from the ruins, where hundreds of

Heroes of the Victoria Cross.

the mutineers perished. Willoughby got into the open country, but was murdered by a band of armed villagers in attempting to reach Meerut; Forest, Rayner, and Buckley survived to receive promotion, and to wear the Victoria Cross, the first who got it in the Indian Mutiny. The result of the explosion was not so important in its material consequences, for there were still large amounts of military stores undamaged, but the moral effect of the heroic design was immense.

"From one end of India to another," says Kaye, in his "History of the Sepoy War," "it filled men with enthusiastic admiration; and when news reached England that a young artillery officer named Willoughby had blown up the Delhi magazine, there was a burst of applause that came from the deep heart of the nation. It was the first of many intrepid acts which have made us proud of our countrymen in India, but its brilliancy has never been eclipsed. Sad to think that Willoughby did not live to wear the Victoria Cross!"

During the siege of Delhi there were several memorable incidents which gained the merited reward of valour, and none more conspicuously than when Major Tombs, every inch a hero, rushed to the rescue of a younger friend, Lieutenant Hills, of the Horse Artillery, equally brave, but who was in peril, disarmed and helpless amidst murderous foes, after maintaining an unequal struggle with several assailants. Tombs and Hills both received the Victoria Cross.

At the critical moment of the storming of Delhi, a small band of gallant men undertook the perilous duty of blowing in the Cashmere gate, led by Lieutenants Home and Salkeld, of the Bengal Engineers, in broad daylight. Under a fierce fire from the walls, they advanced to the gate, planted and fired the powder bags, and opened a way for the attacking column, waiting the result with breathless anxiety. Most of the exploding party were killed, but of the survivors, the two Lieutenants, Sergeant Smith of the same corps, and Bugler Hawthorn of the 52nd Regiment, received the Victoria Cross, the honour of which Home and Salkeld lived only a short time to enjoy. But the fame of their exploit remained to rouse others to heroic efforts, in other posts of danger during the rebellion.

Nor was it only by soldiers that the Victoria Cross was gained during the Sepoy rebellion. Not a few civilians received it for heroic deeds; and several medical officers, though reckoned as "non-combatants," were as brave in action as they were devoted to their professional duties. Some of the most distinguished deeds were done by civilians. Mr. Ross Lewis Mangles, assistant magistrate at Patna, and Mr. Fraser McDonell, magistrate of Chuprah, may be named as examples, and it has been remarked, that "the gallant deed of Mangles solved the question as to whether civilians could share with their military brethren the honour of the Victoria Cross." The occasion was this. Three Sepoy regiments had mutinied at Dinapoor, and after the usual scenes of violence, they hastened towards Arrah, a distance of about twenty-four miles, expecting to surprise the Europeans there. There were only fifteen of them, with a few native Christians, and fifty Sikhs at the station. Mr. Herwald Wake, the magistrate, assisted by Mr. Vicars Boyle, an engineer of the railway, had just time to make a roughly-fortified post of a two-storied house, about fifty feet square. Here for a week the little garrison kept at bay some thousands of infuriated rebels, who swarmed around them, thirsty for blood and for plunder. A relieving force was sent by the civil magistrate of Patna, within whose district Arrah lay. There were nearly five hundred in all, including seventy Sikhs. Two civilians, Mangles and McDonell, volunteered to accompany the force.

It was a disastrous expedition. Arriving near Arrah in the night, suddenly a terrible fire was opened upon them from an ambuscade in a dense grove of mangoes. The assailants could not be seen, and the fire could be met only by random shots, by which friends were as likely to be hit as foes. Captain Dunbar, of the 10th Foot, the leader of the force, was killed by the first volley and during the hours of darkness the men were continually being shot down. When daylight broke, it was apparent to the survivors that their only chance of escape was to return to the river, which they had crossed in their evening advance. The Sepoys crowded after them, shooting many down as they retreated. Happily the boats were in the place where they had been left, but it was with the utmost difficulty they could get away from the crowd of fierce pursuers. Less than two hundred of the whole reached the shore, and of these only about fifty were unwounded. Some gallant deeds were witnessed during the hasty retreat. Lieutenant Ingleby, who led the retiring force, kept the men in heart by his cool and resolute bearing, and was the last to leave the shore. A bullet struck him just as he was stepping into a boat, and his body fell into the stream. Ensign Erskine, of the 10th Foot, had been struck down a little before, and was at the mercy of the rebels, when Private Dempsey rushed back to his aid, and bore him in his arms towards the river—an act of devotion for which, with subsequent services during the mutiny, he received the Victoria Cross. One of these services was carrying through a burning village, with marksmen aiming at him, a bag of powder with which to mine a passage in rear of the enemy's position, a feat of extraordinary risk, which none but a brave and resolute man would attempt.

But to return to the retreat from Arrah. Mangles, although suffering from a severe musket ball wound in the head, several times stopped to staunch the blood and dress the wounds of fallen comrades, and when a private of the 37th Regiment was struck down at his side, a large heavy man, Mangles, though feeble from fasting and from his wound, lifted the wounded soldier, and carried him on his back for six miles, over rough and swampy ground, with the Sepoys close behind, nor left him till he deposited his self-assumed burden in safety in one of the boats.

McDonell's deed of daring was scarcely less conspicuous. After performing many feats of valour during the retreat, he, regardless of his own safety, rendered every assistance to the helpless and wounded, and not till he saw them all off the bank did he leap into the last boat, and push out into the stream. The rebels had taken away the oars, and had lashed the rudder, and the thirty-five soldiers on the boat were drifting to the bank, from which a smart fire was kept up. McDonell saw the danger, and from the bow of the boat called out to cut the rope which lashed the rudder. Not being understood or obeyed, McDonell saw that not a moment was to be lost, and he did not repeat the order. The river boats have a covered roof, upon which he climbed, exposed to a shower of bullets, more than one of which pierced his hat and clothes, but he got to the rope, and cutting it, seized the tiller, and steered the boat into the stream, thus saving the lives of all on board. So he shared with Mangles the honour of a civilian bearing the badge of valour and merit.

In Kaye's "History of the Sepoy Revolt," and in other works relating to that time, we cannot read many pages without meeting with some deeds of heroic enterprise or of noble endurance.* "I may be wrong," says Kaye," but I think this heroism of Patience is grander far than the active gallantry displayed in a perilous charge. It is far easier to rush at an enemy in the fine enthusiasm of battle, than to stand steadfast on a given spot, for an ungiven period, waiting for the order or the opportunity to move, whilst swept by the fire of a hidden enemy. It is waiting that tries the man; and never were men more tried, or more patient under trial, than the troopers of Hope Grant's brigade." This refers to a critical season at the siege of Delhi, when for two hours the cavalry brigade stood firm, exposed to terrible fire, waiting the order to advance. The 9th Lancers mainly thus were exposed, but

---

* There is a good selection of instances of courage during the Indian Mutiny in a work compiled by Edwin Hodder, entitled "Heroes of Britain, in Peace and War" (published by Cassell & Co.), a book which ought to be in every school library, being full of records not only of warlike daring, but of devotion to duty in civil life.

Heroes of the Victoria Cross. 309

with them were Tombs of the artillery, Probyn of the Punjab Horse, and other heroic men, who knew how to wait as well as how to fight.

In the early spring of the same year that the Indian Mutiny broke out, there was a short but sharp war with Persia. Sir James Outram was in command, "the Bayard of the Indian army," whose name afterwards shone brigher than ever as one of the conquerors of Lucknow, along with Havelock and Clyde. The small British force in Persia was on one occasion confronted by an army of double their numbers. The enemy's artillery was soon silenced, and their cavalry routed, but a strong battalion of infantry formed square, and seemed resolved to meet the charge of the British cavalry. The battle might have been prolonged, and many of our men sacrificed, if this square remained firm. Their fire was very galling and destructive, and the square seemed impregnable. The cavalry charge, led by Captain Forbes and other brave officers, was steadily awaited by the Persian infantry with bayonets fixed. Lieutenant Moore, mounted on a splendid charger, in advance of all the others, rode right up to the square, and setting spurs to his horse made him leap upon the bayonets. The poor animal fell dead, and his rider must have shared the same fate, but the confusion caused by the desperate leap left a gap into which other men of the charging squadron rushed. The square once broke, disorder began to appear, and there was a confused *mêlée*. Lieutenant Malcolmson saw his friend Moore on the ground, alive but with his sword broken, and in deadly peril. Cutting his way to the place he told Moore to grasp his stirrup, and wheeling round brought his friend safely out of the surging crowd. By the good fortune which often favours the brave, neither Moore nor his rescuer Malcolmson received the slightest wound, and both received the Victoria Cross for their gallantry on this occasion, and lived to distinguish themselves during the Sepoy rebellion.

We might quote many other examples of heroic conduct in the wars in China, in Abyssinia, in New Zealand, in Afghanistan, and in South Africa, for England has almost always had some conflict on hand, even throughout what is commonly called "the peaceful reign of Queen Victoria." But enough has been said to give an idea of the kind of deeds rewarded by the Victoria Cross, and to incite some of our readers to refer to the books in which the noble actions, inspired by duty and by patriotism, are recorded.

KAVANAGH'S DARING JOURNEY.

IN the history of the Indian Mutiny one of the most memorable events was the relief of Lucknow by Sir Colin Campbell, afterwards Lord Clyde. Next to Delhi, the city of Lucknow was the place on the possession of which the result of the war mainly turned. A large proportion of the Sepoy troops belonged to this part of India, and Oude was the very centre of the rebellion. Immense efforts were used to overwhelm the little band of Englishmen, who against fearful odds defended the Residency, which the brave and good Henry Lawrence held till his death.

Then came the famous march of Havelock, from Allahabad to Cawnpore, to reinforce the now few and feeble, but dauntless defenders. The brave Outram joined the advancing force, and when they had fought their way through the besieging hosts, though entitled to command as the senior officer, with the chivalry characteristic of him, became a volunteer, merely in order that Havelock might have the honour of leading the entry of the troops.

But the relieving force soon found itself closely besieged, and in need of help, although "Havelock's march" was one of the most brilliant exploits in the annals of the British army. The city was beleaguered by countless foes, with every appliance for carrying on the siege. Sorties were useless against the numbers by whom the place was surrounded. It came at last to be a matter of days how long the noble little garrison could hold out, for provisions and ammunition were quickly running short.

At last the rumour reached them that Colin Campbell was on the march to their relief. It was then that the famous incident occurred of the poor Scotchwoman who cheered the fainting soldiers by declaring that she heard the notes of the bagpipes. True, the "Campbells were coming," but they were yet too far away to make this possible, and we must take it as an instance of "second hearing," like the "second sight" of which we read in Highland legends. But Sir Colin Campbell was pushing forward with all possible haste, and at last a native spy came into Lucknow, with tidings that the Commander-in-chief was at Alumbagh, with five or six thousand men.

Mr. Kavanagh, an Irishman, of "the uncovenanted service," was among those shut up in the Residency, with his wife and family, throughout the siege. He was in infirm health at the time, yet he took a gallant part in the defence, and was conspicuous for his deeds of daring, especially in the operations when the approaches of the Sepoy sappers and miners had to be resisted. He was thus engaged when he heard of the arrival of a spy, whose name was Kunoujee Lal, and who was going back to Alumbagh the same night with despatches from Sir James Outram to Sir Colin Campbell. Believing that his local knowledge would be of service in guiding the relieving force into the city, he instantly resolved to volunteer to accompany Kunoujee Lal to Alumbagh. He first went to find the man, and told him he wished to go with him in disguise. Kunoujee Lal objected, describing the dangers of the attempt, and saying that the chances of detection in passing through the enemy's lines would be doubled if two went together. Finding Kavanagh resolved to go, he proposed that they should leave the city by different roads, and meet at some distance outside. Kavanagh objected to this, and left him to make preparation for the perilous enterprise. The result of the journey, and the story of the daring adventure, we give in Kavanagh's own words.

"I had some days previously witnessed the preparation of plans which were being made, by direction of Sir James Outram, to assist the Commander-in-chief in his march into Lucknow, and it then occurred to me that someone with the requisite local knowledge ought to attempt to reach His Excellency's camp beyond or at Alumbagh. The news of Sir Colin Campbell's advance revived the idea, and I made up my mind to go myself. I mentioned it to Colonel R. Napier, chief of Sir James Outram's staff. He was surprised at the offer, and seemed to regard the enterprise as fraught with too much danger to be assented to, but he did me the favour of communicating the offer to Sir James Outram, because he considered, he said, that my zeal ought to be brought to his notice. Sir James did not encourage me to undertake the journey, declaring that he thought it so dangerous that he would not himself have asked any officer to attempt it. I, however, spoke so confidently of success, and treated the danger so lightly, that he at last yielded, and did me the honour of adding that if I succeeded in reaching the Commander-in-chief, my knowledge would be a great help to him.

"I secretly arranged for a disguise, so that my departure might not be known to my wife, as she was not well enough to bear the prospect of an eternal separation. When I left home about seven in the evening she thought I was going on duty for the night in the mines, for I was working there as an assistant field-engineer, by order of Sir James Outram.

By half-past seven o'clock my disguise was completed, and when I entered the room of Colonel Napier no one in it recognized me. I was dressed as a Budmash, or irregular soldier of the city, with sword and shield, native-made shoes, tight trousers, a yellow silk koortah over a tight-fitting white muslin shirt, a yellow sheet thrown round my shoulders, a cream-coloured turban, and a white waist-band or kummerbund. My face and neck and hands were coloured with lamp-black, the cork used being dipped in oil, to cause the colour to adhere a little. I could get nothing better. I had little confidence in the disguise of my features, and I trusted more to the darkness of the night, but Sir James Outram and his staff seemed satisfied ; and after being provided with a small double-barreled pistol, and a pair of broad pyjamahs over the tight drawers, I proceeded with Kunoujee Lal to the right bank of the river Goomtee. Here we undressed and quietly forded the river, which was only four feet and a half deep, and a hundred yards wide at this point. My courage failed me when in the stream, and if my guide had been within reach, I should perhaps have abandoned the enterprise. But he had waded quickly, and was near the opposite bank, where he went crouching up a ditch for three hundred yards to a grove of low trees on the edge of a pond, where we stopped to dress. While here a man came down to the pond to wash, and went again without observing us.

"My confidence now returned to me, and with my tulwar resting on my shoulders, we advanced into the huts in front, when I accosted a matchlock man, who answered my remark that the night was cold, 'It is very cold, in fact, it *is* a cold night.' I passed him, adding that it would get colder by-and-by. After going six or seven hundred yards farther we reached the iron bridge over the Goomtee, where we were stopped, and called over by a native officer, who was seated in an upper-storeyed house, and seemed to be in command of a cavalry picket, whose horses were near the place saddled. My guide advanced to the light, and I stayed a little back in the shade. After being told that we had come from Mundeon (our old cantonment, then in possession of the enemy), and that we were going into the city to our homes, he let us proceed. We continued on along the left bank of the river to the stone bridge, which is about eight or nine hundred yards from the iron bridge, passing unnoticed through a number of Sepoys and matchlock men, some of whom were escorting persons of rank in palanquins preceded by torches.

"Recrossing the Goomtee by the stone bridge, we went by

the sentry unobserved, who was closely questioning a dirtily-dressed native, and into the Chouk, or principal street of Lucknow, which was not illuminated as much as it used to be previous to the siege, nor was it so crowded. I jostled against several armed men in the street without being spoken to, and only met one guard of seven Sepoys talking to some women. When issuing from the city into the country we were challenged by a Chowkedar, or Watchman, who, without stopping us, merely asked us who we were. The part of the city traversed that night seemed to have been deserted by at least a third of its inhabitants.

"I was in good spirits when we reached the green fields, into which I had not been for five months. After going some miles we found we were out of the way, in the Dilkooshal Park, which was occupied by the enemy. My guide excused himself by saying he had missed the way in his anxiety to take me from the enemy's pickets."

[By help of one or two native cultivators watching their crops the right direction was regained, and early in the morning they approached Alumbagh, and an advanced picket of Sepoys actually pointed out the road, Mr. Kavanagh going forward to ask them, "as I thought it safer," he says, "to go up to the picket than to try to pass them unobserved."]

"Kunoujee Lal now begged that I would not press him to take me into Alumbagh, as he did not know the way in, and the enemy were strongly posted around the place. I was tired and in pain from the shoes, and would have preferred going in, but as the guide feared attempting it, I bade him go on to the camp of the Commander-in-chief, which he said was near Bunne, a village eighteen miles from Lucknow, upon the Cawnpore road. The moon had risen by this time, and we could see well ahead. By three o'clock we arrived at a grove of mango trees situated on a plain, in which a man was singing at the top of his voice. I thought he was a villager, but he got alarmed on seeing us approach, and astonished us, too, by calling out a guard of twenty-five Sepoys, all of whom asked questions. Kunoujee Lal here lost heart for the first time, and threw away the letter entrusted to him by Sir Colin Campbell. I kept mine safe in my turban. We satisfied the guard that we were poor men travelling to Umroola, a village two miles this side of the chief's camp, to inform a friend of the death of his brother by a shot from the British entrenchment at Lucknow, and they told us the road. They appeared to be greatly relieved on discovering that it was not their dreaded foes that had disturbed them. We went in the direction indicated by them, and after walking for half an hour, we got into a jheel or swamp, such as are numerous and large in Oude. We had to wade through it for two hours up to our waists in water, and through weeds; but before we found out we were in a jheel we had gone too far to recede. I was nearly exhausted on getting out of the water, having made great exertions to force a way through the weeds, and to prevent the colour being washed off my face; it was almost gone from my hands.

"I now rested fifteen minutes, despite the remonstrances of the guide, and went forward, passing between two pickets of the enemy, who had no sentries thrown out. It was near 4 A.M. when I stopped at the corner of a tope, or grove of trees, to sleep for an hour, which Kunoujee Lal entreated I would not do; but I thought he overrated the danger, and lying down, I told him to see if there was any one in the tope, who could tell us where we were. He had not gone far when I heard the English challenge, 'Who comes there?' with a native accent. We had reached a British cavalry outpost. My eyes filled with tears, and I hastened to shake the Sikh officer in charge of the picket heartily by the hand. The old soldier was as pleased as myself when he heard from whence I had come, and he was good enough to send two of his men to conduct me to the camp of the advanced guard. An officer of H.M. 9th Lancers, who was visiting the picket, met me on the way, and took me into his tent, where I got dry stockings and trousers, and, which I much needed, a glass of brandy—a liquor I had not tasted for nearly two months.

"I thanked God for having safely brought me through this dangerous enterprise, and I thanked Kunoujee Lal for the courage and intelligence with which he had conducted himself through this trying night. When we were questioned he let me speak as little as possible. He always had a ready answer; and I feel that I am indebted to him, in a great measure, more than to myself, for my escape. It will give me great satisfaction to hear that he was suitably rewarded."

Such is the substance of Mr. Kavanagh's narrative. It is not necessary to say more than that the tidings of his arrival soon spread through the camp; that Sir Colin Campbell's rugged countenance beamed with genial sympathy as he heard the recital of the night's adventures; that Kavanagh's guidance was of great service in the advance towards Lucknow, on nearing which he pressed forward to be the first to tell Sir James Outram of the success of the march.

His old comrades received him with enthusiasm, and while the echoes of the cheering still remained, he had the joy of conducting Outram and Havelock into the presence of the Commander-in-chief, who had retained him near his person throughout the advance. In the despatch to the Government of India Sir Colin Campbell recorded in generous terms his obligation to Mr. Kavanagh, and marked his own sense of the enterprise by calling it "one of the most daring feats ever attempted." The Victoria Cross, a handsome present, and an important post, the Assistant-Commissionership of Oude, rewarded the gallant Irishman's services, of which this perilous night journey was the crowning act.

THE LAST OF THE MAMELUKES.

EVERY one who has read anything about the history of Egypt in modern times knows of the terrible massacre of the Mamelukes by order of Mohammed or Mehemet Ali. In his plans for becoming sole despot and ruler, and subsequently making himself independent of the Sultan, the Pasha of Egypt, or Khedive as one would now call him, found the Mamelukes standing in his way, just as Louis XIV. found the French nobles troublesome, before he was able to become absolute ruler, and to say "L'etat c'est Moi."

The Mamelukes, a soldier class of independent chiefs, had long ruled in Egypt, although the country had been nominally governed by a Pasha appointed by the Sultan at Constantinople. When Napoleon invaded Egypt he found the power of these Mamelukes paramount, and the native population oppressed by them. He was, therefore, hailed as a deliverer. But on the departure of the French army of occupation, the Mamelukes regained their power, and retained it till the pashalic of Mehemet Ali, who determined to humble and subdue them. After much conflict he resolved to complete their overthrow by a cunningly-devised act of treachery. Many of the chiefs were residing in Cairo, having been pardoned, and appearing to be on good terms with the Pasha.

It is doubtful whether they were caballing and plotting against Mehemet Ali, as he afterwards asserted, or whether he only said so in order to justify his atrocious treachery, as Louis Napoleon did in his *coup d'etat*. At all events, he resolved to strike a decisive blow, and to get rid of the possibility of danger from these dreaded conspirators.

He consulted with the Albanian chief, Hassan Pasha, the most confidential of all his advisers, nor is it known that any other person was privy to the plot. Dissembling all suspicion on his part, and shunning everything that might excite it in them, he invited the most influential of all the

Mamelukes, looked up to as their chief, to an audience, and appearing to take him into his closest confidence, consulted him as to a holy war which he thought of proclaiming, for the advancement of the Mohammedan faith.

Saim Bey had always been thought a man of great shrewdness and penetration, but he was fairly over-reached by Mehemet Ali and Hassan Pasha. Flattered by the confidence reposed in him, he acceded to the proposal, and named all those whom he thought most likely to be useful in the undertaking. Mehemet Ali thus obtained the names of the leaders of the Mamelukes, but he said he would leave the arrangements entirely to the Bey, and concluded the interview by inviting him to come on the following Friday to consult further on the matter, bringing with him the whole of his friends and adherents.

When Saim Bey retired from the audience he went to those of the Mamelukes who were most in his confidence. One of them, more cautious and discerning than the others, warned the Bey of the whole scheme as savouring of treachery. But Saim replied, "So much the worse for the Pasha if it be so; and if there be danger, we shall not want power or courage to meet it." The result was that the whole of the chief men of the Mamelukes agreed to accompany Saim Bey to the appointed meeting, at the palace, in the citadel of Cairo, mounted and armed.

What occurred on that terrible day we now narrate in the words of one of the Pasha's soldiers, who witnessed the whole scene, and who long afterwards published an account of his adventurous life. His name was Giovanni Finati, an Italian by birth, as many of the Franks in Egypt are to this day, and a soldier of fortune. After leaving the Pasha's service he became a guide to European travellers in Egypt, Arabia, and Syria. In this capacity he accompanied Mr. W. J. Bankes, M.P., in an Eastern tour, and Mr. Bankes thought so highly of him that he translated from Italian into English the book we have referred to, and from which we obtain what follows.

"The Mamelukes coming to the citadel," says Signor Finati, "the Pasha was not idle in concerting his measures for receiving them. Before dawn, upon the Friday named, the drums were beating throughout the city to call the troops together as for some great parade; few, if any of us, had received any intimation of this beforehand, so that all hurried from their quarters to know what it meant, and were marched off to the citadel as they arrived, and stationed there. No specific instructions were given, but each man was strictly charged, after his arms had been examined, on no account to quit the post assigned him, and to wait there for further orders.

"The hour of audience was at hand, and a procession of about five hundred Mameluke officers, of higher or lower degrees, presented themselves at the gate of the citadel, and went in; they made rather a splendid show, and were led by three of their generals, among whom Saim Bey was conspicuous. When entered, they proceeded directly onwards to the palace, which occupies the highest ground; and as soon as their arrival there was announced to Mehemet Ali and Hassan Pasha, who were sitting in conference together within, an immediate order was given for the introduction of the three chiefs, who were received with great affability, both Pashas entering into a good deal of conversation with them, and many compliments and civilities passed. After a time, according to Eastern custom, coffee was brought, and last of all pipes; but at the moment when these were presented, as if from etiquette, or to leave his guests more at their ease, Mehemet Ali rose and withdrew, and sending privately for the captain of his guard, gave orders that the gates of the citadel should be closed; adding, that as soon as Saim Bey and his two associates should come out for the purpose of mounting, they should be fired upon till they dropped, and that at the same signal the troops, posted through the fortress, should take aim at every Mameluke within their reach; while a corresponding order was sent down at the same time to those in the town, and to such even as were encamped without, round the foot of the fortress, to pursue the work of extermination on all stragglers that they should find, so that not one of the proscribed body might escape.

"Saim Bey, and his two brothers in command, finding that the Pacha did not return to them, and being informed by the attendants that he was gone into his harem (an answer that precluded all further inquiry), judged it to be time to take their departure. But no sooner did they make their appearance without, and were mounting their horses, than they were suddenly fired upon from every quarter, and all became at once a scene of confusion, and dismay, and horror, similar volleys being directed at all the rest who were collected round and preparing to return with them, so that the victims dropped by hundreds. Saim himself had time to gain his saddle, and even to penetrate to one of the gates of the citadel; but all to no purpose, for he found it closed like the rest; and fell there pierced with innumerable bullets.

"Another chief, Amim Bey, who was the brother to Elfi, urged the noble animal which he rode to an act of greater desperation, for he spurred him till he made him clamber up the rampart, and preferring rather to be dashed to pieces than to be slaughtered in cold blood, drove him to leap down the precipice, a height that has been estimated at from thirty to forty feet, or even more; yet fortune so favoured him, that, though the horse was killed in the fall, the rider escaped. An Albanian camp was below, and an officer's tent very near the spot on which he alighted; instead of shunning it, he went in, and throwing himself on the rites of hospitality, implored that no advantage might be taken of him; which was not only granted, but the officer offered him protection, even at his own peril, and kept him concealed so long as the popular fury and the excesses of the soldiery continued.

"Of the rest of that devoted number, thus shut up and surrounded, not one went out alive; and even of those who had quietly remained in the town, but very few found means to elude the active and greedy search that was made after them, a high price being set upon every Mameluke's head that should be brought. All Cairo was filled with wailing and lamentations; and, in truth, the confusion and horrors of that day are indescribable, for not the Mamelukes alone, but others also, in many instances, wholly unconnected with them, either from mistake, or from malice, or for plunder, were indiscriminately seized on, and put to death; so that great as the number was that perished of that ill-fated body, yet it did not comprehend the total of the victims. For myself, I have reason to be thankful that though I was one of the soldiers stationed in the citadel that morning, I shed none of the blood of those unhappy men, having had the good fortune to be posted at an avenue where none of them attempted to pass, or come near me, so that my pistols and musket were never fired."

The strange fact of the leap and escape of Amim Bey, and of his asylum in the officer's tent, reached at last the Pasha's ears, who sent instantly to demand him; and when the generous Albanian found that it would be impossible any longer to shelter or screen the fugitive, he gave him a horse, and recommended him to fly with all speed into Asia, where I afterwards saw him, living in the palace of Suleyman Pasha at Acre, at the time of my first visit there with Mr. Bankes.

Thus far the narrative of Signor Finati. At the citadel of Cairo the place is still shown where the desperate leap was made, and the incident is mentioned in all guide-books and histories. But many have wondered, as we have done, what became of the solitary survivor of the massacre, and whether he or his horse escaped from the scene of slaughter. This narrative of the officer who witnessed the scene, and who afterwards saw "the last of the Mamelukes," will be read with interest.

MAN OVERBOARD!

IT is impossible to describe the intense excitement and anxious interest on board a vessel when passengers and crew are disturbed in their usual course by the startling cry, "Man overboard!" The life-buoy is at once thrown over, and the boat is lowered; while those who cannot take part in the rescue, look eagerly over the ship's side, to catch, if possible, a glimpse of the unfortunate, and to direct the course of those who have gone forth upon the waters towards the place where he rises to the surface after his first fearful plunge into the deep.

Sometimes a gallant comrade, or still more gallant and generous officer, does not wait for the boat, but risks his own life in the attempt to save a fellow-creature. Poor Captain Webb, who lost his life in so tragic a way at Niagara, was first brought to public notice by thus leaping into the stormy Atlantic—at night, too—in order to rescue a man overboard! The records of voyages, and those of the Humane Society and other institutions for honouring such noble deeds, contain a bright list of names, in every rank and of every age, from admiral to cabin boy, who have ventured life in this gallant way.

Often the effort is successful and the boat returns, amidst hearty and thankful cheers, with both the rescuer and the rescued. But, alas! often also the attempt has been in vain, and no help has reached the castaway.

A painfully interesting case of this kind has gained undying remembrance from having suggested to Cowper his last and one of his most touching poems, *The Castaway*. The incident is narrated in "Anson's Voyage round the World," one of their best seamen being washed overboard on a stormy night, when they were unable to render any assistance. Many a poor sailor has thus been lost, perishing where no attempt at rescue could be made. Sometimes the cause of failure to rescue has been special, as in the following incident, which was related by captain of much experience, who had himself several times saved men from drowning.

"I never lost a man in this way but once," he said, and a dark shadow came over his brow as he recalled the scene. "The sea was perfectly calm; it was daylight, and everything favourable, but the man never rose to the surface. The men in the boat were quite at a loss; in vain they watched and rowed about the place where he had sunk; he was never seen again. On returning to the ship, after the long and vain search, an old sailor who was intimate with the lost man said, 'I know how it was, sir; it was his belt of gold!' The man, it seems, was coming home from California with his earnings of many years, and had, as he thought, secured them safely by turning them into that which caused his death—a belt of sovereigns worn round his body. Thus weighted, he sank as lead in the mighty waters. The sad incident is told in the first volume of the *Boys' Own Paper*, and the remarks made about it are so sensible and thoughtful that we quote them here.

"This man was doing no wrong in taking good care of his treasure, although he might have chosen better ways of doing so. He may have been taking it home to make provision for his old days, or for those near and dear to him. But when I heard the sad incident I could not help seeing in it a lesson of life, for young and old, and for people on land as well as those on sea. The life of the soul may be endangered by some worldly treasure as fatal as that sailor's belt of gold. There may be something round the heart which keeps from Christ and His salvation. too, may be 'a castaway,' and be lost as that sailor was—

"'But I, beneath a rougher sea,
Am whelmed in deeper gulfs than he.'"

I fancy it must have been good Mr. Kingston, the friend and favourite author of boys, who wrote this in the *Boys' Own Paper*, when I read the closing sentence "Aye, as you value your souls' safety, boys, suffer not the things of this world to cling too closely round your hearts, and overweight you so as to drag you down to destruction."

Another famous naval writer, Captain Basil Hall, in his " Fragments of Voyages and Travels," a book full of interesting reading, has something to say on the subject of " Man overboard."

There are few accidents, he says, more frequent at sea than that of a man falling overboard ; and yet, strange to say, whenever it happens, it takes every one as completely by surprise as if such a thing had never occurred before. What is still more unaccountable, and, I must say, altogether inexcusable, is the fact of such an incident invariably exciting a certain degree of confusion, even in well-regulated ships.

I remember once, when cruising off Terceira in the *Endymion*, that a man fell overboard and was drowned. After the usual confusion, and long search in vain, the boats were hoisted up, and the hands called to make sail. I was officer of the forecastle, and on looking about to see if all the men were at their stations, missed one of the foretop-men. Just at that moment I observed someone curled up, and apparently hiding himself under the bow of the barge, between the boat and the booms. " Hilloa ! " I said, " who are you ? What are you doing here, you skulker ? Why are you not at your station ? " " I am not skulking, sir," said the poor fellow, the furrows in whose bronzed and weather-beaten cheek were running down with tears. The man we had just lost had been his messmate and friend, he told me, for ten years. I begged his pardon, in full sincerity, for having used such harsh words to him at such a moment, and bid him go below to his berth for the rest of the day. " Never mind, sir, never mind," said the kind-hearted seaman, " it can't be helped. You meant no harm, sir. I am as well on deck as below. Bill's gone, sir, but I must do my duty." So saying, he drew the sleeve of his jacket twice or thrice across his eyes, and mustering his grief within his breast, walked to his station, as if nothing had happened.

In the same ship, and nearly about the same time, the people were bathing alongside in a calm at sea. It is customary on such occasions to spread a studding-sail on the water, by means of lines from the fore and main yard arms, for the use of those who either cannot swim, or who are not expert in this art, so very important to all seafaring people. Half-a-dozen of the ship's boys, youngsters sent on board by that admirable and most patriotic of naval institutions, the Marine Society, were floundering about in the sail, and sometimes even venturing beyond the leech rope. One of the least of these urchins, but not the least courageous of their number, when taunted by his more skilful companions with being afraid, struck out boldly beyond the prescribed bounds. He had not gone much further than his own length, however, along the surface of the fathomless sea, when his heart failed him, poor little man ! and along with his confidence away also went his power of keeping his head above water. So down he sank rapidly, to the speechless horror of the other boys, who, of course, could lend the drowning child no help.

The captain of the forecastle, a tall, fine-looking, hard-a weather fellow, was standing on the shank of the sheet anchor with his arms across, and his well-varnished canvas hat drawn so much over his eyes that it was difficult to tell whether he was awake, or merely dozing in the sun, as he leaned his back against the fore-topmast back-stay. The seaman, however, had been attentively watching the young party all the time, and rather fearing that mischief might ensue from their rashness, he had grunted out a warning to them from time to time, to which they paid no sort of attention. At last he desisted, saying they might drown themselves if they had a mind, for never a bit would he help them ; but no sooner did the sinking figure of the adventurous little boy catch his eye, than, diver-fashion, he joined the palms of his hands over his head, inverted his position in one instant, and urging himself into swifter motion by a smart push with his feet against the anchor, shot head foremost into the water. The poor lad sank so rapidly that he was at least a couple of fathoms under the surface before he was arrested by the grip of the sailor, who soon rose again, bearing the bewildered boy in his hand, and, calling to the other youngsters to take better care of their companion, chucked him into the belly of the sail in the midst of the party. The fore-sheet was hanging in the calm, nearly into the water, and by it the dripping seaman scrambled up again to his old berth on the anchor, shook himself like a great Newfoundland dog, and then, jumping on the deck, proceeded across the forecastle to shift himself. At the top of the ladder he was stopped by the marine officer, who had witnessed the whole transaction, as he sat across the gangway hammocks, watching the swimmers, and trying to get his own consent to undergo the labour of undressing and dressing. Said the soldier to the sailor, "That was very well done of you, my man, and right well deserves a glass of grog. Say so to the gun-room steward as you pass; and tell him it is my orders to fill you out a stiff nor'-wester." The soldier's offer was kindly meant, but rather clumsily timed, at least so thought Jack, for though he inclined his head in acknowledgment of the attention, and instinctively touched his hat, when spoken to by an officer, he made no reply, till out of the marine's hearing, when he laughed, or rather chuckled out to the people near him, "Does the good gentleman suppose I'll take a glass of grog for saving a boy's life?"

I could give a pretty long list of cases which I have myself seen, or have heard others relate, where men have been drowned while their shipmates were thus struggling on board who should be first to save them, and instead of aiding so laudable a cause, were actually impeding one another by their hurry-skurry and general ignorance of what really ought to be done. I remember, for example, hearing of a line-of-battle ship, in the Baltic, from which two men fell one evening, when the ship's company were at quarters. The weather was fine, the water smooth, and the ship going about seven knots. The two lads in question, who were furling the fore-royal at the time, lost their hold, and were jerked far in the sea. At least a dozen men, leaving their guns, leaped overboard from different parts of the ship, some dressed as they were, and others stripped. Of course the ship was in

Man Overboard! 327

a wretched state of discipline where such frantic proceedings could take place. The confusion soon became worse confounded; but the ship was hove aback, and several boats lowered down. Had it not been smooth water, daylight, and fine weather, many of these absurd volunteers must have perished. I call them absurd, because there is no sense in merely incurring a great hazard, without some useful purpose to guide the exercise of courage. Now these intrepid fellows merely knew that a man had fallen overboard, and that was all; so away they leaped out of the ports and over the hammock-nettings, without knowing whereabouts the object of their quixotic heroism might be. The boats were obliged to pick up the first that presented themselves, for they were all in a drowning condition; but the two unhappy lads who had been flung from aloft, being furthest off, went to the bottom before their turn came. Whereas, had their undisciplined shipmates not officiously and most improperly gone into the water, the boats would have been at liberty to row towards the men who had fallen accidentally, both of whom, in that case, might to all appearance have been saved.

I remember a bitter kind of story which was current in the navy when I first entered it. In those days, naval punishments were not only more severe than they now are, but they were inflicted with less solemnity than is at present deemed essential to their salutary effect. In a frigate, commanded by a well-known Tartar, as the martinets of the service are generally denominated, one of the crew, I forget from what cause, took it in his head to jump overboard for the purpose of drowning himself. When he began to sink, he discovered that a salt-water death was not quite so agreeable as he had reckoned upon; so he sung out lustily for a rope. The ship being brought to the wind, the man was picked up with some difficulty. The matter was investigated instantly; and as soon as it appeared that he had gone overboard intentionally, the hands were turned up, the gangway rigged, and the offender seized up. "Now," said the captain, "I shall punish you under the sixteenth article of war, which is as follows:—'Every person in or belonging to the fleet, who shall desert, shall suffer death, or such other punishment as the circumstances of the case shall deserve.'" And then, addressing the boatswain, he said, "You will punish this man for desertion, or, which is exactly the same thing, for going out of the ship without leave." "Now, sir," resumed the captain to the trembling culprit, "if you have any longer a desire to go overboard, you have only to ask the first lieutenant's leave. He has my instructions to grant you permission; while I shall take very good care that you are not again picked up."

I was lately told of some incidents which occurred in a frigate off Cape Horn, in a gale of wind, under close-reefed main-topsail and storm-staysails. At half-past twelve at noon, when the people were at dinner, a young lad was washed out of the lee fore-channels. The life-buoy was immediately let go, and the main-topsail laid to the mast. Before the jolly-boat could be lowered down, a man jumped overboard, as he said, "promiscuously," for he never saw the boy at all, nor was ever within half a cable's length of the spot where he was floundering about. Although the youth could not swim, he contrived to keep his head above water till the boat reached him, just as he was beginning to sink. The man who had jumped into the sea was right glad to give up his "promiscuous" search, and to make for the life-buoy, upon which he perched himself, and stood shivering for half an hour, like a shag on the Mewstone, till the boat came to his relief.

At four o'clock of the same day, a man fell from the rigging; the usual alarm and rush took place, the lee-quarter boat was so crowded, that one of the topping-lifts gave way, the davit broke, and the cutter, now suspended by one tackle, soon knocked herself to pieces against the ship's side. Of course, the people in her were jerked out very quickly, so that, instead of there being only one man in the water, there were nearly a dozen swimming about. More care was taken in hoisting out another boat, and, strange to say, all the people were picked up, except the original unfortunate man, who, but for the accident, which might and ought to have been prevented, would in all probability have been saved. Neither he nor the life-buoy, however, could be discovered before the night closed; and it is most distressing to think, that, perhaps, he may have succeeded in reaching this support only to perish before the long winter night of those dreary regions could be one quarter over!

EARLY EXPLORING EXPEDITIONS IN AUSTRALIA.

WHO first discovered Australia? By the "discovery" of a country is meant its being made known to the civilized world. The ancestors of the native inhabitants were of course the first to find the great island or continent of Australia. Sometimes the natives of countries are called Aborigines, as if they grew up there, or developed themselves from some inferior animals. But no one believes this except advocates of the theory of evolution. The Aborigines of Australia migrated thither from other lands or islands, and it is much more probable that they degenerated, as they removed further from the ancient centres of population, than that they were improved by the change. De-civilization is more the natural process than civilization, as we get to the remotest regions of the earth. The Australian natives, when first seen by Europeans, were found to be very low in the scale of humanity.

The question, then, is by what European eyes was the country first seen? It has usually been said that the Dutch have the honour of the discovery, their commercial enterprise having brought them much into the regions nearest to the Australasian waters, and they claim the discovery as having been made by one of their exploring ships in 1605. That very year a Spanish fleet, under De Quiros, sailed from Callao, and discovered some of the island groups of the Pacific. One of Quiros' ships, commanded by Torres, having been separated from the others in a storm, passed through the channel between New Guinea and Australia, since known as Torres' Straits. He descried land on the south, which must have been part of the mainland, probably Cape York, its most northerly point. This was, however, after the date given for the Dutch discovery. Within the last few years a manuscript has been found in the Royal Library of Belgium, containing the personal narrative of the discovery of Australia by Manuel Godinho, a Portuguese navigator, who touched on the coast in 1601. There is no reason to doubt the authenticity of this record, so that the Portuguese may claim priority at least in sighting the great island of the south.

Several navigators, chiefly Dutch, were in these seas in subsequent years of the first half of the seventeenth century, but it was Tasman, who, in 1642, surpassed all his countrymen in successful exploration. It was he who discovered New Zealand, large tracts of the Australian coast, and what is now known as Tasmania, but formerly Van Diemen's Land, so named by Tasman in honour of Anthony Van Diemen, then Governor-General of the Dutch East Indies, for the hand of whose daughter the adventurous explorer was a suitor. Tasman thought that this was part of the mainland, and so it was believed to be down to the year 1798, when Bass proved it to be an island, by passing in an open boat through the strait which now bears his name. On the whole, the Dutch had most to do with the earliest discovery of the great south land, and evidence of this appears in the names of places given by them, while the whole vast island was, till recent times, known to geographers as New Holland.

As no settlement was made nor colony founded by any of these early explorers, their discoveries are now matters merely of historical interest. They attracted little attention in Europe, and, in fact, had almost passed into oblivion (although visited occasionally, as by Captain Dampier), till the time of

in Australia.

the celebrated first voyage of Captain Cook. The chief object of his expedition to the southern hemisphere was not geographical exploration but astronomical observation. He was sent to observe the transit of Venus from a station on the opposite side of the globe. This was successfully accomplished at Otaheite, or Tahiti, June 3rd, 1769. After examining the adjacent group, to which he gave the name of the Society Islands, in honour of the Royal Society at whose recommendation the expedition was sent, Cook proceeded south-westward with a general design of exploration in the Pacific Ocean. He reached New Zealand on the opposite coast to that visited by Tasman, and circumnavigating, he ascertained the division into two main islands, separated by the channel since known as Cook's Straits. He then sailed for Australia, or New Holland, exploring its east coast for more than 2,000 miles, and gave the names since so familiar,—New South Wales, Botany Bay, and Port Jackson, the magnificent bay or harbour on which now stands the eastern colonial capital, Sydney. After a nearly three years' voyage he anchored in the Downs June 12th, 1771, having sailed from England July 3rd, 1768. The subsequent voyages of Cook had no special bearing on Australian discovery.

The first use made by England of the discoveries by Cook was the establishment of a convict settlement at Botany Bay, near Port Jackson, in 1788. It was not till long afterwards that Australia was thought of in connection with colonization or emigration. Very little additional knowledge of the coast-line was obtained for fifty years after Cook's first voyage; in fact, not till the surveying voyages of Captain King, from 1818 to 1822. The interior of the country was then, and long after, wholly a *terra incognita*. Previously to the establishment of the convict settlement of Botany Bay, it is probable that no European had ever gone inland out of sight of the coast. The first to see the interior were escaped convicts, who long gave trouble to the free emigrants on their beginning to be attracted to the settlement. These gradually advanced northward and southward along the coast, and searching for suitable locations penetrated to the base of the Blue Mountain ridge. This lofty and rugged chain long formed the boundary of the colony. Many efforts were made to pass this natural barrier, but without success, till the year 1813, the twenty-sixth year of the settlement, when a terrible season of drought burnt up the lands from the sea to the hills, and the cattle perished in large numbers from want of pasturage. Three agriculturists—Bloxland, Lanson, and Wentworth were their names—resolved to join in an effort to penetrate the highlands, and see if there were not open land beyond, to the westward, for their flocks and herds. By observing and following the course of the rivers and streams, they succeeded in gaining a watershed, or main mountain-ridge, and after a difficult route of above fifty miles, they reached the lofty and rugged brow of a precipice from which they looked down on a vast expanse of open grassy land spread before them, like the pampas or prairies of the New World. A road was soon after commenced, by convict labour, to these pastoral downs, in the midst of which, about one hundred and twenty miles from Sydney, the town of Bathurst was founded. The road to Bathurst, crossing the mountains by what is now called the Victoria Pass, was opened throughout in 1832. A railway now runs from it to Sydney. The town is on the banks of the river, named after Governor Macquarie. The sources of the Lachlan river were about the same time discovered, more to the south.

The first extensive journey into the interior was made in 1817, by Mr. Oxley, the Surveyor-General of the colony. The primary object was to trace the course of the Lachlan. It was ascertained that the Lachlan and also the Macquarie entered a flat, level country, sometimes parched with drought, and at other seasons forming swamps or lagoons, to which no limits were apparent. Not till several years later was the Murrumbidgee river discovered, with the rich tracts of land watered by it, and in 1824 the larger river, the Murray, into which the waters of the Murrumbidgee flow. The colonial government did not seem anxious to prosecute further explanation, the reports of Mr. Oxley as to the Macquarie river being discouraging, but two independent colonists, Messrs. Hume and Howell, undertook a journey to the south-west, expecting to reach the coast near Bass' Strait, where they arrived, at Port Philip, having crossed a fine pastoral district lying to the west of the Warragong Mountains, of which nothing was previously known, and they discovered the country through which flow the Hume, Ovens, and Goulburn rivers. Returning by a more westerly route, they found other rich tracts of land, and their reports were so favourable that many settlers went to that region, and this was the first step towards the foundation of what is now the colony of Victoria.

The Colonial Government in 1827 sent an expedition, under Mr. Allan Cunningham, to explore the country west of what is called the Dividing Range. For four hundred miles the land was mostly dry and sterile, but he then came upon the Darling Downs, and crossed the streams forming the headwaters of the river Darling. In subsequent journeys he connected his first route with Moreton Bay, passing by a gap in the range which divides the coast-flowing waters from those flowing inland. In his last expedition he ascended the Brisbane river.

The next distinguished explorer was Captain Charles Sturt, whose narrative of "Two Expeditions into the Interior of Southern Australia, in 1828—31," although published above fifty years ago, in 1833, is still read with interest. He was accompanied in his first expedition by Mr. Hume. Captain Sturt found the Macquarie was connected in wet seasons, through marshes, with the Darling, but that year the whole region was a parched waste. The idea prevailing that these streams, as well as the Lachlan and Murrumbidgee, emptied themselves into some vast inland lake or sea, Captain Sturt's second journey was made to ascertain the truth of this hypothesis. He started from Sydney in December 1829 to explore the Murrumbidgee, and traced it to its connection with the large river named by him, the Murray. After nine days' voyage down this river, the explorers came to the confluence of another large river, which Sturt rightly conjectured to be the Darling. Having pursued the course of the Murray for 500 to 600 miles from the union of the Lachlan and Murrumbidgee, the boats entered an extensive lake, called by him Lake Alexandrina, from the southern shore of which he gazed upon the ocean, which was found afterwards, at Encounter Bay, to be easily reached by a navigable channel. This expedition caused the exploration of the country between the Murray and the Gulf of St. Vincent, and so led to the formation, a few years later, of the colony of South Australia.

The following years, 1832—36, witnessed most successful expeditions conducted by Major, afterwards Sir Thomas, Mitchell, who, among other discoveries, opened up the magnificent sylvan and picturesque region, named by him Australia Felix, destined before many years to be the busy scene of other settlements than those of pastoral quiet and happiness, being "the gold region" of Victoria. A few graziers from Van Diemen's Land and farmers from New South Wales knew the pastoral fertility of the district, but kept their knowledge secret, in order to monopolize the fine sheep-walks, but Sir Thomas Mitchell at once gave the public the benefit of what he had seen. He was the first European who ever stood on the summit of the famed Mount Alexander (called Mount Bung in his map), and having ridden up he admired the view, little dreaming of the mineral wealth that lay concealed in the neighbouring creeks and gullies.

We must pass with simple mention the expeditions of Lieutenants Grey and Lushington, the first to penetrate into the interior on the north-west side of the continent. They started from Hanover Bay February 1st, 1838, and discovered the Glenelg River, which they followed upwards for about seventy miles from the coast, but were compelled to return by scarcity of provisions, and by the hostility of the natives.

Having lost their boats, they had a most perilous journey, along an inhospitable shore, to the Swan River. In following years Mr. Eyre made several journeys from South Australia. In his last expedition he set out in February 1841, with the purpose of reaching the settled portion of Western Australia. This he accomplished, keeping near the sea-board all the way, and arriving at King George's Sound on July 7th. The distance was above one thousand miles, the latter half of the journey being made with only one native lad, and amidst most distressing privations. On one occasion they were seven days without a drop of water. The country was found to be generally without any timber, the higher ground clothed with scrub, while scarcely a stream or river-course occurred for six hundred miles.

Whilst Mr. Eyre was exploring the western part of the continent, which was found inhospitable, and unsuited for colonization, Count Strzelecki, a native of Polish Prussia, in the course of a scientific voyage round the world, came to Sydney. He was asked by the Governor of New South Wales, Sir George Gipps, to undertake a survey of that portion of the colony between 30° and 39° south latitude, and stretching 150 miles inland from the coast. In 1840 the Count discovered, in the extreme south-east, a fine and well-watered region, which he named Gipps' Land, hitherto cut off from the rest of the continent by the Australian Alps. But he had already made a more startling discovery, which was kept a secret, and of which we must give a separate notice—the gold fields of Australia.

Confining our view meanwhile to the progress of geographical exploration, the next important movement was the attempt to cross the continent from sea to sea. Of the earliest expeditions for this great design we hasten to give a brief account, and can here therefore only mention the names of Austin, the brothers Augustus and Frank Gregory, Kennedy, Warburton, and other explorers who, after Sturt and Mitchell, added to our knowledge of various parts of the vast continent.

Some of the regions traversed by them were not favourable for colonization, but others have been since occupied by an industrious and rapidly increasing population.

We conclude this article by referring to the various divisions, political as well as geographical, of the great continent, and the dates at which they became separate Colonies. The first settlement, as we have seen, dates from 1788, and this was the beginning of the colony of New South Wales. Victoria was separated from New South Wales in 1850, and Queensland in 1859, to form separate colonies; Western Australia was taken possession of in 1829. South Australia, at first a settlement of a private company, became a Crown colony in 1836; and to it was added, in 1863, the northern territory, or Alexandra Land, stretching from latitude 26° south to the north coast, and between longitudes 129° and 138°. The population of this territory is as yet small, but its area is above 523,500 square miles. The densest population in proportion to the area is in Victoria, which has only 88,451 square miles. Colonial statistics rapidly change, and it may be interesting to compare with more recent returns the population in 1874. New South Wales, 584,278; Victoria, 807,756; South Australia, 205,082 (of which only 200 were in the northern territory); Queensland, 160,000; Western Australia, 26,209. The Aborigines were then reckoned at about 50,000. In 1836 Victoria had only 244 persons; in 1851 the population had risen to 77,000; but in consequence of the discovery of the gold fields it increased to 325,000; and in a few years had far outstripped the parent colony. It is owing to the gold fields that the rapid increase of population is due, but the solid prosperity of the colonies will henceforth mainly depend on their ordinary commercial and agricultural industries. The sudden leap into notoriety caused by the gold discovery, and the consequent rush of emigrants, will always mark an epoch in Australian history, and deserve separate notice in these pages.

ACROSS AUSTRALIA FROM SEA TO SEA.

IN 1844 the first attempt was made to solve the geographical mystery of the great *terra incognita* of central Australia. Captain Sturt, already so distinguished in adventurous exploration, undertook, under Government auspices, to lead an expedition from Adelaide to the Gulf of Carpentaria on the north. Following upwards the course of the Murray and the Darling, he thence struck across in a north-west direction through a country hitherto unexplored. It was a dismal journey, mostly through barren desert, and during six months, from November 19th, 1844, to July 2nd, 1845, not a drop of rain fell. The nights were cold even when the days were fearfully hot. No living creatures were seen throughout long tracts of stony wilderness, and even vegetation ceased. Having advanced to within two degrees of the Tropic of Capricorn, and no rain having fallen from July 17th to September 9th, with another summer setting in, it was thought prudent to retreat, and he reached Adelaide January 19th, 1846. He had been out eighteen months, and only accomplished half the distance. The expedition was so far useful as revealing the true nature of large areas of the interior.

While this expedition was in progress Dr. Leichardt, a German naturalist, undertook a journey from Moreton Bay, on the east coast, to Port Essington on the north. The journey occupied fifteen months, and resulted in the discovery of numerous districts, fertile and well watered, large tracts of which have since been occupied as sheep runs. The distance in direct line was 1,800 miles, but above 3,000 miles were traversed before his return in November 1845.

Anxious to make further exploration of the interior Leichardt set out in 1848 on a second expedition, from which, alas! he never returned. Two years passed without any tidings of him. When the third year was drawing to a close much anxiety was felt, and in after years expeditions went in search. In

1852 a report was current among the natives, seven hundred miles in the interior, that he and his party had perished. Thirty years passed without further tidings, and then some relics and the explorer's journal were recovered by a settler from the natives. The interest taken in the lost explorer was as great in the colony as that felt in Europe on the discovery of the Franklin relics. We do not say more now, for the time must be near when some colonial pen will write a full history of Australian exploration, a book which will contain many a story of thrilling interest, and many a record of patient endurance and heroic enterprise.

In 1858 Mr. Macdouall Stuart commenced those expeditions which have made his name famous in the annals of Australian exploration. Three journeys were made into the interior before 1860, each of them with valuable results in opening up new districts. In March of that year he started on a fourth journey, with the purpose of crossing to the northern shore, but the determined hostility of the natives compelled him to turn back when within 220 miles of the western extremity of the Gulf of Carpentaria. He found wide desert belts, but also at intervals rich and well-watered tracts. In 1861 he set out once more, and taking the old track he reached the furthest camping place of his previous journey, and finally reached the north coast at Van Diemen's Gulf, where he hoisted the British flag, nine months after leaving Adelaide. To find a way through the dense scrub was the chief difficulty in the last part of the journey, but the route once being marked out was never again lost, and before ten years a line of telegraph from north to south across the continent brought Sydney and Melbourne into speaking distance with the mother country.

Macdouall Stuart got all praise for his successful enterprise, but historical justice must be done to other explorers who were actually before him in crossing from sea to sea. July 25th, 1862, was the day of Stuart's arrival on the northern shore, but more than a year before, on the 11th February, 1861, the passage had been achieved by Messrs. Burke and Wills. They

DEPARTURE OF THE EXPEDITION FROM MELBOURNE. [*page* 339.

Across Australia from Sea to Sea. 339

perished on their return journey to Melbourne, and so the fact of their having crossed from sea to sea was unknown when Stuart claimed the honour of the first passage. Of this expedition, with its tragic ending, let us give a brief account.

It was a great gala day in Melbourne, when, on the 20th of August, 1860, an expedition, numbering fifteen persons, with horses, camels, and an immense supply of stores, including provisions for twelve months, left the Royal Park, amidst the cheers and good wishes of the assembled population. The funds for the enterprise had been contributed by subscription, and the whole community became interested in the project, which was to cross the continent to the Gulf of Carpentaria. The command of the expedition was entrusted to Robert O'Hara Burke, who had formerly been in the Mounted Constabulary in Ireland, and Acting Inspector of Police in Melbourne He was a man much respected and trusted in the colony. The second in command was William John Wills, a medical man by education, recently arrived as an emigrant, and now appointed as surveyor and naturalist to the expedition. Dr. Ludwick Becker, geologist, nine white men, and three coloured men, one of them an Indian Sepoy, in charge of the camels, formed the expedition. Cooper's Creek was selected as the base of operations, where a large depôt of provisions was to be formed, as the explorers might have to fall back upon it, if necessary. An advance party of eight pushed on from the Darling to Cooper's Creek to establish the depôt, and here all met, and remained from the 11th of November to the 16th of December, making excursions from this centre, and preparing for the perilous and unknown regions to the north.

Burke knew by this time which men seemed best to accompany himself and Wills on the journey, and he selected Gray and King, leaving Brahé in charge of the depôt, with strict orders to remain there, and not quit the place, unless from absolute necessity. Three men were thus left along with

Brahé. The others had been sent back, as not necessary for carrying out the expedition.

Burke, with his party, then started, directing his course along the 140th degree east longitude. He had with him six camels, a horse, and provisions for twelve weeks. He expressed his belief that in less than that time he would be back, though Brahé said he hardly expected so speedy a return.

The journey was less difficult than they anticipated. They divided each day into three short stages, and occasionally travelled by night to get more rapidly over desert tracts. They always carried water, that they might be free to halt at any suitable camping ground, although no streams or springs were near. Thus they advanced, steering "by compass and observation," till they came to a river, which Wills pronounced to be the Albert River, but which others have since thought to be the Flinders River, and others some stream on the other side of the Albert, more to the westward. The date is somewhat doubtful, but it was between the 11th and 14th of February, 1861.

They did not think it necessary to go on to the shore of the Gulf, for they were satisfied that the river on whose banks they were was a tidal river, and the water was decidedly salt. They advanced eighteen miles beyond the spot where they came to this conclusion, but a fear had already possessed them of the provisions failing, and they felt satisfied with what had been done.

About the middle of February the return journey was commenced. A record of their visit was left at the side of the river, and whatever baggage could be spared, including some books, which had been taken to lighten the monotony of the way. Two-thirds of the provisions having been consumed, it was necessary to be upon short rations, eked out with an occasional hawk or crow that came within gunshot. Rains had made the ground in some places heavy, and the camels, enfeebled by over-fatigue and under-feeding, could scarcely struggle on. Four out of the six soon succumbed, and their flesh gave them a few not very wholesome meals. Gray was the first of the four whose strength was exhausted, and he died on the 8th of April. They had scarcely strength to dig a grave deep enough to cover him, and a sense of lassitude and utter helplessness would have made them lie down also to die, were it not that the hope of reaching the depôt at Cooper's Creek sustained their feeble and staggering steps. Another of the camels and the horse "Billy" soon after died of starvation. The bodies were cut, and some of the flesh "jerked," but the dried strips had not a trace of fat, and were mere fibre.

At length, on Sunday, April 21st, they reached Cooper's Creek. The place was silent and deserted. Without uttering a word, they looked round, and when the terrible truth of their being abandoned broke upon them, Burke flung himself on the ground, completely overwhelmed with surprise and vexation, while Wills seemed utterly paralysed and bewildered. So King reported, who alone survived to tell the tale of that terrible scene.

In a few moments all three recovered their self-command sufficiently to examine the place and ascertain the state of matters. On a tree near the spot where they had parted from Brahé they descried the words cut, " DIG, 21st April." The feelings of the men on reading this date can be imagined. The depôt was deserted upon the very day of their arriving there! Yet this allowed a gleam of hope amidst their disappointment, and prevented it turning into despair. It might be possible, after a little rest, to overtake the retiring party, who had left so recently. Yet they had hardly strength to dig the ground under the marked tree. Here they found some flour, oatmeal, dry meat, and sugar. These famished men were thankful for this, but as King said afterwards in his affecting narrative, "they thought they might have left more, as they had nine months' provisions for themselves, without stinting." On further search they found in the *cache* the following letter :—

"DEPÔT, COOPER'S CREEK, *April* 21*st*.

"The Depôt party of the V. E. E. (Victoria Exploring Expedition) leaves this camp to-day to return to the Darling. I intend to go S.E from camp to get into our old track near Bulloo. Two of my companions and myself are quite well; the third, Paton, has been unable to walk for the last eighteen days, as his leg has been severely hurt when thrown by one of the horses. No one has been up here from the Darling. We have six camels and twelve horses in good working condition.

"WILLIAM BRAHÉ."

This letter was enough to drive them to despair. How could half-dying men overtake those who were "quite well," and "with camels and horses in good working condition"?

Nevertheless they took courage, and resolved to endeavour to brace themselves for a last struggle for dear life. They resolved to rest for a few days, for they were too weak to proceed at once, and while thus waiting they anxiously discussed the future. Wills thought they should proceed by the old track homewards, but Burke, being satisfied that the provisions could possibly not hold out, resolved to make for Mount Hopeless, from which to the nearest settlements of the Adelaide territory it would be a shorter journey.

It was a fatal determination, and a second blunder was made in leaving no manifest sign at Cooper's Creek of their having been there. An urgent letter, indeed, was deposited in the *cache*, but no mark such as Brahé had made on the tree. It seems that this man, possibly from some feeling of conscious guilt in leaving contrary to orders, had gone or sent back to the Creek, and seeing nothing, concluded that no one had been there, and hastily resumed his journey.

Abandoning everything but what could be carried for supporting life, Burke and his companions turned their steps towards Mount Hopeless. They found the water-courses dry, and knew that to persevere in this direction would imply

Across Australia from Sea to Sea. 343

certain and speedy death. They returned with difficulty a distance of about forty miles, to a creek where there was plenty of water, but by this time their provisions were almost exhausted. Wills made his way to Cooper's Creek, and deposited another note in the *cache*, telling "where they were waiting." Some natives found them at this creek, and showed much sympathy. They lived chiefly on nardoo, a plant from the seeds of which they prepared a sort of meal, but this diet was insufficient to keep up, far less to restore, their strength. Wills kept his journal day by day, and there were found in it, on its recovery, such entries as these: "All very weak, in spite of having had fish from the natives." This was written on June 7th, and on the 15th he writes: "King out for nardoo, Mr. Burke and I pounding and cleaning it; he finds himself very weak, and I am not a bit stronger."

The natives had by this time left them, and the three travellers were left to their own resources. The last strip of dried camel had been consumed, and nothing remained but the nardoo, of which Wills says: "It appears to be wholly indigestible, and cannot possibly be sufficiently nutritious to sustain life by itself." In a later entry he says: " Unless relief comes I cannot possibly last more than a fortnight." On the 27th June he wrote a touching letter of farewell to his father, evidently intended to be a comfort to him after his death, which he felt was imminent, for it ends with the words, " I think to live about four or five days; my spirits are excellent." He had told of the successful journey, and the causes of its calamitous ending, and said: "Our position, although more provoking, is probably not near so disagreeable as that of poor Harry and his companions"—alluding to his cousin who perished with Sir John Franklin.

As they felt that some effort must be made, Burke and King went out in hope of meeting with some of the natives, leaving nardoo, water, and firewood within reach of Wills, who was too weak to stand. They made their way to Cooper's Creek, and there Burke lay down to die. King stayed a few hours beside his dead chief, and then set out to return to Wills. He found only his dead body. He must have died soon after they left him. Burying the body in the sand, the lonely man set out in quest of natives, for he saw that they had been at the place. He soon found some who told him by signs the " white fellow " was dead, putting their fingers in the ground and covering them with sand, pointing at the same time to the Creek. King made them understand that Burke also was dead, and the poor natives were moved to compassion at his loneliness and misery. They took him to their camp, gave him plenty to eat, and treated him with the utmost tenderness. He stayed with them for about a month, and recovered a little of his strength. They managed to convey a wish to visit the place where Burke had died, and on King conducting them there, they broke into loud wailing and lamentation, and after sitting round in a group looking at the dead chief for a time, they covered his resting place with a pall of green bushes which they gathered. These are the people whom the more savage early colonists, after provoking their hostility by outrages, shot down and killed by poison, as being lower than brutes, and incapable of human feeling ! A happier tone of public opinion now prevails in the centres of colonial life, and Christian influence has been brought to bear on the few survivors, but there is still cause for watchfulness, in remote places, as to the treatment of the natives, whose lands more powerful strangers have taken possession of.

While these tragical events were occurring, great anxiety was felt in Melbourne as to the fate of an expedition which had started with so much promise. A relief expedition was at length formed, and Mr. A. W. Howitt, a son of William and Mary Howitt, volunteered to be the leader. The rescuing party reached Cooper's Creek on the 15th of September, and in the neighbourhood they met with King, still dependent on the natives, who had continued to treat him kindly, but he was in a state of extreme weakness and despondency. The natives hailed with delight the advent of the new-comers, evidently because they thought that their arrival would rouse their poor guest from his gloomy lethargy. Mr. Howitt stayed in the neighbourhood to gather all the relics of the ill-fated expedition, including the journal kept by Mr. Wills almost to the last hour of his life. The remains of the brave explorers were buried with honour, and a record cut on trees beside the graves, over which had been read the grand story of death and resurrection used in the Christian burial service. Mr. Howitt distributed useful presents among the kindly natives, which were received by them with demonstrations of gratitude and joy. On the return to Melbourne, King was received with great honour, and rewarded for his adventurous services. Brahé made the best excuses he could for leaving Cooper's Creek, and his part in the affair was, happily for him, forgotten in the pride felt at the noble way in which the explorers had done their duty. A monument in Melbourne attests the admiration of their fellow-colonists, and their names will ever live in the annals of heroic adventure.

THE DISCOVERY OF GOLD IN AUSTRALIA.

IN our account of early exploring expeditions in Australia, it has been mentioned that Count Strzelecki was engaged in a scientific survey of New South Wales, commencing in the year 1839. In his survey of the hill region in the east of the colony he was struck with the resemblance of the rocks to those in Russia, which were rich in mineral wealth. On making further investigation he discovered that extensive gold-fields existed in the region. He communicated the information to Governor Gipps, who implored him not to divulge the secret, dreading the effect upon the population, which was just settling down to successful industry as colonists. The Count kept his promise to the Governor, and his whole conduct in Australia was generous and self-denying, being a man of philanthropy as well as thoroughly versed in science. He laboured for nearly five years, entirely at his own cost, in exploring the region of which he had undertaken the survey.

How the discovery was so long delayed, after settlers began to spread through the country, seems now strange; but so it was, that not till May 22nd, 1851, was the first public and official notification made. This was contained in a dispatch from Governor Fitzroy to Earl Grey, then minister for the Colonies. In this dispatch the existence of a gold-field is announced, to the westward of the town of Bathurst; at the same time the Governor adds his doubts as to the truth of the report, ."being informed that the gold sent to Sydney for inspection seemed to be Californian gold." At the same time he thought the report to be of sufficient importance to require an efficient police to patrol the Bathurst road.

A communication from Mr. Stutchbury, the geological surveyor, very soon undeceived and enlightened His Excellency. Three days before the date of the dispatch to Earl Grey, the surveyor had written from Summerhill Creek a note, announcing that gold was being found in considerable quantity, with no better instrument than a tin dish; that it was found not only in the creek, but far above its flood-line; and that at least four hundred persons were at work in the locality. The camp of the gold-finders had been named Ophir, and the first public record of the name was in the postscript of Mr. Stutchbury's letter—"Excuse this being written in pencil, as there is no ink in this city of Ophir."

It was not by Count Strzelecki alone that the presence of gold had been affirmed. Sir Roderick Murchison, probably from hearing the Count's report, and himself knowing the geology of the Ural Mountains, had come to the conclusion that the whole Dividing Range was auriferous, and suggested to the colonial minister the adoption of measures to attract gold-seekers. Sir Roderick did not take into consideration the effects of the announcement, which were dreaded by Governor

The Discovery of Gold in Australia. 347

Gipps and Strzelecki. The immediate effects had much admixture of evil, for individuals at least, but the general result to the prosperity and progress of the Australian continent can never be estimated.

Besides this testimony from England, the Rev. Mr. Clarke, a local geologist, had expressed his conviction that gold existed and would be found among the Blue Mountains.

On the 3rd of April, 1851, Mr. Hargreaves, a settler who had gone to California and seen the gold-fields there, was struck with the resemblance of that country in general aspect, or physical geography, for he does not seem to have been a geologist. He returned to Australia with the firm belief that he would find gold, and he found it. He wrote to the Government offering to reveal the locality for the sum of £500! This offer, made on April 3rd, 1851, was refused. On the 30th April he addressed another letter to the Colonial Secretary, naming the locality, and leaving the reward for the information to the liberal consideration of the Government. Whether any other reward was given we do not know, but Mr. Hargreaves, as well as Mr. Clarke and Mr. Stutchbury, received official and well-paid appointments at the gold-fields of Bathurst.

Stranger still it seems that the discovery was so long delayed when the following facts are considered. A shepherd had long been in the habit of bringing lumps of gold to Sydney, at occasional intervals, and disposing of them in the town, but always refusing to tell where he got them.

In 1849, an engineer employed in some iron-works, in the neighbourhood of Berrima, produced to the Colonial Secretary a lump of gold embedded in quartz, and asked a large sum for naming the locality; but it was refused, and Smith kept his secret, with what result to himself is not known to us.

How the rumour first got wings and spread it is not easy now to tell; but very soon after Mr. Hargreaves had set to work the whole colony began to be in excitement. Communication was slow and difficult in those times, and it is a fact that on the very day when the Governor sent off his incredulous report to England, there were already above a thousand people at Summerhill Creek, busily at work on an area of not more than a mile in extent, and finding gold in considerable quantities. More than a week before, a man had brought to Bathurst a lump of gold weighing thirteen ounces valued at £30, and the whole population capable of moving rushed to the goldfield. When the authentic news came to Sydney there was the same excitement there, and tradesmen and labourers of every class and sailors from the ships were soon on the road to the Bathurst Hills.

Three months after the dispatch of Governor Gipps, Lieutenant-Governor La Trobe wrote from Melbourne to Earl Grey that large deposits of gold had been found in Victoria. A proclamation having been issued, announcing arrangements for granting licenses similar to what had been found necessary to be granted in New South Wales, the population poured forth from the city to the gold-fields, especially to Ballarat, the most productive of the various localities where it had been discovered. Previous to this discovery the labourers of Melbourne had been migrating in crowds to the Bathurst diggings. This was soon checked, and not only so, but the tide turned, and the Port Phillip emigrants found their way back again, and with them a large portion of the population of New South Wales, allured by the superior richness of the Victoria goldfields, and the ease with which they are reached, from their vicinity to the city. In a short time not fewer than 20,000 people had arrived at the Victoria mines from the neighbouring colonies. The disorganization of society was threatened, and ruin impended upon all the industrial pursuits of the colony. But things righted themselves gradually. It is not the purpose here to narrate the history of the times subsequent to the first discovery of gold, but having in previous pages described the first discovery of gold in California (*ante*, page 18), it seemed fitting to narrate the parallel event in our own Australian colonies.

HOW CHRISTIANITY WAS INTRODUCED INTO MANGAIA.

ON the morning of March 29th, 1777, the natives of Mangaia were startled by the apparition of a "mighty canoe, without paddles or outrigger," but rapidly approaching the southern coast as if possessed of life. By the time it reached the lee of the island, numbers of armed men had made their way to the outer edge of the reef, and gazed at this seeming monster of the deep with admiration and terror. The famous warrior Potai remarked, "This is unquestionably a visitor from the spirit-world." Another chief oracularly declared that "it was the great (god) Motoro himself."

After some natural hesitation, Mourua and his friend Makatu, both worshippers of Motoro, launched a canoe and approached the huge visitor that had successfully "pierced the solid blue vault." The gift of a string of large blue beads (afterwards shown about as veritable chips off the azure arch), and a few nails (subsequently converted into brad-awls), rewarded their daring. The boat of the *Resolution* rowed along the reef in the vain hope of finding a landing-place. Mourua without hesitation jumped into the boat, and receiving from Captain Cook a large knife, stuck it in his right ear,—the pocket of those days. He was thus sketched by an artist connected with the expedition.

Numbers of natives now took courage, swam off to the boat, and received gifts from the great navigator. To Kirikovi, the then temporal lord of Mangaia, was presented an iron axe, the first ever seen on the island. A general scrimmage now took place; but Captain Cook, with great forbearance, after permitting these unceremonious fellows to possess themselves of all he could spare, returned to the *Resolution*, accompanied only by Mourua, who deemed himself wonderfully brave in venturing on board. This he would not have done but for the assurances of Mai (the "Omai" of the *Voyages*) that he would be perfectly safe. Much to his satisfaction, Mourua was eventually brought back to the reef in the ship's boat. He swam ashore, and related to his admiring countrymen the wonders he had seen; whilst Cook sailed on to Atiu, which lies about one hundred miles north of Mangaia. An important step had thus been taken in civilisation: they had become acquainted with the existence of a race different from all that they had hitherto seen or heard of, wiser, stronger, and more benevolent than themselves.

At the beginning of the present century, an English whaling ship, name unknown, touched at Mangaia. Emboldened by the profitable intercourse of their fathers with Captain Cook, several canoes at once pushed off to the ship. A brisk traffic was for some time carried on; but no native was allowed to board the ship. A chief named Koroa had just concluded a splendid bargain in exchanging a fine octopus for a knife and a tenpenny nail, when a wild fellow called Tairoa paddled up in his canoe, and, watching his opportunity, mortally speared a white man who was holding on to the ship's iron braces, and amusing himself with the scene. Highly satisfied with his valour, Tairoa paddled back to what he considered a safe distance, and watched the confusion on board the vessel. A long bamboo (as it appeared to the natives) was pointed at the aggressor, who did not dream of danger. An unaccountable light and noise issued from this hitherto unknown weapon, and Tairoa fell lifeless at the bottom of his canoe.

All now was consternation amongst the natives. Ngaunui proposed to Koroa to rescue the body of the slain; but Koroa wisely refused to interfere, and cursed Tairoa for having spoiled the traffic. Ngaunui persisted in attempting to get the corpse, when a few swan shot in his shoulders induced him to retire with all convenient speed. A boat was now lowered, the crew of which took possession of Tairoa's lifeless body and his canoe. All being drawn upon deck, the captain made haste to leave this inhospitable island.

About 1814, when Makitaka was lord of Mangaia, and a terrible famine prevailed over the island, another whaler arrived,—the third vessel they had seen. The weather was remarkably fine. The captain, wishing to see something of the island, landed with a companion. The names of the two white men who first landed on Mangaia are unknown. They crossed the reef, and walked in quiet over part of the ground now occupied by the mission premises. Very unwisely one of them displayed a fine pearl oyster shell. A rush was made by the natives to get possession of this wonderful treasure. The fortunate thief was himself chased into the interior by scores of envious countrymen. With this magnificent ornament dangling from his neck, he would be sure to carry the palm at the festive dances. The white men, alarmed for their own safety, fired repeatedly, though without effect, upon the retreating natives. Recollecting the fate of Tairoa, the natives disappeared in the thick bush then growing to the water's edge, whilst their white visitors hastily took their departure.

The next vessel that touched at the island was a schooner, having on board the lamented missionary Williams. This was in 1823. Papehia, Taua, and Haavi, with the wives of the two latter, were landed as the first evangelists of Mangaia. But the very rough treatment they at once experienced induced the five to swim back through the surf to the ship's boat. Their escape in safety was owing to Mr. Williams ordering a charge of powder to be fired from the ship to frighten the heathen, who were plainly intent on killing the men and taking possession of the women. All their property was stolen.

In 1852 good old Haavi revisited Mangaia; and, in an address delivered to a most crowded congregation, he touchingly contrasted the savageness and wretchedness of 1823 with the pleasant and Christian aspect of the villagers before him. Many were affected to tears by his remarks, for not a few of their number had taken part in the attack upon these humble servants of God.

Mr. Williams left behind him a valuable souvenir in the

shape of a couple of pigs. The boar was named Tauiti (*Little Pet*); the sow Makave (*Ringlet*). They were gravely conducted to the *marae*, or temple of the war-god, as foreign divinities. They were wrapped in sacred white cloth, and the best of food set before them day by day. But the speech of these divinities was a great mystery. From their grunting about the *marae* the Mangaians derive the proverb, "Ua aue nga atua,"—"the gods are crying." Eventually the filthy habits of these foreign animals made the heathen suspect that they were no gods after all. The finest of the first litter was solemnly offered to Rongo in lieu of a human victim. They greatly multiplied. In 1852 a grand feast was held, when upwards of a thousand hogs were killed and eaten.

After the departure of the teachers, their little property and books were used as ornaments for the night dances. Nobody suspected that the printed characters had a signification, the islanders regarding them as ingenious cloth-patterns. But soon after dysentery — hitherto unknown — decimated the population. The heathen very naturally referred this scourge to the anger of the visitors' God on account of the ill-usage His followers had experienced at their hands. A vow was registered that, should He ever deign to send messengers again to their shores, they should be duly protected from insult and injury. The leaves of books, which had been worked up into head-dresses, and strips of calico, once the garments of the teachers and their wives, were carefully collected, and thrown down the deep chasms where they were accustomed to bury their dead, hoping that the scourge would disappear with these things.

On June 15th, 1824, their sincerity was put to the test. Two members of the church of Tahaa—Davida and Tiere—were landed on Mangaia by Messrs. Tyerman and Bennet on their voyage to Sydney. With the Tahitian New Testament wrapped up in their shirts, and secured to the top of their heads, these intrepid men leaped into the surf, and swam ashore in the presence of many hundreds of heathen. As

Davida's feet touched the reef a long spear was thrust at him by a warrior, who exultingly shouted, "Thou shalt never catch sharks," meaning that the new God should never win victories on Mangaia. Providentially, the future king of the island—then a young man—was standing close behind the intending murderer, and at the very moment the lunge was being made arrested the weapon.

These humble evangelists landed on the reef, and were at once *literally* taken by the hand by Numangatini, the king, and conducted to his own seaside *marae*, dedicated to Rongo, so as to invest their persons with a sacred character. The crowd dared not follow. After a brief rest the king led them to the interior, where his ordinary residence was. All this had been pre-arranged between the king and principal chiefs, as the schooner had been recognised on the previous evening as "God's ship." The carrying out of their wishes was entrusted to the king and his warlike friend Maungaati, who showed the strangers great kindness.

A feast was prepared for the teachers. The crowd was surprised that the strangers should close their eyes and pray before eating. On this well-remembered occasion the following colloquy occurred between the heathen and their new teachers :

"What are you doing?"—"Thanking God for His gifts."

"Where does your God live?"—"In heaven."

"What is His name?"—"Jehovah."

"Does your God eat food?"—"God is a Spirit. He is not like us; He lives for ever. It was He that made the earth, the sky, the sea, and all things. He made us."

A reed house was now built for the use of the teachers, and a rude hut for worship and daily teaching. The site was the enclosure where human sacrifices were first exposed.

Very diligently did Davida and Tiere labour to instruct the younger men in the mysteries of book-learning, and all who would attend, in the first principles of Christianity. Nor were their efforts vain, for numbers came from all parts of the island to hear the wonderful words that fell from the lips of these devoted evangelists.

At length Davida found himself strong enough to form a Christian village near the sea, where a good site could easily be obtained for the erection of a larger church and school-house. This had been originally suggested by the Rev. J. Williams. The new village was called "God's town." At that period its rocky shore was covered with large ironwood and other trees. It was the custom of the early coverts, like Nathanael of old, to retire at midday to the seclusion of these trees to pray,—each having his own particular tree.

Now, for the first time, husband and wife ate together at meals, and parents tasted food with their firstborn. The oppressive restriction thus broken through had prevailed throughout the South Sea Islands, although no better reason cou'd be assigned for it than that "such was the will of the gods."

In September 1825, Mr. Bourne, the pastor of Davida and Tiere, visited Mangaia, and was much pleased with the striking change so speedily brought about by the blessing of God.

Not long afterwards—in 1826—Tiere passed away to his rest and reward, so that Davida was left to labour alone for some years. Tiere was a man of amiable disposition and winning manners.

Opposite to the *marae* of Motoro and the altar for human sacrifice was the idol-house, known as "The-prop-of-the-kingdom" (*Te kaiara*). Inside were the principal gods of Mangaia, which, with the exception of Rongo, all consisted of rude representations of the human form carved in iron-wood.

The entire family of gods was fed *before* the sun had actually sunk beneath the horizon, as that was the signal for them to go on their travels all over the island. At break of day they were said to rush back with a great noise "like wind in a cocoa-nut grove," ashamed of daylight! Occasionally the idols were sunned to prevent their fine wrappings from getting mouldy. New white cloth was put on them from time to time.

Some time after the introduction of Christianity it happened that one of the regal family was taken dangerously ill. Whilst the heart was softened by affliction, the parent was struck with the glaring absurdity of professed adherents to Christianity keeping up this idol-shrine with its daily oven of food. What should be done with the idols? It was decided by the king, Pirama Simeona, and the other leading men of the day, to surrender these dangerous things to Davida. To the horror of the heathen, but to the great joy of the Christian party, the whole thirteen were carried in triumphal procession to the house of Davida by the sea. The wrappings were thrown away, and for the first time since they were carved by Rori they were exposed to the vulgar gaze. Soon after Messrs. Williams and Platt paid an opportune visit to the island; and they proceeded to Raiatea laden with these idols, which were eventually deposited in the museum of the London Missionary Society.

The day the idols were removed, the house in which they had been kept was set on fire; the *maraes* all over the island were desecrated, the little houses in which the deity was supposed to be invisibly present were burnt; the great stone idol of Rongo at the seaside, where human sacrifices were offered, was smashed to atoms, and (what is much to be regretted) the magnificent native mahogany (*tamanu*) trees were set on fire, on account of their supposed connection with idolatry. Cocoa-nuts were planted on the crest of the *marae* of Motoro in commemoration of this happy event. In their wild excitement the war-dance was actually performed, as if they had gained an important victory!

The constellation of the Pleiades held an important place in the heathen mythology. Its appearance on the horizon at sunset, about the middle of December, determined the commencement of the new year. When at sunset the constellation was invisible, the second half of the year was supposed to have commenced. The reappearance of the Pleiades on the horizon at sunset was in many of the islands a season of extravagant rejoicing, and was welcomed with frantic dances and discordant shell-music.

In July 1845, arrived their first resident missionary, the Rev. G. Gill, who remained at this station until his removal to Rarotonga in April 1857. His labours were incessant, and were owned by the Great Master to the ingathering of many to the fold, and in the general enlightenment of the islanders in spiritual truth. A stone church and a substantial school-house, erected in each of the three villages, testify to his energy. A mission-house of a superior character was built by him at the principal village of Oneroa. Although many years have elapsed since his removal, he still lives in the loving remembrance of the people.

On his arrival it was difficult to travel from one village to another; before he left an excellent road had been made round the island. Several oppressive laws were cancelled by the king and chiefs at his suggestion.

On the 15th of July, 1851, the writer left England in the missionary bark *John Williams*, but did not land at Mangaia until March 1st, 1852. Not long afterwards the character of the people was put to a severe test by the wreck of two vessels within a few months of each other. Most of the property was saved for the captains. Upon the whole there was every reason to be much pleased with the way the people behaved.

Of the men who welcomed the first white missionary in 1845, and myself in 1852, few survive; they were men who knew by bitter experience the cruel bondage of heathenism, and who lovingly embraced Christianity. We thank God that these worthies died as they had lived in the faith of the Gospel.

Our converts do not seem to be troubled with the doubts and fears which affect the highly-cultured European. May not this be owing to the childlike nature of their faith,—just taking God at His word?

MANGAIA. HEATHEN CEREMONIES ON THE RETURN OF THE PLEIADES. (page 336.

Amongst the excellent men whose death-beds it has been my privilege to visit I would refer to Rakoia, chief of Tamarua, who died in September 1865, nearly eighty years of age. He was emphatically a good man, ready for every good word and work. He was never absent from his place in the adult Bible-class or in church, except when ill. During the last two years of his life he became childish; yet I could nearly always fix his attention for a few minutes by referring to the interests of his soul. The last words I heard from his lips a few days before his death were, "I am dying; but I am in God's hands. Jesus alone is the Way, the Truth, and the Life!"

Three months afterwards Tamatangi, chief of Ivirua, died of inflammation of the lungs. I had ridden over twice to administer medicine and to converse with him. On the first Sabbath of December 1865, I spent the entire day at Ivirua. After the morning service I went to see him, and at once perceived that the last hour was near, although he was in full possession of his mental faculties. Tamatangi might be seventy years old, and was reclining on a mat supported by a near relative. Like Jacob, he died in the midst of his people; for perhaps one hundred natives were in the chamber of death. His mind was fixed upon Jesus. Twice we offered prayer on behalf of the dying man; and twice we sung (first a version of "When I can read my title clear," and then a version of "Rock of ages, cleft for me"). I held his hand, uttering such words of comfort as I could think of. He looked around upon his wife and relatives, and then fixed his dying gaze on me. His last words were an exhortation to his clan to cleave to the Word of God. He then said "Farewell,' and expired.

Mauapa died in the same year. He was the oldest man on the island, and had been a valuable deacon for many years. In visiting this worthy old Christian, I have often come away refreshed in spirit, beholding what Christianity can do for one who grew up to mature age in heathen darkness. His mind was clear to the last. He passed away without a cloud.

In October 1866, Paunui, who had been my leading deacon at Oneroa for many years, was called away. His removal was rather sudden. Although by no means faultless—indeed, being possessed of great energy and decision of character, he often occasioned me great anxiety—his death was a brilliant sunset. One Sabbath morning early he sent for me. I was grieved to find him suffering greatly. Gasping for breath, he said, "My teacher, I am going. Do not detain me by your kind prayers and wishes. Let me go. I want to be with Jesus. There we will meet again." To me it seemed incredible that such a robust, noble frame should be so near dissolution. I spoke of his possible recovery, and the medicines I had in my pocket. He again said, "I know I am dying. I wish to go and be with Jesus. Medicines will not avail. Detain me not." I inquired the ground of his hope. He said that he was trusting in Jesus only. He then commended me and the native pastors to the special care of a chief (his relative) who was by his side. This he did partly from kind personal interest and friendship, and partly as devolving a sacred trust derived from his cousin Parima, the first chief who embraced the Gospel, and who thereby was universally considered to be the special protector and helper of the "servants of God." Other chiefs who visited him successively received the same charge, proving how sacredly he regarded the trust committed to him by those who nearly fifty years ago embraced the Christian faith.

I bless God for the many dying testimonies I have met with among these poor natives to the power of the Gospel to take away the sting of death, and to impart in its place a bright hope of a blissful immortality. It should be remembered that these men were all warriors in heathenism, and had freely shed blood without compunction in those days of darkness. They grew up in the practice of a debasing superstition, and yet cordially embraced the teachings and moral requirements of the Gospel.

For the last seven years the contributions from Mangaia to

the general funds of the London Missionary Society, after defraying all local expenses, have exceeded £200, and during the same period, Rarotonga has contributed a much larger sum.

The first complete version of the Bible in the dialect of the Hervey Group was brought by the *John Williams* in 1852. In two years every one of the five thousand copies was disposed of. In 1855 a new edition of an equal number was called for, and a third editon (of five thousand), with marginal references, is in general circulation.

A recent critic, referring to the South Sea Missions, speaks of "the smallness of the results obtained from the enormous expenditure upon Mission-work." Now what are the facts of the case? Sixty-five years ago the whole of the Pacific was heathen. Now upwards of three hundred islands are Christianised. When missions were commenced in the Pacific, commerce did not exist. The commerce of the Pacific is now estimated at £3,000,000. So surely does civilization follow in the wake of Christianity. Idolatry, in the greater portion of the Pacific, is a thing of the past. Education is advancing; 500,000 natives are under instruction; 60,000 are, we hope, "disciples indeed." Wherever a Christian community is ministered to by a native pastor, he is sustained, not by contributions drawn from Europe or America, but by the freewill offerings of his own people. All this has, under God, been done by various Protestant Missionary Societies at little more than the total cost of the Alexandra Palace,—less than a million sterling!

Seven complete translations of the Scriptures have been made by missionaries into dialects hitherto unwritten. Thirteen others are proceeding at the present moment. That the message of love should thus be conveyed in twenty barbarous dialects is itself a wonderful feat, whether regarded from a literary or a religious point of view.

The writer has not yet discovered an island of saints. If he were in search of one, he would naturally look for it not amongst those who within his own memory were heathen, but nearer home, where Christianity has been professed for nearly eighteen centuries. None are so conscious of the manifold defects of their converts as the missionaries themselves; but they believe that they are equal to the church at Corinth (who were honoured by an epistle from an inspired apostle), and certainly far superior to those hordes who in the Middle Ages cast aside their idols, and became the founders of our modern Europe.*

TWO ATTEMPTS TO ASCEND CHIMBORAZO.

'FEW of the works of nature," says Mr. Prescott, in his "History of the Conquest of Peru," " produce impressions of higher sublimity than the aspect of this coast, as it is gradually unfolded to the eye of the mariner sailing on the distant waters of the Pacific, where mountain is seen to rise above mountain, and Chimborazo, with its glorious canopy of snow, glistening far above the clouds, crowns the whole as with a celestial diadem."

Until comparatively recent times, the Andes were generally supposed to include the highest mountains of the world, and Chimborazo was regarded as the highest of the Andes. It is now known that there are peaks in the Andes loftier than Chimborazo, and that there are mountains in the Himalayas higher than any in the Andes. The present century was, however, well advanced before these facts were discovered, and at the time that the celebrated Alexander von Humboldt was travelling in South America it was universally believed that Chimborazo was the highest mountain in the world. There is no doubt that it was this which principally stimulated the traveller to try to reach the summit, and he was profoundly vexed that he did not succeed.

* From "Life in the Southern Isles," by the Rev. W. Wyatt Gill, B.A. (Religious Tract Society).

Two attempts to ascend Chimborazo.

Humboldt had been travelling three years in South America at the time that he made his attempt to ascend Chimborazo. He left Quito for the expedition on the 9th of June, 1802, and on June 23rd he reached the mountain. He says, that upon arriving at the elevation of 15,600 feet the way became narrower and steeper. "The natives, with one exception, refused to accompany us farther, and were deaf to entreaties and threatenings, maintaining that they suffered more than we did from the rarity of the air. We were left alone— Bonpland, the botanist, Carlos Montufar, a younger son of the Marquis de Selvalegre, a half-cast Indian from the neighbouring village of San Juan, and myself.

"By dint of great exertion and considerable patience, we reached a greater height than we had dared to hope for, seeing we had been almost constantly enveloped in mist. In many places the ridge was extremely narrow. To our left was a precipice covered with snow, the surface of which shone like glass from the effects of frost. This thin sheet of ice was at an inclination of about thirty degrees. On the right was a fearful abyss, from 800 to 1,000 feet deep, from the sides of which projected huge masses of naked rock. We leant over rather more to this side than the other, for it seemed less to be dreaded than the precipice on our left, where the smooth sides afforded no opportunity of checking a fall by catching hold of projecting pieces of rock, and where the thin crust of ice furnished no security against being buried in the loose snow beneath.

"The rock became more friable, and the ascent increasingly difficult and dangerous. At certain places, where it was very steep, we were obliged to use both hands and feet, and the edges of the rock were so sharp that we were painfully cut, especially on our hands. In addition to this, I had for some weeks been suffering from a wound in my foot. The loose position of the stones upon the narrow ridge necessitated extreme caution, since many masses that appeared to be firmly attached proved to be only embedded in sand.

"We advanced all the more slowly, as every place that seemed insecure had first to be tested. Fortunately, the attempt to reach the summit of Chimborazo had been reserved for our last enterprise among the mountains of South America, so that we had gained some experience, and knew how far we could rely on our own powers. It is a peculiar characteristic of all excursions on the Andes that beyond the line of perpetual snow Europeans are always left without guides just at the point where, from their complete ignorance of the locality, help is most needed. In everything Europeans are left to take the lead.

"We could no longer see the summit, even by glimpses, and were therefore doubly anxious to ascertain how much of the ascent had still to be accomplished. We opened the tube-barometer at a spot where the ridge was wide enough to allow two persons to stand side by side in safety. We were only at an elevation of 17,300 feet, and therefore scarcely 200 feet higher than we had attained three months previously upon Antisana.

"After an hour's cautious climbing, the ridge of rock became less steep, but the mist unfortunately remained as thick as ever. One after another we all began to feel indisposed, and experienced a feeling of nausea, accompanied by giddiness, which was far more distressing than the difficulty of breathing. Blood exuded from the lips and gums, and the eyes became bloodshot. There was nothing particularly alarming to us in these symptoms, with which we had grown familiar by experience.

"The stratum of mist which had hidden every distant object from our view began, nothwithstanding the perfect calm, suddenly to dissipate. We recognised once more the dome-shaped summit of Chimborazo, now in close proximity. It was a grand and solemn spectacle, and the hope of attaining the object of all our efforts animated us with renewed strength. The ridge of rock, only here and there covered with a thin sprinkling of snow, became somewhat wider; and we were hurrying forward with assured footsteps, when our further progress was suddenly stopped by a ravine, some four hundred feet deep and sixty feet wide, which presented an insurmountable barrier to our undertaking. We could see clearly that the ridge on which we stood continued in the same direction on the other side of the ravine, but I was doubtful whether, after all, it really led to the summit. There was no means of getting round the cleft. On Antisana, after a night of severe frost, Bonpland had been able to travel a considerable distance upon the frozen surface of snow, but here the softness of the snowy mass prohibited such an attempt, and the nature of the declivity rendered it equally impossible to scale the sides.

"It was now one o'clock in the day. We fixed up the barometer with great care, and found we had now reached an elevation of 19,286 English feet.

"We remained but a short time in this dreary waste, for we were soon again enveloped in mist, which hung about us motionless. We saw nothing more of the summit of Chimborazo, nor of the neighbouring Snow Mountains. We were isolated as in a balloon; a few rock lichens were to be observed above the line of perpetual snow, at a height of 16,920 feet; the last green moss we noticed was growing about 2,600 feet lower. A butterfly was captured by M. Bonpland at a height of 15,000 feet, and a fly was observed 1,600 feet higher; both had been carried up into the higher regions of the atmosphere by the currents of air originating in the warmer plains beneath. We did not, however, see any condors, which are so numerous upon Antisana and Pichincha, where, in those vast solitudes, from being unaccustomed to the sight of man, they are wholly devoid of fear.

"As the weather became increasingly threatening, we hurried down along the ridge of rock, and, from the insecurity of our footing, found that greater caution even was necessary than during the ascent.

"When we were at a height of about 17,400 feet, we

encountered a violent hailstorm, which gave place to snow twenty minutes before passing the limit of perpetual snow, and the flakes were so thick that the ridge was soon covered several inches deep. The danger would indeed have been great had the snow overtaken us at a height of 18,000 feet. At a few minutes past two we reached the spot where we had left the mules."

Humboldt was evidently very proud of this expedition, although he completely failed to reach the summit; and to the end of his long life he was never tired of mentioning and of drawing attention to it. Only a few years before his death, after he had travelled in many countries and seen many other mountains, he remarked to Bayard Taylor, "I still think that Chimborazo is the grandest mountain in the world."

In 1831 an attempt to ascend Chimborazo was made by M. Boussingault, the French Academician, who had been residing many years in South America. He was accompanied by an American, Colonel Hall, and says, in his published account, that, viewed from Riobamba (that is, from the east), the mountain exhibits two slopes of very different inclinations. "The one facing the Arenal, the sandy plain on the south of the mountain, is very abrupt, and there are to be seen, coming out from under the ice, numerous masses of the rock called trachyte. The other, descending towards the place called Chillapullu, not far from the village of Mocha, is, on the contrary, little inclined, but of a considerable extent.

"After having well examined the environs of the mountain, it was by this slope that we resolved to attack it, and, on the 14th of December, 1831, we went to lodge at the farm of Chimborazo, where we found dry straw to lie on, and some sheepskins to keep us from the cold. The farm stands on an elevation of 12,350 feet, so the nights are cool there, and, as a resting-place, it is not agreeable, because wood is scarce.

"On the 15th, at seven in the morning, we put ourselves *en route*, under the guidance of an Indian from the farm. We followed, in ascending, a rivulet enclosed between two walls

Two attempts to ascend Chimborazo. 365

of trachyte, whose waters descend from the glacier; but very soon we quitted this fissure, in order to direct our steps towards Mocha, going along the base of Chimborazo. We rose very gradually, and our mules walked with trouble and difficulty through the *débris* of rock which has accumulated at the foot of the mountain. The slope then became very rapid, the ground was unstable, and the mules stopped almost at every step to make a long pause; they no longer obeyed the spur. The breathing of the animals was hurried and panting. We were then precisely at the height of Mont Blanc, for the barometer indicated an elevation of 15,626 feet above the level of the sea.

"After we had covered our faces with masks of light gauze, in order to preserve ourselves from snow blindness, we began to ascend a ridge which abutted on a very elevated point of the glacier. It was midday. We went up slowly, and, as we got farther and farther on to the snow, the difficulty of breathing in walking became more and more felt, but we easily regained our strength by stopping at every eight or ten steps, without, however, always sitting down. As we went on we felt extreme fatigue from the want of consistency in the snowy soil, which continually gave way under our feet, and in which we sank sometimes up to the waist. In spite of all our efforts we were soon convinced of the impossibility of advancing; in fact, a little farther on the loose snow was more than four feet deep. We went to rest on a block of trachyte, which resembled an island in the midst of a sea of snow. The height noted down was 16,623 feet, so that, after much fatigue, we had only reached 997 feet higher than the place whence we set out.

"At six o'clock we were back at the farm. The weather had been splendid, and Chimborazo had never appeared to us so magnificent, but, after our fruitless journey, we could not help looking at it with a feeling of spite. We were determined to attempt the ascent by the abrupt side—that is to say, by the slope, which looks towards the Arenal. We knew that it was on this side that Humboldt had ascended this mountain, for they had pointed out to us at Riobamba the place which he had reached, but it was impossible for us to obtain exact information as to the route which he had followed to get there, for the Indians who had accompanied that intrepid traveller were no longer living.

"At seven o'clock the next day we took the road towards the Arenal. The sky was remarkably clear. On the east we perceived the famous volcano of Sangay, in the province of Macas, which, nearly a century before, La Condamine had seen in a state of permanent eruption. In proportion as we advanced the land rose sensibly. In general the trachytic plateau, which supports the isolated peaks with which the Andes are, as it were, bristling, rises gradually to the base of these same peaks. The numerous and deep crevasses which furrow the plateau seem all to start from a common centre; they become narrower as they get away from this centre. We could only compare them to the lines on the surface of a cracked glass.

"We were at a height of 16,071 feet when we took to journeying on foot. The ground had become altogether impracticable for the mules, and, besides, those animals, whose instinct is extraordinary, tried to make us understand the great fatigue which they felt; their ears, usually so straight and attentive, were quite drooping, and, during the frequent halts which they made for breath, they never ceased looking towards the plain. Few riders have probably taken their steeds to such a height, and to travel on the back of mules, over a moving soil beyond the limits of the snow, requires perhaps several years' experience in riding in the Andes.

"After having examined the locality in which we were, we saw that, in order to gain a ridge which ascended towards the summits of Chimborazo, we must first climb an excessively steep ascent just in front of us. It was formed in great part of blocks of rock of all sizes, disposed in slopes. Here and there these fragments of trachyte were covered by sheets of

Two attempts to ascend Chimborazo. 367

ice more or less extensive, and in several points you could clearly see that the *débris* of rock lay over hardened snow. They proceeded consequently from the recent falls which had taken place in the upper part of the mountain. These falls are frequent, and in the midst of the glaciers of the Cordilleras what one has most to fear are the avalanches, in which there are really more stones than snow.

"At eleven o'clock we finished crossing a very extended sheet of ice, on which we had been obliged to cut notches in order to make sure of our steps. This passage was not without danger, for a slide might have cost us our lives. We entered, then, afresh on the *débris* of trachyte, which was firm earth to us, and from that time we were able to ascend more rapidly. We marched along in a file, I first, then Colonel Hall, and my negro last. He followed my steps exactly, in order not to endanger the safety of the instruments which were entrusted to him. We kept an absolute silence during our march, experience having taught me that nothing exhausts so much as a sustained conversation at this height ; and during our halts, if we exchanged a few words it was in a low voice.

"We had now reached the ridge at which we were aiming. It was not what we had thought it from a distance, for, in fact, there was a little snow on it, and its sides were so steep that they were very difficult to climb. We were obliged to make almost unheard-of efforts, and such gymnastics are painful in these aerial regions. At last we arrived at the foot of a perpendicular wall of trachyte, which was many hundred feet in height. There was a feeling of discouragement when the barometer told us that we were only at a height of 18,460 feet. This was little for us, for it was not even the height to which we had attained on Cotopaxi. Besides, Humboldt had ascended higher on Chimborazo, and we wished at least to attain the point at which that learned traveller had stopped."

Boussingault arrived at this point at a quarter to one, and

then became enveloped in cloud for a time. When this disappeared they found a precipice on their right hand, but succeeded in forcing a passage on the left of their "perpendicular wall of trachyte." They then found soft and loose snow lying over ice, and nearly came to grief through M. Boussingault slipping. "We were all in imminent danger. This incident made us hesitate, but, taking new courage, we resolved to go on," and by half-past one they got again to their desired ridge. There they were convinced that "it was impossible to do more," for they were "now at the foot of a prism of trachyte, of which the upper part, covered with a cupola of snow, forms the summit of Chimborazo."

"The ridge at which we had arrived was only some feet in width. On all sides we were environed with precipices, and surrounded by the strangest sights. The deep colour of the rock contrasted in the most striking manner with the dazzling whiteness of the snow. Long stalagmites of ice appeared suspended over our heads, so that one might have thought that a magnificent cascade had frozen there. The weather was beautiful, some light clouds only being visible on the west; the air was quite calm, so that the view was very extensive. The situation was new, and we felt a lively satisfaction in it. We were at a height of 19,513 feet, which is, I believe, the greatest height to which men have ever climbed.

"After some moments' repose we found ourselves recovered from our fatigues, and neither of us experienced those uncomfortable sensations which most persons who have ascended high mountains have done. Three-quarters of an hour after our arrival my pulse, and also Colonel Hall's, beat 106 in a minute; we were thirsty, and evidently under a slightly feverish influence, but it was not a painful state. All sounds seemed to me, however, thinned in a remarkable manner, and the voices of my companions were so much changed, that under any other circumstances it would have been impossible to recognise them. The slight noise which the blows of my hammer on the rock made also surprised us very much."

Towards 3 P.M. the weather began to change, and when they had descended about a thousand feet they got into cloud and a hailstorm. Night surprised them before they got off the mountain, and it was 8 P.M. when they arrived at the farm. No more attempts upon Chimborazo were made by Boussingault or his friend, who separated from each other shortly afterwards.

Besides these attempts to ascend Chimborazo, others have been made by Professor Wagner, Garcia Moreno, the late President of Ecuador, Dr. Stübel, and M. Remy, but never with success, till Mr. Edward Whymper, of Alpine celebrity, "came, saw, and conquered," as our next article narrates.

TWICE TO THE TOP OF CHIMBORAZO.

THE name of Edward Whymper is widely known as a daring climber and adventurous explorer. As a mountaineer he has few rivals, and his book of Alpine travel contains many feats as wonderful as the first ascent of the Matterhorn. It was natural that so successful and ambitious a climber should long to attack the lofty peaks of the Andes, and the more so because of the recorded failures of other explorers. Towards the close of 1879 he accordingly sailed on this adventurous expedition.

It must not be supposed that for successful mountaineering the main requisites are strength of muscle, firmness of nerve, and other animal properties in which man is excelled by the sheep or the chamois. These material qualities are necessary, to some extent, but there are higher mental endowments needed for achieving results worthy of record. Before starting, there ought always to be much study and planning ; and careful preparation is as essential as readiness of resource when the time of action comes. The qualities that go to make a first-rate mountain traveller are as remarkable and as rare as those of a general in arranging for a difficult campaign.

Mr. Whymper's experience in Switzerland, Greenland, and other snowy regions stood him in good stead; and he took with him to the New World a tried and trusty companion, well known to readers of the "Ascent to the Matterhorn," Jean Antoine Carrel, with his cousin Louis Carrel, also a skilful and practised cragsman.

The party sailed from Southampton on the 3rd of November, in the West India mail steamer, the *Don*. While the ship was at Kingston, Jamaica, the travellers stretched their legs by going up five thousand feet to Newcastle, and from their highest point saw both the northern and southern sides of the island. After crossing the isthmus to Panama little time was lost, for on December 15th the party was mounting from the low-lying land on the Pacific side of the State of Ecuador. By this time the expedition comprised Mr. Perring, an interpreter, and a train of mules with attendants. A few days of continuous ascent brought them to the ridge of the outer range of the Andes, which was crossed at a height of about ten thousand feet, and on December 18th they arrived at the village of Guaranda, which Mr. Whymper resolved to make his head-quarters, hiring a house there, and beginning his observations and plans for the ascent of Chimborazo. A prospecting journey, with the Carrels, to the highest level of the Arenal, or sandy plain, at the base of the mountain, confirmed his opinion as to this being the best side for attempting the ascent. The Carrels were sent on a second prospecting journey, to select a suitable station for the first camping, which they did, at a height of about 16,000 feet. All was ready on the 23rd, but as the muleteers would not be away from Guaranda on Christmas Day, the departure was delayed till the 26th. On that day the journey commenced, the party consisting of Mr. Whymper, the two Carrels, Mr. Perring, two Indians as porters, three arrieros or muleteers, with fourteen mules. The camping-ground was reached at 5.30 P.M., a little below the summit of the Arenal. "It was a superb night, with a brilliant moon," says Mr. Whymper,* "and the great cliffs of Chimborazo, with their snowy dome, 7,000 feet above us, were indescribably grand."

Some days' delay took place, partly from the exhaustion and illness of several of the party, the desertion of the Indian porters, and the tidings brought up of the house at Guaranda being broken into by robbers. While Mr. Perring went down with a letter to the authorities, asking for a guard to the baggage, Mr. Whymper and the Carrels prepared a second camping station, at a height of 16,600 feet above the sea, and a third at 17,400 feet. These preparations having been made, the mules and arrieros were sent back, and, on the arrival of Mr. Perring with three Indians, to replace those who had deserted, the whole of the necessaries for the final ascent were got up to the third camp by the 2nd of January, 1880. The result we give in Mr. Whymper's own words.

"Being now well established, and provided with sufficient food and firing at our high station, I considered that we might prudently attempt to make for the summit, and on the 3rd of January, 1880, we started, at 5.35 A.M. At that time it was calm, and we mounted for a thousand feet without any great difficulty, excepting such as arose from shortness of breath. Our course led up the ridge on which our two camps were placed. On one side of us, and deep down below, there was a large glacier, and on the other very extensive snow-fields.

"Soon after 7 A.M. wind began to spring up, and at 7.30 it blew so hard as to render farther progress highly dangerous. At this time we had mounted little more than a thousand feet above our third camp, and as it was certain that we could not

---

* In a communication to the editor of the *Leisure Hour*, in which magazine an account of the expedition was given in the number for January, 1881. In Mr. Whymper's great work on the Andes, published by John Murray, all the details of the expedition will be found, with magnificent illustrations.

reach the summit on that day, we came down again, holding ourselves, however, in readiness to start again on the following morning.

"On January 4th I started at 5.40 A.M., with the two Carrels, leaving Perring in charge of the camp. It was a very fine and nearly cloudless morning. We followed the track of the previous day, and benefited by the steps which had then been cut in the snow. At first the line of ascent was on the southern side of the mountain, but after the height of 18,500 feet had been attained, we commenced to bear round to the west, and mounted spirally, arriving on the plateau on the summit from a northerly direction.

The ascent was mainly over snow, and entirely so after 19,500 feet had been passed. Up to nearly 20,000 feet it was in good condition, and as we sank in but slightly, we progressed at a reasonable rate until 11 A.M. We had met with no great difficulties, and up to that time had experienced fine weather, with a good deal of sunshine.

"We were now 20,000 feet high, and the summit seemed within our grasp. We could see the great plateau which is at the top of the mountain, and the two fine snowy domes, one on its northern and the other on its southern side. But, alas! the sky became clouded all over, the wind rose, and we entered upon a large tract of exceedingly soft snow, which could not be traversed in the ordinary way, and it was found necessary to flog every yard of it down, and then to crawl over it on all fours. The ascent of the last thousand feet occupied more than five hours, and it was 5 P.M. before we reached the summit of the higher of the two domes of Chimborazo.

"On the immediate summit the snow was not so extremely soft; it was possible to stand up upon it. The wind, however, was furious, and the temperature fell to 21° Fahr. We remained only long enough to read the barometers, and left at 5.20 P.M.; by great exertion succeeded in crossing the most difficult rocks which had to be passed over just as the last gleam of daylight disappeared; but we were then benighted, and occupied more than two hours descending the last thousand feet, arriving at the camp about 9 P.M."

Thus was achieved the first recorded ascent of Chimborazo. Mr. Whymper had been compelled to leave the summit before taking all the observations which he had intended, and he desired, therefore, to make a second ascent before quitting the mountain. One of the Carrels was so disabled by frost-bitten feet that the purpose had to be postponed for some months, while medical help was necessary. Mr. Whymper returned at the beginning of July, many important journeys having been made in the interval, including the ascent of Cotopaxi, the great volcano of the Andes. On the 3rd of July, after encamping at a height of about 16,000 feet, the summit was again reached, and more than an hour was passed on the top. Two natives, on this occasion, accompanied him, and as there was very general incredulity in Ecuador as to the possibility of ascending the mountain, one of these natives, Javier Campana, of Quito, made a solemn declaration before H. B. M. Consul at Guayaquil, as to the highest summit of the mountain being reached by himself, along with Mr. Whymper, the two Carrels, and David Beltram, of Machachi. This signed and attested document contains a detailed narrative of the incidents of the ascent : "As we approached the very highest point, we saw that there was something strange upon it, and when we got up we found the pole of the flag which Mr. Whymper had put up on January 4th, 1880. It stood above the snow, but very little of the flag remained, as it had been torn to pieces by the wind. I took a small piece of the flag to show to my friends below, and was filled with joy at being the first Ecuadorian to reach the summit of the great Chimborazo."

The reader of this account of the ascents of Chimborazo will look with keener interest for the work in which Mr. Whymper gives the personal narrative of his adventures among the Andes.

THE WIDOW AND HER MONEY-BAGS.

A PERSONAL RECOLLECTION BY THE LATE LORD LAWRENCE.*

IT was my practice in India, where every one who wishes to preserve health either walks or rides early in the morning, instead of taking a mere constitutional (as it is called), to endeavour to join that object with business, or, at any rate, with amusement. There was always some end in view—a village to visit, a new road to be made, or an old one to be repaired, or the spot where a crime had been committed to be examined. If I was in tents, making my annual visits in the interior of the district, which seldom occupied less than five months of the year, there was plenty to engage the attention. I seldom failed to visit every village within a circle of seven or eight miles before the camp moved on another march. Their locality, the nature of their soil, their means of irrigation, —a point of much importance in the East,—the general appearance of the inhabitants, and the character they bore among their neighbours, were all points on which I was much interested; for all such information was of infinite value in the performance of my daily duties.

I had in truth so much to occupy me, or, what is pretty much the same thing, made so much occupation for myself, that, though often the sole European in the district, and literally without any one with whom I could exchange a word in my native tongue, I do not think that I ever felt listless for a day. I sometimes rode alone, but more frequently with a single horseman, who either carried my rifle or boar spear. Thus, if anything in the way of game turned up, I did

---

* "Life of Lord Lawrence." By B. Bosworth Smith (Smith, Elder, and Co.). A book worthy of the great man whose career it records. In this incident of his early days as a district magistrate, we see the energy of character, the devotion to duty, and the high principle, which afterwards shone so conspicuously in John Lawrence, when Governor of the Punjab, and Viceroy of India.

The Widow and her Money-Bags. 375

not lose a chance; and if a messenger was required, or anything was to be done, an active fellow was always ready. More than once I have in this way brought home a buck; and many is the good run I have had with wolf, hyena, and wild boar. It would have no doubt enhanced the pleasure to have had a friend with whom to contest the spear, and to talk over the turns and chances of the field when ended. Still, when I look back on those days, it is surprising how much I enjoyed them in my comparative solitude.

In these journeys my follower was instructed to ride at a respectful distance, so that I might freely converse with any one I might pick up by the way. One or more of the headmen, or some of the proprietors of the village I was visiting, usually mounted his mare, and rode with me to the next village; thus acting as a guide, and at the same time beguiling the tedium of the way, often with useful information, at any rate, with amusing gossip.

I had one morning mounted my horse for such an expedition, but had not proceeded far when I met the *kotwal*, or chief police-officer, of the neighbouring town, bustling along in quite unwonted haste. On seeing me, after making the usual salutations, he reported that a burglary had occurred in the town during the previous night, and that he was anxious that I should visit the spot myself, as neither he nor any of the police could make anything of the case.

I at once assented, and as we rode along, I ascertained that the party robbed was a poor widow, who, with her niece, lived in a large and substantial, but rather dilapidated, house in the neighbouring town. The robbery, it seemed, had created much sensation, from the circumstance that the widow asserted that she had lost a large sum of money, whereas she had hitherto been deemed miserably poor. "Some of the neighbours," remarked the policeman, "deny that she has been robbed at all, and indeed to me it appears suspicious; I suspect there is some *fareb* (deceit) in the matter. Where could such a helpless creature get so much money? It was but the other day that she was exempted from her quota of the watch-tax, as *mooflis* (a beggar), and now she asserts that she has lost one thousand and fifty rupees." "Well, well," said I, "that will do; we will hear what she has to say for herself. Don't you pretend to make out that she was not robbed. I suppose there are marks about the house of a forcible entry?" "Oh yes," he replied, "I don't deny there is a hole in the wall by which the door has been opened. There were two marks of footsteps about the interior of the courtyard, but the ground was so hard we could make nothing of it. I have, however, sent for the *khojia* (tracker), and if anything is to be discovered, I am sure he is the man to do it."

By this time we had arrived at the house, where we found some policemen, some of the neighbours, and the widow. The khojia, or personage celebrated far and near for his powers of recognising and tracing the marks of biped and quadruped, had already examined the premises. He informed me that the footsteps were difficult to trace, from the hardness of the soil, as well as from the passing and repassing of the people; but that he had satisfied himself that there had been two thieves, that the two had entered the house, but that only one appeared to have left it, and that he had followed those traces, through various turnings and windings, till they finally stopped at the house of a man who was said to be the nephew of the widow herself. He then showed me the different marks, from the interior of the widow's house up to the very threshold of that of the nephew. There were certainly some traces, but so very indistinct to my eye that I could form no opinion. The tracker, however, seemed perfectly convinced. "One foot," he observed, "is small and delicate, which goes to the nephew's house; the other, a large, broad foot, I cannot trace beyond the courtyard." The nephew was summoned, his foot was compared with the print, the khojia insisted that it exactly corresponded, and it certainly answered to the description he had previously given.

The Widow and her Money-Bags.

We then entered the house, and carefully examined the premises. The thieves, it seemed, had picked a small hole in the side of the wall, so as to admit a man's hand, and had thus opened the outer door. It was clear that the theft was perpetrated by someone who was well acquainted with the premises, for the money had been concealed in three earthen pots, buried in the ground floor within a small recess. The ground had been dug up in the exact spot where the pots lay, and it must have been the work of only a few minutes, for they were close to the surface. It seemed that there was some suspicion of the nephew in the mind of both the old woman and her neighbours, for he was a man of reckless and dissolute habits. "But, widow," I said, "did he know of your treasures? Did he know of the place where you concealed them?" "No," she replied to my query, "I can't say he did. I never let him come into the house for many years, though he has sometimes come as near as the door, and asked me to make friends; but I was afraid of him, and never let him pass my threshold." "Well," I remarked, "it seems a bad business. That you have been robbed is evident, but there seems no clue as to who did it; and as to your loss, you must have told a lie, for I hear it was only a few months ago that, under the plea of destitution, you were exempted from the watch-tax." "My lord," replied the widow, "it is very true that I pleaded poverty, and poor enough I am; nevertheless, I have been robbed of a thousand and fifty rupees. You may believe me or not, as you please; my history is this. Some forty years ago, or more, my husband was a merchant, well-to-do in this town; but after a time his affairs fell into disorder, and when he died his creditors seized everything but this house in payment for his debts. When dying, he told me that certain moneys had long been due to him in the holy city of Muttra. Accordingly I went there, and collected something more than two thousand rupees, with which I returned here, and I have lived ever since on this sum." "What!" I interrupted, "have you lived on this money for forty years, and yet have a thousand and fifty rupees, nearly half, left?" "Yes," said she, "I opened my treasure once a month, and took out two rupees, which lasted me and my niece for the month." "Why," I remarked, "at this rate you had enough for the next forty years; why could you not pay the tax?—how much was it?" "Two pyce a month," she replied, "and all widows are exempt." "Yes," remarked a bystander, "if they are poor; but you are as rich as Lakhsmi" (the Hindu goddess of fortune). "I believe that Kali has sent this misfortune on you for your lying. Do you recollect when you were assessed at one anna, how you wept and tore your hair, and said you were starving? You are a sad liar by your own account, and are well served. I hope if you ever recover your money, the Sahib will make you pay it up with arrears." "Oh," said the widow, clasping her hands, "restore me my money, and I will pay for the rest of my life."

As I suspected, from the different circumstances which had transpired, that the nephew was in some way connected with the robbery, I directed his house to be searched, but nothing which could in any way implicate him was found. Despairing, then, of discovering the criminal, I mounted my horse, and after telling the police to be on the look-out, I set off towards my tents. I had ridden some little way, conning the matter over in my mind, when it struck me how very singular it was that the khojia should persist in it that only one of the thieves had left the house. As the walls were very high, and as there was but the one door to the courtyard, it seemed as if the thief must still be inside. "Pooh, pooh!" I cried, "the thing is out of the question; did we not search the house? And, after all, what could a thief be doing there? The khojia is trying to mystify me." However, I was not satisfied. After riding a little farther, I turned round and galloped back. I said to the police, who had not left yet, "We must have another search," and upon this my myrmidons spread themselves over the premises. While they were searching, I began to pace up and down, with some little impatience, I confess, as the thought struck me of the bootless errand on which I had returned.

Suddenly I heard a policeman exclaim, "I have not seen *him*, but I have seen his eye," and as he spoke he pointed to one side of the courtyard near where he stood. On examining the spot, we discovered what appeared to be a small air-hole to some vaults, and from this the man persisted he had seen an eye glisten. Turning to the widow, I demanded what places there were underground, when she explained that there were subterraneous vaults, which had never been opened since her husband's death, and which she had not thought of mentioning when we first searched the house. "A second case of Guy Fawkes," thought I. "Show me the entrance. I daresay someone is down there; though why any one should be such a fool as to hide there passes my understanding." The old dame accordingly showed me a small door in a retired part of the courtyard, which had hitherto escaped observation. By it we descended to some very extensive vaults, and after some search, dragged out a man. He had not the money about his person, but, after some little hesitation, showed us where it was concealed, at the foot of one of the pillars. He confessed that he belonged to a village in the vicinity, that the nephew had induced him to join in robbing the old lady, whose treasures he had for a long time suspected. It seemed that the thief had slept part of the night in the nephew's house, and that they had been prevented from effecting the robbery till late in the night, from the presence of the people who were about, and consequently the morning had broken before they had time to divide the booty, or dispose of it in any safe place. In the hurry and confusion it had seemed best that he should hide in the vaults, where it was supposed that none would think of looking; for the nephew was afraid to conceal him in his own house, or to allow him to pass out of the town with such a large sum in silver, lest, being recognised by some of the guards at the postern as a stranger, he should be stopped and searched. When the nephew was confronted with his accomplice, his effrontery forsook him, and he confessed that he had seen the old woman smoothing the earth in the recess one day as he stood at the threshold; and from this circumstance, coupled with her always being in that part of the house, he had suspected that she had property concealed.

When the coin was produced, the woman recognised her money-bags; and on opening and counting the money, we found the exact sum she had stated—namely, one thousand and fifty rupees, or about one hundred and five pounds in English money; so that this poor creature had lived on about four shillings a month, and even supported part of that time a little niece! While the money was being counted, and her receipt written out, I said, "You had much better give this money to a banker, who will allow you seven or eight per cent. for it, and in whose hands it will be perfectly safe; otherwise, now that folks know you are so rich, being a lonely, helpless old woman, you will certainly have your throat cut." "No, no," cried the old harridan, as she grasped her bags in an agony lest I should take them from her; "no, no! I will bury it where no one will ever know." I accordingly allowed her to go off with her treasures; and out she trotted, bending under the weight of her money-bags.

I may have failed in giving an interest to this story, but it certainly made a considerable impression on my mind at the time. The avarice and parsimony of the old woman, who, bending under the weight of old age, and possessed of wealth which she could never hope to enjoy, yet grudged the payment of two pyce a month to defend her from spoliation, if not from being murdered; the villainy of the nephew, with his utter want of common sense and prudence in concealing his accomplice in the very premises they had just robbed; the acuteness and discernment of the tracker, in so ably, I may say, deciphering the history of the transaction from the very faint footmarks, altogether formed a picture which it was not uninteresting to contemplate. Of the subsequent fate of the widow I do not recollect anything, as I shortly afterwards left that part of the country; but if she escaped being robbed, she concealed her treasures in some out-of-the-way place, which, when she dies, her heirs will fail to discover. In this way, no doubt, large sums are annually lost, for although property is remarkably safe in this country, and a very large rate of interest always to be got, the people are very much addicted to concealing coin and jewels, probably from habits they acquired in former times, when seldom a year passed that a village or even town was not laid under contribution, or stormed and plundered by the Mahratta and Pindari hordes.

COMMODORE BYRON IN PATAGONIA.

UNTIL comparatively recent times very little was known about Patagonia, the southern region of the American continent. Commodore Byron, in the narrative of his voyage round the world, visited the coast in 1764, and for fifty years afterwards his report was always given as the most authentic account of the country and its people. Now that we know a great deal more about these regions, it is interesting to read this early record of Byron's visit.

When Commodore Byron had landed his men on the coast, he drew them up on the beach, with the officers at their head, giving orders that none should leave their station. "I then," says he, "went forward alone towards the Indians, but perceiving that they retired as I advanced, I made signs that one of them should come near. The chief approached me; he was of a gigantic stature, and seemed to realize the tales of monsters in human shape; he had the skin of some wild beast thrown over his shoulders, and was painted so as to make the most hideous appearance I ever beheld; round one eye was a large circle of white, which was surrounded by a circle of black, and the rest of his face was streaked with paint of different colours. I did not measure him, but if I may judge of his height by the proportion of his stature to my own, it could not be much less than seven feet. When this frightful colossus came up, we muttered somewhat to each other as a salutation. I then walked with him to his companions, among whom there were many women. Few of the men were less in stature than the chief. I heard their voices at a distance; and when I came near, I perceived a good number of old men who were chanting some unintelligible words in the most doleful cadence I ever heard, with an air of serious solemnity, which inclined me to think that it was a religious ceremony. They were all painted and clothed nearly in the same manner; the circles round the two eyes were in no instance of one colour, but they were not universally black and white, some being red and white, and some red and black. Their teeth were as white as ivory, remarkably even, and well set; but, except the skins which they wore with the hair inwards, most of them were naked, a few only having upon their legs a kind of boot, with a short, pointed stick fastened to each heel, which served as a spur.

"Having looked upon these enormous goblins (some of whom were six feet six inches high, though the greater part of them were from five feet ten to six feet in stature) with no small surprise, I took out a quantity of white and yellow beads, which I distributed among them, and which they received with very strong expressions of pleasure: I then took out a whole piece of green ribbon, and giving the end of it into the hands of one of them, I made the person who sat next take hold of it, and so on as far as it would reach; they all sat quietly, and appeared to be more pleased with it than with the beads. While the ribbon was thus extended, I took out a pair of scissors and cut it between two of the Indians that held it, so that I left about a yard in the possession of every one, which I afterwards tied about their heads, where they suffered it to remain without so much as touching it while I was with them. Their peaceable and orderly behaviour on this occasion certainly did them honour, especially as my presents could not extend to the whole company.

Commodore Byron in Patagonia. 383

"These people were not wholly strangers to European commodities; for upon closer attention, I perceived among them one woman who had bracelets of brass or very pale gold upon her arms, and some beads of blue glass strung upon two queues of hair, which, being parted at top, hung over each shoulder before her. One of the men showed me the bowl of a tobacco pipe, which was made of red earth, but I soon found that they had no tobacco among them, and this person made me understand that he wanted some; upon which I beckoned to my people, who remained upon the beach, drawn up as I had left them, and three or four ran forward, imagining that I wanted them. The Indians no sooner saw them advance, than they all rose with a great clamour, and were leaving the place, as I supposed, to get arms, which were probably left at a little distance. I desired only one of my people to come and bring with him all the tobacco he could collect from the rest. As soon as the Indians saw this, they recovered from their surprise, and every one returned to his station, except a very old man, who came up to me and sung a long song; but before it was finished, Mr. Cumming brought the tobacco, and I could not but smile at the astonishment which I saw he expressed in his countenance, upon perceiving himself, though six feet two inches high, become at once a pigmy among giants; for these people may indeed be more properly called giants than tall men. Of the few among us who are full six feet high, scarcely any are broad and muscular in proportion to their stature, but look rather like men of common bulk, run up accidentally to an unusual height; and a man who should measure only six feet two inches, and equally exceed a stout well-set man of the common stature in breadth and muscle, would strike us rather as a being of gigantic race, than as an individual accidentally anomalous; our sensations, therefore, upon seeing five hundred people, the shortest of whom were at least four inches taller, and bulky in proportion, may be easily imagined.

"During our pantomimical conference, an old man often laid

his head down upon the stones, and shutting his eyes for about half a minute, first pointed to his mouth, and then to the hills, meaning, as I imagined, that if I would stay with them till the morning, they would furnish me with provisions; but this offer I was obliged to decline. I observed that they had with them a great number of dogs, with which I suppose they run down the animals that serve them for food. Their horses were not large, but nimble, and well broken. The bridle was a leathern thong, with a small piece of wood that served for a bit, and the saddles resemble the pads that are in use among the country people in England. The women rode astride, and both men and women without stirrups; yet they galloped fearlessly over the spit upon which we landed, the stones of which were large, loose, and slippery.

"Every one of them had a missile weapon of a singular kind tucked into the girdle. It consisted of two round stones, covered with leather, each weighing about a pound, which were fastened to the two ends of a string about eight feet long. This is used as a sling, one stone being kept in the hand, and the other whirled round the head till it is supposed to have acquired sufficient force, and then discharged at the object. They are so expert in the management of this double-headed shot, that they will hit a mark not bigger than a shilling with both the stones, at the distance of fifteen yards; it is not their custom, however, to strike either the guanico (an animal that resembles the deer), or the ostrich, with them in the chase, but they discharge them so that the cord comes against the legs of the ostrich, or two of the legs of the guanico, is twisted round them by the force and swing of the balls, so that the animal, being unable to run, becomes an easy prey to the hunter."

Such is Commodore Byron's account. His statement as to the size of the Patagonians has been confirmed by subsequent voyagers, at least in regard to some of the tribes. Lieutenant Musters, who travelled through the country in 1869, describes the Patagonian hunters as being "tall and of fine proportions." It has usually been stated that the people of Tierra del Fuego, the island to the south of Patagonia, were of very diminutive size (as some of them may be); but a French traveller, M. Pertuiset, who travelled there in 1873, describes the Indians of the interior as being " well grown and of as good proportions as the Patagonians," and, like them, living by fishing and hunting. The eastern slopes of the mountains in the northwest of Patagonia are occupied by a race less nomadic than the Patagonians proper, possessing cattle and sheep, and cultivating the soil. They much resemble the Araucanians, on the corresponding opposite slope in southern Chili, a fine race, descended apparently from ancient Indian tribes driven south by the Spanish and Portuguese invaders. The area of Patagonia, including Tierra del Fuego and the islands, is almost as large as that of France and Spain together, but is sparsely inhabited. The climate is, in most parts, inhospitable, with long, severe winters, and even in summer often cold and stormy.

The Argentine Republic and Chili both claim possession of parts of Patagonia; and under the protection of these States settlements have been recently formed at various stations near the coast—one of them a Welsh colony at the mouth of the river Chupat. The Chilians have a penal settlement, and a coaling station for ocean steamers near the Strait of Magellan, a seam of coal being worked in the neighbourhood by the Chilian Government.

The condition of the Patagonian people has long excited the charitable attention of Christian people, and the South American Missionary Society—an offshoot of the Church Missionary Society—has stations in these regions. As long ago as 1830 Captain Fitzroy, a benevolent man as well as distinguished explorer, brought some of the natives to England that they might be instructed at his own expense. He thought well of the capabilities of the race. The first formal attempt to establish a mission, under the superintendence of Captain Allan Gardiner, came to a sad conclusion, but the death of these early martyrs was not in vain, and in the reports of the

South American Mission many satisfactory and cheering statements of the results of subsequent labours will be found.

THE TRAVELS OF MARCO POLO.

OF all travellers, ancient or modern, who have left written records of their adventures, no name is surrounded with more mysterious and romantic interest than that of Marco Polo, of Venice. Some of the remote regions of Asia which he describes, as he saw them six hundred years ago, have only been very recently revisited by European explorers, who all bear testimony to the accurate observation and strict veracity of the old Venetian traveller. For instance, he tells how he came to a district in Central Asia " said to be the highest in the world, a plain between lofty hills, through which flows a great river, issuing from a large lake ; and this plain, is the best pasturage in the world, for a lean animal becomes fat in ten days." Here he says " the fire does not burn so clear, nor with the same colour, as in other places, nor does it cook victuals so well "—facts which indicate the lofty elevation of this tableland. The plain is the tableland of Pamir ; the river is the Oxus ; the lake the Sir-i-kol in which the river has its source ; and the hills are the beginning of the principal mountain-chains of Asia. No European in after ages knew the place, till at length it was reached, in February 1838, by Lieutenant Wood of the Indian navy. After surmounting immense difficulties, and escaping many dangers, Lieutenant Wood stood on the tableland of Pamir, and saw the source of the Oxus, and thus confirms the story of Marco Polo: "This tableland of Pamir is about 15,000 feet high, little lower than the summit of Mont Blanc. The natives' call it *Bam-i-duniah*, or the Roof of the World ; and it would appear to be the highest tableland in Asia, and probably in any part of our

The Travels of Marco Polo.

globe. Before us lay stretched a noble sheet of water, from whose western end issued the infant river of the Oxus. According to the Kirghis, the grass is so rich that a sorry horse is brought into good condition in less than twenty days."

Here is a singular confirmation of Marco Polo's narrative, and many other of his remarkable statements have in like manner been verified by modern travellers. His book has recently been re-edited by Colonel Yule of the Royal Engineers, the man of all others best qualified for such an undertaking, and his two volumes, with their minute and learned commentaries, form a mine of curious and valuable information on Asiatic geography and history. Some of the old traveller's reports still contain mysterious statements, but this is Colonel Yule's judgment of the whole narrative: " With all the intrinsic interest of Marco Polo's book, it may be doubted if it would have continued to exercise such fascination on many minds, through successive generations, were it not for the difficult questions which it suggests. It is a great book of puzzles, whilst our confidence in the man's veracity is such that we feel certain every puzzle has a solution."

In earlier years of the thirteenth century several travellers had penetrated to various parts of the interior of Asia, and had brought back reports of what they saw. One of them, Carpini, an Italian, crossed the desert east of the Caspian on his way to the ruler of the Mongols, and tells how he everywhere on these sandy steppes saw heaps of bones and skulls, marking the track of the terrible conqueror Genghis Khan. A few years later, William de Rubruquis, a Fleming, sent by Louis IX. of France, as envoy to the Mongol Emperor, travelled from Constantinople to the Crimea, thence reaching the Don, the Volga, and the Ural, returning by Astrakhan and the Caucasus, after an absence of two years and three months. These expeditions served to increase the curiosity in all European lands about the East, whilst the fear entertained as to the movements of these restless conquerors in Central Asia induced the Governments to seek every information and to send ambassadors to court the friendship of the Mongol Potentate. It was with this purpose that Marco Polo set out from Venice, in the year 1271, to make his way to the Court of Kublai Khan, the greatest of the successors of Genghis Khan. Kublai Khan had at this time completed the conquest of the northern part of China, having overthrown the reigning dynasty, and established himself at Pekin, as the capital of his mighty empire.

It would take too long to tell how the young Venetian, at first accompanying his father and uncle, but left at last to his own resources, after many wanderings and perils, was received with favour at the Court of Pekin. The Emperor took him under his protection, made him an officer of the Imperial household, employed him in various confidential affairs, and appointed him governor of one of the provinces. Marco had long adopted the dress and customs of the country, and had taken such advantage of his opportunities that he was well versed in the history and politics as well as the language of the Chinese and of their Mongol conquerors.

After many years the desire to return to his native land grew too strong to be resisted, and as he could not obtain permission from the Emperor he quitted China by stealth, and sailing from a port in the province of Fokien reached southern India. At Sumatra and other islands in the Indian Archipelago he was long detained, but at last he made his way through Persia and by the Persian Gulf to Trebizond and Constantinople, arriving at Venice in 1295, after an absence of about twenty-four years. In all the places through which he passed, or where he resided, he made careful observations, and he included in his notes all the trustworthy information that he could gather from others as well as what he himself witnessed. What he tells about China was for a long time the only source of our knowledge of the internal affairs of that empire, and his account of the city of Pekin, written more than six hundred years ago, contains much that will be recognised as applicable to our own time, when Europeans first obtained access to the long secluded capital. One of the chapters of his book, relating to Pekin, will give a good idea of the style of Marco Polo.

THE CITY OF CAMBALUC (PEKIN).

You must know that the city of Cambaluc hath such a multitude of houses, and such a vast population inside the walls and outside, that it seems quite past all possibility. There is a suburb outside each of the gates, which are twelve in number, and these suburbs are so great that they contain more people than the city itself (for the suburb of one gate spreads in width till it meets the suburb of the next, whilst they extend in length some three or four miles). In those suburbs lodge the foreign merchants and travellers, of whom, there are always great numbers, who have come to bring presents to the Emperor, or to sell articles at court, or because the city affords so good a mart to attract traders. There are in each of the suburbs, to a distance of a mile from the city, numerous fine hostelries, for the lodgment of merchants from different parts of the world, and a special hostelry is assigned to each description of people, as if we should say there is one for the Lombards, another for the Germans, and a third for the Frenchmen. And thus there are as many good houses outside of the city as inside, without counting those that belong to the great lords and barons, which are very numerous.

You must know that it is forbidden to bury any dead body inside the city: If the body be that of an idolater it is carried out beyond the city and suburbs to a remote place assigned for the purpose, to be burnt. And if it be of one belonging to a religion the custom of which is to bury, such as the Christian, the Saracen, or what not, it is also carried out beyond the suburbs to a distant place assigned for the purpose. And thus the city is preserved in a better and more healthy state. Guards patrol the city every night in parties of thirty or forty; looking out for any persons who may be abroad at unseasonable hours—*i.e.*, after the great bell hath stricken thrice. If they find any such person he is immediately taken to prison, and examined next morning by the proper officers. If these find him guilty of any misdemeanour they order him a proportionate beating with the stick. Under this punishment people sometimes die; but they adopt it in order to eschew bloodshed, for their Bacsis say that it is an evil thing to shed man's blood. To this city also are brought articles of greater cost and rarity, and in greater abundance, of all kinds, than to any other city in the world. For people of every description, and from every region, bring things (including all the costly wares of India, as well as the fine and precious goods of Carthag itself with its provinces), some for the sovereign, some for the court, some for the city, which is so great, some for the crowds of barons and knights, some for the great hosts of the Emperor, which are quartered round about, and thus between court and city the quantity brought in is endless.

"As a sample, I tell you, no day in the year passes that there do not enter the city one thousand cartloads of silk alone, from which are made quantities of cloth of silk and gold, and of other goods. And this is not to be wondered at; ·or in all the countries round about there is no flax, so that everything has to be made of silk. It is true, indeed, that in some parts of the country there is cotton and hemp, but not sufficient for their wants. This, however, is not of much consequence, because silk is so abundant and cheap, and is a more valuable substance than either flax or cotton. Round about this great city of Cambaluc there are some two hundred other cities at various distances, from which traders come to sell their goods and buy others for their lords, and all find means to make their sales and purchases, so that the traffic of the city is passing great."

HOW BLAKE MADE VAN TROMP TAKE THE BROOM FROM HIS TOP-MAST.

IN the middle of the sixteenth century the Dutch were the acknowledged "masters of the sea." The States of Holland, having carried on a successful trade at home and abroad, even in the remotest East, had reached a height of naval power, and of wealth, which caused them to treat all other nations with the insolence of superiority. The navy of Spain, once supreme, had been declining ever since the defeat of "the Invincible Armada." The English followed up that victory by carrying war into the Spanish dominions in America, under such sea-kings as Cavendish and Drake. But all this naval greatness had departed during the inactive reign of James I., and the civil commotions during the time of Charles I. and the Long Parliament. The Dutch saw their opportunity, and aimed at the empire of the sea. When war between the two Commonwealths of England and Holland broke out in 1652, the English were unprepared, while the Dutch had a splendid fleet, with commanders the most renowned, whose names are still famous in history—De Witt, De Ruyter, and Van Tromp.

Having long been making preparations they equipped a powerful fleet, without any apparent need of it for purposes of defence. The English were naturally suspicious of their aims, and resolved to fit out a fleet for the security of their merchantmen and for the protection of their coasts. Robert Blake, who had already distinguished himself by his naval services against the Portuguese and the French, was appointed admiral of the fleet.

The Portuguese war arose in this wise. Prince Rupert had taken refuge in the Tagus, having gone there after escaping from Kinsale Harbour where Blake was watching for him. Blake demanded leave from the Portuguese Government to attack Prince Rupert's fleet, as belonging to the foes of the English Commonwealth. On being refused permission he fell upon a

Portuguese fleet then returning from Brazil, burning three of their ships and capturing seventeen. The King of Portugal ordered Prince Rupert to attack Blake and recover the Brazilian ships. The Prince declined the honour, and quitted the Tagus, where he could no longer be protected, while Blake was taking home his Portuguese prizes.

The French war in 1650-51 arose out of the raids of privateers on English merchant ships. Blake was then in the Mediterranean, where he had blockaded Prince Rupert in the port of Malaga, and attacking him there had destroyed three of his ships, and forced him to quit the sea, and take refuge at the Spanish Court. A French war-ship heaving in sight soon after, Blake ordered the captain to come on board, meaning to ask why privateering was carried on against merchant ships of a friendly nation. The captain was asked to deliver up his sword, in token of surrender of his ship. He gallantly refused, although in Blake's power; and Blake said " he was at liberty to go back to his ship and defend it as long as he could." After a fight of two or three hours the Frenchman struck, and surrendered his sword.

These seem rather high-handed proceedings, but the Dutch war, which soon followed, was a war of duty and of self-defence. On the 18th of May, 1652, Van Tromp appeared in the Downs with a fleet of forty-five men-of-war; Blake had only twenty. On the approach of the Dutch admiral three shots were fired as a signal, to intimate that a foreign fleet ought in courtesy to lower his flag in entering the seas of another nation. Van Tromp answered with a broadside. Blake, perceiving that this point of honour and international usage was disregarded, anxious also to prevent an open rupture and a general action, advanced alone with his flagship, in order to treat with the Dutch commander. The Dutch, disregarding the customs of war, closed upon him, and fired on him with their whole fleet. It was some time before the English ships could come to his assistance, and although receiving a vast number of shots little damage was done,

take the Broom from his Top-mast.

while two of the Dutch ships were destroyed. Only fifteen men were killed in the admiral's ship, for which Blake acknowledged the special preservation of God, and ascribed his success to the justice of the cause, the attack being both unprovoked and treacherous.

For some months the war continued with varying success, the Dutch having the superior armaments; but their losses being so great, De Ruyter and De Witt were superseded, and Van Tromp was entrusted with the sole command. Blake had to weaken his fleet by sending detachments to protect the coasts and the shipping, and he had less than forty sail in the Downs ill-manned and ill-supplied, for the Parliament had begun to be jealous of allowing undue power to officers either on land or sea. Van Tromp, desiring to distinguish his resumption of command by a decisive victory, steered for the Downs with eighty ships of war and ten fire-ships. More than half of Blake's ships had had to lie idle, without engaging, for want of seamen. To have retired before so overwhelming a force would have been no dishonour, but Blake had too much personal valour, and too sensitive a jealousy for his country's honour, to do so without a fight. Every one of the twenty-two ships he took into action was assailed by two or three of the enemy, and he lost two men-of-war and four frigates, but not without a gallant resistance, for of the Dutchmen one was blown up and two or three disabled, when Blake withdrew his fleet into the Thames. It was then that Van Tromp raised the broom on his top-mast in his triumphant passage through the English Channel. But his triumph was short.

On the 18th of February, 1652-3, Blake led eighty ships against a nearly equal force of the enemy. For three days and nights the battle continued, and at last the Dutch had to retire into their ports, or behind the shoals, which they were able to do from the less draught of their vessels, while the English ships could not follow. In one of the actions above a hundred men were killed on board Blake's ship, the

Triumph, and as many in the *Fairfax*, under Captain Lawson, and the admiral himself was wounded, but no ship was taken. The Dutch lost several ships in the three days' fight; their own writers confessing to eight men-of-war and twenty merchant ships, probably an insufficient estimate, for the news of the defeat caused such popular discontent, that the people compelled the States General to ask for peace, which was not, however, yet to be obtained.

In April of the same year, 1653, the form of government in England was changed, and Cromwell became Lord Protector of the Commonwealth. Blake, and his naval comrades, like Hale and Milton, and the greatest and best men of the nation, declared that they were ready to stand to their duties to the country, notwithstanding change in the administration. "It is not the business of a seaman," said Blake, "to mind state affairs, but to hinder foreigners from fooling us!"

On the 30th of April, Blake, with Monk and Dean, sailed with a large fleet, and soon drove all Dutchmen in the Channel into the Texel. They then set out in quest of Van Tromp, who was in the north seas, protecting the fishing vessels. Van Tromp steered towards the Sound, and so eluded his pursuers. Several engagements took place during the early summer, notably one on the 4th of June, during which Van Tromp boarded the ship of Admiral Penn, but was beaten off, and his own vessel boarded, when he was relieved by the advance of De. Ruyter and De. Witt, whose services were again in requisition. After this battle the Dutch were clamorous for peace, and the States had to obey their wish. The admirals were summoned to give their opinion. Van Tromp said that "without great reinforcements of large men-of-war he could serve them no more;" and De Witt exclaimed, "Why should I be silent before my lords of the states? The English are our masters, and by consequence masters of the sea."

In November 1654 Cromwell sent Blake with a powerful fleet to the Mediterranean. While there the English admiral was protector of the sea, his superiority being recognized by the haughty Spaniards and the lawless Algerians, as it already was by the surly Dutch. At Tunis many English captives were said to be in slavery; Blake demanded their surrender. The Governor drew up his ships under the guns of the forts, Castle Goletta and Porto Ferino, "on which," he said, "you may do your worst." For ships to engage at close quarters fortresses on land, was a thing unheard of heretofore in naval warfare, but Blake went at them. In less than three hours every gun in the castle was silenced, and while he kept pegging away at the fortifications, nine well-manned and well-armed boats were sent inside, and every piratical ship was sunk or fired, with a total loss of only twenty-five of Blake's men killed, and forty-eight wounded. The admiral then went to Tripoli and other nests of pirates on the African coast, collecting a tribute from the rulers, and threatening vengeance if the capture of Christians for slavery were continued. Nor was it renewed till Cromwell and Blake had gone to their rest, and under the inglorious reigns of Charles II. and James II. the sun of England's greatness was darkened. In those reigns all was lost, even English honour. The nation was subservient to the Crown, and the Crown to France; and again the Dutch flag was seen in the Thames unchallenged and unresisted! It was time for the national awakening, which ended in the Revolution of 1688, and the accession of William III.

The respect with which Blake caused the name of England to be treated is seen in a story which Bishop Burnet records. When he lay at Malaga, some of the sailors on shore meeting a procession of the host refused to kneel as it passed, as all around did. The priest in charge incited the people to attack them. On returning to the ship, and telling of this ill-treatment, Blake sent to the Viceroy or Governor of Malaga, demanding that the priest should be sent aboard his ship. The Governor replied that "he had no authority over persons ecclesiastical." Blake sent to say that "he did not inquire into the Governor's authority, but if the priest were not sent within three hours he would bombard the town."

The priest was sent, and pleaded the provocation given by the sailors. To which the admiral replied, that if complaint had been made to him, the sailors would have been punished severely, for he would not let his men affront the religion of any place, especially of a friendly power; but he was angry that the Spaniards assumed that power, and "he would have all the world know that an Englishman was only to be punished by an Englishman." So, having used the priest civilly, he sent him back, being satisfied that he was in his power.

When the news of this came home, the conduct of Blake pleased Cromwell greatly, and he read the letter in Council with much satisfaction, saying, " he hoped to make the name of an Englishman as great as even that of a Roman had been."

In 1656 war with Spain was declared, and both on the coasts of the old kingdom, and in their dominions in the New World the ships of Blake had a series of glorious successes. The destruction of the Spanish fleet at Santa Cruz, a fleet of great power, under the guns of strong fortresses, was an achievement never surpassed in the annals of the English navy. The least of the Spanish ships was larger than the greatest of Blake's, yet he shattered the forts, and destroyed the fleet. "The whole action," says the historian Clarendon, "was so incredible, that all men who knew the place, wondered that any sober man, with whatever courage endowed, would ever have undertaken it." The Admiral cruised for some months longer, and intercepted many of the rich Spanish trading ships, but broken by the fatigue of the last three years, he resolved to return home, and died before he came to land.

His body was embalmed, and having lain in state at Greenwich, was laid with all honour in Westminster Abbey. The nation mourned his loss, and not a man who ever had served under him but lamented his loss as that of a father.

The opinion of Lord Clarendon as to his courage has been quoted, and we give that of another Royalist to "his lofty character and spotless integrity." So Dr. Johnson speaks of him, in telling of his noble deeds, and says:—"Nor is it without regret that I am obliged to relate the treatment his body met with a year after the Restoration, when it was taken up,* by express command, and buried in a pit in St. Margaret's churchyard. Had he been guilty of the murder of Charles I., to insult his body had been a mean revenge; but as he was innocent, it was inhumanity and ingratitude. But that regard which was denied his body, has been paid to his better remains, his name and memory."

DAVID DOUGLAS, THE BOTANICAL COLLECTOR.

MANY of the stately trees and lovely flowers now familiar to us were unknown to our forefathers, and have been introduced from foreign lands to English parks and gardens. A few of them have been sent or brought home by residents in distant regions, or by those who have gone there in the course of ordinary voyages and travels, but the larger part have been obtained by regular collectors sent out for the purpose, either by public bodies or by private persons of wealth. There are always numbers of botanical collectors thus wandering in various parts of the world, some of them in the common course of trade, at the cost of nurserymen and florists, who find it pays them well to employ such travellers.

One of the earliest and most successful of these botanical travellers was a Scotchman, David Douglas, whose name is attached to the magnificent pine tree, the *Abies Douglasii*, the seeds of which he first brought to this country from British Columbia. A brief account of his adventurous life, too soon cut short by a tragical death, will be read with interest.

He began his career by being apprenticed to the head

* The same indignity was put on the remains of Cromwell and other men who had made England great. Thus was illustrated the Eastern apologue about the monkeys pulling the dead lion's beard!

gardener at Scone Palace, where he worked, from the age of twelve, for seven years. When nineteen he obtained a situation at Culross, in the garden of Sir Robert Preston. At this place were many exotic plants, which greatly excited his curiosity, and at the mansion there was a good library, including books on botany, which he was permitted to use, so that the two years he was at Culross were very pleasantly and profitably spent. He then obtained employment in the Botanic Garden at Glasgow, under the superintendence of Sir William Jackson Hooker, the father of Sir Joseph Hooker of Kew Gardens. Dr. Hooker took much notice of the young and enthusiastic gardener, and allowed him to attend the lectures on botany, which were given to the medical students of Glasgow University. He also took him as his companion in excursions during the summer months in the Scottish Highlands and islands. He thus was prepared for his life-work under the most favourable auspices.

In 1824 the Hudson's Bay Company resolved to send a botanical collector to the vast regions of British Columbia, then under their authority. Dr. Hooker being asked to recommend a suitable person, David Douglas at once received the appointment. In those times the only way to reach the western regions of North America was by a long sea voyage, in a sailing ship, round Cape Horn. The voyage lasted about nine months, for the ship did not anchor in Columbia River till April 8th, 1825.

Of the incidents of the voyage a record was kept by Douglas in his Journal. There was much to interest him, and nothing pleased him more than a visit to Juan Fernandez, on which island, strangely enough, another Robinson Crusoe was found. On the second day after their arrival, while Douglas and some companions were exploring, an uncouth-looking skin-covered man startled them by springing from among the bushes. His name was William Clark, and he had come from London five years before. He seemed contented to stay there, and satisfied with the occasional intercourse with his fellow-men when a ship touched at the island. As he did not discover himself on the first day, it is likely that he reconnoitred the strangers before making his appearance, so as to judge whether their company would be agreeable or safe. He had a few books, among which were "Robinson Crusoe" and "Cowper's Poems." From the latter he had committed to memory the piece upon Alexander Selkirk. Douglas says in his Journal: "No pen can correctly describe the charming and rural appearance of this island." He took away specimens of the native plants, and in return sowed various seeds of fruits and vegetables, which have enriched the island since his visit.

Arrived at Columbia Douglas soon found his way to Fort Vancouver, where the chief factor, a fellow countryman, Dr. M'Lauchlan, gave him a warm welcome. He lost no time in commencing his explorations from this place as his headquarters. His labour was at times interrupted by the rainy weather, but he made such large collections of seeds and plants that his deer-skin tent was too straitened to hold his treasures, and a larger hut of dried oak bark had to be built for their reception and preservation. When the ship was ready to return, at the end of four months, he was able to despatch a large collection of specimens. His hut he expected would be useful for winter shelter, but as long as he was able to move about he preferred rougher quarters. At the beginning of his first autumn he wrote: "I have been in a house only three nights since my arrival in North-Western America, and these were my first after my debarkation."

On his journeys he used to wander about, with his gun across his shoulder, and his *vasculum*, or botanical box, strapped on his back, attended only by his faithful Scotch terrier, rough and shaggy as his master. The Indians all knew him, mostly taking him for a "big medicine." The forest was his home. The fur traders' well-appointed stations never tempted him to stay long. He preferred to sleep under one of his own pine-trees. The trappers called him the "Grass Man."

He sacrificed everything for the sake of his plants. On one occasion we find him wearing a damp shirt, in order to keep the dry one to wrap around his specimens. On another, when he crossed the Columbia river, he congratulates himself that, while he had lost all his provisions, he had saved his plants. Having formed the resolution to cross the continent from the Pacific to the Atlantic, a journey of more than three thousand miles, he describes his outfit: "My store of clothes is very low, nearly reduced to what I have on my back—one pair of shoes, no stockings, two shirts, two handkerchiefs, my blanket, and cloak. Thus I adapt my costume to that of the country, as I could not carry more without reducing myself to an inadequate supply of paper, and such articles as I required for *my business.*"

As an instance of his self-denial and perseverance, we may recount what he did and endured in the discovery of the *Pinus Lambertiana*, which is now scarcely less famous than the pine-tree called by his name. Having secured one of its remarkably large cones from the Indians, he resolved to visit the place in the following spring. After many difficulties he reached the grove, and saw the precious cones hanging like sugar-loaves from the pendulous branches. He secured three of these with almost fatal result. He could neither climb the tree nor hew it down; he therefore attempted to shoot down the cones. The Indians, hearing the report of his gun, speedily surrounded him in warlike array, with their bows, arrows, bone-tipped spears, and knives. He had invaded their sacred grove; he had dared to fire upon their sacred trees. He managed to allay their wrath, and betook himself to the depths of the forest. In returning he encountered greater dangers. He lost his way; he again was opposed by hostile Indians; he was exposed to a pitiless storm. Twelve days he spent in extreme misery and danger, during which his horse perished, before he came out on the Columbia and was taken care of by his friends.

Shortly after this he made a journey into California, and

whilst there exploring its rich herbage and wonderful arborage, had the good fortune to fall in with a kindred spirit, Dr. Coulter, who had been collecting in Mexico, and with great joy writes to Dr. Hooker, "As a salmon-fisher he is superior to Walter Campbell of Islay—the Izaak Walton of Scotland—besides being a beautiful shot with a rifle, nearly as successful as myself! And I do assure you from my heart it is a *terrible* pleasure to me thus to meet a really good man, and one with whom I can talk of plants."

He manifested the greatest prudence in dealing with the Indians, many of whom had never seen the face of a white man before. When one was boasting of his superiority to the King George men, Douglas quietly lifted his gun and brought down a bird which was flying overhead. They never shoot anything on the wing. This manifestation of his power caused them to lay their hands upon their mouths in token of fear. "My fame was hereupon sounded through the country. Ever since, I have found it to be of the utmost importance to bring down a bird flying when I go near any of their lodges, taking care to make it appear as a little matter, not done to be observed." On another occasion, having finished a piece of salmon in the presence of a large number of Indians of whom he was not sure, he brought from his pocket some effervescing powder which he carried as medicine, put it into some water, stirred it with his finger, and drank it before them. This had immense effect. A man that could swallow *boiling water* was not to be interfered with, especially one who could boil it with his finger! Sometimes he struck terror into their hearts by lighting his pipe with a lens, and greatly impressed them by putting on his blue spectacles. A friendly chief having done him a service, the "Grass Man" bored a hole through his only shilling, and suspended it by a brass wire to the septum of his nose, which was pierced according to the custom of his tribe. Another chief was rewarded for similar service by being shaved after the fashion of white men. In sailing up one of the rivers he was accompanied by Madsue, or "Thunder," who was long famous in the region around the Columbia Thunder would not taste liquor, but he made up for it in smoking. In self-defence Douglas smoked also. In this, however, he astonished his companion by putting out the smoke from his mouth, which these Indians did not do. "Oh!" cried Thunder, "why do you throw away the smoke? See, I take it in my belly."

Having made journeys with many perils through Oregon, Washington Territory, and California, he started to go farther north through British Columbia and Russian America. In crossing the Fraser river, up near Quesnelle, his canoe was dashed to pieces against the rocks, all his provisions and specimens lost; himself cast into the waters, and thrown benumbed and bleeding upon the shore. This was a great disaster. It not only discouraged him from proceeding on that journey, but made him eager to return home. More than four hundred specimens, the result of laborious toil, were there destroyed in a few minutes. His misfortune was felt all the more from the fact that the ten years' toil and exposure had already told severely upon his frame. He could not shoot well, as his eyesight had begun to fail. He became lonely, desolate, despondent, and acknowledges that but for the companionship of his Bible, which he carried with him and perused in all his wanderings, and the sympathy and support of the Faithful Redeemer in whom he believed, he must have perished in utter hopelessness.

He therefore made preparations for his return to Britain, and left the Columbia river in October 1833. The ship touched at the Sandwich Islands, and had to wait there for cargo. He therefore set out to explore the country—especially the volcanic region. On the 7th January, 1834, he started to visit the volcano Mauna Kea. Returning from the summit of the mountain, hungry, thirsty, blistered, and jaded, he wrote: "Gratified though one may be at witnessing the wonderful works of God in such a place, it is with thankfulness that we approach a climate more congenial to our natures, and welcome the habitations of our fellow-men, where we are refreshed with the scent of vegetation and soothed by the melody of birds."

In the last of his letters to Professor Hooker he said : " May God grant me a safe return to England. I cannot but indulge the pleasing hope of being soon able in person to thank you for the signal kindness you have ever done me." But in this he was disappointed. He had resolved to visit Mauna Kea once more. At six o'clock in the morning of the 12th July he called at the house of Edward Gurney, an Englishman who had a house in the region of the mountain. He stated that his servant had failed on the way, and requested him to show him the best path. After breakfasting together Gurney accompanied him for about a mile, pointed out the different paths, and specially warned him of the pit-traps, of which there were many, for the catching of wild cattle. He had not gone more than two miles when he came to one of these, into which a bullock had fallen. He looked into it, passed by, and went up the hill. There, some idea induced him to turn. Laying down his bundle, beside which his faithful terrier remained, he proceeded to examine the pit more minutely.

While doing this he missed his footstep and fell down into the pit beside the enraged bullock. Two natives who were passing were attracted by his cries, and saw Douglas under the feet of the animal. They ran as quickly as they could for Gurney, who shot the bullock, but found that Douglas was already dead. After removing the mangled body, Gurney took charge of the dog, and the bundle, and the other things which he had in his pockets, which were duly forwarded. Thus ended the life of Douglas when thirty-five years of age. Exactly ten years after his first embarkation for America his body was brought down to Oahu for burial. His death was all the more unfortunate as he had not completed his account of his explorations in the north-west. He had lost four hundred of his last collected specimens in attempting to cross the Fraser river. His subsequent sickness and despondency had prevented him describing them.

Notwithstanding these misfortunes and his death ere he had reached middle life, Douglas had done noble work, and attained a character that will ever rank high among those who have advanced the interests of humanity. On the reverse side of his monument, "erected by the lovers of botany in Europe" to his memory in Scone churchyard, there is given a list " of a few of the numerous trees, shrubs, and ornamental plants introduced by Douglas." Among these we recognise many of the annuals now common in our gardens, and of the trees and shrubs that are favourites in our grounds. Thus are his name and memory perpetuated not only by his monumental stone, but by the widely-distributed Douglas pine and other trees in many lands. Their waving branches, moved by the winds, will sound forth the melancholy requiem of him who loved so well the old forests.

His early friend and patron Dr. Hooker published his Journal, or as much of it as reached home; and long years after, a Scotch clergyman, Mr. Somerville, gathered many traditions from those who knew him in British Columbia. From these sources we have obtained most of the facts of the foregoing narrative.

Printed by Hazell, Watson, & Viney, Limited, London and Aylesbury.

BY THE SAME AUTHOR.

Fourth Edition, Completing Ninth Thousand.

ALL TRUE.

Records of Peril and Adventure by Sea and Land—Remarkable Escapes and Deliverances—Missionary Enterprises and Travels—Wonders of Nature and Providence—Incidents of Christian History and Biography.

With Twelve Illustrations. Crown 8vo, cloth, gilt, 5s.

"Dr. Macaulay has a peculiar genius for the work he has undertaken in this volume. He thinks a collection of true incidents may be made as attractive as the story books which are provided in such abundance. We can only advise every father who has boys growing up around him to be sure and have a copy."—*Congregationalist.*

"'All True' is a record of adventure and enterprise, of the wonders of nature, the goodness of Providence, and generally of such matters as young people are or ought to be interested in hearing about. Young people never like a story the worse because it is true."—*The Times.*

"A more delightful miscellany could scarcely be found."—*British Quarterly Review.*

"A book full of what is useful and true, forming, with its nice binding and well-executed pictures, a capital and handy school-prize or Christmas present."—*Nonconformist.*

"The selection of incidents has been carefully made, and the illustrations are numerous and appropriate."—*The Standard.*

"All the articles are good, and as they are also short, there is a most agreeable and entertaining variety."—*Liverpool Daily Post.*

"A book which cannot but recommend itself to the patronage of book buyers and readers."—*The Bookseller.*

"'All True' contains records of adventures by sea and land, remarkable escapes and deliverances, missionary enterprises, etc., is as entertaining as the majority of such books are depressing, and may be welcomed as a welcome present for children. The illustrations are above the average of those vouchsafed to us in children's books."—*The Spectator.*

"The present volume verifies the saying that 'Truth is strange, stranger than fiction.' It is made up to about seventy short narratives, which cannot fail to rivet the attention and add to the intelligence of the reader."—*The Scotsman.*

"Among the numerous story-books designed for the young, this certainly occupies a high place, containing a collection of true incidents, which, while securing attention, and exciting interest, may also help in the formation of sound principles and Christian character in the youthful mind."—*Melbourne Daily Telegraph.*

"A splendid book for young people."—*Daily Review.*

"No man is better qualified to cater for the intellectual amusement of old and young, and our opinion is that 'All True' is one of the most valuable collections he has given to the public."—*Edinburgh Courant.*

"A book difficult to put down. It takes the mind captive. There are twelve first-class illustrations. We have here thrilling adventure, brave conflicts, missionary enterprises—indeed, seventy short narratives make up a volume of true incidents, some of them more marvellous than any fairy stories; and best of all, the Saviour is honoured and glorified throughout."—*Evangelical Magazine.*

LONDON: HODDER AND STOUGHTON, 27, PATERNOSTER ROW.

BY THE SAME AUTHOR.

Third and Cheaper Edition.

ACROSS THE FERRY.

First Impressions of America and its People.

Nine Illustrations. Crown 8vo, cloth. Price 5s.

"It is needless to commend Dr. Macaulay to our readers; they know too well how graphically and instructively he can tell the story of his travels. And many of them are acquainted with this very book, and have assigned it a place amongst their favourites; but this edition is illustrated by nine engravings that add much to its interest, and has also a new introduction, making interesting reference to incidents that have occurred since the 'First Impressions' were originally published, and also to the first impressions of other visitors to America. The immense mass of information supplied by these records makes them very valuable, and it is worked into the 'Impressions' with charming facility."—*Literary World.*

"Dr. Macaulay not only records his own impressions, but he incorporates with them much of the useful and interesting information which an intelligent traveller not only picks up, but takes special pains to furnish himself with. The volume is a series of photographs of America as it was in 1870, and is full, therefore, of practical interest." *British Quarterly Review.*

"It contains a large mass of information, and is full of suggestive matter."— *Spectator.*

"Dr. Macaulay's sketches are marked with good sense; they are full of solid information; and yet they are anything but dull. The present edition has the further advantage of being illustrated."—*Scotsman.*

"The description he presents of social life in the great cities of America, of the wonderful growth of some of its centres of population, of the position of its labouring classes, and of its educational and ecclesiastical organisations, is exceedingly instructive. Altogether, the book contains a mass of information which will be regarded as both pleasant and useful by every one who takes an interest in the new world 'across the ferry.'"—*Scotsman.* (*First Edition.*)

"A model in its way of what a book of American travels ought to be."—*London Society.*

"The best and most sensible articles on our country that have ever appeared in England."—*Philadelphia Ledger.*

"Well worth reading, throwing quite a new light upon many things of which we know too little in this country."—*The Graphic.*

"'Across the Ferry' is extremely full of information. It modestly professes to give 'First Impressions,' but they are both vivid and valuable, and written with a deep insight into whatever is best worth knowing in the United States."—*People's Magazine.*

"A very lively, entertaining, and generally accurate description."—*Appleton's Journal.*

"A book written in a genial Christian spirit. Not admiring without discrimination, or finding fault without reason! We confess to have learnt more from it of what we really care to know, than from any other volume which has come under our notice."— MR. SPURGEON's *Sword and Trowel.*

"The author's visit was a short one, but he made good use of his time; and the result of his observations is given in a popular form, embracing a great variety of topics, and without the bias which has destroyed the value of much that has been published in England respecting the United States."—*The Times of India.*

LONDON: HODDER AND STOUGHTON, 27, PATERNOSTER ROW.

BY THE SAME AUTHOR.

Second Thousand.

GREY HAWK:

Life and Adventures among the Red Indians.

AN OLD STORY RETOLD.

Eleven Illustrations. Handsomely Bound. Gilt Edges. 5s.

"The editor of the *Leisure Hour*, having come across a romantic story of real life, has worked it up into a genuinely interesting Indian story. The illustrations and handsome style in which the book is got up make it very suitable for presentation."—*Sheffield Independent*.

"A book of such thrilling adventures as are dear to the souls of boys, and is well worth the reading of older people than the boys who will certainly delight in it."—*Literary World*.

"The story itself is told with the simplicity of Robinson Crusoe, and brings the details of savage life among savage people before the reader's eyes with the same vivid reality."—*Guardian*.

"Dr. Macaulay is at his best in 'Grey Hawk.'"—*Liverpool Daily Post*.

"There is a mysterious fascination about the subject which is of itself sufficient to secure for it a wide popularity."—*Congregationalist*.

"The story is graphically told, and will be sure to become a favourite with boys."—*Globe*.

"These adventures are spirit-stirring as the wildest romance; and Cooper might have borrowed his heroes from the 'ower true tale' without scruples. Not only is the story of 'Grey Hawk' an amusing and instructive book for boys, but it is likewise a most valuable book of reference as to the condition of the Indian race at the period of the tale, compared with what is now beheld at the present day."—*Court Journal*.

"A splendid boy's book."—*Derby Mercury*

"The narrative is very interesting."—*Queen*.

"This is a picturesque story of a time which now seems curiously remote."—*Daily News*.

"The story is written in the first person, and the mingled ease and simplicity of the style make it very pleasant reading. It may be regarded as a description of the life of the North American Indians, regarded from their own point of view. There is much strange, exciting incident and adventure, and many interesting matters of American history are embodied."—*School Board Chronicle*.

"Dr. Macaulay has revived with excellent effect a true story of Indian life. The story has a thoroughly genuine look. But though the savage pictured here is scarcely 'noble' he is not wholly ignoble. In fact, to use a famous phrase, there is a good deal of human nature in him."—*Pall Mall Gazette*.

"Dr. Macaulay has given us in this volume an account of life among the Indians in the form of a personal narrative. The incidents are drawn from the statements of one who, some years ago, was taken prisoner and kept amongst the Indians when young, and who, growing up amongst them, acquired the knowledge of their ways which he afterwards made public. The story is told in a spirited fashion, and forms extremely pleasant reading."—*City Press*.

LONDON: HODDER AND STOUGHTON, 27, PATERNOSTER ROW.

THE LATE W. H. G. KINGSTON'S STORIES.

I.

Crown 8vo, gilt edges, handsomely bound, 5s. Eight Illustrations.

FROM POWDER MONKEY TO ADMIRAL:
A Story of Naval Adventure.

WITH AN INTRODUCTION BY DR. MACAULAY.

"This story is equal to any ever written by its author. It is full of life and adventure. In the stirring days of the French War Bill Rayner was a London Arab, and the story tells how by good conduct and bravery Bill rose from the position of powder monkey to that of Admiral He is, early in his career, wrecked and taken prisoner, with another lad his own age, and the pair go through some exciting adventures before they are again afloat. No detailed description is possible of a story which is from end to end crowded with adventure and incident."—*Standard.*

II.

Crown 8vo, gilt edges, handsomely bound, 5s.

JAMES BRAITHWAITE, THE SUPERCARGO.
The Story of His Adventures Ashore and Afloat.

Eight Illustrations, Portrait, and Short Account of Mr. Kingston's Life.

"Mr. Kingston's books for boys are too well known to need many words. It will be welcome to boys as a pleasant memorial of an old and valued friend."—*Athenæum.*

III.

Crown 8vo, gilt edges, 5s. Eight Illustrations.

PETER TRAWL;
The Adventures of a Whaler.

"A whaling story by the late Mr. Kingston, and promises well. It is a manly sort of book, with a good deal of information in it as well as the adventures which boys love. A true story of a gallant skipper who, with the assistance of the ship's carpenter, amputated his own leg, is amongst the notable occurrences recorded."—*Athenæum.*

IV.

Fifth Thousand. Crown 8vo, gilt edges, 5s. Five Illustrations.

HENDRICKS THE HUNTER;
Or, The Border Farm. A Tale of Zululand.

"'A Tale of Zululand.' A very appropriate region to take a boy in at this time. We have nothing to do, however, with the late war, though there is plenty of fighting before Hendricks' tale is told. The illustrations are quite in the spirit of the book. No one who looks at the frontispiece but must turn to page 201 to learn the issue of the startling scene depicted."—*Times.*

V.

Cheap Edition. Fcap. 8vo, Eight Illustrations. 2s. 6d.

JOVINIAN.
A Tale of Early Papal Rome.

VI.

Seventh Thousand. Crown 8vo, cloth, price 3s. 6d.

CLARA MAYNARD;
Or, The True and the False. A Tale of the Times.

"A very charming love story, told with singular grace and power, by a writer gifte with an excellent command of language and a keen insight into the workings of human emotions in their best aspects."—*Standard.*

LONDON: HODDER AND STOUGHTON, 27, PATERNOSTER ROW.